THE SPHAS

Oct 20, 2014

To Steve:
To a tennis fan, basketball
is a real sport.

Enjoy
Doug Stark

THE **SPHAS**

THE LIFE AND TIMES OF BASKETBALL'S GREATEST JEWISH TEAM

Douglas Stark

Foreword by Lynn Sherr

TEMPLE UNIVERSITY PRESS  PHILADELPHIA

TEMPLE UNIVERSITY PRESS
Philadelphia, Pennsylvania 19122
www.temple.edu/tempress

Published 2011

Library of Congress Cataloging-in-Publication Data

Stark, Douglas (Douglas Andrew), 1972–
The SPHAS : the life and times of basketball's greatest Jewish team / Douglas Stark ; foreword by Lynn Sherr.
p. cm.
Includes bibliographical references and index.
ISBN 978-1-59213-633-9 (cloth : alk. paper) — ISBN 978-1-59213-635-3 (e-book)
1. Philadelphia SPHAS (Basketball team)—History. 2. Jewish basketball players—Pennsylvania—Philadelphia—History. 3. Basketball—Pennsylvania—Philadelphia—History. I. Title.
GV885.52.P455S73 2011
796.323'640974811—dc22

2010047388

♾ The paper used in this publication meets the requirements of the American National Standard for Information Sciences—Permanence of Paper for Printed Library Materials, ANSI Z39.48-1992

Printed in the United States of America

2 4 6 8 9 7 5 3 1

For my mother and father

It was the team for all Jewish people in Philadelphia. We were the best and we were Jewish. It was an amazing combination.

—Harry Litwack

In my time, I got involved in lots of things, lots of them. But the SPHAS, that's what I loved.

—Eddie Gottlieb

It was the pinnacle of athletic achievement just to be able to wear that jersey with those four Hebrew letters on it. The money meant nothing. The goal, the fulfillment, was to play for the greatest basketball team in the world, the South Philadelphia Hebrew Association.

—Brookman (Yock) Welsh

Oh, those were great times. I can still picture this long line of girls waiting to come in for the dance after the game was over. The SPHAS were very popular. They were broadcast on radio, and almost every game was a sell-out.

—Dave Zinkoff

CONTENTS

FOREWORD

It used to be a joke, the snide answer to one of those "Thinnest Books in the World" riddles, a wisecrack so common it turned up in the 1980 movie farce *Airplane!*

> *Flight attendant*: Would you like something to read?
> *Passenger*: Do you have anything light?
> *Flight attendant*: How about this leaflet, "Famous Jewish Sports Legends"?

Me? I never thought it was funny. Because my father *was* a genuine Jewish sports legend, and I grew up knowing how very talented and famous he and his teammates were. Thanks to Douglas Stark, the story of the Philadelphia SPHAS is finally available to a much wider audience, taking its proper place in the history of the game. This is neither a thin book nor a leaflet; it is a critical piece of the legend that is American basketball today.

Nearly a century ago, the SPHAS were the team that helped turn professional basketball into a national mania—a feisty, hungry and, by all accounts, gifted group of athletes who, then as now, saw the sport as a way out of the urban ghetto. As the author points out, it was their "search for the American dream." That was certainly my dad's story.

His name was Louis Sherr, and he was born in Philadelphia in 1905. By a happy coincidence, just after his parents immigrated to America from

Eastern Europe, a fellow named James Naismith invented the game of basketball in Springield, Massachusetts. For my dad—a hunk of an athlete with wavy red hair atop his 6'½" frame—it was the perfect outlet for his powerful natural ability. As a first-generation Jew with little money and no access to an established sport like baseball, he was not only welcome but sought out for this new form of recreation that was igniting the interest of so many fans. From the time he was recruited to jump center at South Philadelphia High School, "Reds" Sherr was a local star.

It was a time when basketball was played in a cage—with chicken wire or chain-link fencing surrounding the court to keep the ball in bounds and to speed up the pace. It was a time when you could make a few bucks a night playing ball—big money back in the 1920s—and then cool off at the dance held immediately afterward on the very same court. That's what passed for social media a century ago. And it was a time of quick passes, two-handed set shots, and foul shots tossed underhand. Scores were low—double-digits that rarely exceeded the 40s—and as far as I can tell, my dad, often high scorer, never went beyond 25 points a game. But it was exciting and pioneering and, yes, it started in Philadelphia and was mostly Jewish.

Among the myriad teams sponsored by various synagogues and other Jewish organizations, the SPHAS—named for the social club, the South Philadelphia Hebrew Association, that gave them their first uniforms—became the most successful of all. My father played for three incarnations of the team over a period of eight years, under the leadership of his high school pal Eddie Gottlieb, who would go on to found the Philadelphia Warriors. As the game grew more popular, the arenas got bigger, the cages disappeared, and fans paid up to $1 a game. The fouls got more ferocious, too, with players regularly getting pummeled and elbowed if they stood in the way of victory. And the floors got so slippery, the coaches often had to wipe them down with rosin bags so the after-game dancing could get under way in the converted ballrooms. It was still being promoted as a big party.

But it was also becoming big-time. In Reds Sherr's last two seasons with the SPHAS, they won the Eastern Basketball League Championship, an accomplishment that would, many years later, earn them a special exhibition in the Naismith Memorial Basketball Hall of Fame in Springfield, Massachusetts. My dad left the game in 1932, because, as he wrote to another team owner who was trying to recruit him, "there is so little money offered for playing basketball."

Some of this I know because I heard the stories when I was a child, some because I have letters and programs and a set of scrapbooks filled with blaring headlines ("REDS SHERR STARS AS SPHAS TRIUMPH") on yellowing articles clipped from newspapers by his loving grandfather. But mostly my understanding of the impact of the SPHAS comes from the recognition that my father and "Gotty" and all of their pals got from the people who had seen them play. They were celebrated throughout their lives—and even after.

On the day of my dad's funeral, in 1977, we solemnly filed into the limo for the unbearably sad trip to the cemetery. As my sister and I settled into the back seat with our husbands, my mother sat up front, newly alone, her body shrunken with grief. Just before we drove off, the driver turned to her and said, politely, "Excuse me, ma'am, but was your husband Lou Sherr?"

"Yes," she said, sighing.

"Lou Sherr the basketball player?"

"Yes," she said, sitting up a little taller.

"Well, when I was a boy, I used to pay my money and go watch him play. He was a real star."

My mother beamed. The memories revived her. They *were* stars, all of the SPHAS. This is their amazing story.

Lynn Sherr

To play for the SPHAS in Philadelphia before the NBA was the tops. You could not get any better than that.

—Louis (Red) Klotz

The SPHAS were to Philadelphia what the Original Celtics were to New York. People in other areas of the country wanted them to come and play. Their fame just spread. They carried Philadelphia's name with them and it was good for them, for Philadelphia, and for basketball.

—Bill Himmelman

If you could play basketball, your dream was to play for the SPHAS. Your life would be fulfilled.

—Ed Lerner

PREFACE

> The SPHAS were very popular with the Jewish people. They were our heroes. They gave us something.
>
> —SAM (LEADEN) BERNSTEIN,
> INTERVIEW BY THE AUTHOR

On October 17, 1959, the Philadelphia SPHAS played a game against the Harlem Globetrotters. The contest was held at Madison Square Garden, and 17,932 basketball fans saw two games that early autumn evening. The doubleheader featured the Harlem Globetrotters versus the Philadelphia SPHAS, and the College All-Stars against the home team New York Knicks. The Globetrotters won 68–42, and the College All-Stars, behind Wilt Chamberlain, won 123–113. This contest against the Globetrotters marked the last official game for the SPHAS. Shortly thereafter, the team was reconstituted as the Baltimore Rockets. When the Baltimore Rockets played the Harlem Globetrotters in New York City, on December 31, 1959, the Rockets roster bore a striking resemblance to the SPHAS team in October. The only difference was that the team's name had changed.

The day after the October game the *Philadelphia Inquirer* made only a brief mention of the encounter. In a five-paragraph article filed by an Associated Press reporter, one sentence was devoted to the SPHAS. It said, "In the opening game the Harlem Globetrotters clowned their way to a 68–42 victory over the Philadelphia Sphas."[1] There were no editorials. No box score. Nothing was written remembering the SPHAS or their humble beginnings in 1918 as a group of Jewish high school graduates who formed a basketball team to compete against other local squads. There was nothing written about how the club grew into one of the finest basketball teams of all time, winning multiple championships in various professional leagues. Nothing about the anti-Semitism and racial insults heaped on the players as they played games throughout the Midwest or traveled on the East Coast. No mention of the sold-out Saturday nights with 3,000 fans at the Broadwood Hotel. No reference to the dancing that followed, where young Jewish men and women met their future spouses. No history of the wonderful players, including David (Cy) Kaselman, Joel (Shikey) Gotthoffer, Louis (Inky) Lautman, Moe Goldman, George (Red) Wolfe, Howard (Red) Rosan, Alexander (Petey) Rosenberg, Herman (Chickie) Passon, Harry Litwack, Eddie Gottlieb, Gil Fitch, announcer Dave Zinkoff, or the many others who were a source of pride for the Jewish community in Philadelphia. Sadly, there was nothing.

With that, the SPHAS quietly passed into history, another team whose memory would live on with those who had had the privilege of watching them. On the eve of 1960, forty-one years after their inauspicious beginnings in 1918 as a team representing the South Philadelphia Hebrew Association, the SPHAS ceased operation.

In that game, the SPHAS did not resemble the team of the 1930s that filled armories, ballrooms, and gymnasiums, dazzling the crowds with their passing, shooting, and teamwork. This was not the gang that traveled in an unheated car at the end of December, going from one town (Akron, Oshkosh, and Sheboygan) to another (Flint and Clarksburg) in the Midwest, playing games and facing hostile crowds, all in the hopes of growing professional basketball (something they would, indeed, accomplish). The SPHAS of October 1959 were most certainly not that team.

For the previous ten years, the SPHAS had been a traveling team with the Harlem Globetrotters. The Globetrotters of the 1950s were basketball's most popular and exciting team. They regularly filled arenas in every town in America no matter the size or location, single-handedly keeping the National Basketball Association (NBA) afloat the first several years. The Globetrotters often played doubleheaders to help the financially struggling NBA stay in business. Eventually, they took their show across the globe. The Globetrotters, with Meadowlark Lemon, Marques Haynes, and countless others, amazed crowds with their stunts, their skill, and their flair. They always won. As one of several traveling teams with the Globetrotters, the SPHAS played a close game, but they always lost in the end. And this SPHAS team was not Jewish. Unlike the teams of the 1920s, 1930s, and early 1940s, this SPHAS squad carried only the team name, not its community identity.

On this particular October night at Madison Square Garden, the Globetrotters and SPHAS were a mere warm-up act for the marquee matchup between the New York Knicks and the College All-Stars, who had Wilt Chamberlain. In that first game, "fans were treated to the antics and court magic of the Harlem Globetrotters,"[2] who easily handled an unseasoned SPHAS roster of Brennan, Mitari, Griboski, Josephs, Schreiber, Schayes, Lennox, and Corey. These SPHAS scored 42 points.

The SPHAS that night were only a shell of their former selves, like rodeo clowns as a foil for the real talent on the court. But that end belies the history of their glory days on the court from 1933 to 1946 and the impact they had on basketball.

Here is their story.

1

ON THE ROAD

I remember the team getting off the train once in a little town in Ohio and a group of people staring at us. They said we looked pretty normal—like they had never seen Jews before.

—Shikey Gotthoffer,
quoted in the *Jewish Exponent*

On Sunday night, January 1, 1939, an estimated 13 million Americans around the country, including in the greater Detroit area, turned on their radios to listen to the popular weekly address of Father Charles Coughlin. Father Coughlin, the country's most well-known radio priest, oversaw the Shrine of the Little Flower in Royal Oak, Michigan, a suburb of Detroit. Throughout the 1930s, Coughlin grew increasingly disenchanted with President Franklin Roosevelt and the New Deal. As the decade drew to a close, his rhetoric increasingly became anti-Semitic. Newspapers and radio were the two modes of keeping up with the news at that time, and radio proved widely popular as families would often gather around and listen to news, sports, and variety shows. Many listened to Father Coughlin.

Traveling that same New Year's weekend in an unheated car from Michigan to Wisconsin was a group of seven basketball players, their manager, and public address announcer. They hailed from Philadelphia, and they were all Jewish. The team was known as the Philadelphia SPHAS, which stood for South Philadelphia Hebrew Association. The SPHAS began as a club team in 1918; by the 1930s, they were regarded as one of the nation's top basketball squads. The team played in the American Basketball League (ABL), the premier professional basketball league in the country at the time. The SPHAS dominated the league; prior to the 1938–1939 season, they had captured three championships in five seasons and were gunning for another title.

For several years, Eddie Gottlieb, the team's manager and coach, took his team on the road between Christmas and New Year's when the ABL did not schedule any games. Gottlieb believed it was important to spread basketball through the Midwest and keep his team sharp before league play resumed. It also served as a way to add a few extra dollars to the bottom line. Above all, Gotty was a brilliant promoter, and keeping his team in the news and making some extra money would pay dividends in the future. The team began this Midwest ritual in 1936–1937; by 1938–1939, it had become an important aspect of the SPHAS itinerary and identity.

Moe Goldman, a regular on those trips, remembered traveling through the Midwest:

> We'd make a Christmas trip out west each year and play the teams out there for about ten days in cities like Chicago, Oshkosh, and Sheboygan. The league had no games during the holidays. So we'd go out in Eddie Gottlieb's car. There would be seven of us. He had a specially built car that seated nine with three across. We'd leave Saturday night after a ball game. We'd stop in Harrisburg, Fort Wayne, and all the other towns. We'd travel for hours and hours.
>
> Gottlieb kept us going. We went on the trips and we would come back and make very little money. Money was not there for a trip like this. I would say, "Eddie, why can't we take Christmas off instead of making this trip?" He said, "We are not making this trip for money. We are pioneers for the future of professional basketball."[1]

The America of the 1930s was in a deep economic depression, and the rise of Nazism and anti-Semitism both devastated and united the American Jewish community. Jerry Fleishman played on the SPHAS during World War II and accompanied the team on a few of these trips. He recalled:

> We went into towns like Oshkosh or Sheboygan in Wisconsin and we would have the Jewish star on our jerseys, and it took courage to do that. Most people were for us because of our ability to play. Each team always had one football player who would bully us. The Jewish star on the jerseys got us into trouble. We got into fights, but we got out of it. We were proud to represent the Jews, who were supposedly the weak ones. But we could handle ourselves. We became life friends with the basketball players who played with us and against us.[2]

The SPHAS traveled all through the Midwest and were a popular attraction wherever they went. Venlo Wolfson was a youngster in Wisconsin when he first saw them play. He later studied at the University of Pennsylvania and attended games at the Broadwood Hotel. "I grew up in Wisconsin, and the SPHAS came to Milwaukee to play Oshkosh and Sheboygan. This was around 1940, or during the early war years. The SPHAS would travel and play everyone. The roster at that time had seven or eight players at most."[3]

In the car on that January 1, 1939, night trip from Michigan to Wisconsin were the three-time ABL champions.

Howard (Red) Rosan, a 5'9" guard, graduated from Temple University (Philadelphia) in 1935. Rosan joined the SPHAS for the final three games in 1934–1935 and thereafter became a regular part of the rotation. During the 1936–1937 championship series against the Jersey Reds, Rosan was instrumental as the team rebounded from a 3–1 game deficit to win the title in overtime in the seventh game. He averaged 5.7 points during that championship series. A mild-mannered person, Rosan was a strong defensive player on the court.

George (Red) Wolfe, a 5'11" guard/forward, had been with the SPHAS since 1929–1930 when the team played in the Eastern Basketball League. Wolfe was dependable; he held the team record for playing the most seasons (15) and was second in total games played with 457. The 1938–1939 season marked Wolfe's tenth year as a member of the SPHAS, and he had already been a part of six championship teams.

Meyer (Mike) Bloom, a 6'5" center, led Temple University to the first ever National Invitational Tournament (NIT) championship in 1938. He joined the SPHAS for the final five games of the 1937–1938 season. His lone full season with the SPHAS would be 1938–1939. Bloom then jumped from team to team before finding a home with the Trenton Tigers and Baltimore Bullets. He was eventually twice voted the ABL's Most Valuable Player (MVP).

Joel (Shikey) Gotthoffer, a 6' forward, joined the team in 1933–1934 when the SPHAS first entered the ABL. A tough player, Gotthoffer was considered by many to be the best SPHAS player. For his efforts, he won the ABL MVP award. In his first five seasons, he averaged more than 7 points per game three times, which was considered high for that time.

Louis (Inky) Lautman, a 6'1" forward, came directly from high school to join the SPHAS for the 1933–1934 season. A reliable player, Lautman played fourteen seasons, second on the team only to George Wolfe, and missed only nine regular season games and one playoff game in his career.

He retired in 1946–1947, long after all his teammates had stopped playing. During his career, he averaged 7.2 points per game.

Alexander (Petey) Rosenberg, a 5'10" guard, joined the SPHAS after playing one season of college ball at St. Joseph's College (Philadelphia). The 1938–1939 season was his first, and in thirty-three games, he averaged 7.2 points. He helped the SPHAS win two championships in his first three years. A terrific dribbler, Rosenberg would often run out the clock to seal another victory.

David (Cy) Kaselman, a 5'10" guard, became a member of the SPHAS for the 1929–1930 campaign after graduating from Temple University. Known for his two-handed set shot, Kaselman was regularly a top scorer in league play. His high-arcing shots from nearly half court would swish cleanly through the nets. In his first six seasons, he led the team in scoring each season, and twice he averaged more than 10 points per game. In his thirteen seasons, he won eight championships.

Eddie Gottlieb was a born promoter and helped found the SPHAS in 1918 with friends Hughie Black and Chickie Passon. After a brief career on the court, Gottlieb turned his attention to managing the club and was instrumental in signing the players, booking the games, and promoting the team. Along with basketball, Gottlieb promoted wrestling and baseball and was a key figure within Negro League baseball.

Dave Zinkoff became part of the SPHAS family as a Temple University student and served as the team's publicity manager, public address announcer, and publisher of the *Sphas Sparks*, a part-program, part-gossip-column magazine that was available at every home game. He and Gottlieb were inseparable and both played major roles in the development and growth of the NBA after World War II. Zinkoff later became the announcer for the Philadelphia Warriors and 76ers.

Moe Goldman, the team's starting center, did not accompany his teammates on this particular trip.

League play had ended on December 24, 1938, with a home victory over the Brooklyn Visitations, 50–38. The win raised the team's record to 11–4. Their trip would take them to Ohio, Michigan, and Wisconsin, where they would play six games in nine days. The SPHAS were not due back in Philadelphia until January 7, 1939, for a home contest against the Kingston Colonials.

The first stop, on December 28, 1938, was Akron, where the SPHAS faced the Goodyears, a top team in the recently formed National Basketball League (NBL).[4] A preview article in the *Akron Beacon Journal* stated: "Philadelphia, rated by eastern sports scribes as the greatest team in basketball and a worthy successor to the New York Celtics of Holman, Lapchick, Dehnert, Barry and Banks, is intent upon extending its supremacy to the Midwest."[5] The SPHAS did not disappoint, and before 2,700 fans, defeated the Akron Goodyears 48–33. The game was close at the outset, but baskets by Rosan and Lautman gave the SPHAS a lead they would not relinquish. Rosan led all scorers with 15, while Lautman chipped in with 13 points.

The SPHAS then traveled to Flint, Michigan, for a Friday night game against the Fisher Body team. The game was scheduled for 8:30 at the I.M.A. building on the eleventh floor. A preliminary game between two girls' teams preceded the main event. This marked the SPHAS' first trip to Flint, and the excitement was apparent in the *Flint Journal.* Al Zingone, a local basketball fan and former ABL player with Paterson and Ft. Wayne who had followed professional basketball since the 1920s, testified to the prowess of the SPHAS. "The Celtics are good and so is Renaissance. But if you want to see the best professional basketball team in the country, then you want to see the Philadelphia Hebrews."[6] The SPHAS lived up to Zingone's advanced billing and defeated Fisher, 40–34. Fisher fought back valiantly, but could not overcome a 19-point second period outburst by the SPHAS that gave them a 27–12 lead. Gotthoffer led the scoring with 9 points.

With two wins in two games, the SPHAS made the drive to Wisconsin for three games against the Oshkosh All-Stars, a rising team in the NBL. Faced with the difficult challenge of containing LeRoy "Cowboy" Edwards, Oshkosh's improving big man, the SPHAS dropped three straight to the All-Stars. On January 2, 1939, the SPHAS lost 47–36 in Fond du Lac. The following night, Oshkosh again held serve, 37–32, in West De Pere. In their final matchup, the SPHAS fell again, 36–31, at the Merrill Junior High School in Oshkosh.

Three straight games. Three straight losses, but the SPHAS did not have time to think about their losses. They had a 457-mile trip from Oshkosh to Detroit to face the New York Renaissance, the best black basketball team in the country. Before 1,500 fans at the Light Guard Armory, the SPHAS, behind Petey Rosenberg's 17 points, defeated the Rens 51–45 to earn a split of their six-game trip.

After the last game of the road trip, the team piled into Gottlieb's car for the 586-mile drive back to Philadelphia. Despite three straight losses to Oshkosh, the trip was deemed a success. The SPHAS played before sold-out crowds, made their first trip to Flint, and stayed sharp for the stretch run in league play. As the team drove back through the Midwest and Mid-Atlantic, the players had time to reflect on the games played and how far basketball had progressed since they started playing. Gottlieb was thinking about the future. Even though his team lost three games, he knew they had been winners. It was all part of the journey of professional basketball. Years later, these games and many others like it would prove instrumental in the evolution and growth of basketball in the country.

2

A JEWISH GAME

> Every Jewish boy was playing basketball. Every phone pole had a peach basket on it. And every one of those Jewish kids dreamed of playing for the SPHAs.
>
> —Harry Litwack, quoted in Jon Entine, *Taboo*

Much like the game of basketball, the city of Philadelphia was the result of one man's vision. William Penn was granted a charter from the King of England in 1681 for what eventually became the Pennsylvania colony. Twenty years later, Penn himself issued a charter that established Philadelphia as a city. Quickly, Philadelphia became important for trading and government. The city improved and grew rapidly in the 1750s and 1760s, in large measure due to the efforts and direction of Benjamin Franklin. By the time of the American Revolution, Philadelphia was a central location for the colonies and acted as the host for the First Continental Congress, the Second Continental Congress (at which the Declaration of Independence was signed), and the Constitutional Convention. The city also served for a brief time as the capital of the United States. Eventually, the state and federal governments left Philadelphia, but the city remained an important political and economic hub due to its size and location along the Atlantic coast. Philadelphia continued to grow and in 1876 celebrated the first Centennial Exposition. By the late nineteenth century, the city's population had swelled as immigrants from Europe, including Russia and Eastern Europe, flooded the city. Among these new residents was a heavy concentration of Jews who were fleeing persecution and seeking a new life.

After the game's invention in December 1891, basketball spread quickly and soon made its way to cities up and down the eastern seaboard, including

Philadelphia. It is not known exactly when this new winter game showed up in Philadelphia, but it is safe to presume that some time in 1892, the sport was being introduced to YMCAs throughout the city. On January 15, 1893, an article appeared in the *Philadelphia Inquirer* about the YMCA and some of its activities, remarking, "Among the other features of the evening will be a game of basket ball between West Philadelphia and Northwest teams. A gymnasium exhibition, the Y.M.C.A. Orchestra and the High School Banjo Club will furnish the music."[1] Several weeks later, an article reported that a game between the Camden (New Jersey) and Philadelphia YMCAs was played and that Philadelphia had held on for a 2–0 win. It is interesting to note that, less than two years after basketball's invention, contests between different cities were being arranged. The game's popularity continued to spread in Philadelphia and soon reached the college level. In 1894, basketball was added at Temple University; the first game was a 3–1 victory over the Purple Crescent Athletic Club, a team based in Philadelphia. The Temple Owls finished that first season 8–3, playing mostly YMCA teams, with one game against Haverford College.

Concurrent with the rise of basketball through the YMCA and regional colleges, the game also spread quickly in the Young Men's Hebrew Association (YMHA). The YMHA was impressed by the organization of the YMCA in the 1850s and 1860s. A few YMHAs began in the 1850s, but the association did not gain momentum until 1874 when the New York YMHA was established. A year later, the first YMHA in Philadelphia was established at the northeast corner of Broad and Spring Garden Streets. The YMHA stayed at that location until 1883, when it moved to the Odd Fellow Hall across the street. Over the next fifty years, the YMHA had several locations, until 1926, when it found a permanent home at Broad and Pine Streets, where it is still located today. The YMHA was a communal organization sponsoring programs that focused on educational, religious, and athletic classes. Clubs and classes on athletics became an avenue for Jewish immigrant children to participate safely in sports while becoming more American.

Basketball became particularly popular with immigrants, especially Jewish immigrants. The game, which was still so new that the sport itself had yet to be formalized or codified in any significant way, was a vehicle for Jewish children to assimilate and become American. As opposed to football or baseball, which required large, open areas to play, basketball was an inexpensive sport for children to play. "The Jews never got much into football or baseball. They were too crowded then," Harry Litwack recalled.[2] Not much was required except a hoop and a ball. It could be played almost anywhere—on a playground, behind a tenement house, or on the back of a wall. More so than other sports, basketball is an urban game, and its growth and emergence in the early twentieth century can be traced to the cities and urban demographics. City populations reflected ethnicity and the immigrant communities. Teams were based on ethnic populations; there were teams that were Irish, black, German, and Jewish. Jews gravitated immediately to basketball because it was accessible.

Jews quickly developed their own style relative to the game, and before long, basketball was referred to as a Jewish game. A new style emerged that was predicated on cutting without the ball, with constant movement, ball control, passing, and defense. Ossie Schectman, who grew up playing basketball in Brooklyn, remembers how he learned his distinctive style: "Playing basketball in those days was confined to smaller areas. The physical setup was not too much. The ceilings were low, and there were ten men on the court. You played in a figure-eight and there was lots of movement. It was devoid of long set shots."[3] Sam (Leaden) Bernstein, who grew up in South Philadelphia playing basketball, recalled, "Basketball was a slower game. It was a mental game. If you were a dumb ballplayer, you could not play in the game. If you were slow or could not concentrate or were not capable of playing, then you did not play. You had to be the best to play. There was a lot of competition."[4] With the amount of competition, Jews immediately became good players and the sport was quickly associated with the Jewish community.

A short seven years after the game was invented, basketball was a professional sport with its first official organization. The National Basketball League, which debuted in 1898–1899, was anything but national in scope. The league had six teams based in the greater Philadelphia-Trenton corridor. Three of the teams dropped out that first season, leaving the Trenton Nationals to defeat the Millville, New Jersey, team for the first championship. The league continued for another four seasons and eventually fielded teams in Wilmington and New York, although the New York team played no home games. After the National Basketball League, professional leagues sprung up on the East Coast and in the Mid-Atlantic region. These organizations included the Philadelphia Basketball League, New England Basketball League, Western Massachusetts Basketball League, Eastern League, Hudson River League, New York State League, Pennsylvania State League, and Interstate League.

Basketball was growing in Philadelphia, and the Eastern League was composed of teams from Pennsylvania and New Jersey. The league lasted from 1909–1910 to 1922–1923. One of the top teams in the Eastern League was DeNeri, which represented the South Philadelphia community. Prior

The DeNeri Reserves featured a number of future Philadelphia SPHAS players, including Hughie Black (*front row, far left*) and business manager Abe Radel (*back row, far left*). (*Courtesy of Diane Moskowitz.*)

to the contests featuring the DeNeri team, a preliminary game was often played that featured the DeNeri Reserves, in a match similar to a junior varsity match prior to the varsity match. The DeNeri Reserves of 1915–1916 were a successful team that included a young player by the name of Edwin Black. Forever known as Hughie, Edwin Black may have been the least well-known of the SPHAS' three founding members, in contrast to Eddie Gottlieb and Chickie Passon. By the late 1920s, Black had retired from basketball to focus on teaching and his family, and his status with the SPHAS receded into history. Still, he played an important role in the team's founding and early years.

Born in Russia in 1898, the same year as his future basketball partner Eddie Gottlieb, Black grew up in a small town called Moldavia with his two older sisters, Gussie and Ida. Life in Russia at the turn of the century was particularly difficult, and the rise of pogroms and persecution made life untenable for Russian Jews. His parents, seeing the difficult future ahead, decided to leave Russia and settle in America.

Black's son Marvin, who continues to pass down the story of the SPHAS and his father's role in the team's formation, remembers the dramatic family story of how his father and two sisters left Russia:

> He was born in 1898, and he came to the United States when he was about 6 years old. That was around 1904. He came over with his two sisters and settled in South Philadelphia at Fourth and Reed Streets. His sisters talked about how he walked out of Russia. He would talk about being a child in Russia and hiding when the Cossacks would come looking for young children. They would steal kids from their families. My father and his sisters would hide in closets, in boxes, to hide from these Cossacks. He walked across a secret open area with a sister in each hand to leave Russia. They snuck out of Russia. They snuck out as kids. Apparently, their parents sent them ahead. . . . They came over on a boat and landed in Baltimore as immigrants. They made their way to Philadelphia and always lived as a family in Philadelphia.[5]

After successfully arriving in America and settling in Philadelphia, Black's family sought to build a new life. His father, Louis, became a tailor. His mother was a homemaker, tending to the apartment and the children. The family lived in a heavily Jewish neighborhood, and Black often played with the local children after school. One game that caught everyone's attention was basketball, which by the early 1910s was two decades old.

Black and his neighborhood friends played basketball any chance they had.

Edwin (Hughie) Black was a founding member of the Philadelphia SPHAS, along with Herman (Chickie) Passon and Eddie Gottlieb. He played with the SPHAS during the 1920s before retiring to focus on teaching and running his camp. (*Courtesy of Mickey and Marvin Black.*)

"South Philadelphia was full of immigrant kids. They slept, ate, and loved basketball. They played basketball all the time," Marvin said about the neighborhood in which his father grew up.[6] In an interview given as he neared his ninetieth birthday, Hughie Black recalled playing basketball and how it defined his early years. "Although we didn't know it at the time, it was a very unique team. I had been playing basketball since I was about 9 years old. A group of us who lived in South Philadelphia used to play basketball every minute we could—after school, after dinner—whenever."[7]

With so much time on the courts, Black and his friends soon joined some of the early professional basketball teams that dotted the greater Philadelphia area, including the DeNeri Reserves. Soon thereafter, they enrolled in high school and continued playing together. "They all went to the same high school, South Philadelphia. He played four sports, a four-letter man at South Philadelphia High School. He is a member of the Sports Hall of Fame at South Philly. He played football, baseball, basketball, and he even ran track and field. He was very athletic. He was a good student. He loved children. He was a very charismatic guy all the time. He was able to be very successful as a teacher and had a very good junior high school teaching record," his son noted.[8]

During Hughie Black's high school years, South Philadelphia High School won three consecutive city basketball titles. "South Philadelphia became city champions and that team became the Philadelphia SPHAS," Marvin Black noted. "They organized themselves in 1918. They had no money for uniforms. They formed an association so they could afford to buy uniforms. They even started a sporting goods store called Passon, Gottlieb, and Black."[9]

After high school, Black joined his friend Eddie Gottlieb at the School of Pedagogy, which later became known as the Normal School. His son Marvin recalled:

> He went to Normal School. In those days it was a two-year Normal School at Temple University. He graduated as a teacher. He was the first Jewish physical education teacher in Philadelphia. Physical education instructors were usually German. For a while, my father worked in the meat business with his brothers-in-law and played for the SPHAS. He retired from the SPHAS in the late 1920s when I was a few years old. He left as a player and then became the manager and they made some financial deal with Gottlieb. He went

from player to manager and then retired. He stayed with the meat business a little bit longer even when he was a teacher. And then he just taught.[10]

With Black, Gottlieb, and Passon leading the way, the SPHAS began their first season of professional basketball in 1917–1918 in the American League of Philadelphia. The American League was considered a minor basketball circuit at the time and featured six teams based in the greater Philadelphia region. In that first season, the team was known as the YMHA, and in a short season, they compiled a 4–11 record, which tied them for last place with Port Richmond. The team continued playing in the American League under the support of the YMHA for one year.

A year later, the YMHA, citing the rough play associated with the sport, decided to withdraw its sponsorship of the team. Undaunted, Gottlieb, Black,

The 1918–1919 Philadelphia SPHAS featured the following players: Harry Passon and Lou Schneiderman (*front row, left to right*); Charlie Newman, Mark (Mockie) Bunin, Edwin (Hughie) Black, Herman (Chickie) Passon, and Eddie Gottlieb (*middle row, left to right*); and Bob Seitchick (*back row*). (*Courtesy of Naismith Memorial Basketball Hall of Fame.*)

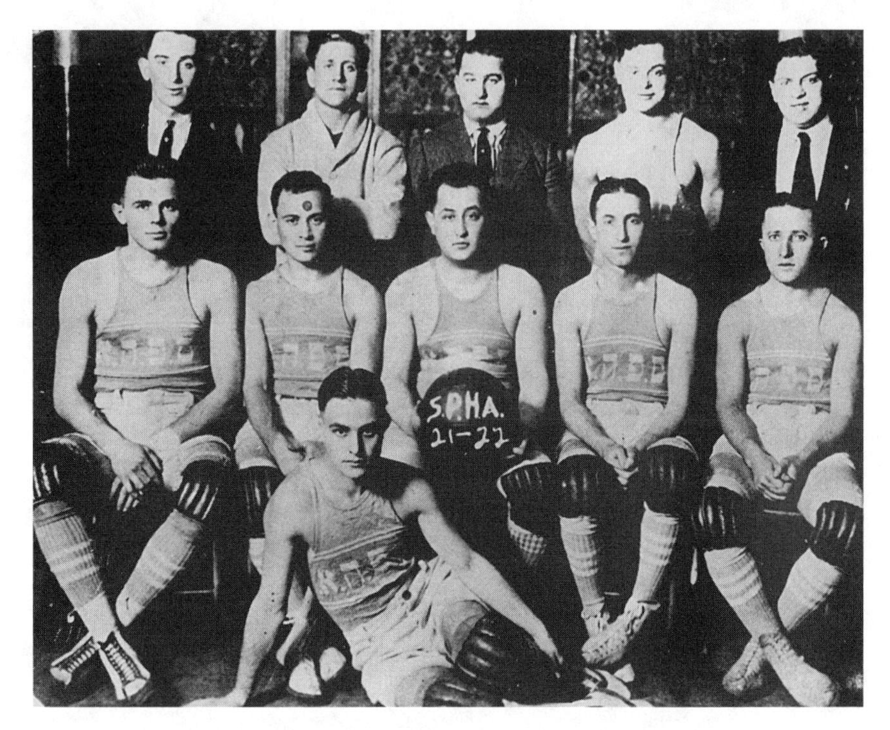

The 1921–1922 Philadelphia SPHAS competed in the American League of Philadelphia. In this photo a young Eddie Gottlieb is shown seated in the center holding the ball. (*Courtesy of Naismith Memorial Basketball Hall of Fame.*)

and Passon approached the competing South Philadelphia Hebrew Association at Fourth and Reed Streets about sponsoring the team. The Association agreed and provided uniforms with the Hebrew acronym SPHAS across the front of the jerseys. Now known as the SPHAS, the team continued playing, but their association with the South Philadelphia Hebrew Association did not last long. The Association withdrew its sponsorship, and for the second time, the SPHAS were without a sponsoring organization. This time, however, the team was more financially sound than in years past and could afford to buy their own uniforms. In the early 1920s, Gottlieb, Black, and Passon opened a sporting goods store, P.G.B., otherwise known as Passon, Gottlieb, Black. Eventually, Passon bought out Gottlieb and Black in their shares of the store and renamed it Passon Sporting Goods. Passon Sporting Goods became one of the most successful sporting goods stores in Philadelphia. For years, Gottlieb kept an office above the store.

With their own store, the trio created the team's uniforms, consisting of plaid shorts and jerseys with the name SPHAS across the front in Hebrew letters. The threesome decided to keep the team name SPHAS as a way to remember their heritage and neighborhood. For a number of years, the team was known as the Wandering Jews, because the team did not have its own home court. Instead, the SPHAS were willing to travel anywhere to play a game.

After their break from the Association, the SPHAS continued to play in the American League and then spent one season, 1922–1923, in the Manufacturer's League, a minor division that comprised company-based teams. That same season, the SPHAS joined the Philadelphia League, which consisted of teams in the Philadelphia region. A number of the teams were represented by religious entities, such as Cathedral, St. Peter's, and Holy Name. In that first season, the SPHAS finished the first half in second place with a 7–3 mark, only to sputter to a 1–8 record in the second half, good for a last-place finish.

The following year, the Philadelphia League added more games to the schedule and the SPHAS finished the first half with a 14–13 record. In the second half, the team finally began to find its groove. It finished in first place with an 11–3 mark and met the first-half champions Tri-Council in the championship round. In the first game, the SPHAS won 31–23. The SPHAS also won the second game to capture their first professional title. This was just the first of many championships in the decades to come.

A championship under their belt, the SPHAS entered the 1924–1925 season with confidence and renewed purpose. The team sprinted out to a 15–4 first-half record, easily distancing themselves from the second-place team. The second half saw the SPHAS falter, but they still earned a trip to the championship round. For the second year in a row, the SPHAS defeated Tri-Council to win the league title. Two championships in three seasons in the Philadelphia League positioned the SPHAS as one of the best local teams. The following season, the SPHAS entered the Eastern League after the demise of the Philadelphia League. Unfortunately, the Eastern League was short-lived as well. The SPHAS finished the first half with an 8–6 record and jumped out to a 6–0 record in the second half before the league ceased operations. Despite this organizational failure, the SPHAS were hitting their stride, and the person most responsible was Eddie Gottlieb.

From the moment the SPHAS were formed, it was evident that the driving force behind the team was Eddie Gottlieb. One of the founding three members along with Hughie Black and Chickie Passon, Gottlieb held a place with the team longer than anyone else. Gottlieb's association began in 1918, when World War I was still raging, and ended as the Eisenhower Administration was concluding its eight years in the White House. By 1959, when the NBA welcomed Wilt Chamberlain into the league, the game was less Jewish than when Gottlieb started four decades earlier. Throughout, it was he who kept the SPHAS going, signed the players, arranged for the games, did advance press, and traveled with them on the road. Ralph Kaplowitz, who played a half season with the SPHAS in 1946, sums up the importance of Gottlieb. "I believe that when you say SPHAS, you have to mention Eddie Gottlieb. He was not only a promoter, but he was the sweetest person you ever wanted to meet. So when you mention the SPHAS, you mention Eddie Gottlieb in the same voice. He was the SPHAS."[11]

Gottlieb was born in 1898 in Kiev, Ukraine, only seven years after basketball was invented. It marked the same year that the National Basketball League debuted. After immigrating to the United States, his family settled in Harlem, where his father, Morris, operated a candy store. Gottlieb lived with his parents and sister, Bella, in an apartment at 107th Street and Madison Avenue. In 1908, the family relocated to Philadelphia to an apartment at 762 South Broad Street. Morris worked as a tailor there, but died shortly thereafter. From then on, Gottlieb helped his mother and sister with tending to the apartment and providing for the family.

Growing up, Gottlieb was attracted to sports, particularly football, baseball, and basketball. His days were spent on the streets with his neighborhood friends playing sports. "Before we moved to Philadelphia, when I was 9 years old, we lived in New York City and I would hitch rides on the back of ice trucks to watch the New York Giants play at the Polo Grounds. I was an average player. Two things were wrong with me as a catcher. I couldn't hit very well and I couldn't throw very well, but I was an A-1 receiver."[12]

When it came time for high school, Gottlieb and his friends all enrolled at South Philadelphia High School, where they continued to play basketball. Southern, as the school was known, had an outstanding basketball team and won the city championship in 1914, 1915, and 1916. Gottlieb captained the team in 1915, and he was joined on the team by Hughie Black, Herman (Chickie) Passon, Mockie Bunin, Moe Ingber, and Charlie Newman. This group, which led Southern to basketball glory, later formed the first SPHAS team in 1918. Gottlieb was part of the regular rotation, a good but not great player. As Gottlieb recalled years later, "I was considered a tough kid. And not to blow my own horn, but I was also always considered a player with a pretty good noodle."[13]

After graduating from Southern in 1916, Gottlieb enrolled at the School of Pedagogy, where he studied teaching for two years and graduated in 1918. While a student in 1917–1918, Gottlieb joined with old friends Chickie Passon and Hughie Black and formed a basketball team under the auspices of the YMHA. The YMHA provided the team with uniforms and affiliation, while the three friends ran all the business and strategic aspects of the team.

Eddie enjoyed playing, but it soon became apparent that his talents did not lie on the court. It was behind the bench, where he could manage the game and utilize his extraordinary capacity for working with numbers. "Eddie Gottlieb was the Mogul. He had the brain of a computer," Sam (Leaden) Bernstein remembered. "He was tough and sarcastic, but he had to be that way. He had a temper and was on the cheap side, but he knew the game. He left a good name. There was nobody like him."[14]

Indeed, there was nobody like him, and Gotty, as he was known, stood out in the pack in a number of ways. To start, he was short, 5'7", heavy-set, and shaped like a pear. He always had bags under his eyes as if he never slept. His office was his coat and pants pockets, with papers, bills, and receipts stuffed in every crevice of his clothing. His appearance gave the impression of being disorganized and disheveled. But in Gottlieb's case, appearances were deceiving. He was an extremely smart man and had exceptional recall, especially for numbers. Years later, he could remember exact details of games, including attendance figures. His capacity for figures and his ability to count attendance in an arena would be remarked upon by nearly everyone who came into contact with him. Long after his players stopped playing for him, they fondly remembered Gottlieb as a fair, honest, and caring person. But above all, in a game where everyone wanted to win, nobody wanted to win more than Gottlieb.

"Eddie was a wonderful man. He stuck to his word," Jerry Fleishman, who played for the SPHAS during World War II, recounted. "He would keep talking until he ran out of breath. One time, we were playing in Detroit and we lost. We are in the bathroom of the airport, and Matt Goukas says he wanted to win in the worst way. Eddie says that he wanted to win more. So, Eddie locks the door and they argue over who wanted to win more. The people in the airport had to call security because Eddie would not let anyone in the bathroom."[15]

Shikey Gotthoffer, one of Gottlieb's best players of the 1930s, remembered the type of person he was:

> Eddie Gottlieb was fair. He was honest and he was fair. He believed in principles. If you're supposed to play 45 minutes, give me 45 minutes. Don't give me 20. He also believed that a ballplayer had to start out with a certain amount of ability to play for him. Eddie learned basketball in Philadelphia. He played in the Jewish League

> way before my time. Eddie wasn't a good basketball player in the sense of using his body. Eddie was very burly and short, but he had a good head on him. He could analyze things and think out things. He was literally the driving force behind the NBA. Eddie created the schedules and did a lot of the organizational work. Eddie was a big wheel in the NBA. He was a teacher. He had taught for a while. Eddie had a lot of logic and brains.[16]

If you played for Gottlieb, then you were expected to play a certain way. He stressed teamwork and fundamentals. It was an essential part of the way the SPHAS played the game. "He was a tough coach. You would not want to be in halftime listening to what he had to say," Louis (Red) Klotz, who later formed the Washington Generals, noted. "He was a fundamental, smart coach, but he was strict, and if you made a mistake, you were in trouble. In those days, the ball moved around. It would not hit the ground unless you were going to drive. The movements were smart; there were picks and blocks."[17]

Gottlieb was obsessed with winning; Jerry Rullo, who played for and later coached the SPHAS, remembers the type of person Gottlieb was. "He was a good coach. He knew what he wanted to do. He was a very competitive man. He always took care of business prior to the game because if we lost, he could not do business too well. He took losing hard. He was a good guy. If he told you something or promised you something, he stuck by his word. He backed up his promises."[18]

In addition to playing and winning in the moment, Gottlieb had a sense of the future and where he thought the game was going. He once remarked to *Sports Illustrated* writer Frank Deford, "We set up the guys who are making all the money now."[19] His ability to plan ahead and to see where the game was headed was not lost on his players. Jack (Dutch) Garfinkel, one of his star guards during World War II, noted, "During the war years, he wanted the league to continue so he called his players and other players and had them play for other teams. He did that so the league could go on. He was quite a promoter."[20]

Moe Goldman commented, "Gottlieb was a very nice fellow. Crazy, but he only wanted to win. He was tough. He was our coach in all the years I played. He was the father of professional basketball. During the war, when the best teams could not hold up, Eddie was taking care of the expenses of some other teams. He had foresight. He kept it moving."[21]

By 1925–1926, under the watchful eye of Gottlieb, the SPHAS were regarded as one of the top teams in Philadelphia. The SPHAS played a strong schedule and were known to travel throughout the region to play any team. Aside from playing in the poorly managed Eastern League, the SPHAS played teams in the American Basketball League (ABL), the first major attempt to create a national basketball league. The ABL was founded in 1925–1926 and was run by Joe Carr, who also served as president of the National Football League. The league stretched from the East Coast to Chicago, shunning the strict regionalism of earlier incarnations. Teams were located in Brooklyn, Washington, Cleveland, Rochester, Ft. Wayne, Boston, Chicago, Detroit, and Buffalo. Gottlieb scheduled games against the ABL as a way to see where his team stood against the elite professional teams. In a six-game stretch that saw the SPHAS play the Brooklyn Arcadians, Ft. Wayne Caseys, Cleveland Rosenblums, Washington Palace Five, and Paterson Legionaires of the Metropolitan League, the team won five contests.

Emboldened by their success against the ABL teams, Gottlieb decided to up the ante and schedule games against the two foremost barnstorming teams in the country. In 1926, the SPHAS played the Original Celtics and New York Renaissance in a total of five games. Against the Original Celtics, the SPHAS lost the first game, 32–24, shooting a miserable 10 of 27 from the foul line. In the second game, the SPHAS won on a last-second shot by Davey Banks. In the final game of the series, the SPHAS easily defeated the Celtics, 36–27, to claim the three-game series.

With the Original Celtics defeated, the last challenge remaining for Gottlieb and his team were games with the New York Renaissance. In the first game, the SPHAS won in overtime, 36–33, as the defense held the Rens without a shot at the basket in overtime. In the second contest, the SPHAS won, 40–39. Both games were held at the Palais Royal at Broad and Bainbridge Streets. The victories over both the Celtics and Rens significantly boosted the confidence of the SPHAS and, most importantly for Gottlieb, gave the team increased exposure within the basketball community. Writing the review for the SPHAS in the *Reach Basket Ball Guide*, Abe Radel, the team's business manager, declared, "Scribes, basketball historians and other notables were unanimous in proclaiming the 1926 edition of the South Philadelphia Hebrew Association one of the greatest, if not the greatest, combinations in basketball history."[22]

With the quick demise of the Eastern League and the SPHAS' recent success against elite teams, Gottlieb was faced with the challenge of where the team should play. Should they join another league or should they play as an independent team? Gottlieb wisely chose to join the ABL for the 1926–1927 season. After a successful initial season, the ABL looked forward to another year of professional basketball. Gottlieb entered his team and changed the name from the SPHAS to the Warriors. The Philadelphia Warriors (later the team name in the Basketball Association of America [BAA] in 1946–1947) played two seasons in the ABL and acquitted themselves quite well. In 1926–1927, the Warriors finished the first half at 14–7, in third place. In the second half, the team slipped to 10–11 and into fourth place. The following year, the league reorganized into Eastern and Western Divisions. The Warriors finished the season in second place in the Eastern Division with a 30–21 mark, a full nine games behind league leader New York. The Warriors earned a trip to the playoffs where they were defeated by New York in two games.

During their two-year stint in the ABL, one of the team's key players off the bench was Louis Sherr. Reds, as he was affectionately called because of his shock of red hair, was a fixture in the Philadelphia basketball community during the 1920s. In many ways, Reds's journey as a player during the Roaring Twenties was indicative of the game during that time. Basketball in the 1920s was still a loosely organized proposition. Many leagues sprung into action, while most struggled as they faced financial difficulty. Teams started and then abruptly withdrew. Players did not have contracts and often played on different teams in different leagues, offering themselves to the highest bidder. Reds's own career reflected the unsettled nature of the sport.

Louis Sherr was born into an Orthodox family on February 2, 1905. As a child growing up in Philadelphia, he quickly gravitated to sports, where his talent was readily apparent. He first played basketball at McCall Grammar School and later joined the Ardentes Juniors in the Philadelphia Playground League, and Anchor in the Philadelphia Amateur League. When it came time for high school, Sherr enrolled at Southern. In his sophomore season, he started jumping center for the team, and by the time of his graduation in 1922 earned

Louis (Reds) Sherr was a standout player and student at the University of Pennsylvania before he joined the Philadelphia SPHAS. During the 1920s, Sherr played for the SPHAS in several different professional leagues. (*Courtesy of Lynn Sherr and Lois Sherr Dubin.*)

the unique distinction of receiving the Athletic Medal of Honor and was elected a member of the Philadelphia All-Scholastic basketball team. This duality between academics and athletics followed him as he enrolled at the University of Pennsylvania.

While a student at Penn, Sherr continued playing with Judaic Union of the Jewish Basketball League. Many players in the Jewish Basketball League hoped to one day play for the SPHAS. Sherr played for a number of teams and periodically joined the SPHAS for random games in the Philadelphia and Eastern Leagues. As a college student, Sherr was a two-time letter winner in 1925 and 1926 and helped guide the Penn team to 17–5 and 14–7 records in his years on the varsity. He graduated college in 1926 and earned the Frazier Prize, which recognized the athlete with the highest academic standing. His high school and college record allowed him to pursue a law degree at Penn.

Sherr continued playing through law school and joined with Eddie Gottlieb when he played for the Philadelphia Warriors in the ABL. In 1926–1927, he played in twelve games and averaged 2.7 points per game. The following year, Sherr became the primary option for Gottlieb off the bench and saw action in twenty-five contests, scoring a total of 80 points. He played in both playoff losses in 1928 to New York and averaged 3.5 points per game. Sherr continued playing in the evenings and on weekends even after graduating law school in 1929, months before the stock market crashed. He played in the ABL and then rejoined the SPHAS in the early 1930s, when the team was dominating the competition in the Eastern Basketball League.

After two seasons in the ABL, the SPHAS spent the 1928–1929 season as an independent team traveling on their own and scheduling their own games. Prior to the start of the 1929–1930 season, Gottlieb welcomed a new addition to the team in Harry Litwack. The team was now entering the Eastern Basketball League and Litwack became the team's newest star. For the rest of their lives, Litwack and Gottlieb were extremely close friends.

Born on September 20, 1907, Harry Litwack was only 3 years old when his parents made the journey from Galicia, Austria, to Baltimore, Maryland. His parents, Jacob and Rachel, had saved enough money to move Litwack and his five sisters to America. Eventually, the family settled in Philadelphia, where his father worked as a shoemaker and his mother raised the family. Litwack and his siblings learned English, adapting to their new country, while their parents spoke only Yiddish at home.

Basketball soon attracted Litwack's attention and he began playing this new game on the streets with the neighborhood boys. "The Jews never got

Harry Litwack, who joined the SPHAS for the 1929–1930 season, became known for his accurate outside shot. After his playing career, Litwack went on to become a Hall of Fame coach at Temple University. (*Courtesy of Diane Moskowitz.*)

much into football or baseball. They were too crowded then," Harry Litwack reflected many years later. Basketball was easier to play and cost less. Football and baseball required more space and in the Jewish neighborhood in South Philadelphia, space was at a premium. Basketball was conducive to the tight spaces of the streets and tenement buildings. Soon the Jews in those neighborhoods developed their own playing style; as Litwack noted, "It was a quick-passing running game as opposed to the bullying and fighting way which was popular other places."[23]

Litwack soon excelled at this new game, enrolling at Temple University, where he became a very good player. A four-year team member, he captained the Owls his junior and senior seasons. While at Temple, he played basketball on the side with the Hakoahs in the Philadelphia League. In his senior season, he began teaching at a junior high school and joined the SPHAS when he graduated. Litwack was a perfect addition to the team.

A smart, seven-season player, Litwack knew how to fit in with his teammates. He was sound in fundamentals and rarely made mistakes. Louis (Red) Klotz, who first played with the SPHAS Reserves during the late 1930s, grew up watching the SPHAS, particularly Litwack. "Harry Litwack was my idol as a player. As a kid, he was the player I watched on the SPHAS all the time. He was my man, and he became a great teacher and coach at Temple. His style of play is not lost today."[24]

"Most people know that Harry Litwack was a great coach, but most people do not know that he was a great player, too," Sam (Leaden) Bernstein, who saw the team play at the Palais Royal, recalled. "I am left-handed and I watched them play and I wanted to play just like Harry. He was strong, beautiful eye, and was smart. He knew how to play the game. Litwack had a good outside shot. He possessed a good hook shot and he had it all. Guys used to say do not fool around with him because he was a quiet man, but do not get in a fight with him."[25]

Bernstein's advice about not picking a fight with Litwack was not heeded by the Jersey Reds one night in a game in northern New Jersey. As Litwack remembered it, "Because we were Jews, we often had hostile crowds. They wanted to see us get killed. One time in Jersey City or Hoboken, the ball went out of bounds and a fan grabbed it. I tried to get it back from him to put the ball into play quickly, and that started a big fight. I was hit over the head with a Coke bottle by an irate fan, and had to be taken to the hospital."[26]

The incident was long remembered by some of Litwack's teammates who, decades later, could recall every moment of that incident. As Gil Fitch noted, "They'd throw stuff at you. I saw Harry Litwack get smashed on the head with a Coke bottle during a game in Union City, and blood was oozing down his face."[27] Lou Forman, the team's starting center before the arrival of Moe Goldman, recalled, "I remember that time in Jersey City when Harry Litwack got hit over the head with a bottle. Harry tried to get the ball away from a fan, and that started a free-for-all with the six of us and Gotty up against the wall throwing punches at the fans."[28]

During Litwack's playing days, the game of basketball was still rough and it was not uncommon for fights to break out between teams or between the teams and the fans, who often sat very close to the action. "I heard stories about Harry Litwack and Chickie Passon and what they went through," Sam (Leaden) Bernstein recalled. "They threw things at guys like them. They were so good on the floor, and fans were so anti-Semitic. They would throw cans at them—anything at them. They do not talk much about this, but they were tough."[29]

When Litwack joined the SPHAS for the 1929–1930 season, the team was joining the Eastern Basketball League after spending a year playing as an independent team in the greater Philadelphia region. This was the third edition of the once-successful Eastern Basketball League. The league comprised six teams in the Philadelphia area, with one team as far north as Camden, New Jersey, and another as far south as Wilmington, Delaware. The regular season was divided into two halves, with the winner of the first half facing off against the second-half winner for the championship.

In their four years in the Eastern Basketball League, the SPHAS were clearly the top team and the biggest draw. The team won the championship

The 1929–1930 Philadelphia SPHAS won the first of three consecutive championships in the Eastern Basketball League. Counted among the team members were Cy Kaselman (*front row, second from the left*), George Wolfe (*front row, second from the right*), Harry Litwack (*front row, far right*), Coach Eddie Gottlieb (*second row, middle*), and Abe Radel (*second row, far right*). (*Courtesy of Diane Moskowitz.*)

the first three years and made it to the finals in the fourth season. In 1929–1930, the first year, the SPHAS finished in second place in the first half with a 16–4 record, a game behind the Philadelphia Elks. The team won the second half with a 14–3 mark. The SPHAS edged the Elks for the championship in five games. The following season, the SPHAS picked up where they left off and led the first half with a 17–3 record. They faced the Camden Skeeters in the championship and won in four games. In 1931–1932, the SPHAS de-

This trophy was awarded to the Philadelphia SPHAS for winning the 1929–1930, 1930–1931, and 1931–1932 Eastern Basketball League championships. (*Courtesy of Naismith Memorial Basketball Hall of Fame.*)

feated the Philadelphia Moose to capture their third consecutive title. The next season was the last for the Eastern States Basketball League, and the SPHAS finally met their match, the Trenton Moose, who bested them in the finals. In 1929–1930 and 1930–1931, the Eastern Basketball League was a minor league, but in 1931–1932 and 1932–1933, the renamed Eastern States Basketball League was a major league. The two teams would meet again the following year in a new league and under different circumstances. By then, Gottlieb had assembled a strong team that was starting to peak at just the right time.

3

A NEW LEAGUE, A NEW TEAM

Goldman, You're At Center.

—Eddie Gottlieb, quoted in Moe Goldman, interview by Robert Peterson

On October 30, 1933, a meeting occurred at 120 Wall Street in New York City. It marked the first league meeting for the reconstituted ABL. After two years during which all league operations had ceased due to the Great Depression that engulfed the nation, John J. O'Brien reorganized the league and made it more regional as opposed to national in scope. Eddie Gottlieb, representing the Philadelphia SPHAS, was present, along with promoters for the Trenton Moose, Brooklyn Jewels, Brooklyn Visitations, Bronx Americans, Union City Reds, Newark Bears, Hoboken Thourots, Camden Brewers, and New Britain Palaces. The league would have teams as far north as New Britain, Connecticut, and as far south as Philadelphia, with the greatest concentration of teams in New Jersey, just outside of New York City.

The meetings, which occurred monthly, always at O'Brien's New York law offices on Wall Street, covered all aspects of league operations with an emphasis on oversight of the games. For instance, at the November 13 meeting, the league's second, the starting times for all home games were agreed upon. Philadelphia would tip off at 9:00 P.M., while the other teams started between 9:00 and 9:45 P.M. Only Union City had an early start time, 4:45 P.M.

The meetings also dedicated significant time to discussing rules and administrative issues. In December, the owners agreed that a jump ball could not take place in the foul zone area but only on the foul line. A player would be allowed to pivot once in any direction following a legal dribble. A horn would be sounded to denote the last five minutes in the final period. Over the next two decades, until the ABL disbanded in 1952–1953, the league continued to have monthly meetings, and Gottlieb had a strong presence in the league's operation.

Since withdrawing his Philadelphia Warriors after the 1927–1928 season in the original ABL, Gottlieb had returned his team to the greater Philadelphia area and the success he enjoyed in the early 1920s. In 1928–1929, his team, again known as the SPHAS, played independently before joining the newly established Eastern Basketball League in 1929–1930. In four years in the Eastern Basketball League, Gottlieb was able to rebuild the team, shedding some of his players from the early years and adding new ones who would be instrumental in the team's success over the next decade. With an eye toward the future and working his connections throughout Philadelphia, Gottlieb built a team that, by the mid-1930s, was regarded as one of the best teams in America. He quickly rejoined the ABL when it started anew in 1933–1934.

The 1933–1934 ABL season began on November 18 at the Broadwood Hotel as the SPHAS hosted the Hoboken Thourots. The game saw the introduction of three fifteen-minute periods, a rule that had been discarded by the old Eastern League more than twenty years earlier. The game witnessed many out-of-bounds plays, but behind Cy Kaselman's extraordinary shooting (15 points), the SPHAS cruised to an easy 34–20 win. A week later the SPHAS were back in action at home versus the Union City Reds. The league was still experimenting with different rules and game operations, and this game was notable for introducing the practice of having two officials. One official called the infractions, and the other tossed the ball after each made basket. The second official for this particular game, interestingly, was Hughie Black, a founding member of the SPHAS in 1918. Black received a warm ovation from the crowd. Despite the good feelings in the building, the SPHAS lost a close game, 41–38, to drop to 1–1 early in the season.

Throughout the first half, the SPHAS were paced by Cy Kaselman, who led the team in scoring in fifteen games during this period. His offense, though, was not enough to keep the SPHAS from playing inconsistently during the season's first half. Except for a five-game winning streak in late December/early January, the SPHAS could not gather any momentum or string together a successful winning streak. Two losses to the Newark Bears and Trenton Moose dropped the SPHAS' record to 15–12 as the season's first half came to a close.

AMERICAN BASKETBALL LEAGUE

OFFICIAL SCORE BLANK

Visiting Team Hoboken vs. Home Team So. Phila. Hebrew Assn. Date Nov. 18/1933

Hoboken Player		Field Goals	Foul Goals	Number Foul Chances	Assists	Total Points
Adams	F	1	1	3	0	3
McEnroe	F	0	0	0	0	0
Stekowitz	F	2	1	4	3	5
Bosch	F	0	0	0	0	0
Jacobs	C	0	1	2	0	1
Berger	G.	1	0	1	1	2
Kist	G.	3	3	3	1	9
Total		7	6	13	5	20

Sphas Player		Field Goals	Foul Goals	Number Foul Chances	Assists	Total Points
Wolfe	F.	1	2	2	3	4
Kaselman	F.	6	4	6	1	16
Lautman	C	1	0	0	0	2
Forman	C	0	0	0	1	0
Gotthoffer	G.	2	3	7	2	7
Litwack	G.	2	1	2	1	5
Fitch	G.	0	0	0	0	0
Total		12	10	17	8	34

REFEREE Dr. Louis Sugarman

Score, End First Period: Visiting Team 10 Home Team 9

Score, End Second Period: Visiting Team 16 Home Team 23

" " Third Period " " 20 " " 34

DISQUALIFICATIONS: Visiting Team / Home Team

REMARKS

SCORER Phil Silverman TIMEKEEPER Abe Radel

File immediately with John J. O'Brien, 120 Wall Street, New York

This scorecard from the first game the Philadelphia SPHAS played in the American Basketball League records the team's 34–20 victory over the visiting team, the Hoboken Thourots, on November 18, 1933. (*From the ABL Collection, courtesy of Naismith Memorial Basketball Hall of Fame.*)

As the second half of the 1933–1934 season began, the SPHAS welcomed a new addition to the team. Over the next nine years, Moe Goldman would be a mainstay for the squad, providing solid leadership and a strong interior presence. His arrival came at an opportune time. Teams that possessed strong inside games, such as the Trenton Moose with Tiny Hearn and the Brooklyn Jewels with Mac Kinsbrunner, repeatedly punished the SPHAS, shoving them around and controlling the ball off the center jump.

In thinking about his team for the second half and its chances to contend with the Trenton Moose and Brooklyn Jewels, Eddie Gottlieb realized he needed a young, athletic center to offset these lumbering opposing centers. Finding a versatile big man would allow his team to play the up-tempo style he favored. He needed someone to control the center jump. He needed Moe Goldman.

Basketball happened later for Moe Goldman than it did for other players of his generation. Born in the Brownsville neighborhood of Brooklyn in 1913 to immigrant parents, Morris Goldman did not immediately gravitate to

Moe Goldman joined the SPHAS for the second half of the 1933–1934 season and helped revolutionize the center position over the next decade. (*Courtesy of Bill Himmelman.*)

basketball. A smaller child growing up, Goldman played other popular games such as stickball and handball. Even when he entered Franklin K. Lane High School, Goldman played only recreationally and rarely had contact with the basketball team. "I learned to play basketball in high school. We played a little bit on the playgrounds but not much," Goldman remembered many years later.[1] He was small and had little interest in the game.

All of that changed during the summer before his senior year when he grew six inches to 6'2", becoming the tallest person in his class. When he returned to school in the fall, the other students assumed he was a basketball player, so he joined the team. "When I came back to school, the basketball coach took one look at me and said, 'Oh, you've got to be a basketball player.'"[2] Without ever having played competitive basketball in his life, Goldman was now the starting center for the 1929–1930 Franklin K. Lane boys' basketball team.

In his only year of high school basketball, Goldman performed tremendously, leading his team to the New York Public School Athletic League (PSAL) basketball championship. Selected to several all-scholastic teams, Goldman led Lane to a 12–1 record and a 24–23 overtime victory over previously undefeated Textile High for the city championship. Injured during the game, Goldman refused to come out, "fully realizing that his presence was essential to his team's success."[3] In becoming the first Brooklyn winner of the PSAL championship since 1922, Lane defeated three powerhouses in New Utrecht, Bryant, and Textile in the same week. "A cool, dependable player, [Goldman] constantly out-tapped the highly touted Moe Spahn [in the Bryant game], and then repeated the same opposite Johnny La Rocca, Textile star and adjudged the best centre in Manhattan and the Bronx."[4]

Nearing the end of his high school career, Goldman was approached by an assistant coach at City College of New York (CCNY), who asked if he would like to play college ball. "Nat Holman did not recruit me; somebody else did, but I don't remember who it was. I think it was an assistant coach who asked me to come. Some of the older ballplayers at City College, like Moe Spahn, also asked me to come," Goldman noted. "I had the scholastic average to get in, and I wanted to play basketball and study."[5] So, in 1930, he joined the Beavers program.

When Goldman joined the Beavers in 1930, CCNY basketball was in the process of building a basketball legacy led by legendary New York City player Nat Holman. Holman was one of the game's first great basketball players, and he was instrumental in promoting basketball among Jewish immigrants in New York City. He would become a very important figure in the rise of New York City basketball in the first half of the twentieth century.

Born Nathan Helmanowich on October 19, 1896, Nat Holman grew up on the Lower East Side of New York City as the seventh of ten children. His father owned a grocery store, and all the children took turns helping with various tasks around the store. Along with his brothers, Holman gravitated toward sports and soon developed into a good athlete. Basketball, still relatively new during Holman's childhood, proved a popular game for Nat and other immigrant children to play. Holman joined the various social clubs and the Educational Alliance and Henry Street Settlement, where he learned to play basketball. As he recalled, "The settlement houses played a significant role in the life of every Jewish youngster on the Lower East Side. They provided us with homes away from home. There were a variety of sports and cultural activities, plus functions."[6]

He soon became a good player and joined the Roosevelt Big Five, a team of Jewish kids from the Lower East Side. He kept improving and continued playing while enrolled in P.S. 62 and P.S. 75 before entering Commerce High School in 1912. As a high school student, Holman played basketball, baseball, and soccer. During his sophomore season, he led Commerce High School to the PSAL championship in basketball and over the remaining three seasons took an active role in coaching the team. Holman graduated Commerce and, instead of accepting an offer to pitch in the Cincinnati Reds farm system, enrolled in the Savage School for Physical Education (later part of New York University [NYU]), where he led the team to a 30–0 record in his two years.

While a student at the Savage School, Holman began a professional basketball career that over the next seventeen years saw him become one of the game's premier players. He led Germantown to the 1921 Eastern League championship before embarking on a career with the world famous Original Celtics. Holman's brilliant passing and savvy as a floor general made the

Original Celtics the game's best team and biggest gate. His talents earned him an unheard-of contract of $12,500 per season and the reputation as the game's greatest attraction. Holman became known as "Mr. Basketball" during the 1920s, a moniker later attributed to George Mikan of the Minneapolis Lakers, widely regarded as basketball's top player in the 1950s.

When Moe Goldman enrolled in college, Holman had been coaching at CCNY since graduating from the Savage School in 1918. Hired as a tutor in the Hygiene Department and as varsity soccer coach and freshman basketball coach, Holman soon took over the varsity basketball program. Within a short time, the Beavers developed into a top team not only in New York but also on the entire East Coast.

Steeped in the fundamentals of the game, much of which made him one of the game's best players, Holman introduced that basics-first style to his players. Possession of the ball and smart shot selection became characteristics of his teams. He urged his players to control the ball, work it around for a good shot, and play as a team. He was hard on his players, demanding, but year in and year out, he fielded strong, competitive teams that played sound basketball. During a 1987 interview, Goldman recalled:

> Nat Holman was very disciplined. He was a master of fundamentals, and he insisted that you do all the things he wanted you to do. He wanted you to pass the ball and get your shot inside rather than outside. He was tough, but he was fair. He was a good coach.
>
> Nat Holman would have everybody on his teams do the same thing. For example, everybody had to shoot fouls underhanded. I was a pretty good foul shooter, but I couldn't shoot underhand. So, in practice, I would shoot overhand and he would kick me in the behind and say "Underhand." But he finally had to give in because my average overhand was very good. I was actually the first ballplayer who changed foul shooting from underhand to overhand.[7]

When Moe Goldman was in college, the center jump defined how the game was played and coached. After each basket scored, the players gathered at half court and jumped the ball. This stopped any momentum that the offensive team may have generated. The game was possession-oriented, and each team sought one big man capable of winning the center jump. As Goldman recalled, "At the beginning, we jumped center after each basket. There was no such thing as taking the ball out."[8]

As center, fully grown at 6'2", Goldman figured prominently in the outcome of most games, and his ability to score made him a double threat. "We used the center jump after each basket. I could jump pretty well. I'd get rebounds from the big fellows," Goldman noted. "I could outjump them. I could jump and run, and I was one of the few center men who could shoot from a distance fairly accurately, the two-handed set shot."[9]

The center jump figured prominently in the strategy employed by players and coaches. "We had plays off the center jump. If the other team had a tall center that could outjump me, we had set plays for defense off the center jump," Goldman recalled in 1987. Meanwhile, if Goldman knew he could outjump his center opponent, they had set plays for that too. "I would usually give a signal to where I was going to tap it by nodding. We would give a signal like a face here or a nod there. We didn't use numbers or by talking to each other. For every jump ball, you had a moment to walk to it and while you're walking, I'd say 'I'll try and get it to you.'"[10]

During his three seasons with the Beavers, Goldman became one of the finest college centers of his era; according to Goldman, "If it were today I would probably be chosen as a number-one draft choice."[11] As a sophomore, his first with the team, he helped CCNY compile a 16–1 record. The following year, the team finished 13–1 and repeated as eastern champions.

A three-time All-Metropolitan selection (twice on the first team), he captained the Beavers his senior year while earning All-America honors. Goldman put forth an outstanding effort all year. Toward the end of his senior season, City College traveled to Philadelphia to play Temple University. The game marked the seventh time CCNY and Temple played, and the new rivalry had been one-sided, with Holman's team losing only once. That one loss, 33–29, had been the only blemish on CCNY's 1931–1932 season.

A contender for national honors in 1933–1934, CCNY was ready to stamp out Temple's hopes of an upset. Writing the next day in its game coverage, the *Philadelphia Inquirer* stated, "That band of tartars from Upper New York ripped up and down Mitten Hall court with a vicious attack and when the fight was over the Cherry and White of Temple University was trailing in the dust by a 33–29 count."[12]

Goldman proved to be the difference in the game. His ability to gain the center tap kept a feisty Owls squad at bay. Temple sent three different players at Goldman, including future SPHAS teammate Howard (Red) Rosan, but all fell short in their attempt to outjump Goldman. As the *Inquirer* reported, "The great Lavender pivot was the bulwark of the attack for the City College team. He was all over the court and gave out many timely assists. He played well in the back court and was constantly getting the ball out of scrimmage to zip it forward to his mates."[13] His 16 points led all scorers. As Goldman noted, "We beat them, which was very unusual because in those days each home team got their own referees. There was no such thing as a referees' association. They assigned referees."[14]

Back at the hotel after the game, one of Moe's teammates came into his room and said, "Moe, there's somebody here to see you. He said he's Eddie Gottlieb."

"I don't know who Eddie Gottlieb is," Goldman said.

"He's the owner of the Philadelphia team," his teammate replied.

"Okay, I'll see him," Goldman told his teammate, even though he had never heard of the SPHAS or Gottlieb.

With nothing to lose, Goldman met with Gottlieb for a few minutes. Gottlieb told him about the team and the newly formed ABL and how professional basketball operated. He mentioned his need for a center and how Goldman was the last piece of the puzzle, the perfect complement for his young team.

"Moe, how would you like to play for the SPHAS?" Gottlieb asked.

"I don't mind, but I have two more college games to play," Goldman replied.

"I'll offer you $35 a game," Gottlieb explained. "Now Saturday night you're playing NYU. That will be your last game. Sunday night we'll be in Brooklyn playing against the New York Jewels in the American League. So you meet us at Arcadia Hall in Brooklyn."

Goldman and Gottlieb shook hands, and Goldman became a member of the SPHAS. "I accepted, because it was good money, comparatively speaking," Goldman recalled.[15]

A day after his college career ended with a heartbreaking 24–18 loss to archrival NYU, Goldman "took a bus by myself to what we called Arcadia Hall.[16] Arcadia Hall was a dance hall that they converted to basketball. It could seat a couple of thousand. On an average night, the Jewels would have drawn 1,000 to 1,200. Usually, there were dances before the game, or after the game.[17] I got to the gate and the gate people wouldn't let me in."[18]

"I'm playing for Philadelphia," Goldman said.

"I don't know you from Adam," the guard, who would not let Goldman inside, replied.

Gottlieb finally came down and said, "Yeah, he's one of my players." He escorted Goldman into the locker room to meet his teammates and receive a uniform. "I got a uniform and I figured I'd go upstairs and watch them play," Goldman said.[19]

As the team huddled up on the sideline, Gottlieb announced, "Goldman, you're at center." Without ever having played professionally, let alone even met his new teammates, Goldman joined Shikey Gotthoffer, Cy Kaselman, Red Wolfe, and Inky Lautman at center court against the Jewels. "I'd never even played with those fellows before," Goldman remarked. "But I'll tell you this much, it didn't matter. You can always break in with a team if you know some of the fundamentals."[20]

With Goldman starting at center, the SPHAS were on their way to becoming the dominant team in the league.

After winning the first two games of the season's second half over the Newark Bears and the Bronx Americans, the SPHAS welcomed Goldman to the team with a road game against the Brooklyn Jewels at Arcadia Hall on March 4, 1934. "Greatly enforced by the presence of Moe Goldman, former City College of New York captain making his professional debut, the Philadelphia Hebrews upset the Brooklyn Jewels 30–24,"[21] the *Philadelphia Inquirer* wrote the following day. Goldman opened the scoring for Philadelphia with a foul shot but was badly outplayed by his center opponent Matty Begovich, who outscored him 10–4. Sensing Goldman's first-game nervousness, veteran George (Red) Wolfe, a New York native himself, paced the SPHAS with 9 points to lead the team to their third straight victory.

With a week before his Philadelphia debut, Goldman had time to adjust to the professional game and leave his college career behind. On March 10, 1934, Goldman made his Broadwood Hotel debut, pacing the SPHAS with 9 points to lead them to a 41–36 victory over the Brooklyn Visitations. Despite miserable winter weather that night, the Jewish community turned out "to get a look at Goldman, who has been touted as one of the best centre men to come from college ranks." His four long set shots "were carefully set tries that went cleanly through the nets."[22] The game was a tough defensive struggle as Inky

George (Red) Wolfe was a 5'11" guard/forward from New York City who held the team record for playing the most seasons (15) and was second in total games played (457). (*Courtesy of Naismith Memorial Basketball Hall of Fame.*)

Lautman chipped in with 9 points to help the SPHAS pull out their fourth straight win.

Goldman still needed to work on mastering the center jump and on adjusting to the physical nature of the pro game. He had been outplayed by the Visitations' Frankie Moore and Red Conaty. But the SPHAS were winning and had found their much-needed center, one who would be with them until World War II.

With Goldman came winning and more winning. The SPHAS compiled a 14–0 record in the second half, the last twelve wins coming with Goldman in the lineup. The SPHAS simply dominated their opponents. With the exception of a 21–17 victory versus the Brooklyn Visitations and a 27–25 win against the New Britain Palaces, the SPHAS were never seriously challenged. In their other ten games, the SPHAS won by an average of 10.1 points per game, easily the best in the league.

The team scored and scored. Seven times in the second half of the season, they scored more than 40 points, including a season-high 69 against the Bronx Americans in early March. Goldman led the team in scoring in only one game, but his youth at the center position enabled the SPHAS to play a more up-tempo game. With Goldman in the lineup, the other players could focus on their positions and not worry about rebounding and interior defense. Instead of relying on the slow, methodical game of the 1920s, the SPHAS introduced a more fast-paced game indicative of their personnel. According to Goldman, "There was continuous movement toward the basket, continuous passing. A few teams have it, but in our day it was all passing. You tried to get under or near the basket. Your shots were taken near the basket."[23]

Prior to Goldman's fourth game, the *Philadelphia Record* summed him up as "the main reason for the Hebrews' success. For in acquiring Goldman, Eddie Gottlieb has ended his search for a tapoff artist who lives up to all qualifications, a good scorer, an excellent floor man and one adept in getting the jumps. Goldman's acquisition has rounded the SPHAS into a winning combination, as Gottlieb's aggregation has won three straight with the gangling Jewish youngster at the pivot post."[24]

The SPHAS sailed through the regular season, winning the second half comfortably over the New Britain Palaces, and setting the stage for a matchup against the Trenton Tigers, first-half winners, for the championship.

The first championship series for the reconstituted ABL matched two teams that knew each other well. Ever since professional basketball had begun in 1898, Trenton and Philadelphia had fought for supremacy of this new sport. Through various professional leagues over the previous thirty years, basketball power had shifted back and forth across the Delaware River frequently. The 1933–1934 championship series was largely a repeat of the championship in the Eastern States Basketball League the year before, when the SPHAS defeated the Trenton Moose in four games. Mostly intact from the previous season, Trenton sported a well-rounded squad with Rusty Saunders, future Basketball Hall of Famer John (Honey) Russell, George Glasco, Tiny Hearn, and Lou Spindell. The SPHAS, meanwhile, were a younger team with the freshmen additions of Inky Lautman, Shikey Gotthoffer, and Moe Goldman. Cy Kaselman, Red Wolfe, Harry Litwack, Gil Fitch, and Lou Forman had been with the team for several seasons. It was a testament to Eddie Gottlieb that he was able to add three new players in the first year of the ABL, all of whom became key contributors until World War II.

Two contrasting styles with teams going in different directions set up the storyline for the series. A veteran team, Trenton slowed the tempo and directed their offense from the pivot. Meanwhile, Philadelphia aimed to spread the floor and use their speed to open up the offense for easy baskets. After the series, the Trenton franchise folded. In 1935–1936, the Trenton Bengals joined the league for a season, and in 1941–1942, the Trenton Tigers joined for a few seasons. But this series marked the last go-round for the great Trenton teams of the late 1920s and early 1930s.

Youth and speed paid immediate dividends in the opening game. Moved to Trenton High School from the arena downtown to accommodate the overflow crowd, the game saw the SPHAS "run wild on the spacious enclosure," according to the *Philadelphia Inquirer*. Using their quickness and passing ability, the SPHAS "unleashed a glittering offense with which the home forces were totally unable to cope," the *Inquirer* reported.[25] Newcomers Gotthoffer, Goldman, and Lautman tallied 21 points as they cruised to a 28–21 victory. With their convincing opening win, the SPHAS were "overwhelming series favorites" and looked to take advantage of the home court in the second game at the Broadwood Hotel.[26]

After being outclassed on their home court in Game 1, the Moose reverted to the play that earned them a 24–6 first-half record. Playing a ball-control offense, they frustrated a youthful SPHAS team looking to continue their winning ways. In his first year with Trenton, Rusty Saunders, the Moose captain, proved one of the league's best all-around players. Now in his ninth professional season, Saunders was in his prime. Since turning professional in 1924–1925 as an 18-year-old high school senior, Saunders had played in nearly every professional league that existed. Twice during the mid-1920s, he led the first ABL in scoring, though it was his pivot play that made him a truly exceptional player.

Looking to even the series, Trenton turned to Saunders to get them on track. As the *Inquirer* reported:

> Russ Saunders stood at the foul mark and worked the one count pivot play in such a manner that the Sphas were unable to deflect the ball. Back and forth the leather traveled between George Glasco and Saunders, Spindell and Saunders, Russell and Saunders, with Tiny Hearn right in the job to intercept any wild pass. The Sphas looked as if they were bewildered, they could not get the ball, goal after goal was piled through the net, nine in all, to send the Gottlieb clan down to one of its worst defeats of the season.[27]

Trenton's 19–6 third period helped even the series at a game apiece.

The acquisition of Moe Goldman in February had defined the SPHAS' fortunes. The past and future of the center position in basketball was on display with Tiny Hearn and Goldman. Goldman had had a strong opening game but had been outplayed by Hearn and had scored only 2 points in Game 2. "Not considered a heavy scorer," Hearn "was in the right place on two occasions," the *Philadelphia Inquirer* wrote in its article on the game.[28] A plodding center whose primary objective was to play defense, Hearn had rebounded the ball and had won the center jump after each basket. Scoring would fall to his teammates.

"Trenton had Rusty Saunders and Tiny Hearn. They were big and they would hit you and that's all. From hitters we became basketball players. At the beginning, these fellows would hit you to prevent you from scoring and they wouldn't run too fast. They would get in there and bang away," Goldman noted. "Rusty Saunders was a very outstanding ballplayer, but he wasn't much of a scorer. He could handle the ball well and pass the ball well and keep you from scoring. Tiny Hearn couldn't score 2 points a ball game. He was in there to get the tip and to get rebounds, and that's about all," Goldman added.[29]

Goldman signified a new style in which the center was more agile and more integral to the success of the team on offense. No longer was the tallest player on the floor relegated only to winning the jump ball. While in college, Goldman had learned the fundamentals from Nat Holman and had developed an offensive game to complement his defensive talents. Bernie Fliegel, a future SPHAS teammate and Goldman's successor at center for CCNY, remembered the impact Goldman had on the center position:

> From the inception, Moe had to compete against the old vintage centers (all taller, heavier, and brawnier) and very rarely were centers expected to do anything but rebound and block out. Moe changed the perception of a center from the start. His outstanding speed, outside shooting, touch underneath the basket, and dribbling (as a left-hander) were unmatched and confusing to the centers of his day—who just could not stay with his quickness, alertness, and anticipation. He more than matched the other centers in his controlling the boards and in his rebounding by blocking out the other taller, heavier centers and then quickly reacting to the ball bounces. Moe gave new meaning to what centers in pro ball were expected to and could do. He reset the standards for outstanding centers in pro ball. Moe was most responsible in changing the image of a "center" from a lumbering hulk to an outstanding team leader, one who is quick, a scorer, and superb all-around player.[30]

Jack (Dutch) Garfinkel, later a member of the SPHAS and a great player in his own right, grew up in Brooklyn and often went to Arcadia Hall to watch ABL games while a high school student. Garfinkel remembered many years later:

> I saw Moe perform with the Sphas at the old Arcadia Hall in Brooklyn against such outstanding teams as the Brooklyn Visitations, Jersey City Reds, and Brooklyn Jewels. He played with finesse and had great ability. Moe was an outstanding ballplayer of his time. He was the first center who could play like a forward or guard. He could shoot, pass, dribble, and was outstanding on defense.[31]

Later in life, as he reflected on his basketball career, Goldman explained, "I was the first center man in those days who could run and shoot. The rest of the center men were tall, gangly, and couldn't run. All I had to do was fake and go. I could shoot if they stayed back. So I would say, without trying to be boastful, that I revolutionized the center position. I think I was the first center to be able to run and shoot, to dribble and pass, to do all those things."[32]

Goldman's all-around ability enabled the SPHAS to play all five players on offense, as opposed to Trenton, who played four, with Hearn relegated to rebounding. The individual battle between Goldman and Hearn encapsulated the direction of both teams and the future of the center position.

Goldman's play in Game 3 and the rest of the series would determine whether the SPHAS could outlast the Moose. The SPHAS quickly jumped to a 12–2 lead and "went on to win as much as they pleased. Trenton was thoroughly outclassed, especially in the nimble art of betting about the spacious floor."[33] Using his speed, Goldman paced the SPHAS with five field goals. Three times in the final period, Goldman scored key baskets to keep the SPHAS in the lead and the Moose's rally at bay. At one point, he "outsprinted both Hearn and Russell to score under the basket" and later in the period he "proceeded to score a Spha field goal with all the nonchalance in the world."[34] His 11 points paced his team to a 32–20 victory.

The fourth game resembled the second game. For two periods, the SPHAS kept in front, using their quickness to keep Trenton off balance. Goldman, Lautman, and Gotthoffer continued to pace the SPHAS. As the final period began, Trenton found its rhythm. With three minutes left on the clock, Lou Spindell scored 2 of his 11 points to give Trenton a lead. From then on, the Moose fell back on their ball-control offense. As reported in the *Philadelphia Inquirer*, "Saunders settled on the foul line. With Glasco, Russell, Spindell, and Hearn, he hurled the ball back and forth and never gave the SPHAS a chance to intercept the ball. The 3,000 fans, the majority followers of the Sphas, could not help cheering this dazzling piece of play. To keep possession of the ball for three minutes in a game like the American League rules provide, with the slightest infringement causing the ball to be given to the other side out of bounds, is a notable feat."[35] Trenton held on for a 3-point win to tie the series at two games apiece.

After four games, the series was even, but a study in contrasts. When Trenton was able to control the ball through Saunders in the pivot, the Moose neutralized the speed of the SPHAS. The SPHAS found success utilizing their quickness and open-court passing ability. Which style would offset the other? Game 5 was scheduled for a neutral court, Arcadia Hall in Brooklyn, the site of Goldman's first game as a professional.

From the earliest days of professional basketball, the two-handed set shot had been the game's most reliable offensive weapon. Teams moved the ball around until finding a player open long enough to shoot the two-handed shot. Many of the game's early players excelled at the game's most fundamental shot. Stars such as Barney Sedran, Nat Holman, and Bobby McDermott made their reputations by consistently hitting the set shot.

The set shot found its greatest artist and proponent in Cy Kaselman. David (Cy) Kaselman was regarded as one of the greatest basketball players to ever come out of Philadelphia. Known as a "lady killer" for his handsome good looks, Kaselman developed into one of the best set shooters and foul shooters of his era. "Cy Kaselman was a great shooter," Phil Rabin, a former teammate, remembered, "He had a unique way to fake, cut to the basket, and you would give him a bounce pass to the basket."[36]

Kaselman joined the SPHAS in 1929–1930, the first year the team played in the Eastern Basketball League, and he continued with them until 1941–1942. During his career, Kaselman came off the bench to give the team a much-needed spark offensively. In many ways, he was the team's all-important sixth man, long before the sixth man became a popular concept. His high-arcing, two-handed set shots were a feature of most games played at the Broadwood. "Kaselman had one of the greatest three-point shots that ever was," Louis (Red) Klotz, another teammate of Kaselman's, recalled. "He would shoot it a mile in the sky and it was beautiful to watch. He could shoot that thing."[37]

Kaselman's outside shooting in the fifth and sixth games propelled the SPHAS to the championship, eliminating any chance Trenton had of winning. In Game 5, the *Philadelphia Inquirer* noted, he "was a constant menace. He penetrated the Trenton defense continually and scored 14 points."[38] After falling behind 2–1, the SPHAS displayed "an exhibition of floor work and swift passing which completely bewildered their rivals."[39] They scored 13 unanswered points to take a 14–2 lead that swelled to 25–12 after two periods. They cruised to an easy 32–22 victory.

In the deciding sixth game, Kaselman was at his best and "was the principal instigator in the denting of the net."[40] His onslaught in the opening period lifted the SPHAS to a 21–7 lead, making the outcome a foregone conclusion. The *Philadelphia Inquirer* reported, "Three times he split the cords for baskets that came from deep center, two of the three coming right after the tap-off to start the SPHAS off in the lead never to be headed for the rest of the game. Kaselman's third basket of the opening period came just as time was up and was the result of calls to 'shoot' as only a few seconds remained to finish the period and Cy let the ball go from a guard's position."[41]

This trophy was awarded to the Philadelphia SPHAS for winning the 1933–1934 American Basketball League championship. (*Courtesy of Naismith Memorial Basketball Hall of Fame.*)

With Kaselman's extraordinary shooting and the addition of Goldman, the SPHAS captured the inaugural championship in the reconstituted ABL. Goldman's play in the pivot—his ability to score, rebound, and run the floor—would usher in a new standard for centers. For the next decade, Goldman would anchor the middle for the SPHAS and help lead them to multiple championships. Their archrivals defeated, the SPHAS had now captured titles in three separate leagues.

4

PROSPECT HALL AND THE VISSIES

> There's no question about it, playing away from home was always tough, but the toughest place was Prospect Hall, the home of the Brooklyn Visitations. They made the fans check their guns at the door there.
>
> —Eddie Gottlieb,
> quoted in *Today* (*Philadelphia Inquirer*)

By the mid-1930s, the Great Depression had swallowed up the country hard and the economic crisis threatened the very future of America. Millions of Americans were without jobs and the prospects for employment of any sort were bleak at best. With the rise of anti-Semitism in Europe came an increase in anti-Jewish sentiment in America. The terrible economic situation and isolationist mentality of the country led to a rise in anti-Semitism, which was a fact of life in this country in the 1930s. The SPHAS were not immune to insults or threats. In a harsh environment, the team, referred to as the "Hebrews" on their road jerseys and in the sports pages, encountered more than their share of difficult and threatening situations. The SPHAS players came of age at a time when resentment toward Jews was at its peak.

"We all grew up with anti-Semitism around us. On the way to and from school, Christian kids would yell 'kike' or 'Christ-killer' at us," Gil Fitch recalled. "It may be hard for people today to understand this, but all of us had experiences of being beaten up because of our religion."[1]

Like other American cities of the time, South Philadelphia in the 1920s and 1930s was an area separated along ethnic lines. Sam (Leaden) Bernstein, later a star sandlot baseball player, grew up in Philadelphia during that time and remembers well the neighborhood and the daily battles he fought:

> South Philadelphia was all divided. Ninth Street past Broad Street was all Italians. East of Ninth Street was all Jews. As you came towards Center City, it became Polish and Irish. Everyone lived in his or her own neighborhoods. We had synagogues every block. The churches are still there today. South Philadelphia would not exist today without the Catholic churches. We were a tough bunch of guys.
>
> My parents moved to South Philadelphia, the end of South Philadelphia, and there was a river to the right and one to the left. In between, there was a dump, railroad tracks, nothing. My parents moved into this neighborhood and it was Jewish, and all around us was Irish families. When we went to school, we had to pass a church. We passed all these Italian kids. We had it rough. I used to fight them every day until I became their friends. After a long time playing ball, we all became friends. We started out and they didn't like us. They were out to get us. We were tough Jews and we knew how to fight back.[2]

The hostility translated onto the basketball court. Even in the mid-1930s, forty years after the game was invented, basketball was still a rough sport marred by aggressive play, hard fouls, fights, and ethnic divisions. The SPHAS were not immune to any of that. "They'd throw a drink at you as you went by or touch you with a lighted cigarette as you stood there to take a ball out," Gil Fitch stated, about playing on the road against a tough crowd.[3]

The players faced a lot of anti-Semitism on the road, but they played through it. Shikey Gotthoffer often told one particular story, recounted by his wife, Muriel, years later, about barnstorming during the off-season in either southern Ohio or southern Illinois. "We arrived by train, and there was a huge crowd waiting to greet us. Upon stepping off the train, I asked one of the local men if basketball was that popular here. The local responded that it was not, but nobody had ever seen a Jew before. In those days, there existed the cliché that Jews had horns on their heads."[4]

Perhaps more than other ethnic groups in that era, Jewish athletes in the 1930s represented their communities, their neighborhoods, and their religion. Jewish communities took great pride in the achievements of their sons and daughters who stood up to the prejudice. Succeeding in athletics instilled great pride in the Jewish community.

Peter Levine, in his extremely well-written book *Ellis Island to Ebbets Field: Sport and the American Jewish Experience*, about Jewish athletes during the interwar years, notes the importance for Jewish children of succeeding in athletics:

> The visible success of Jewish athletes also served an important symbolic purpose. Jewish physicality became a badge of being comfortable as an American. Triumphs in the ring, on the basketball court, baseball diamond, or football gridiron diminished stereotypes about Jewish weakness and countered anti-Semitic charges that Jews were unfit to be full Americans. They also invigorated Jews with a sense of pride in their physical abilities that contributed to a positive sense of Jewish identity. This theme became most apparent in the 1920s, 1930s, and 1940s, when economic depression, American anti-Semitism, and worldwide threats to Jewish existence contributed to a definition of Jewishness that included a visceral, physical dimension committed to the struggle for Jewish survival.[5]

Levine's observation accurately depicts the experiences of many of the SPHAS players during the 1930s. "We knew there would always be obstacles against Jews, and there was nothing we could do or say to change the situation. On the court, at least, we had a way to fight back a little bit," Petey Rosenberg remarked.[6]

"We played harder because we were representing our people. Because we were Jews, we often had hostile crowds who wanted to see us killed," Harry Litwack remembered many years later.[7]

"There was so much anti-Semitism then that Eddie wanted to jam it down everyone's throat and let the world know that his team was Jewish and a Jewish team could hold its own," Gil Fitch stated with great pride many decades later.[8] "Gotty said the best way to answer them was to be the best team in basketball. When people in the crowd said 'get those Jews' or 'kill those Jews' we played extra hard," Litwack remembered. "We had to stick together, and we had to fight to defend our people."[9]

No place gave the SPHAS more trouble than Prospect Hall. Located in South Brooklyn, Prospect Hall served as the home court for the Brooklyn Visitations, a top team in the ABL from 1933–1934 to 1938–1939.

Originally built in 1892, Prospect Hall served as a social gathering place for Brooklyn residents, and the building was noteworthy for being the first in Brooklyn with electricity and an elevator. Prospect Hall proved widely popular with the social elite of Brooklyn until the turn of the century. However, on December 11, 1900, the building was destroyed by a fire shortly after the conclusion of a performance. Undaunted, the community rallied, and owner John Krolle rebuilt Prospect Hall. When it reopened a few years later, it was even grander. The new facility featured a beer hall, bowling alleys, meeting rooms, and a dance hall. Over the next few decades, performances, speakers, and large gatherings highlighted the building's calendar. In 1908, Presidential hopeful William Jennings Bryan held a campaign event at Prospect Hall, and in 1914, the Women's Suffrage Party formally began its national campaign there. In the 1920s, Al Capone was a regular attendee for movies, vaudeville, dancing, and boxing. During the Depression, FDR's Works Progress Administration showed theater productions, and by then the makeup of the audience had shifted from the elite of the Victorian era to the common man of the early decades of the twentieth century.

The centerpiece of the building, though, remained the dance hall located on the second floor. The hall featured ornamental boxes and seating for 1,500 people. Two balconies encircled the entire room and looked down on the dance floor. This dance hall served as the home court of the Brooklyn Visitations. During their six years in the ABL, the Visitations made it to the championship round twice, winning in 1934–1935. Throughout, the Vissies, as they came to be known, proved to be one of the SPHAS' toughest adversaries. In its passion from the fans, players, and both cities, the rivalry was one of the fiercest of its day.

Eddie Gottlieb recalled with some humor years later:

> There's no question about it, playing away from home was always tough, but the toughest place was Prospect Hall, the home court of the Brooklyn Visitations. They made the fans check their guns at the door there.
>
> They used to have a balcony that hung over the court where the spectators sat and they'd serve the fans bottled beer and sandwiches. Whenever something would happen down on the court those Brooklyn fans didn't like, they'd send those bottles down on us.[10]

As Moe Goldman remembered:

> When we went to the Visitations I don't think there were any Jewish spectators. I think it was mostly Prospect Hall. Prospect Hall at that time was a non-Jewish area.[11] At the Brooklyn Visitations, they'd sit in the front row with no supervision, no cops or anything. They could throw a drink as you went by, or touch you with a lighted ciga-

> rette as you stood there to take the ball out. Little things like that.[12] We'd get a lot of anti-Semitism when we went to some places. Our traveling uniform had the name SPHAS in Hebrew on it. If we traveled to the Brooklyn Visitations, in an area where they were all Catholics, we'd have some trouble.[13]

Even Shikey Gotthoffer, who was one of the toughest players during his era, encountered his challenges when he faced the Visitations. "There were a lot of brawls, but we made up afterward. A team called the Brooklyn Visitations was particularly tough on us. The spectators would get involved, too. One time I had the ball for a throw-in from the side. The spectators sat very close. One guy takes a cigar he was smoking and jabbed me in the thigh with it. I almost jumped into the balcony. Yeah, we had them drop flower pots from the balcony on us."[14]

Prospect Hall, with its passionate fan base, was the site of a tense playoff series at the end of the 1934–1935 regular season between Philadelphia and Brooklyn. The best-of-three series determined the winner of the season's second half, who would face the New York Jewels, winners of the first half, in a five-game series for the championship. Confident in defending their title, the SPHAS were stunned to find themselves locked in a playoff series with the season on the line. During the season's final week, the SPHAS had held a slim lead on the Brooklyn Visitations in the race for the second-half crown. As the SPHAS headed to Prospect Hall on March 24 for their last regular-season game, the team controlled its own destiny. A win and the team clinched a berth in the championship round. A loss and they would be rooting for New Britain to upset Brooklyn the following week. Riding a two-game winning streak, including a thumping of the Jersey Reds, 44–30 the night before, the SPHAS figured they had found enough late-season momentum to propel them back into the finals.

The moment the game began, the SPHAS sensed that it might not be their night. Playing for its season, Brooklyn jumped to a quick 3–0 lead on a basket by Bobby McDermott and a foul shot by Pete Berenson. The SPHAS answered quickly with a basket by Shikey Gotthoffer, a free throw from Gil Fitch, and another Gotthoffer basket to open a 5–3 lead. That was their one and only lead. "With Bobby McDermott, Pete Berenson and Carl Johnson running wild, the Visitations, after the first few minutes, assumed a lead which in the second period assumed gigantic proportions," the *Philadelphia Inquirer* reported the next day.[15] A first-period 15–7 lead swelled to a 31–13 advantage after two periods. Paced by three players in double digits, the Visitations cruised to a 39–31 win, setting the stage for a key game the following week against third-place New Britain. A Brooklyn win would force a playoff series against Philadelphia. A loss would end the season.

After winning the inaugural ABL title, the SPHAS figured to be in the hunt again for the championship. As soon as the first season ended, ABL President O'Brien and team owners went to work on improving the league for the following season. Changes were afoot for the 1934–1935 season. Among the first order of business was securing the commitments of franchises to field a competitive schedule. The Trenton Moose and Bronx Americans withdrew, while the Newark Bears changed their name to the Newark Mules, the New Britain Palaces became the New Britain Jackaways, and the Union City Reds became the Jersey Reds. The New York Jewels and Brooklyn Visitations returned. The only new franchise belonged to the Boston Trojans. Seven teams started the season, and it was a positive sign that strong franchise stability had marked the beginning of the ABL's second year.

With the teams intact, O'Brien and the owners instituted a few changes aimed at improving play. All newspapermen were issued cards of admission, a precursor to the modern-day media pass. Teams were told to strictly comply with the starting times; failure to do so would result in fines and penalties levied by O'Brien. To avoid players jumping between professional leagues, no ABL players were permitted to play in the Eastern League, a minor league based in the greater Philadelphia region. Finally, "stringent measures are to be adopted, curving [sic] the use of profanity by the players at all times."[16]

Eddie Gottlieb forgot to bring the league memo to the locker room prior to the SPHAS opening game against the Newark Mules. Ronald Friedenberg, writing the next day in the *Philadelphia Inquirer*, noted, "Fists flew furiously, tongues wagged wildly and goals dropped deliriously" as the SPHAS overcame a 17–13 third-period deficit to win 25–20.[17] Frustrated as the Mules "guarded so well during the first two periods, the Sphas were able to make only five field goals," the SPHAS showed their own defensive tenacity by holding the Mules to 3 third-period points. The SPHAS scored 12 points to win the game.[18] Five of those points came courtesy of Cy Kaselman, whose "goals were the kind no guard is very well able to prevent and the first of these was particularly noteworthy. It was served on a shot fully three-quarters the length of the floor, the distance being necessitated by the fact that the tocsin was about to sound just as the leather cut the strings."[19] Kaselman's 8 points led all scorers.

David (Cy) Kaselman was known for his good looks and deadly outside shot. In thirteen seasons with the SPHAS, he led the team to eight championships. (*Courtesy of Diane Moskowitz.*)

Of all the talented players that Eddie Gottlieb assembled during his years, none could shoot a basketball quite like David (Cy) Kaselman. Born in 1909 in Philadelphia, Kaselman grew up playing basketball. As a 19-year-old, Kaselman joined the SPHAS for the 1929–1930 season, when the team was in the Eastern Basketball League and had finished their barnstorming days. In his thirteen seasons with the SPHAS, he was part of eight championship squads. Many viewed Kaselman, who was known for his handsome good looks and popularity with the young women at games, as one of the best Jewish basketball players ever to come out of Philadelphia. His two-handed set shots had no equal, and he was known for hitting foul shots blindfolded, a feat he used to do to entertain crowds at the Broadwood Hotel. In his obituary in 1971, the *Philadelphia Inquirer* noted, "His accuracy at the foul line was unerring in a period when one player on a team shot all the fouls."[20] His reputation was so highly regarded that, later in life, Eddie Gottlieb asked him to teach Wilt Chamberlain to change his foul-shooting technique from overhand to underhand.

All those who saw him play would never forget the sight of him shooting a basketball. His high-arcing shots "were the type that almost touch the ceiling and drop through the cords without touching the hoop."[21] Marvin Black, son of Hughie Black, one of the three original SPHAS, became an usher at SPHAS games in the early 1940s. "My father was able to make me an usher," Marvin remembered. "Abe Radel, the manager of the SPHAS, would pay the ushers a silver dollar at the end of every game. You would go into the locker room and receive a silver dollar. I loved to go into the locker room. My spot was in the balcony. I was an usher in the balcony and liked to watch the games."[22]

From his vantage point in the balcony looking down at the court, Marvin had the best view to see Kaselman shoot his set shot as it arced high in the air before falling cleanly through the nets. "When I was watching the SPHAS, I liked Cy Kaselman. He was a handsome guy. He would shoot two-handed set shots high arched that were unbelievable. He could put in two-pointers. There was no such thing as three-pointers in those days. His set shots were beautiful."[23]

Louis (Red) Klotz, who played with the SPHAS Reserves before joining the team in the early 1940s, remembered well Kaselman shooting the ball. "Kaselman had one of the greatest three-point shots that ever were. He would shoot it a mile in the sky and it was beautiful to watch. He could shoot that thing."[24]

Several years prior, in the early 1930s, Sam (Leaden) Bernstein recalled watching Kaselman shoot in the Palais Royal, one of the SPHAS' home courts prior to the Broadwood Hotel. "He was the greatest shooter I ever saw. There were stories about him making shots blindfolded. He was an ideal man. He was quiet and had an easy way about him. He was smart. His hands would stand still but his feet would be moving."[25]

With Kaselman's shooting magic, the SPHAS looked to get off to a quick start in league play. After their season-opening victory against the Newark Mules, the SPHAS found themselves playing inconsistently throughout the first half. Other than two three-game winning streaks, the SPHAS often found themselves playing from behind throughout much of the game. As Kaselman went, so, too, did the team, an ominous sign that would figure prominently in the end of the season.

The SPHAS finished the first half at 13–10, three games behind the first-place Jewels. The season's second half began with a convincing home win over the Brooklyn Visitations, 39–25. The SPHAS pushed their record to 3–1 before losing a home-and-home series to the New Britain Jackaways to drop them to .500. Over the course of the next month, from mid-February to mid-March, the SPHAS went on a 7–1 run to push their record to 10–4. Their run began and ended with close victories over first-half winner New York Jewels. With five regular-season games remaining, the SPHAS appeared to be in command for a return trip to the championship round. Or so they thought.

After losing two straight to the New York Jewels and New Britain Jackaways to drop to 10–6, the SPHAS found a late-season final push. On March 20, the SPHAS traveled to Brooklyn to play a neutral-site game against the Boston Trojans, a team they had handled easily in their last two encounters. After increasing their lead to 18–14 midway through the

Displayed here are warm-up pants and a jacket worn by Cy Kaselman. (*Courtesy of Naismith Memorial Basketball Hall of Fame.*)

second period, the SPHAS lost their focus as the Trojans went on a 10–2 run to close the period with a 24–20 lead. With their season on the line, the SPHAS responded brilliantly by outscoring the Trojans 16–7 to claim a 36–31 victory. In the final period, Kaselman connected on three outside shots to pace the team with 10 points.

Three nights later in their last regular-season victory at home, the SPHAS crushed the Jersey Reds, 44–30, as Kaselman again led the team with 10 points. Early in the second period, with his team trailing, 20–18, Gottlieb inserted super-sub Kaselman, and the fortunes of the game turned immediately. "Kaselman scored two long-range field goals and after that the visitors were never in it," Ronald Friedenberg wrote the following day in his article. "Kaselman's goals were of the kind your basketball follower refers to as those 'that no one can stop.' They were of the type that almost touch the ceiling and drop through the cords without touching the hoop."[26] With the SPHAS in high gear, the team was surprised to find itself in a battle with the Brooklyn Visitations for second-half honors.

After Brooklyn defeated New Britain, 35–30, in its final regular-season game, the SPHAS set their sights on a best-of-three playoff series against the Visitations to determine who would face the Jewels in the championship round. The regular season series had been a closely fought affair as the teams split their eight games. With the series set to begin on April 5, the SPHAS had had nearly two weeks to prepare since last losing to the

Visitations. Sharp and rested, the SPHAS went into Brooklyn and convincingly defeated their rivals, 24–15. All season long, playing at Prospect Hall had given the SPHAS troubles. The team was 1–3 in Brooklyn and had lost their last two games there. Instead, their surprisingly easy victory placed them in the driver's seat to return to the championship round and defend their title. True to form, Kaselman entered the game midway through the second period and instantly provided an offensive spark. His 10 points on three field goals and four foul shots led the team to an easy victory. Shikey Gotthoffer, serving as the team's defensive stopper, put the clamps on Bobby McDermott, limiting him to 2 points, as the SPHAS won.

The series marked an interesting contest between two of the league's top scorers. Kaselman was enjoying one of his finest offensive seasons to date. He finished second in league scoring with 322 total points on 110 field goals and 102 foul shots. In twenty-one games during the season, he led the team in scoring and posted a high of 17 on November 15 against New Britain. His high-arcing shots sparked his team when he was summoned from the bench in the middle of the second period. His counterpart, Carl Johnson of the Visitations, led the league with 346 points on 115 field goals and 116 foul shots. His 116 points from the foul line led the league and served as a testament to his ability to draw contact and get to the foul line in close games. Kaselman and Johnson served to keep both defenses on their toes.

When the series shifted to Philadelphia and the Broadwood Hotel the following night, the SPHAS looked to build on their momentum and close out the series. It was not to be. Many times during the season, slow starts had put the team in a position of playing catch-up, a task they did not handle well. The Flatbushers got off to a great start; "in a wild orgy of first period scoring the visitors made nine of their twin pointers and held the advantage, 22–11, a bulge the Sphas were never able to puncture."[27] Led by Johnson and newcomer Bobby McDermott, who each scored 15 points, the Visitations were never seriously threatened. Despite the heroics of Gotthoffer, who scored 15 points, the SPHAS were never in the game. They came as close as 4 points in the closing minutes when the game had already been decided. Kaselman, who had paced the team the night before, scored only 3 points, all on foul shots.

The season on the line, the SPHAS and Visitations engaged in arguably the finest game the season had to offer. The third and final game, winner takes all, lived up to its expectations. From the opening tip, both the SPHAS and Visitations flexed their muscles defensively as the offenses took their time looking for the best shot. A tight, low-scoring game looked to be on hand.

The Visitations ended the first period leading 8–7. The second period mirrored the first as Brooklyn held a slim 16–15 lead. At the start of the final stanza, Brooklyn opened with a 4–2 run and built their largest lead, 20–17. Time was slipping away for the SPHAS—who had not led at any point and needed to find a way not only to match Brooklyn shot-for-shot but also to generate a run of their own. It was now or never for the SPHAS.

Shikey Gotthoffer, who earlier in the week had been named the league's MVP, came down the court and hit an outside shot to cut the deficit to one, 20–19. With just minutes remaining, the Broadwood crowd was in near hysteria as 3,500 Philadelphians were yelling and screaming, on their feet cheering for their hometown team. Writing the next day in the *Philadelphia Inquirer*, beat writer Ronald Friedenberg captured the mood in those final minutes: "Imagine for yourself the scenes of hilarious happy disorder a moment later when the same Shikey pounded to the strings for his third field goal of the night a twin-pointer that gave the Gottlieb crew their first advantage of the engagement. That made it 21–20 and the Sphas seemed to be getting somewhere after trying frenziedly for goals but missing by inches, with the hoop taking a beating but with the strings unswished."[28]

With its first lead, 21–20, the SPHAS needed a defensive stop. Brooklyn's Pete Berenson, a thorn in their side all game, was fouled and went to the foul line where he made one shot. The score now stood tied at 21–21.

On its next possession, the SPHAS worked the ball around and found Moe Goldman, who was having a good game and had already connected on three baskets. Goldman calmly sank another shot. A month earlier, Goldman had hit the winning shot against Brooklyn on the same floor in the same spot for a 21–19 win. As Friedenberg noted, "You remember it was Moe who beat Brooklyn 21–19 with a last-minute double-decker in the regular second-half campaign several weeks ago in the same floor."[29] The crowd and players from both teams wondered if history would repeat itself.

Leading 23–21, the SPHAS finally got their much-needed defensive stop. With the ball and leading by 2 points, the SPHAS did not settle for an outside shot but drove to the basket, looking to draw contact. "Problematical that may be but one thing was sure and that was that the Sphas were cutting for the basket now in a repudiation of their former policy of sticking it from 15 to 20 feet away," Friedenberg wrote. Inky Lautman, who was having a quiet night, "pounded down to the scoring station, the ball hovered on the rim and then dropped contently downwards."[30] His foul shot made it 24–21. Moments afterward, Kaselman hit a foul shot to make it 25–21.

With a 4-point lead and just a minute remaining, the SPHAS looked to close out the series and advance to the finals. "Then it happened and I won't tell you again how the tables were turned and the second half title went to Brooklyn. It hurts to think of it," Friedenberg wrote.[31] Brooklyn summoned their best as "the Flatbushers were away on their mad spurt to goals, gelt and the second-half crown."[32]

Brooklyn quickly regained their composure and worked the ball around to center Howie Bollerman, who connected on a basket. The SPHAS' lead had been cut to 25–23. After getting a defensive stop, Brooklyn's Carl Johnson scored to tie the game at 25–25. Johnson, who led all scorers with 9 points, outplayed his counterpart Kaselman, who did not have a basket and scored all 4 of his points from the foul line. With the score tied at 25 and less than a minute remaining, the SPHAS came down the floor looking to score the winning basket. They missed. Brooklyn grabbed the rebound and came down the court as "Pete Berenson, one of the league's best scorers, dropped the penalty toss that shoved the Sphas off the throne."[33] After another missed opportunity, Brooklyn's Bobby McDermott had a chance to increase the lead but missed his foul shot. The 1-point margin stood, and Brooklyn had defeated the defending champion SPHAS. The Visitations were on their way to the finals against their Brooklyn rival, the Jewels. The following day, the headline in the *Brooklyn Daily Eagle* proclaimed, "Sphas Dethroned as King of Courts."[34]

A series that had started with so much promise with a rare road victory at Prospect Hall quickly turned sour as the SPHAS lost two games at home. It marked the first time all season that the SPHAS lost two in a row on their home court. They had lost only once all season at home to Brooklyn, and that had happened in the season's second game back in November. Kaselman, the shooting star and team's sixth man who had sparked the SPHAS all season with his scoring off the bench, was uncharacteristically quiet in the last two games. After scoring 10 points in the opening-game win, Kaselman did not score a field goal in the last two games, both defeats. His 7 points all came from the foul line. A season with so much promise had ended in bitter defeat.

5

SHIKEY

> After the games, we would go out and there were lots of girls who were groupies. They used to say, "Oh, I touched Shikey Gotthoffer. I touched Shikey Gotthoffer."
>
> —Muriel Gotthoffer, interview by the author

In the 1920s, Hank Greenberg and Joel (Shikey) Gotthoffer were childhood friends growing up just blocks from one another in the Bronx, New York. Both enjoyed sports and could often be found playing baseball, basketball, and other sports of the day with the neighborhood kids. When it came time for high school, they enrolled locally at James Monroe High School and continued their athletic pursuits. Basketball was popular, and each joined the team, eventually advancing to the varsity squad. Behind their play, James Monroe won three consecutive PSAL championships from 1926 to 1928. For Greenberg, that was the high point of his basketball career, as he turned his attention to his first love, baseball, and embarked on a Hall of Fame career. Gotthoffer, meanwhile, was just beginning his basketball stardom. Although they went their separate ways, Greenberg and Gotthoffer, along with boxer Barney Ross, were among the best American Jewish athletes in the 1930s. In a ten-month stretch in the mid-1930s, with the Depression at its height, the rise of Adolf Hitler and Nazism, and growing American anti-Semitism, Greenberg and Gotthoffer achieved the pinnacle of their athletic careers. In so doing, they gave great pride and comfort to the Jewish community.

Several weeks prior to the start of the 1935–1936 basketball season, the eyes of the sports world, and most specifically the Jewish community, shifted their attention to the Midwest, where Hank Greenberg was preparing to lead his Detroit Tigers against the Chicago Cubs in baseball's most cherished event, the World Series. The Fall Classic featured a sterling matchup and promised to be one of the finest World Series in recent memory. For the second year in a row, the Detroit Tigers captured the American League pennant and this time set their sights on avenging their seven-game World Series defeat to the St. Louis Cardinals the previous year. Led by Greenberg and Charlie Gehringer, the Tigers had a second chance at their first World Series title. The Cubs, meanwhile, had edged out defending champion St. Louis in the National League and finished 100–54. Behind two twenty-game winners, Bill Lee and Lon Warneke, the Cubs anticipated winning their first World Series since 1908.

As the country geared up for the Series, the Jewish community looked forward to following the exploits of Detroit's first baseman. In only his third major league season, "Hammerin' Hank" had blossomed into one of baseball's best players. In 1935, Greenberg compiled one of the best seasons of any player. He led the league in runs batted in (170) and total bases (389) and tied for first in home runs (36). In averaging .328, he was second in the league in doubles (46), triples (16), and slugging percentage (.628) and third in the league in runs scored (121). His 103 runs batted in at the All-Star break that year still stands as a record. His fabulous season on the field led him to the first of two league MVP awards. Despite his on-field heroics, it was the one day that he did not play that made him a hero to the Jewish community.

The year before, during a heated pennant race, Greenberg became a symbol for Jewish pride and solidified his position as the most popular Jewish athlete in America at that time. With a few weeks remaining in the 1934 season, the Detroit Tigers faced the lowly Boston Red Sox. Detroit was fighting for first place against the hated New York Yankees, and Greenberg contemplated skipping an important game against the Red Sox to observe Rosh Hashanah, the Jewish New Year. After much reflection and consultation with his rabbi, Greenberg decided to play. His two solo home runs, including one in the ninth, accounted for Detroit's only runs in a 2–1 victory. Ten days later, Greenberg decided to skip an important game against the New York Yankees in observance of Yom Kippur, the Day of Atonement, and the holiest day on the Jewish calendar. He instantly became a hero to Jews around the country as newspapers and radio programs extolled his decision to observe his religion and not play a baseball game.

When the 1935 baseball season started, Greenberg's popularity had reached a new level. That season, he compiled some of the best numbers of any baseball player in history and had his Detroit Tigers ready to play in the World Series. The World Series was supposed to be Greenberg's chance to shine on a national level. In the opening game of the series, the Cubs blanked the Tigers 3–0. Greenberg was 0 for 3 with a walk. The following day, the Tigers jumped on the scoreboard first as Greenberg hit a first-inning two-run home run. In the seventh, Greenberg tried to score from first on a single to right. A collision at home plate left Greenberg with a broken bone in his wrist. He was done for the series. He watched from the dugout as the Tigers won the World Series in six games. Despite being on the sidelines, his Tigers were victorious, and his exploits throughout the season earned him admiration from fans everywhere.

Shortly after the World Series concluded, the SPHAS gathered at the start of the season planning to avenge the previous year's devastating end. The loss in the playoffs to the Brooklyn Visitations had left a sour taste with the SPHAS. All summer, the players wrestled with what might have been. After winning the first game in Brooklyn, the SPHAS lost the next two at home, where they had sported a 17–6 record during the regular season. A golden opportunity to win a second consecutive championship slipped through their grasp. With the 1935–1936 season on the horizon, the team was determined to recapture the form that had earned them a championship two seasons earlier.

With the oncoming Brooklyn Visitations in the backs of their minds, the SPHAS quickly dispatched the Kingston Colonials, 52–36, to begin the season. Against Kingston, the previous year's champions of the New York State League, the SPHAS took advantage of a mismatch inside, as Moe Goldman, now recovered from the previous season's shoulder injury, scored 15 points to lead the SPHAS. Their easy victory was a precursor of things to come.

The SPHAS pounced on their competitors as they raced out to a league-leading 8–2 mark. Gottlieb, seeking to shake up his lineup a bit, substituted players on a more regular basis and advocated for an up-tempo style. It worked. In the season's third game, the SPHAS' balanced attack proved too much for the team from Paterson, New Jersey. The Panthers, in their first year in the ABL, could not contain the SPHAS, as eight players scored at least two field goals apiece en route to an easy 43–26 win. After dropping their first game against the New York Jewels a week later, the SPHAS compiled a four-game winning streak, highlighted by a second victory over the

Brooklyn Visitations. Beating the Vissies twice in the season's first month was an added boost to the team's morale, even though it did not make up for the previous year's playoff defeat.

On January 4, with two games remaining on the schedule, the SPHAS claimed first-half honors with a stirring 37–24 win over the Jersey Reds. The SPHAS were playing at an advanced level that impressed their opponents, the crowd, and even the media. One commentator noted, "For this game, Eddie Gottlieb was taking no chances and the Sphas were akin to a college football team in its big contest in that they pulled plays out of the bag that hitherto they had not displayed. For instance, there was a revolving pass that had the leather shooting back and forth in such fashion as to bewilder the opposition. Again there were spot passing plays with the champions scoring several of their goals as a result of the stratagem."[1]

The momentum and high-level play in the season's first half carried over to the start of the second half, which began with a split in a home-and-home series with the Brooklyn Visitations. The SPHAS won the first game and then lost the second one. After the loss, the SPHAS suddenly stalled. The team staggered to a 4–3 record after seven games, which included dispirited losses to the Passaic Red Devils and the New York Jewels. After that, the wheels fell off. A five-game losing streak left them limping into the postseason as the team barely played .500 the rest of the way.

Although the team finished the second half with a disappointing 9–11 record, the one constant was Shikey Gotthoffer. Twelve times during the regular season, Gotthoffer had paced the team in scoring. He led the team with an average of 6.7 points per game and finished sixth in the league in scoring. For his efforts, he garnered some votes as the league's MVP.

Of all the players to have suited up for the SPHAS, Joel (Shikey) Gotthoffer might have been the most complete. Through the years, the SPHAS featured some of the greatest players of their generation, many of whom had enough talent to play in the NBA. But Gotthoffer was the one who stood out from the rest. Sam (Leaden) Bernstein, a longtime SPHAS fan from Philadelphia, remembers watching Shikey play. "Shikey Gotthoffer was tough. He may have been the toughest. He was not a bully, but he played tough. He had a good body, he could run, and he played a hard-nosed game. He was one of the toughest guys I ever saw play in those days. He was a winner."[2]

"Shikey was one of the great players for the SPHAS. The reputation he had was of being one of the greatest," Ralph Kaplowitz, later a SPHAS player after World War II, remarked. "I never saw him play. I heard a great deal about him."[3]

A strong, burly player from New York City, Gotthoffer earned his reputation as a fierce competitor who did not back down. His temperament, ability, and determination made him one of the ABL's finest players. In his ten years with the team, he averaged more than 6 points per game and was a member of six championship squads. He won several league MVP awards and was consistently regarded by teammates and opponents as one of the league's toughest players and best defenders.

"Shikey Gotthoffer was sensational. He went to Monroe High School. He was named MVP in the ABL for a number of years. He was short and stocky, but smart and fast," Bernie Fliegel, a former teammate and opponent, recalled. "I will always remember the one lesson he taught me. I was guarding him and I kept one arm on his to feel where he was, but I always kept watching everyone else. One time, he throws me into the stands. So, I learned to touch my opponent but do not let him throw you into the stands."[4]

His toughness almost certainly was a result of where he learned the game of basketball. A product of New York City, Gotthoffer was born on January 1, 1911, on East Eighth Street, in what today is known as Greenwich Village. He parents left Austria, arriving in New York City through Ellis Island and settling on East Eighth, where they began to create a life for themselves in a new country. To support his growing family, Gotthoffer's father "was a designer for women's clothes. He had his own business in the garment district in Manhattan. He made women's coats and suits."[5] As a youngster, Gotthoffer used sports as a social outlet where he met and befriended the other kids on the block. Basketball in particular drew his interest, and he grew up playing with the neighborhood boys all day and into the night, until his mother summoned him from the window of their apartment. "I was called Shikey from childhood. When my mother called me, it must have sounded like 'Shickey' or 'Shikey,' and the kids picked it up."[6] When he heard his mother yelling "Shikey," Gotthoffer knew it was time to stop playing and return home for dinner and an evening of school work.

Basketball and Gotthoffer were synonymous from the beginning:

> I guess I started playing basketball before I could read. I can't recall not playing. We had a unique situation when I moved to the Bronx from Manhattan. I was getting old enough to handle a basketball. We had a group that was very much entrenched in basketball and we consequently built a basketball court behind the buildings that we lived in. There were a group of youngsters like myself who were basketball minded. We had the Bronx Owl Seniors, Bronx Owl Juniors,

In the eyes of many, Joel (Shikey) Gotthoffer was the SPHAS' best all-around player. His efforts earned him a Most Valuable Player award and respect from teammates and foes alike. (*Courtesy of Naismith Memorial Basketball Hall of Fame.*)

and Bronx Owl Midgets. All were basketball teams. One generation moved up to the other, and all of us together built a basketball court behind the tenement houses we lived in. It was between 165th and 163rd Street on Union Ave in the East Bronx.[7]

As a schoolboy, Gotthoffer would rise early, eat a quick breakfast with his family, and grab his school bag before meeting his friends and walking to school. "I can't recall when I didn't go to school dressed underneath with my basketball things so that at 3 o'clock I could stay in the playground and play basketball. The school had a gym, but when we played after school it was on the outdoor court. They had an indoor gym and they had playgrounds."[8]

Years later, Gotthoffer was asked whether he would focus on basketball as much as he did growing up if he could go back in time.

If I could do it all over again, I would. You betcha. I didn't know there were girls around until I was 17 years old. I didn't go to parties. We didn't have time. It sounds ridiculous. I'd go to school, come out of school and go to the schoolyard and play. At night, I would go to play some more—all the time playing basketball. I played basketball, basketball, basketball. But I didn't have to roam around because the Bronx Owls had a structure. We always were there and we played as a team and ultimately we went to college and into the professional ranks.[9]

With all his time on the courts, Gotthoffer soon became a good player and attracted the attention of many individuals looking to make a quick dollar on the game. His desire to play basketball and make some money, something he carried through to his college days, began in junior high school. It was a pattern that greatly impacted his basketball career prior to joining the professional ranks. As Gotthoffer noted:

I played basketball for [name unmentioned] and I received a dollar for playing. Somehow or other the Public School Athletic League of the city found out that I had received a dollar and when I graduated junior high school and came to James Monroe, the Public School Athletic League wouldn't let me play my freshman year because they claimed that I had received money for playing on the outside. And since I couldn't actually defray the dollar expense at that time—after all, a trolley car was a nickel a ride, a frankfurter was a nickel—

a dollar was a lot of money to get rid of. And I had difficulty getting rid of it, I remember.[10]

Despite not playing his freshman year, Gotthoffer joined the team in his second year and quickly became an integral part of the Monroe basketball team. Monroe won the city championship three consecutive years in 1926, 1927, and 1928 with future baseball great Hank Greenberg, Gotthoffer's grade school friend, at starting center. Gotthoffer's ability soon attracted the attention of many colleges looking to build their basketball programs with New York players.

Toward the latter part of my years at Monroe before I was graduated, I received offers from people who wanted me to play for their team. They were representing themselves as a team that would go out and play against another team, and *X* amount of dollars would be paid to the individual who was organizing this, and he in turn was giving a certain amount of money to the players. That happened to be $5 in my case. I played and the individual I played for later turned out to be a bone in my throat and was responsible for keeping me out of college.[11]

Again, the issue of money haunted him. His college career, which was greatly affected by having accepted money to play on the side, never amounted to what Gotthoffer had hoped. Although he would not confirm the identity of the coach he played for, in an interview in 2007, his wife, Muriel, discussed how Gotthoffer's college career was doomed from the start. "After high school, he went to Providence College and Duke University to play basketball. Prior to that, he played on a team organized by Nat Holman, the coach at CCNY, and he was paid $5 to play. He was considered a professional because he was paid. Holman told both schools that Joel was a professional, and both schools did not let him play. He eventually finished at New York University, although I do not think that he played for NYU."[12]

Gotthoffer's college journey, a sad one, is best explained in his own words:

I received scholarship offers from Brown, Providence, Temple, University of Pennsylvania, Duke, and Princeton. When the time came that I graduated high school, I received this Princeton offer. The coach's name was Whitman, and he asked me to come out to Princeton, New Jersey, because he wanted to talk to me. I went out there and spent the weekend, and I looked around and lived that life two or three days. It was much too rich for my blood—not that it was too rich for my blood, but I just couldn't handle it, put it that way. I felt that I would be a tag-on to all the kind of people I saw there. So at the end of the weekend, I told him that I didn't think Princeton was for me. He was quite annoyed with that because he felt everything was settled. I had told him my story, and he rightfully told me that Princeton would not bargain my professionalism with anybody. I know that the Ivy League colleges had had players that had received money because I played with some, and I know that Columbia had a ballplayer that had played with me, and they didn't want to talk about it. They just turned it off. I just didn't feel that I belonged frankly, that was it. I thought I wouldn't be accepted for me. I would be accepted because I was a ballplayer. So I told him I'm sorry and I went home.

I decided that I was going to go to college and I wrote to Providence College, which had offered me a scholarship. The coach told me to come up to Providence, which I did. We worked out a situation that I would get a scholarship for basketball. When the term began I started at Providence. When the time came for the basketball team to start practicing, I became part of that situation. Apparently I must have been highly touted because there was quite a crowd in the gym. I wondered why they were there and someone told me that they were there to see me. So naturally I didn't have any trouble becoming part of that team.

When the basketball schedule came out, there was a college on that schedule whose coach was someone I had played with once; he had recruited me to play an exhibition game. He was cruel because he recruited friends of mine who were also thrown out of college for the same reason. I had picked Providence because it was a small school and I thought no one would know about it. But this team appeared on the schedule and when my name was on the roster, this party wrote and said that I was a recognized professional on the Eastern Seaboard and that they would not play. I was called in when Father received that letter and he questioned me about it, and I admitted to it and I said that I didn't understand what makes me different than anyone else. The fact that I got $5 doesn't make me an iron man. He said the rules are the rules and they would have to take my scholarship; however, they would let me finish out the year. I did and then left.

I think it might have been two times for $5. So the big amount might have been $10. One time I played in Port Chester and the other time in New Jersey. Maybe I was aware that college players were supposed to be Simon-pure, but I felt what I was getting didn't represent anything. It was like a minuscule amount. How can you take a dollar and turn that into professional—or even $5? True, $5 was a lot more than it is today, but it never dawned on me that it would cause me to be a professional. I never heard the word used. All I knew who were professionals were the Original Celtics and the Harlem Renaissance. To me, a professional was a man who takes a shot and never misses. That was my concept of professionalism. I didn't think anything like that would be attached to me. It turned out that they gave me a year's grace at Duke, and now I have two years of college. And then I went to NYU and had to pay. I didn't finish. I was nine credits short. But I realized I didn't want to teach, and that was why I was studying Physical Ed and health education. I realized that I didn't want to teach. It was not something I was interested in. So that closed my college career.

I didn't play at NYU. Howard Cann was then the coach of NYU and he found out that I was going to health education, so he sent word that he would like to talk to me. I knew he couldn't possibly want me to play basketball for NYU with all the commotion that had gone on with me, but I went to him and he said, "I know you've got basketball experience. I know you're pretty good. I've heard about you. I want to ask a favor of you. I'd like you to sit with me during practice sessions and point out problems that exist and how I can alleviate them. It wouldn't be conducive to have you at the games because people would recognize you."

I said that I have no desire to sit with you at the games but I could be helpful. So I said fine, I'll do that. So there were many days I spent at the uptown gym of NYU. What struck me as being strange—some of the ballplayers who were out there were playing for money on the side at the time. I never said anything to Howard Cann. I doubt that he knew it because he was a pretty strait-laced type of guy.[13]

The pay-for-play concept was nearly as old as the game of basketball. Since 1896 when the first basketball players were paid to play, being a professional basketball player had been a goal for which every player strived. Throughout the 1910s, 1920s, and 1930s, players often played for multiple teams in different leagues, seeking to earn as much money as they could. College players, too, sought to make extra money and moonlighted on semiprofessional or professional teams during their college careers. This was clearly in violation of their status as college students on scholarship. Earning extra money was a tremendous benefit to these kids, many of whom were children of immigrants, where every little bit was needed. Gotthoffer was not any different than the other players except that he was caught.

Even though he was not playing for Cann's Violets, Gotthoffer kept in basketball shape by playing semiprofessional games in and around the New York metropolitan area:

> While I was at NYU, I was playing semipro ball. I was playing with pickup teams like the Knights of Columbus [K of C]. That went on for some time until one day I received a call from the Yonkers K of C. They told me they were entering the American Basketball League and they were looking for ballplayers. I got what I considered good money, so I started playing with the Yonkers K of C. This was 1932 or 1933. They had some pretty good ballplayers. Joe Lapchick played for us for a while and others who were well known in basketball circles.
>
> Then the time came when the American Basketball League was going into high gear. Cities were beginning to join in. Max Posnak of St. John's Wonder Five was playing with the SPHAS, and he wanted to go with the New York Jewels who were made up of the old Wonder Five—they wanted Posnak to play with them. So Eddie Gottlieb, who was the owner of the SPHAS, told John J. O'Brien, who was president of the league, "Fine, you can have Posnak if I can have Gotthoffer from Yonkers." So they ended up paying $2,500 for me. That was big, big, big bucks and I joined the SPHAS.[14]

Even though Gotthoffer had not had a traditional college career, Gottlieb thought highly enough of him to spend an exorbitant sum in the Depression for Gotthoffer to join his team. It proved to be a shrewd move by Gottlieb.

With the acquisition of Gotthoffer, Eddie Gottlieb sought to remake his team as they moved from the Eastern States Basketball League to the ABL. Gotthoffer became a SPHA at the outset of the ABL in 1933–1934. Joining him that season were Moe Goldman and Inky Lautman. Together, the three became mainstays for the SPHAS for the next decade. Gotthoffer was finally playing basketball for a living, his goal since high school, and as he would soon discover, he was a part of one of the best teams. By the end of his professional career, he would be earning $100 a game, a far cry from the dollar he was paid while in junior high school.

After a few seasons, the SPHAS were household names in the Philadelphia Jewish community, and one of the more popular players with the fans, especially the women, was Gotthoffer. During the summers, Gotthoffer worked in the Catskills, a resort community in New York State, helping the guests, playing basketball, and being available for the recreational activities. One night, he met a beautiful young woman, Muriel, with whom he danced at one of the evening functions. Muriel became a Broadway performer, but years later clearly remembered meeting her future husband. "I originally met my husband when I was 17 years old. I was dancing in the Catskills, and he was my partner. He told me I was a cute girl but to come back in five years. We were married in 1940, five years after I met him," Muriel said. "I traveled with the team once or twice on the road but Gottlieb did not like the wives too much. He intimidated everybody. He resented the fact that they married. He saw his players as his children. George Wolfe was the first to get married and then Joel."[15]

During his professional career, Gotthoffer was remarkably consistent, and his steadiness kept the SPHAS ready to play on a nightly basis. The SPHAS finished the 1935–1936 regular season winning four of five games, and the late spurt had them ready for the championship series against their old rivals the Brooklyn Visitations. All season, the SPHAS had wanted revenge from their disappointing loss the previous year, and now the time had come. The Visitations had won the second half with a 12–8 record and were the defending ABL champions. The third ABL championship series pitted the league's last two winners.

The series opened on March 28 in Philadelphia with a capacity crowd of 3,500 boisterous fans. The SPHAS won Game 1, 30–28, while outscoring the Visitations 14–7 in the final period. As written by Ronald Friedenberg of the *Philadelphia Inquirer* the next day, "Trailing 13–10 in the first chukker and 21–16 in the second session the Sphas struck savagely in the wind-up spasm. They moved the ball with unbelievable celerity, they scored on spine-tingling long tries for the nets, they were in possession most of the time and more surprising than ever, Cy Kaselman was on the loose as of yore."[16] The Visitations led, 24–23, but behind Kaselman the tide turned. "Cy had gone into action late in the second period, but nothing was the result. All season he had proven a cipher and he wasn't breaking the losing habit. So when the ball was passed to him beyond mid-floor and Kaselman let fly, nobody's heart stopped beating. Not until the leather knifed the cords and the Sphas were on the long end, 25–24."[17] Kaselman's basket pro-

The 1935–1936 Philadelphia SPHAS defeated the Brooklyn Visitations to win the championship. *Left to right:* Abe Radel, Harry Litwack, George Wolfe, Gil Fitch, Inky Lautman, Moe Goldman, Howard Rosan, Shikey Gotthoffer, Cy Kaselman, and Eddie Gottlieb. (*Courtesy of Bill Himmelman.*)

pelled the SPHAS in the game's final stretch. Tied at 28 with less than a minute remaining, Gotthoffer took a pass from Red Wolfe under the basket to score the decisive basket.

The following night, the series shifted to Prospect Hall in Brooklyn, where the Visitations protected their home court advantage with a nail-biting 27–24 overtime victory. The SPHAS led 17–10 midway through the second period and looked to be in good position to take command of the series with an important road victory. But Brooklyn soon found its rhythm and reeled off 8 straight points to take an 18–17 lead. The SPHAS scored the next 4 for a 21–18 advantage at the close of the second period. From that point until the game's conclusion, the SPHAS found themselves in a dog-fight as the Visitations clawed their way to a series-tying win. Gotthoffer scored only 3 points, but continued to play an all-around game that benefited his teammates.

Two close games, one settled on the game's last play and another in overtime, signaled that tempers might be fraying. And they were. A close contest in the third game grew heated as Inky Lautman and Brooklyn's Pete Berenson exchanged punches on the court. The fisticuffs spilled over to the fans, as some had to be escorted off the floor by police. Once order was restored, the SPHAS held onto their slim margin. Bruised, Lautman still led the way with a game-high 17 points and stellar defense on Bobby McDermott. Considered by many to be the game's best player, McDermott, in only his second professional season, was on the verge of leading the Visitations to a second championship. In the first two games, he had led all scorers, and his long shots from nearly half-court thrilled the entire crowd. Lautman's defensive effort was instrumental in the SPHAS taking a 2–1 series lead.

Playing without their star center, Moe Goldman, the SPHAS suffered their worst defeat, 31–24, in Game 4. With no big man to grab the center jump for the SPHAS, Brooklyn's Howie Bollerman had his way and scored 6 points. The SPHAS were lackluster throughout and trailed, 29–16, in the third period before Brooklyn emptied its bench. Even Gotthoffer, one of the SPHAS' most consistent players, was held to 1 point on a lone foul shot. It was the SPHAS' worst showing by far.

The series was deadlocked at two games apiece. Now, with the fifth game of a tightly contested series looming, the SPHAS looked to Gotthoffer for his experience. His strong defensive presence reliably set the tone for the game. The SPHAS opened strong and led 10–4 after the first intermission. The second period, however, was a reversal of fortune as Brooklyn outscored Philadelphia 12–5 on five field goals. In keeping with the earlier flow of the game, the SPHAS took control of the final frame and held the Visitations scoreless until two minutes remained. Despite McDermott's attempted late-game heroics, it was too little, too late. The defensive effort by the SPHAS, along with solid foul shooting (12 of 17 from the line) proved the key factors in the SPHAS taking a 3–2 series lead.

Game 6 was set for the following night at Prospect Hall, and its intensity lived up to the previous five matches. Leads changed with each possession. The SPHAS led 10–9 after the first session, but the Visitations won the second period. The third period was tense and frantic, as the series hinged on each basket. With under a minute remaining, the contest came down to two men. Red Wolfe was fouled by the Visitations' Red Conaty. Wolfe calmly sank the foul shot to even the game at 30 apiece. Their season on the line, Brooklyn advanced the ball up court and found Conaty in the pivot. He made his move to the basket and was fouled by Wolfe. A possible hero a moment earlier, Wolfe now watched as Conaty sank the foul shot to save Brooklyn's season and force a seventh and deciding game.

For six games, the players had battled for each point, with victory and reputation hinging on each basket. Except for Brooklyn's 7-point win in Game 4, each game's final margin had been 3 points or less. One had gone into overtime, and two had been unsettled until the final play of the game. The home team had won every game. By all accounts, it had been a well-played series up until that point. Many figured the seventh game to be a tight, physical game that would not be decided until the final gun was sounded. But they were wrong.

The first period did not disappoint and went according to plan as the SPHAS held a slight 11–9 lead. After that, the SPHAS broke loose and ran away with the game. The SPHAS easily outclassed and outhustled the Visitations, leading by no fewer than 10 points in the final ten minutes for a convincing 47–34 win. A well-played six games ended in a blow-out victory. At last, after a heartbreaking defeat the year before, the SPHAS had their revenge. In a hotly contested and hard-fought series, the SPHAS had outlasted their bitterest rival. Two championships in three years made the SPHAS the class of the league. By April 1936, the best basketball team was a Jewish team from Philadelphia.

In the summer of 1936, several months after the SPHAS' triumph, newspapers across the country discussed the coming Olympics and the deteriorating situation in Germany. Through the heat of the offseason, debate centered on whether the United States should participate, let alone field a basketball team. Basketball was added to the Olympic roster for the 1936 Berlin Games for the first time since the game had been played as a demonstration sport in 1904 (St. Louis Olympics). The invitation for basketball to join the Olympics reinforced the sport's status as a global game only forty-five years after its invention. On August 1, the Berlin Olympics started. Later that week, on August 7, basketball officially debuted.

Despite the game's popularity and the quickness with which it spread, especially internationally, the notion of basketball being an Olympic sport had not received the necessary support. At the 1904 Olympics in St. Louis, basketball was played as an exhibition game in which medals were not contested. Thirty-two years later, basketball was added to the roster and over time became one of the Olympics' greatest spectacles.

By the mid-1930s, basketball inventor James Naismith had settled into life as a revered professor and dean at the University of Kansas. Naismith had devoted his career to teaching physical education and serving as a mentor to thousands of students since moving to Kansas in 1898. He left basketball behind as he chose to focus his attention on other matters that he deemed more important and rewarding. Basketball, though, was not ready to leave him.

His former pupil, Kansas basketball coach Phog Allen, spearheaded the effort for basketball to be an Olympic sport and for Naismith to travel to see the game played on an international stage. Allen's efforts to include basketball at the 1932 Los Angeles Games failed to garner the requisite amount of support. Shortly thereafter, he worked earnestly to have basketball be part of the 1936 Berlin Olympics, and within time his goal was realized.

With basketball now an Olympic sport, he focused on his second goal, raising enough money to send Naismith and his wife, Maude, to Berlin. Allen's objective was simple: to honor the game's founder as basketball was to be played for the first time in Olympic competition. With the support of the National Association of Basketball Coaches, the week of February 9–15, 1936, was designated "Naismith Week" and one penny from every ticket sold at a basketball game in the United States was set aside to pay for Naismith's trip overseas. Nearly $5,000 was raised.

The Olympic Basketball Committee soon formed with the charge of determining how to assemble a team and finance the outfit's trip to Germany. Eventually a system was established that would lead to a three-day Olympic basketball tryout finale at Madison Square Garden. It was determined that the final field in New York would include the top two teams from the Amateur Athletic Union (AAU) National Championships held in Denver, Colorado; the winner of the Young Men's Christian Association (YMCA) National Championships in Peoria, Illinois; and five college teams selected from an elaborate playoff system. The winning team would be awarded seven players on the Olympic team, the second-place team would have six players, and the final spot would be selected from the remaining six teams. A total of fourteen players would make up the U.S. Olympic basketball team.

To reduce the college field to five teams, a system was devised in which the country was divided into ten districts. Each district would reveal one winner, and the ten district winners would play each other, thus reducing the field to five finalists to make the trip to New York. The second district was composed of teams from New Jersey, Pennsylvania, Maryland, and the District of Columbia.

Temple University was joined by the University of Arkansas, DePaul University, Utah State College, and the University of Washington. Universal Pictures and McPherson Oilers represented the AAU, and Wilmerding (Pennsylvania) YMCA won the YMCA tournament.

On the opening day of the tryouts, anticipation filled the air as eight of the nation's finest basketball teams readied for a trip to the Berlin Olympics. For months, the rise of Nazism and the political and social climate in Germany became known to the outside world. German Jews were no longer considered citizens; they were stripped of all their rights, and their businesses were often ignored by the larger population. Debate centered on whether the Americans should participate in the Games. In his preview article for the *New York Times*, Arthur Daley captured the uncertain climate when he wrote, "No one can guess what the crowd will be. Various anti-Nazi organizations have made plans to picket the Garden even though Temple has four Jewish players on its squad and the Universals two."[18] Set against this political climate, Madison Square Garden was bursting at the seams as the first game was set to tip off.

The quadruple header did not disappoint. In his article the following morning, Arthur Daley wrote, "In a brilliant show, jammed to the utmost with thrills, spectacular playing and the most amazing shotmaking ever seen in New York, the final Olympic tryouts sped away from the starting mark in Madison Square Garden last night while a crowd of 12,000 sat spellbound throughout six hours." The evening was also noteworthy for Naismith. "There was even a touch of sentiment as Dr. James Naismith, 74-year-old physical education instructor who invented the sport forty-five years ago, officially opened the tournament."[19]

Notable in the first night of competition was that four of the five college teams lost. Universal Pictures defeated Arkansas 40–29, Wilmerding YMCA held off Utah State 62–48, Washington trounced DePaul 54–33, and McPherson beat Temple 56–48.

In the semifinal round, Universal Pictures defeated Wilmerding YMCA 42–29, and McPherson Oilers overtook the University of Washington 48–30. The final game between Universal and McPherson was a rematch of the AAU championships played two weeks before. This time, Universal avenged their loss and squeaked out a 44–43 victory. The Olympic team was set and included Frank Lubin, Carl Shy, Duane Swanson, Art Mollner, Don Piper, Sam Balter, and Carl Knowles from Universal and Francis Johnson, Joe Fortenberry, John (Tex) Gibbons, Jack Ragland, Willard Schmidt, and William Wheatley from McPherson. The final player chosen was Ralph Bishop from the University of Washington.

Basketball was finally an Olympic sport. Twenty-two nations, hailing from four of the five continents, were entered. All of the games were played on outdoor clay courts, a sign perhaps that the Germans did not fully appreciate or understand the game. The United States carried fourteen players. The coaching staff decided that the group would be split into two smaller teams and would alternate playing games, with the stated purpose that everyone would have the chance to compete. It also allowed the players to stay fresh and rested.

The United States opened Olympic competition by defeating Spain, 2–0, who forfeited on account of the start of its Civil War. In the second round, the Americans faced Estonia and handily won, 52–28. The Americans jumped out to an early lead and led, 26–7, at the end of the first half. The game was notable in that Sam Balter, a left forward for the U.S. team, became the first Jew to play in an Olympic basketball game. An All-American at UCLA in 1929, Balter continued playing after graduation on a team sponsored by Universal Pictures. He was on the starting five that defeated the McPherson Oilers at the Olympic basketball tryouts in New York City and scored 3 points in that clinching game. As a result of Universal's triumph, he was selected to the Olympic team, but shortly thereafter some doubt and concern crept into his mind about whether, as a Jew, he should participate in the Berlin Olympics.

"I was told by others that it was absolutely imperative that I play," he remembered decades later. "But more important, what kind of propaganda tool would we have if . . . there were no Jews on the American team?"[20] After assurances from U.S. Olympic President Avery Brundage that the athletes would not encounter any problems, Balter joined his teammates for the transatlantic journey to Berlin.

When he arrived, he and his teammates moved into the Olympic Village. The doubt he had felt several months earlier again crossed his mind when he saw many anti-Semitic magazines on sale on every block, as well as propaganda brochures distributed freely throughout the village. "The magazine has caricatures of hooked-nosed people, and it lays blame for everything on the Jews,"[21] Balter recalled. Despite any unease he may have felt, Balter forged ahead and played with extra purpose and determination as if to make his own personal statement to Hitler and Nazi Germany. Against Estonia, he scored 7 points on three field goals. In the semifinal contest against Mexico, Balter led all scorers with 10 points.

After another bye, the Americans moved into the fourth round, where they squared off against the Philippines, whom they defeated, 56–23. The Americans started slow, but forged ahead to stay. In the semifinals, a strong Mexico squad could not keep pace and fell to the United States, 25–10. The United States held Mexico to 2 first-half points.

In the gold medal game, Canada faced off against the United States. The pairing of his birthplace and his adopted homeland no doubt pleased James Naismith, the game's inventor, who joined with 1,000 other spectators as they watched the final in a driving rain. "If you dribbled, it was a splash and it floated away," Balter noted. The score at halftime was 15–4 in favor of the Americans. "These two teams supposedly consisting of the best in the world, and each scored only 4 points in the second half," Balter said.[22] A sloppy game ended with the United States claiming a 19–8 victory and basketball's first Olympic Gold Medal.

In its first Olympic go-round, basketball proved to be a success, and it would only get better in the decades to follow. The day after the gold medal game, the *New York Times* provided this insight into basketball as an Olympic sport: "More remarkable than the guaranteed American victory, however, was the generally high level of play shown by teams from all parts of the world. The mere fact that the three final games today were played by nations so far apart geographically and historically as the United States and Canada on the one hand and Poland and Mexico and the Philippines and Uruguay on the other is evidence enough of the place the 'YMCA game' has taken in the world."[23]

In the ten months from Greenberg's World Series to the Olympic Games in Berlin, much had changed for the Jewish community. The situation for Jews continued to deteriorate at an alarming rate. As concern grew, participation in sport "carried special symbolic import for American Jews concerned both with American acceptance and with Jewish survival."[24] Athletic success and achievement allowed the Jewish community to find some respite from the horrific situation in Europe and America. Hank Greenberg's powerful home runs, Shikey Gotthoffer's tough defense and baskets, and America's basketball triumph at the Berlin Olympics with Jewish players "emphasized the defiant, strong, tough Jew capable of surviving, regardless of the horrors of historical reality."[25] These athletic triumphs gave the Jewish community great pride in fighting for Jewish survival and standing up to the evil and oppression in the world.

6

HOWARD THE RED

He was a quiet man and he looked like he did not belong in sports. But he could play defense.

—Sam (Leaden) Bernstein,
interview by the author

Late in the afternoon of Wednesday November 4, 1936, Red Rosan, Cy Kaselman, Inky Lautman, and Gil Fitch piled into Eddie Gottlieb's car for the drive from Philadelphia to Kingston, New York. Meeting them there would be Shikey Gotthoffer, Moe Goldman, and Red Wolfe, who had traveled together from New York City. Another basketball season was set to commence, and the SPHAS looked to begin defense of their ABL championship with a victory over the Kingston Colonials, who were in their second year in the league. The year before, the Colonials had finished near the bottom of the standings in both halves and had rarely distinguished themselves on the court. The season-opening game was tight throughout, but the SPHAS pulled it out, 30–27, in the last two minutes on a basket by Inky Lautman and a foul shot by Moe Goldman. With the first game in the win column, the SPHAS headed back to Philadelphia to prepare for its home opener against the same Colonials on November 7.

The 1936–1937 campaign marked the fourth year for John J. O'Brien's ABL. Relative stability had settled over the league, and the league president and team owners looked forward to another promising season. In the season's first half, the league welcomed a new team, the Atlantic City Sand Snipers, who fared poorly and withdrew after dropping their first ten games. The Brooklyn Visitations, champions the previous season, played their first game in Paterson, New Jersey, but quickly returned to Brooklyn, where they enjoyed much of their success. The New York Jewels, who played many of their home games at Arcadia Hall in Brooklyn, officially became the Brooklyn Jewels at the start of the second half of league play. Finally, the famed Original Celtics joined the league in the second half and finished a modest 10–10. Their best years behind them, this Original Celtics squad was a shadow of its former self. Otherwise, the league make-up was quite similar to the prior season's.

While the league was enjoying stability with its franchises, the same could be said of Eddie Gottlieb's team. In three short years, Gottlieb had developed a solid, well-balanced team where players understood their roles and how to play with one another. The only major change in terms of personnel was the loss of Harry Litwack, a stalwart on the team since 1929–1930, who retired as a player to focus on his coaching career at Temple University. Jim Fox, another Temple graduate, assumed his place on the roster for a mere seven games. For the most part, Gottlieb had few concerns in filling out a lineup card each night. The roster included Shikey Gotthoffer, Cy Kaselman, Inky Lautman, Moe Goldman, Red Wolfe, Gil Fitch, and Red Rosan, who would be entering his second full season with the team. This core group of seven players became Gottlieb's best squad and the one most associated with the glory days of the team. The SPHAS were entering their prime. With two titles in three seasons, the SPHAS set their sights on back-to-back championships. In the course of the 1936–1937 season, the SPHAS waged one of the best campaigns in league history, and when the season concluded in mid-April, they were indisputably regarded as basketball's best team.

The home opener on November 7 was the first time the SPHAS had played before a Philadelphia crowd since their clinching win in the previous year's championship series. Primed and ready to put on a good show for the home fans, many of whom were anxious for another season, the SPHAS quickly jumped out of the gate and never looked back. Playing with a renewed defensive intensity, the SPHAS hounded Kingston, cutting in the passing lanes and stealing the ball to lead to numerous easy baskets. Their splendid all-around play left everyone with the feeling that "if last night's exhibition is a sample of what's to follow the race will be a canter for Eddie Gottlieb's pupils."[1]

Ronald Friedenberg of the *Philadelphia Inquirer* observed, "Those Sphas youngsters have been together several seasons now and while they usually work like machinery, the engine was pepped up faster than I have ever seen it and Kingston, with all its stars, was never really in the game, although fighting to make a bristling battle, which it proved."[2] The SPHAS led 16–6 after the first intermission and cruised to a 40–27 win.

The Philadelphia SPHAS won consecutive championships in 1935–1936 and 1936–1937. *Clockwise from the bottom right:* Eddie Gottlieb, Howard Rosan, Inky Lautman, Gil Fitch, George Wolfe, Moe Goldman, Cy Kaselman, and Shikey Gotthoffer. (*Courtesy of Bill Himmelman.*)

The following night, the SPHAS headed back on the road and lost, 30–21, to the New York Jewels. Playing without Moe Goldman, benched for an ankle injury, and Shikey Gotthoffer, who was nursing various injuries, the SPHAS could never get going and played catch-up all evening. A week later, the SPHAS hosted the Jewels and returned to their winning ways. A close game early in the second period soon turned on the efforts of Red Rosan, whose "goal in the second period brought a lead never lost on a brilliant play and his doubledecker earlier in the session came from the centre of the floor to give the Hebrews a 13–12 advantage."[3] On the next possession, Rosan stole the ball from Max Posnak and scored a layup. The basket broke a 15-all tie and propelled the SPHAS to their third victory of the young season. Rosan (8 points) led the SPHAS in scoring, the first of eleven times in the regular season he would do so. In only his second full season, Rosan played like a veteran, and during the course of the 1936–1937 campaign, he was one of the team's most consistent players. It was the best year of Red Rosan's career.

To look at Howard Rosan, one would not think he was an elite ball player. "Red Rosan was a star Temple player. He was the best defensive player in those days. He was not that big and not that strong, but he was all hands and legs," Sam (Leaden) Bernstein recalled. "He would play all the better players, even Bobby McDermott, who was the best player I ever saw."[4]

Growing up in Philadelphia, Howard (Red) Rosan was a good athlete. He entered South Philadelphia High School (Southern) and looked to become involved in athletics. He played basketball and football. Rosan graduated Southern and enrolled in Temple, where he became a key contributor on the basketball team. His sophomore season, the Owls compiled a 15–6 record. The team took a step back the following year with a 9–12 mark. Rosan looked to put Temple back on its winning ways as a senior. In a sensational season, the Owls compiled a 17–7 mark, including victories over Ohio State, Pittsburgh, Notre Dame, Drake, and West Virginia.

After his college career came to an end, Rosan played in the final few games of the 1934–1935 season for the SPHAS. He became the latest Temple player, following Litwack, Kaselman, and Fitch, to sign on to play for Gottlieb, who wasted no time in incorporating new players onto his team. And Rosan was no different.

With four games left in the 1934–1935 regular season, Rosan joined the team in time for a key contest against the New Britain Jackaways, who were fighting the SPHAS for second-half honors. The game was the featured matchup of a basketball tripleheader staged at Philadelphia's Convention Hall to benefit the welfare fund of the Philadelphia Sports Writers Association. More than 7,000 fans packed Convention Hall to watch the game, along with two other matches: the Brooklyn Jewels against the Boston Trojans and the Brooklyn Visitations against the New York Renaissance.

Late in the third and final period, Rosan saw his first professional action. "A good many persons among the 7,000 must have come out for a glimpse of Howard (Red) Rosan, ex-Temple ace, who made his professional court debut with Eddie Gottlieb's South Philadelphia passing wizards," Ronald Friedenberg wrote in the *Philadelphia Inquirer* the next day. "I say this because Rosan was accorded an ovation when he replaced Gil Fitch with eight minutes of the final chukker gone." Friedenberg continued, "Rosan wasn't at all nervous. He fitted into the scheme of things nicely and he made good on a pair of tries from the 15-foot line. It began to look as though Rosan was to adorn the bench when New Britain overcame a 9–3 first-period lead, tied the count at 12-all in the second session, and went ahead 18 to 14 soon after the final chukker had ended. But Eddie Gottlieb, Sphas pilot, has great confidence in Rosan and this confidence was not misplaced."[5] Rosan saw plenty of action that night and scored 2 points, both on foul shots.

Rosan did not score in the remaining few games he played, but the experience of being with his teammates and witnessing the intensity of a bitter playoff defeat to the Brooklyn Visitations proved invaluable, positioning Rosan to be a key contributor the following season. In his years with the SPHAS, he was a consistent performer, averaging between 5 and 6.5 points per game a year. His lone breakout season was 1936–1937, when he averaged an outstanding 8.4 points per game.

The team's win over the New York Jewels on November 14, 1936, was the start of a four-game winning streak. Two victories over the Brooklyn Visitations and another over newcomer Atlantic City propelled the SPHAS to a 6–1 record and a match-up with the Jersey Reds. Against Atlantic City, Rosan came to the team's rescue as he led all scorers with 15 points, including "dropping in three on the dead run that brought cheers from those who weren't gasping."[6] In the second win over Brooklyn, Gottlieb welcomed back Shikey Gotthoffer, and for the first time all season, the SPHAS were playing at full strength.

On November 29, the SPHAS, sporting a 6–1 record, traveled to North Bergen, New Jersey, to face the Jersey Reds in an early-season matchup of the league's two best teams. Jersey came into the game riding a five-game winning streak. The SPHAS and Reds fought back and forth all season and waged a great league race in both the first and second halves. In the end, both would engage in one of the toughest and most thrilling championship series in league history to determine the winner.

The Jersey Reds, in their fourth season, were an original franchise of the ABL. Their first season, the team played as the Union City Reds, but soon became the Jersey Reds and played their home games at Columbia Park in North Bergen, New Jersey. Unlike the SPHAS, Jersey started slowly and were not much of a factor in league play their first few years. In the second half of the 1935–1936 season, their third in the league, Jersey finished 11–9, good for second place. The momentum of their best-ever finish stayed with them and high hopes followed them as they started the 1936–1937 season.

In the first matchup between the two best teams of the season, Jersey and the SPHAS waged a hard-fought battle, setting the tone for the rest of the season. Jersey jumped out early and held an 11–6 lead after the first intermission. In the second period, Jersey extended their lead to 10 points, but the SPHAS battled back and cut the deficit to a single point entering the final period. Back and forth the action went in the final frame, and Jersey held on for a 38–36 win. In the season-long battle between the two squads, Jersey struck first.

Handed their second road defeat of the young season, the SPHAS headed home with a week to prepare for a rematch against Jersey. The second time around the SPHAS rebounded nicely and won comfortably, 42–30. A healthy Gotthoffer led the way with 14 points.

Midway through the first half of the season, the SPHAS hit a snag, often following up a win with a loss and being unable to get back on a winning streak. After defeating Jersey, the SPHAS lost to the New York Jewels, defeated Atlantic City, and then lost to Kingston on the night ABL President John J. O'Brien presented the team with its 1935–1936 championship trophy. The loss to Kingston dropped the SPHAS' record to 8–4, only a half-game ahead of Kingston in the standings. The SPHAS were in second place behind Jersey, who at 9–1 were running away with first-half honors.

Jersey's lead, once thought insurmountable, would slowly diminish as the SPHAS started to make a late run. Now in the home stretch of the season's first half, the team traveled to Kingston for a Christmas Day game against the third-place Colonials. This marked the fourth matchup against Kingston in the first half, and the SPHAS held a 2–1 edge, although Kingston had won the previous game two weeks earlier. Second place was on the line, and the SPHAS had a quick start, holding a 15–12 lead at the conclusion of the first period. After that, the Colonials found their mark, and behind Phil Rabin, who continued to have his best games against the SPHAS, outscored Philadelphia 35–15 the rest of the way. Kingston cruised to a 47–30 win and, more importantly, moved into second place.

The SPHAS found themselves in a three-way battle with Kingston and Jersey and needed to step up if they wanted to gain first-half honors. The SPHAS won their next three games to set up a final home-and-home series with the Reds to decide league honors. After their dispiriting loss to

Kingston on Christmas, the SPHAS headed back to Philadelphia and the next night defeated the Brooklyn Visitations to gain a tie for second place with idle Kingston. The following night, the team traveled to Brooklyn for another game against the Visitations. Playing their third straight game in as many nights, extremely rare in league history, the SPHAS won for the first time in the borough of Brooklyn all season. A renewed defensive intensity propelled the SPHAS as "their defensive work during the first two-thirds was their best of the year, for all the home team could garner during this period was 10 points, three in the second period."[7] Behind Gotthoffer, who scored 11 points, and Rosan, who added 9, the SPHAS were now back in sole possession of second place for the first time since December 12.

Two games remained, and the SPHAS faced a crucial home-and-home series against Jersey to determine first-half honors. Jersey sported a 13–3 mark, while the SPHAS were 11–5. A win by the Jersey Reds in either game would clinch first-half honors. If the SPHAS won both games, a one-game playoff would be played to determine the winner. Writing in the *Philadelphia Evening Ledger*, Bill Dallas stated, "The zero hour for the Sphas is at hand. Naturally, the followers of the Sphas are wildly excited to see their favorites stage a great comeback in the closing weeks of the race to jump right into the title running."[8]

The Broadwood Hotel on January 9, 1937, was absolutely jammed with 3,500 fans, "a crowd that filled seats, all available standing room and moved out on the playing floor."[9] The SPHAS came out ready to play and, paced by Gotthoffer and Lautman, led 16–4 after the first period. The SPHAS extended their margin to 21–8 early in the second frame before the Reds, displaying their offensive scoring punch, came storming back in a hurry. Behind Willie Scrill and Moe Frankel, Jersey made a game of it and took their first lead, 23–21. The second period ended with Jersey leading 31–30. In that period, Jersey outscored the SPHAS, 27–14, including 15 unanswered points. Their effort to get back into the game left them with little fight in the final period as the SPHAS pulled away for a 49–41 win.

The following afternoon, the SPHAS traveled to Columbia Park in North Bergen, New Jersey, for a second game against Jersey in less than 24 hours. The SPHAS still needed a win to force a one-game playoff. In their lone game against Jersey on the road, the SPHAS had lost. Jersey had yet to lose a home game, and with the first half on the line, this would not be the time. For two weeks, Jersey had tried to clinch the title, but nerves and poor play had hampered their effort. Finally, Jersey broke through with a 29-point first period and cruised to a 56–33 win. A local newspaper chronicled the Reds' romp to the title:

> As Red rooters looked on in a state bordering on frenzy, Captain Willie Scrill and his men just tore the park wide open in that never-to-be-forgotten first session. The pent-up fury of two weeks exploded with a terrific detonation. Swooping down upon the poor unsuspecting Phils like a Texas hurricane, the locals, playing like men possessed, flashed the most brilliant 15 minutes of offensive play local pro basketball has ever known—to crush the Hebrews, to clinch the championship, and, believe it or not, to shatter the scoring record which only the night before they themselves had set in Philadelphia.[10]

After their loss to Jersey, the SPHAS traveled across the Hudson River to face the Brooklyn Jewels to begin the season's second half. Showing some effects from their loss earlier in the day and playing their third game in two days, the SPHAS squeaked out a 37–36 win to begin their chase for second-half honors. In many respects, the season's second half was similar to the first. The SPHAS started out splitting their first four games before embarking on a four-game winning streak. A road game against Jersey halted their winning streak, much like their November loss versus the Reds had stopped an earlier streak. Undeterred, the SPHAS started another four-game winning streak. Two consecutive losses put the SPHAS on the edge of the playoffs looking in before the team rebounded to win its last four games and claim second-half honors.

In their victory over the Jewels to start the second half, the team was led by Red Rosan, who tallied 13 points. In the season's first half, Rosan had led the team in scoring in six games. After his strong game against the Jewels, Rosan was largely absent as a scoring leader and did not resurface again until seven games remained in the regular season. In those games down the stretch, Rosan led the team in scoring four times, including in a crucial win over Jersey on March 13. His strong play came at an opportune time as the SPHAS made their final push of the season.

Midway through February, the SPHAS held a 6–2 record as they headed into New Jersey for another battle with the first-place Reds. Columbia Park proved one of the more difficult places to play, and the Reds had yet to lose a home game all season. The *Philadelphia Inquirer* even referred to Jersey's home-court dominance and the SPHAS' inability to win there as the "Columbia Park jinx." Knowing how important the game was to his club, Gottlieb scheduled only one game that week, which was the night before, when the SPHAS handily defeated Kingston in a tune-up for their contest with the Reds. Jersey, meanwhile, canceled two exhibition games that week to save their legs for the SPHAS. It was good strategy for Jersey.

Determined to finally break through against Jersey on the road, the SPHAS jumped off to a good start and stayed close, trailing by one, 14–13, after the first period. Feeling confident that they were not being blown out in the first period like their last trip to Columbia Park, the SPHAS kept forging ahead and soon opened a commanding 21–14 lead. "Gotthoffer pumped in a foul to knot the count at 14–14 and a few seconds later he followed with a field goal to put his team 2 points in front. Rosan then cut the cords with a free throw and Goldman, shifting Al Benson into such a state of helplessness that big Al actually fell on the floor, broke away to score a sucker shot from underneath. Cy Kaselman then entered the game and immediately made his presence felt by ripping the lace with a hawker to make the score read 21–14."[11]

Then it all fell apart. Twice before, the SPHAS had fallen victim to scoring outbursts by Jersey that left them bewildered and playing catch-up. Again it happened. Trailing by 7, 21–14, Jersey hit a field goal to quickly stop the SPHAS' momentum. "That free throw seemed to light the fuse to the scoring dynamite the Reds possess. For, without any warning whatsoever, the locals changed from their unorganized team play into a smooth clicking machine, and scoring bombs soon began blasting their way through the basket in the most electrifying style the Park fans have seen this season."[12] Willie Scrill, Moe Frankel, and Moe Spahn all took turns, and when the smoke had cleared, Jersey was in front, 24–21. The hometown fans went wild. "The fans roared and they howled. They hugged one another and slapped each other's backs. It was a madhouse of unconfined joy for Red rooters that was broken only by a time out called by the amazed Phillies."[13]

The SPHAS hung tough in the final period but could not overcome a Jersey team playing its best basketball. The SPHAS fell, 43–35, and were a full two games behind Jersey in the standings. Jersey had now won 16 consecutive home games. They were considered the team to beat.

The SPHAS left New Jersey licking their wounds but vowed to get back at them. Eleven games remained in the regular season; the SPHAS were two games behind in the standings but had three games remaining against Jersey, including two at the Broadwood. Their first chance at a rematch was on February 27. In between, the SPHAS had three league games: one against Kingston and two with the Brooklyn Jewels. Beating up on the weaker opponents was a much-needed tonic. Against Kingston, the SPHAS handed the Colonials one of their few home defeats. More importantly, the team was now only a game behind Jersey, who lost their first game after besting the SPHAS.

The way the schedule fell, both the SPHAS and Jersey faced a home-and-home series against the Brooklyn teams. The SPHAS played the last-place Jewels while Jersey faced the Brooklyn Visitations. Much would be determined by the outcomes of these games, and Jersey needed to keep winning, as the SPHAS were closing the gap. On February 21, the SPHAS easily defeated the Jewels, 33–23, and moved a half-game behind Jersey. The following afternoon, the Visitations went into Columbia Park and snapped the Reds' sixteen-game home winning streak, 31–30. It was the biggest upset of the season. The SPHAS and Jersey now shared first place.

Both Jersey and the SPHAS faced the second half of their back-to-back matchups. The results were the same. The SPHAS defeated the Jewels, and the Visitations again took one from Jersey. After their defeat to Jersey a week before, the SPHAS had made up three games and now had a one-game lead going into their February 27 game against Jersey.

Jersey, looking for their first win in Philadelphia, set the pace early and "advanced the ball up the court with such passing and dribbling speed as to fairly bewilder the Hebrews."[14] Jersey held a 16–9 first-period lead that swelled to 22–9 early in the second period. But much like the last game in New Jersey, the home team righted the ship, quickly reversed course, and pulled away for a clear victory.

The SPHAS quickly came to life as Lautman, Kaselman, and Goldman connected on inside and outside shots that narrowed the gap to 28–26 with only seconds left in the period. The fortunes of the game turned at that moment. Again, it was Kaselman who came to the rescue. "A few seconds before the whistle the visitors were ahead 28–26, when Kaselman secured possession with the tocsin about to sound. He was only a few feet from the opposite basket, but Cy let loose with the longest shot of the year. It penetrated the strings as the crowd roared and the session came to an end."[15] Tied 28–28, the SPHAS had outscored Jersey 19–4 after being down 22–9 early in the period. Kaselman's miracle shot broke Jersey's spirits.

The SPHAS kept the heat on in the final period and advanced to a 42–38 win. The SPHAS now held a two-game lead with seven to play. Next up for the SPHAS was a home-and-home series with the Brooklyn Visitations. A week before, this same Visitation team had taken two games from Jersey, knocking them out of first place. Looking to play the spoiler, the Visitations again pulled the upset and defeated the SPHAS twice within a week.

Only four games remained. The SPHAS hosted Jersey, traveled to face the Original Celtics, and then finished up with two games at home versus the Kingston Colonials and Original Celtics. Jersey, meanwhile, traveled to Philadelphia and Kingston before concluding with Kingston and the Brooklyn Jewels at home. Jersey held a one-game lead, and the weekend of March 13 and 14 had the potential to settle the league race. If Jersey swept both road games in Philadelphia and Kingston, then they would almost be assured of capturing the second half and being declared league champions. As Jersey would find out, playing two league road games in the heat of a close race is no easy task.

With the fate of their season staring them in the face, the SPHAS responded brilliantly against Jersey. With a week to prepare, Gottlieb sought answers for his team to break its three-game slide. He implemented a few new wrinkles in practice that week in the hopes of catching Jersey off guard. It worked. As Ronald Friedenberg wrote in the *Philadelphia Inquirer*, "Eddie Gottlieb's bag of tricks apparently isn't exhausted. A lateral passing play was developed last night with three assisting players lined up in a straight line from basket to basket. Then a scoring or would-be scoring courtman would take a pass from the first, pass to the second, take it from the second and so on until the basket was reached and he was dropping one through. Rosan came through with two double-deckers with this newly devised stratagem."[16] Rosan led all scorers with 15 points on five field goals and five foul shots. It was the third time in four games that Rosan had paced the team in scoring, and he was finding his touch at the right time. The SPHAS easily won, 51–34. It was Jersey's worst defeat all year.

Now tied for first place, the SPHAS traveled to New York, where they defeated the Original Celtics. The victory, coupled with Kingston's 42–41 win over Jersey, left the SPHAS with a one-game lead in the standings. Two crushing road defeats left Jersey in a tough position. Several weeks earlier, the Visitations had played spoiler in the race when they swept four games against Philadelphia and Jersey. Now, Kingston was looking to play spoiler. After defeating Jersey at home, Kingston headed to Philadelphia, where the SPHAS faced their third game in as many nights for the second time that season.

Seeking at least a share of first place, the SPHAS came out firing on all cylinders, picking up where they had left off in their win over Jersey two nights earlier. A 19–8 first-period lead was all the SPHAS needed as their offense left the Colonials powerless to respond. The SPHAS easily won, 55–29, opening up a 1½ game lead and securing no worse than a tie for first place.

Kingston's defeat in Philadelphia by no means discouraged them from playing hard and having an impact on the race. A few days later, they traveled to Jersey and handed them a second defeat in a week. Jersey's loss guaranteed the SPHAS second-half honors with one game to play. A tremendous second-half battle was finally over. The championship series was set: the SPHAS versus Jersey, seven games to determine a winner.

By all accounts, the Philadelphia-Jersey series figured to be a battle. If the regular season had been any indication, this series would go down to the wire. In eight regular-season matchups, each team had won four, holding serve in all their home games. Each team had won close games and each had had a blow-out win. They were as evenly matched as two teams could be. During the head-to-head matchups, the SPHAS averaged 40.1 points per game while Jersey tallied 39.6 points per game. Both the SPHAS and the Jersey Reds were at full strength and ready to get started. Tough, physical games marked the regular season, and that figured to carry over to the playoffs.

The series opened on March 27 in Philadelphia, and 3,500 fans packed the Broadwood Hotel to witness the first game. Jersey surprised many by winning for the first time in Philadelphia all season. The game started well for Jersey, who opened an early lead and took a 14–10 advantage heading into the second period. Their lead increased in the second session as Jersey "played closely, they hung on and they stole the leather many times when the Hebrews just seemed to be getting somewhere."[17] Jersey played smothering defense and held the SPHAS to two field goals, both by Cy Kaselman, in a twenty-eight-minute span of play. For the game, the SPHAS managed only nine field goals and made a last-ditch effort to get back in the game after trailing, 34–25. Two minutes remained when the SPHAS made a run, started by Kaselman, who "came through with the most difficult and sensational goal of the game, a shot on the dead run, made from side court with the right arm sending the ball in a short arc over Kaselman's head clean through."[18] Wolfe and Fitch followed with baskets and the SPHAS now trailed 34–31 with less than a minute remaining. Their last-gasp effort fell short as Jersey's Paul Adamo made a basket to help preserve the win, 36–31. Late in the second period, Moe Sphan collided with Red Rosan, causing Rosan to leave the game with "a deep gash over his left eye."[19] This physical play would be a trademark for the rest of the series.

Down a game and having lost the home court advantage, the SPHAS traveled to Jersey and hoped to return the favor by stealing a road game.

The SPHAS dominated the first period, while Jersey outplayed the SPHAS in the second. At the end of thirty minutes, the score stood dead even at 19 apiece. The teams continued to trade baskets in the final period and with seven minutes remaining the game was deadlocked at 26. It was at that moment that the game and possibly the series changed on a freak accident. Jersey center Al Benson tripped while chasing Moe Goldman as the SPHAS pushed the ball up the court. It was a bitter blow to Jersey, as Benson had been outplaying Goldman to that point. As Benson fell, Goldman continued to the basket and scored the go-ahead basket to make the score 28–26. The SPHAS would not look back. As the *Hudson Dispatch* reported, "[Benson] was examined and was declared in no shape to continue, his old ankle having been aggravated to such an extent that he could hardly walk back to the bench."[20] It was an injury that would haunt Jersey for the rest of the series.

With Benson sidelined, the SPHAS took advantage. After the basket by Goldman, he won the tap at the next center jump. He "ran underneath the basket, received a pass from Cy Kaselman, and scored another double decker."[21] That made it 30–26, the largest lead for the SPHAS since the opening session. Jersey made a comeback and trailed, 32–29, with a few minutes remaining, but Goldman hit another shot, and the SPHAS held on for a 39–36 win to even the series. The win was the SPHAS' first in Jersey all year.

In the first two contests, Kaselman had led the SPHAS in scoring while proving to be a difficult defensive assignment for Jersey. Prior to the start of the third game, Jersey manager/coach Phil (Muggsy) Miller made a lineup change in the hopes of finding a solution to contain Kaselman's offensive outbursts. He decided to move Moe Spahn from his forward position and put him at guard opposing Kaselman. Mike Michelotti switched to the forward position and faced Inky Lautman. A local newspaper explained the rationale for this defensive switch: "The Redleg mentor is aware that Kaselman is plenty loose on the defense, and that Spahn should have little trouble getting away from him. If the brilliant Spahn can check Kaselman and still go out and get his points, Miller is certain the Reds will win."[22]

The change in strategy worked for Jersey as Kaselman was a nonfactor, scoring only 6 points after tallying 9 and 13 in Game 1 and 2, respectively. His lone field goal came in the opening session. Jersey started slowly, down 12–3 after the first period, as the SPHAS "were in full hue and cry. They passed rings around their foes, scored four field goals and the same number of fouls, and performed generally in magnificent style."[23] As had been the case in many of their games versus Jersey, the SPHAS were susceptible to quick swings in the action and huge offensive explosions by their opponent. The SPHAS were largely ineffective after their initial onslaught, scoring only 16 points the rest of the way. Jersey tallied 31 points and cruised to an easy 34–28 win. Al Benson played with a heavily wrapped ankle until the end of the second session before reinjuring himself. He was again helped off the floor, and Moe Spahn shifted from guarding Kaselman to playing center. For the second time in the series, Jersey won on the road and regained home court advantage.

Fresh off their third-period blitz of the SPHAS the night before, the Reds picked up where they left off and held a 15–5 lead midway through the first period in the fourth game. Gottlieb then made a key substitution and replaced Rosan with Kaselman. Since injuring his eye in the first game, Rosan had been largely ineffective. He had not scored in the first game, had been held out as a precautionary measure in the second, and had scored only 1 point in the third game. By the fourth game, Gottlieb had seen enough, and sensing the series might be slipping away from his team, inserted Kaselman into the game earlier.

Kaselman had given Jersey fits offensively all season. This time, Kaselman made his mark defensively by guarding Hagan Andersen, who had had his way with the SPHAS all series. His defensive job on Andersen allowed the SPHAS to get back into the game, as they trailed by one point, 15–14, after the first period. The SPHAS kept the pressure on and led, 18–17, early in the next session. Gottlieb then made another substitution; unlike the first one, this one backfired. Sensing that Kaselman might need a rest, he pulled his star and replaced him with Red Wolfe. Kaselman had held Andersen scoreless, but with this change of defensive players, Andersen found an opening and took advantage. Andersen immediately got back in the scoring column as he "shoved [Wolfe] off in the southeast corner of the court, took a pass, and laid up a dazzling double decker, putting the Reds ahead." Moments later, a "wild dash for the goal ensued and Wolfe was unable to keep Andersen from getting ahead of him. A 3-point play resulted—and the Reds moved on Easy Street, 22–18."[24] Jersey did not look back as they won 34–30 to open a commanding 3–1 series lead.

Down two games and facing elimination, the SPHAS needed a win on its home court. The SPHAS had played brilliantly at the Broadwood all season, and yet in this series, they had lost two home games. The SPHAS faced a confident Jersey team looking to close out the series. Winning one game would seem a difficult task. Winning three in a row to capture the series would be next to impossible.

The 1936–1937 Philadelphia SPHAS came back from a deficit of three games to one, defeating the Jersey Reds to win their third championship in four years. (*Courtesy of Philadelphia Jewish Archives Center in Urban Archives of Temple University Libraries, Philadelphia.*)

The scorecard of Game 5 reads more like an injury report than a roster of a healthy basketball team. Moe Spahn and Moe Frankel "walk onto the floor barely before the game began, Spahn's nose covered with bruises and minor cuts and Frankel with tape over his right eye, and wondering how they had escaped with their lives when the car in which they were being driven to the game figured in a bad accident near Hazelton, Pa., and turned completely over."[25] Dazed and shaken, Spahn and Frankel played tentatively to start the game as the SPHAS, with their season on the line, got off to a quick start. Leading 4–0, the action shifted underneath the basket where a great collision occurred. When the dust cleared, Gil Fitch was laying on the ground in pain. "A doctor, called out of the crowd, examined him, declared there was indications of a break near the knee-cap and ordered him rushed to a hospital for X-rays."[26]

With Fitch out, Gottlieb brought in Kaselman, and the move paid immediate dividends. Kaselman's scoring opened a 17–5 edge, "a fat lead that later in the game saved them from being routed and eventually enabled them to win by a point."[27] The tide slowly turned, and Jersey made their move in the second period. Spahn found his legs, and Jersey outscored the SPHAS 12–8 in the second frame. The intensity was so high that "there were half a dozen occasions when the going became so intense on the floor that the referees had to pry players apart."[28] At one point, Shikey Gotthoffer hit Paul Adamo under the chin with an elbow. Willie Scrill suffered a bloody nose, and play was suspended until they stopped the bleeding. Later, Scrill and the referee nearly came to blows. At the end of the second period, ABL President John J. O'Brien informed the referee that both Scrill and Kaselman were to be fined $10 for using abusive language. The start of the third period was held up by ten minutes as Kaselman, Scrill, and the referee heatedly discussed their differences of opinion.

The third period began, and the SPHAS held a 25–17 margin. Jersey, injured and exhausted, refused to give up and slowly chipped away at the lead. Down by 2, Jersey turned to its best player, Spahn, "who jiggled right through the Philadelphia defense and blotted one in to tie the count at 33–33."[29] By now, the game had reached an unbearable point. The fans, loud and boisterous, kept pushing their way onto the court and had to be pushed back by the police officers. It was hot, and the fans were on top of the court. The game was tied, and the SPHAS' season was on the line. Jersey gained possession with a chance to take their first lead. They worked the ball around and Scrill found Andersen open in the corner, but "Hook, although heading for the basket, didn't have his eyes on the leather and the ball sailed out of bounds."[30]

The SPHAS had the ball, and they found Kaselman, who led the SPHAS in scoring with 10 points. Kaselman took the ball and drove past Andersen, who fouled him. He went to the line and made the foul shot for a 1-point lead. Jersey still had a chance. As Jersey worked the ball around, Andersen fell out of bounds, and in his attempt to get back on the floor, "one of the spectators punched him. Andersen punched back. The fans roared onto the floor and it looked as though a real riot was going to ensue."[31] It took ten minutes for the police to restore order. The Reds had one more shot and missed. The SPHAS escaped with a 34–33 series-saving win. Lost in the commotion was Rosan's best game of the series with 9 points. It appeared that Rosan was returning to form at a pivotal moment in the series.

The SPHAS headed to New Jersey still down a game, having survived by the narrowest of margins. If the SPHAS wanted to force a deciding seventh game, they would need to win another tough game. The injury to Al Benson had proven costly to Jersey. When healthy, Benson was a difficult assignment for Goldman, often winning the center jump and controlling the boards. Benson's injury forced Muggsy Miller to use Spahn at center. This was the case in Game 6, and it proved to be the difference. At the outset, Goldman controlled the jump, and the SPHAS were off and running. They led 18–9 after the first period and increased their margin to 30–10 after the second intermission. Their smothering defense limited Jersey to one foul shot in the period. The third period was a formality as the SPHAS captured the most lopsided game of the series, 45–23.

A week earlier, a seventh game had looked to be a long shot for the SPHAS. But after clawing and fighting, the SPHAS were back in the series. Momentum was with them. Jersey was reeling, and the seventh game was moved to the Philadelphia Arena, where more than 5,000 fans could watch the culmination of an outstanding championship series.

The key for Jersey continued to be the injury to starting center Al Benson. Benson played sparingly in the previous game, and Muggsy Miller decided to take a chance and start him in Game 7. A day before the final game, Miller explained his decision in an interview with the Jersey media. "We can't get away from it. Ever since Al was hurt, we've been trying this and that move in order to overcome the handicap of having our center on the sidelines. It's true we did win a couple of games without Al, but you can't keep doing that forever against any good club. You saw what happened in the first period the other night when they managed to work a few of their plays while we had to wait until they lost the ball before we could start any offense on our own."[32] Benson would play valiantly in the seventh game, but would score only 3 points.

Game 7 would not be a blowout win by either team. The sixth game was an aberration, while the final game from the outset resembled the rest of the series. True to form, the game started off close, and after the first session the SPHAS held a slim 14–13 lead. The SPHAS led 30–26 entering the final period. The Reds battled back and the score was tied at 33, 35, and 36. The SPHAS broke a 36-all deadlock and needed one defensive stop to win the championship. Jersey had battled all series, and they were not about to stop now. They worked the ball across half-court and found Mike Michelotti, who "caressed the cords from mid-floor" to send the game into overtime.[33]

In the overtime period, Inky Lautman dribbled the length of the floor for a basket to put the SPHAS in the lead for good. Kaselman then found Rosan alone under the basket for an easy 2 points. Rosan scored two foul shots, and the SPHAS held off the Reds for a 44–43 overtime win in the seventh game to win the championship. A tough series came down to a 1-point victory. When the season had begun in November, the SPHAS were the defending champions, seeking to add another trophy to Gottlieb's collection at his office at Fifth and Market. In a tightly fought season against the Jersey Reds, the SPHAS had emerged on top, becoming the first ABL team to win back-to-back championships. Three championships in four seasons established the SPHAS as the ABL's first dynasty.

7

SATURDAY NIGHT SPHAS HABIT

> The big deal back then was to come to a Sphas game, meet a nice girl at the dance, win the suit and get married.
>
> —Dave Zinkoff, quoted in *Today* (*Philadelphia Inquirer*)

Growing up in South Philadelphia in the 1930s, Ed Lerner had a ritual every Saturday night during the winter months. After dinner with his family, Lerner took either the bus or subway to the corner of Broad and Wood Streets. When he arrived—always by himself—he paid his 40 cents and walked up the stairs to the balcony of the Broadwood Hotel. He sat in the same seat. It was in the middle of the balcony in the second row. He preferred that seat so he had an unobstructed view of the court below, where he could watch his SPHAS unfurl their precision passing attack from above.

Lerner always arrived early. He did so to read the *Sphas Sparks*, a part program, part gossip column that Dave Zinkoff, the team's publicity director, wrote, edited, and printed each week. Lerner sat in the balcony alone for two hours before the game, reading the *Sphas Sparks*, watching the team practice, and seeing the crowd arrive. It was his routine, and he performed this ritual each and every week without fail.

"During the Depression, I was about 12 years old and everybody followed the SPHAS," Ed Lerner recalled. "They were the kings of the world. If you could play basketball, your dream was to play for the SPHAS. Your life would be fulfilled. I would watch the games like God came down from heaven."[1]

Lerner was not alone. Helen Liebovitz was a high school student in the mid- to late 1930s. In the evenings, Liebovitz took the trolley car to the

YMHA at Broad and Pine Streets to swim. After swimming, she made her way to the Broadwood Hotel, where she met some of her girlfriends. Together, they sat in the balcony, awaiting a SPHAS game.

Nearly seventy years later Liebovitz remembered:

> After the game, there was dancing. The games usually started around 9:00 P.M. and the dancing would follow the games. We usually danced until 12:00 or 1:00 o'clock.
>
> One of the players, Gil Fitch, had a band, and he would play after the games. The singer Kitty Kallen got her start with the band. She was a very pretty girl. The dancing was sometimes straight and sometimes a little crazy with some twirling around.
>
> One night I arrived at the Broadwood Hotel, and my girlfriends and I found our seats in the balcony. Behind us was a group of single fellows who were there to watch the game. One of the fellows, Albert, started talking to me, and we talked for a while. There was an empty seat next to me and he asked if he could sit there. I said, "Sure." After the game, we went dancing. When we finished dancing, Albert and I went for a sandwich at Linton's. He asked me if he could call me again. We started dating. He was six and a half years older, and he was ready to settle down. I was still dating other fellows then. We were married in 1939. We were married for sixty-three years, until my husband passed away three years ago. That is how I met my husband at a SPHAS game. As you can see, basketball will always be my favorite sport.[2]

Sam (Leaden) Bernstein was a scrappy kid growing up in South Philadelphia. As a child, he loved playing sports, all sports, including basketball. Later in life, he became a great sandlot baseball player in Philadelphia, but as a youngster, he was drawn to the SPHAS. Growing up, his older brothers took him to games at the Palais Royal, and he watched Harry Litwack, Chickie Passon, and other stars of the late 1920s. He loved the SPHAS, read about them in the newspapers, talked about them with his friends, and by the mid-1930s was old enough to attend the games alone.

> It was around 50 cents to see a game. You went to see a game and after the game, one of the players, Gil Fitch, was the orchestra leader and he ran the dance afterwards. Kitty Kallen sang at the dances. It was the most beautiful place to attend. People later in life swear that was where they met their spouses and married. I did not go to the

> dances. I was a ballplayer kid. I used to watch the games and go home. It was always crowded, and the price was right. It was mostly young Jewish people who attended the games.[3]

Lerner, Liebovitz, and Bernstein are three of the thousands of Philadelphia Jews whose identities were shaped by attending games at the Broadwood Hotel. It was a time to watch basketball, meet friends, read the *Sphas Sparks*, dance, or find your future spouse. Saturday night was SPHAS night at the Broadwood.

The 1936–1937 season marked Gil Fitch's fifth full season with the SPHAS. Born in Philadelphia, Fitch was drawn to basketball like all the other children with whom he grew up. Playing on the streets after school, Fitch developed into a good player. After graduating from Central High School, Fitch enrolled at Temple University and over three years led the Owls to records of 18–3, 17–4, and 13–7. He graduated in 1932 and became one of many Temple graduates to continue his basketball career by playing for the hometown SPHAS. He joined the team in 1932–1933, the last year the team played in the Eastern States Basketball League. He appeared in twenty-three games that season as the SPHAS lost to the Trenton Moose in the championship round.

Over the next several seasons, Fitch became a key member of the team. A solid contributor off the bench, Fitch scored little but was known for his defensive abilities and overall teamwork. He never averaged more than 4 points per game in any season, but Gottlieb valued him for his basketball intelligence and team play. His best year was 1936–1937, when he averaged 4.6 points per game during the team's seven-game championship series against the Jersey Reds. In his six years with the team, he was part of three championship teams and played

Gil Fitch was a solid team contributor off the bench, but his first love was music. His orchestra entertained the dancers after the games on Saturday night. Eventually, Fitch retired from basketball to pursue a full-time career in music. (*Courtesy of Naismith Memorial Basketball Hall of Fame.*)

in more than 200 games. Fitch loved music even more than basketball, and this love became integral to the SPHAS and their success. He eventually left the SPHAS after the 1937–1938 season to pursue a full-time career in music. As he recalled:

> I always loved music and began playing the alto saxophone at age 11. When I turned 14, I quit school and toured with the Major Revue, a wonderful group of talented child performers. After 8 months, I decided to go back to Central High School. But my music never left me. After graduating from Central High, I went to Temple University on an athletic scholarship in 1928. By 1932, my senior year, I was captain of the basketball, baseball, and soccer teams. In September of that year, Eddie Gottlieb asked me if I would play for the SPHAS.
>
> Four years after I joined the SPHAS, in 1936, I told Gotty I was going to form a band. He liked the idea and suggested that we play after each Saturday night at the Broadwood Hotel. It boosted ticket sales and packed the house. It was a great social evening. At the same time, I needed a songstress. I heard Kitty Kallen on the Kiddy Hour WCAU. What a voice she had. So at age 15 she came to sing with us. Her mother wouldn't allow her to come to the Broadwood by herself. So I always picked her up and took her home. The band became very popular and we began to play at the Bellevue Stratford and other major hotels in the Philadelphia area. By 1939, I had so many bookings, I decided to devote full time to the band and my music.[4]

As a businessman and promoter, Eddie Gottlieb was always on the lookout for new ideas to help promote his team and build solid fan support. Offering dances after the games seemed like a reasonably good way to attract a younger audience, and in signing Fitch, he had a basketball player as well as a band leader to help with the dances and the gate at the games. Beginning in 1936, Fitch's orchestra started playing after the games. At the time, there was dancing between periods, but mostly the dances were held after the games. Sports were not big market draws in those days, so creating any type of additional incentive was an idea always explored, particularly by Gottlieb. Since the SPHAS played their home games in the Broadwood Hotel on a ballroom floor, it was not a stretch that dancing could be held afterward.

Built in 1923, the Broadwood Hotel stood on the corner of Broad and Wood Streets, several blocks from City Hall in downtown Philadel-

The Broadwood Hotel, at Broad and Wood Streets, served as the home court for the Philadelphia SPHAS during the 1930s. The Saturday night games, which were followed by dances, often brought in 3,000 fans. (*From the Karl Lutz Collection, courtesy of the Athenaeum of Philadelphia.*)

phia. Philadelphia Lodge No. 2 of the Benevolent and Protective Order of Elks built the building at a cost of $4 million. The building served as a hotel and as the official offices for the Elks and was known as the Elks Hotel. In constructing the new edifice, the Elks convinced the city that it should expand the hotel business north of Vine Street. In 1930, at the outset of the Great Depression, the Elks foreclosed on the building as a result of dwindling attendance and business. Over the next few years, several companies claimed ownership of the building, and at different times, the hotel was known as the Broadwood Hotel and the Hotel Philadelphia.

In 1947, after the war, the Basketball Association of America (BAA), a forerunner to the present-day NBA, began, and the SPHAS were no longer a major draw. Eddie Gottlieb, who owned the Philadelphia Warriors of the BAA as well as the SPHAS, moved both teams to the Philadelphia Arena, which seated 11,000. Rather than see the hotel fall into disrepair, Joseph Richman, a retired lawyer, and his son Willard, a builder and stock broker, bought the building for slightly more than $800 and spent $1.2 million to renovate it as a health club. Eventually, the Philadelphia Athletic Club became the sole owners. The building closed in 1961. In August 1991, Hahnemann University purchased the building for $2.35 million and turned it into a parking garage, which is what it is today.

In 1933–1934, as the SPHAS joined the reconstituted ABL, Gottlieb began searching for a new home for the team. For a number of years, the Palais Royal at Broad and Bainbridge had served as the team's primary home in Philadelphia. As the team grew in popularity, the Palais Royal's crammed quarters were too small to accommodate the growing number of people clamoring to watch the SPHAS play. Many fans had to be turned away, and this no doubt greatly upset Gottlieb, who was always looking to make a profit. The team was getting better, and it needed a better home venue to show off its talent. In searching for a new home, Gottlieb found the Broadwood Hotel. For $50 a night, the hotel became the SPHAS' new home court until the end of World War II.

The ballroom was on the third floor. Visitors made their way up the stairs and entered through two large doors. Ushers took visitors' tickets, helped them to their seats, and passed out copies of the *Sphas Sparks*. A floor, about 65 feet by 35 feet, greeted the visitors, and two portable basketball hoops were set up on either side. At the far end of the floor was a stage; at times, an overflow crowd sat there and watched the games. Afterward, Fitch's orchestra assembled on the stage, and the dancing commenced on the floor. During the games, chairs were set up on either end of the long side of the ballroom for visitors. "It was usually a full crowd with chairs around the court. The chairs were on risers. You could see everything or as much as you wanted," Venlo Wolfson, who often attended games as a student at the University of Pennsylvania during World War II, said.[5] Upstairs was a balcony with upholstered chairs. The balcony hung slightly over the ballroom floor, creating an intimate setting with the fans and the players. The ballroom floor, balcony with upholstered seats, ushers, and guests wearing suits and dresses all created a beautiful environment to watch a game.

The magnificence of the Broadwood Hotel and the dancing was not lost on the players, many of whom stayed at the hotel and sometimes participated in the dancing afterward. Jerry Fleishman, a player with the SPHAS during World War II, remembered it well in a 2007 interview:

> The Broadwood Hotel where the SPHAS played was a family hotel. The ballroom could hold 3,000 people. It was a fine hotel for residents who lived there. It was on Broad and Wood Streets. It did not have a big lobby. The ceilings were high for a dancing room. The baskets were removable and we would put them away after games. There would be a dance at halftime and after games. At halftime, we asked them not to put wax on the floors. We did not want to skid on it. Three thousand people came to the games and it was always the same 99 percent who came. Saturday night was the place to meet people. The stage was good for shows. Many groupies went to the dances.[6]

The slippery floor was remembered by many players, including Dutch Garfinkel, a teammate of Fleishman's during World War II, who sometimes traveled with him to the games from New York City. "Most of the players at that time were in the service. I was stationed at West Point and would come down every weekend by train. But the games were still sellouts. One thing I remember about the Broadwood. They kept the floor waxed and slippery because of the dancing afterwards."[7]

During the 1940s, Gottlieb expanded the team's makeup. Half the players were from Philadelphia, and the other half hailed from New York, so the two dominant cities in the development and promotion of basketball were well-represented. Along with Fleishman and Garfinkel, Ossie Schectman was another star New York City college player who played for Gottlieb during the war.

> There were four or five of us from New York who were on the team, and on Saturday night we would leave New York Penn Station on a 6:00 P.M. train, and it would take two hours. We arrived at Market Street in Philadelphia and would walk over to the Broadwood Hotel. It was a four or five block walk. The ballroom was on the second or third floor. The ballroom was where we played the game, which could seat about 2,000 or 3,000 people. We dressed downstairs in the health club and would take a small elevator in the back to the game. Eddie would come down and see if all the guys had come in. He had a habit of walking up to us and straightening out our jerseys. Today I can still see Eddie Gottlieb, between periods, yelling at us, "Give me a period." We would play the ballgame, and at halftime the stage would be set up for music and dancing. Behind the stage, there was a dressing room, and he would talk to us there during the half.[8]

Bernie Fliegel, a contemporary of Schectman's, has his own recollections of the SPHAS home court: "The Broadwood Hotel was a nice hotel. There was a game and a dance. They had nice showers. It was a good clean place. The games were incidental. The dances were the top thing. It was always crowded with 2,000 to 3,000 people, mostly young and Jewish.[9]

One of those young, Jewish fans was Marvin Black, whose father, Hughie, was a founding member of the SPHAS in 1918. Marvin had worked as an usher during his high school years.

> The Broadwood Hotel was the center of social activity for any Jewish single. They had the ballgame and Gil Fitch, one of the players, would get dressed right away. He was the orchestra leader. There was a stage. The court became a dance floor. Gil would lead the

> orchestra and all these people would stay and dance. It was just music and dancing, but I do recall seeing a woman singing, and I think it was Kitty Kallen. Many people met and married because of the SPHAS. The Broadwood had a main floor and a balcony. I would have to guess a couple thousand people came to the games and dances. As an usher, I would sit people and watch the game. I was just interested in watching the game. It was around 65 cents to go to a game in those days.[10]

Every Saturday night, nearly 3,000 spectators arrived either by foot or public transportation to watch the SPHAS play. A SPHAS game at the Broadwood represented an important social event in the Philadelphia Jewish community. Second-generation Jews looked to assimilate and become American. Attending a SPHAS game and a dance afterward represented one way to achieve this new status. As Stephen M. Kolman noted in his graduate thesis:

> The second generation wanted to Americanize and at SPHAs games they found it possible to do so without entirely abandoning their Jewish heritage. At SPHAs games, Philadelphia's younger Jews were surrounded by people much like themselves, who wanted to Americanize, but who felt more comfortable doing so among people with whom they had a shared experience. The games became much more than athletic contests. They were social engagements for the young Jewish community, where young Jews, men and women, could go to meet and mingle. The atmosphere at SPHAs games created a non-religious, ethnically Jewish social club for assimilating second-generation Jews.[11]

Attending a SPHAS game appealed to many people in different ways. For Helen Liebovitz, it was a chance to spend time with her girlfriends, meet eligible young men, and dance the night away. For Ed Lerner, it provided time to read the *Sphas Sparks*. And for Sam Bernstein, it was a chance to watch the greatest basketball team he had ever seen: "The Broadwood was a beautiful building. It was about six or seven stories high, and on one of the floors was the auditorium. Basketball was played in the auditorium. The atmosphere was perfect, and you could see the game from anywhere. It was paradise. Every Saturday night was unbelievable. After the game, we stopped off somewhere for a milkshake. It was always about the SPHAS. They were our heroes."[12]

Nearly all those in attendance were Jewish, and many of them were knowledgeable fans who closely followed the SPHAS and the opposing teams. "The crowd was generally basketball enthusiasts. They were extremely knowledgeable. There were no novices," Ed Lerner noted.[13] It was not uncommon for some fans to attend games just to see the opposing teams. Before attending Temple University to play basketball and embarking on a professional career that included stints with the SPHAS and later the Philadelphia Warriors, Jerry Rullo was like every other basketball-obsessed fan. He wanted to see the best basketball played. That often meant attending a SPHAS game. Rullo remembered:

> Before I went to Temple, I would walk to the Broadwood and watch the SPHAS. I went to see the SPHAS when they played the Harlem Renaissance and Fort Wayne Zollner Pistons. There would be 4,000 people. The place was packed. I saw the greatest exhibition by a guy named Bobby McDermott. He shot the ball from the foul line set shot. The next time he would move back and shoot. He did this seven different times until he was at the opposite foul line, where he took a shot and missed. The crowd went nuts and gave him a big hand.[14]

Gambling was also a popular pastime during the 1930s that appeared at SPHAS games. Although there is no record that Gottlieb ever gambled or supported the industry, several dozen gamblers showed up for every home game and formed their own group off to the side, where they conducted business. The gamblers, wearing their hats and overcoats, and smoking cigarettes and cigars, took bets on the SPHAS and other games in the ABL. It was a small sideshow repeated at nearly all basketball games, college and professional, during the 1930s. It probably had no effect on the outcome of any SPHAS game nor did it involve any of the players.

Sam (Leaden) Bernstein, a regular at the games during the 1930s, remembers the one time he came upon the gamblers and bookies at a game. "I remember one SPHAS game. The SPHAS are playing and everyone was betting for the SPHAS. I picked the SPHAS, and the other team was winning, and they made a bad call, and the SPHAS won. That was the only time I gambled, and I gave my money back to the guy. I did not think it was fair."[15]

Max Patkin, long before he became the "Clown Prince of Baseball," was a basketball player who enjoyed a brief career with the SPHAS before embarking on his baseball pursuits. In a 1991 interview for the *Philadelphia Inquirer* about the history of the Broadwood Hotel, he remembered

COMPLIMENTARY

Basketball Game & Dance
SOUTH PHILA. HEBREW ASS'N
BROADWOOD HOTEL BALLROOM
Broad and Wood Sts.
—Every Saturday Evening—

Gov't Tax .... .06
State Tax .... .03
Service Charge .06
Total .... .15

Admission to a Philadelphia SPHAS game at the Broadwood Hotel included dancing afterward. Saturday night was SPHAS night at the Broadwood. (*Courtesy of Naismith Memorial Basketball Hall of Fame.*)

his surprise at how public the gambling was. "The funniest thing, and I couldn't believe it as I walked through the doors, were about 50 or 60 people standing in the doorway betting on the games. You'd hear these guys: 'I got the Jewels.' 'I got the Sphas.' I got the Renaissance.' And they'd be openly betting there in the doorway."[16]

Besides the basketball and the gambling, it was the dancing and the social aspect that brought people to the games and made the evenings memorable.

Louis (Red) Klotz, who started playing for the SPHAS Reserves against college teams and teams from the Jewish Basketball League before the main event with the SPHAS, still recalled sixty years later how popular those dances had been:

> The Broadwood Hotel has a beautiful grand ballroom with stage, balcony, and a dance floor large enough for a basketball court. So every Saturday night, Gotty would sell out. About 1,500 people—65 cents for men, 35 cents for women. Gil Fitch, one of our players, had a band. So after each game, he'd rush out, shower, change, climb on the stage, and become band leader for the dance that followed. Singer Kitty Kallen got her start there. It was a wonderful social event and a place where men would meet their girlfriends. People would dress immaculately. Even the young kids wore suits. Women were dressed in their finest to impress. How many met at the SPHAS' games is anyone's guess. Scores of Philadelphians have probably told their grandchildren about how Grandpop and Grandmom met at a basketball game at a Broad Street hotel.[17]

Dancing became quite popular, and after each home game, the floor quickly cleared and the crowd rushed on and started dancing. "Lots of people got married from going to SPHAS games. Every Saturday night, there would be 3,500 people. You could not get a seat if you stood on someone's head," Ed Lerner recalled. "The crowd was 98 percent Jewish and was young to middle age. If you were a girl and had no interest in basketball but were interested in getting married, then you would go to a SPHAS game."[18]

Moments before the end of the game, Fitch ran backstage, changed into his tuxedo, and came out to lead his orchestra. If he had time, he showered. If not, he simply put on his tuxedo and ran back out to the stage. "He made a very pungent orchestra leader," Dave Zinkoff, the team's publicity man, noted years later.[19] The dancing lasted several hours until the crowds made their way to local restaurants for a late-night snack before heading home.

Along with Fitch's orchestra, the emergence of singer Kitty Kallen represented one of the highlights from the many dances. Long before she became a star singer, first for Jimmy Dorsey and Harry James and later on her own, Kitty Kallen was a child prodigy who enjoyed singing and performing. Born on May 25, 1922, she grew up with her family in South Philadelphia. As a youngster, Kallen was outgoing and talented and loved performing and listening to music. She had an affinity for impersonating contemporary singers and eventually won an amateur contest doing these imitations. For her efforts, she was presented with a camera, which she ran home with to show to her family. She was very excited, but her father thought she stole the camera and punished her accordingly. Not until some neighbors dropped in to congratulate Kallen on her prize did her father realize his daughter had won it in a contest.

Undeterred, Kallen continued singing and entering different contests. She was a regular performer on the radio program "The Children's Hour," which showcased the talents of many Philadelphia children. Sponsored by Horn & Hardart, a chain of cafeterias in New York and Philadelphia known for their creamed spinach, "The Children's Hour" was hosted by Stan Lee Broza and aired on WCAU radio, 1170 AM on the dial. A poster from the time period advertised the show as hearing the "Radio Stars of Tomorrow." The show aired every Sunday morning from 10:30 to 11:30 A.M. Kitty Kallen got her start on this show, which became the station's longest-running show. Kallen gained great admiration for her exceptional singing voice and later had her own show on WCAU.

Soon enough, Gil Fitch had tapped her to sing with his band after SPHAS games. At age 15, she was a regular. "Her mother wouldn't allow her to come to the Broadwood by herself," Fitch noted. "So I always picked her up and took her home."[20] After a year with the SPHAS, she became a vocalist with Jan Savitt, a band leader and violinist and member of the Philadelphia Orchestra. During that time, Kallen roomed with Dinah Shore, who was also looking to make a singing career for herself.

Long after Kallen gained national fame with her singing, many Philadelphians remembered her singing at the dances after the games. Reflecting back many years, Dave Zinkoff recalled, "Oh, those were great times. I can still picture this long line of girls waiting to come in for the dance after the game was over. The SPHAs were very popular. They were broadcast on radio, and almost every game was a sell-out."[21]

The responsibility of orchestrating the team's publicity fell to Dave Zinkoff. For more than sixty years in Philadelphia, Zinkoff became a legend with his distinctive voice and outgoing personality. By the time he joined the Philadelphia Warriors and later the Philadelphia 76ers, "the Zink" was a household name, whose voice was heard throughout every arena in the city. Generations of fans remember Zinkoff with his "Gola Goallll!" after Tom Gola, a star player with the Philadelphia Warriors, scored a basket or "Dipper dunkkkkkk!" whenever Wilt Chamberlain, the Big Dipper, scored. With two minutes remaining in a quarter, Zinkoff would yell, "twoooooooooooooo minutes!" His most popular saying came with his introduction of Julius Erving, Dr. J, at every home game: "And at the other forward, from the University of Massachusetts, Number 6: Julius Errrrrvinnnnnnnnnnnng."[22] His trademark sayings made him a household name and endeared him to thousands of fans. "Dave Zinkoff had a beautiful voice, and he had a gimmick," Sam (Leaden) Bernstein remembered. "He became one of the greatest announcers. He had a lot of personality and he was good."[23]

Zinkoff was born in Russia in 1910. He moved with his parents when he was a year old as they fled persecution and pogroms in Czarist Russia. His family settled in West Philadelphia, where his father operated a grocery store and delicatessen for forty years at 5211 West Girard Avenue. Zinkoff lived there with his parents and sister.

After graduating Central High School, Zinkoff enrolled at Temple University and studied commerce, completing the four-year major in three years. Despite finishing his degree early, he was not, by his own account, much interested in his studies. "I was a kibitzer in college. I was the one who always put the tacks on the professor's seats. But I was never. . . . My muscles would never permit me to make any of the teams. That was never meant to be. I had two left feet which I still have. I'm not coordinated. I just could never make it. When I saw all those athletes getting all that applause, and I couldn't become an athlete, I came up with the great idea of being the announcer."[24]

Zinkoff often spent his free time in the athletic department, talking with the students and becoming friendly with the athletes and coaches. Finally, he had his chance to announce a sporting event when he took over for the regular announcer at a boxing match. It was 1934, and the match featured Temple hosting Army at Mitten Hall on campus. Prior to the match, Bob Geasey, Temple's publicity man, said to Zinkoff, "All right, Zink, you raise so much hell around here, let's see what you can do."[25] He performed so well—"he had lots of gall and everyone seemed to like him"[26]—that he became the regular announcer for all of Temple's sporting events after that. He was paid $5 for that game.

"I was too dumb to have any fear," Zinkoff, said, reflecting on his first announcing job decades later. "I was amazed when the crowd was supposed to be quiet, they were quiet. When they were supposed to cheer, they cheered. I remember Temple's athletic director told me, 'You have a voice that's God-given. If you know how to direct it, you'll do very well for yourself.'"[27]

Soon enough, the Zink was on his way and eventually landed with the SPHAS.

Despite his early success with announcing and the love he had for it, Zinkoff still needed to convince his parents that this was the right profession for him. Many immigrant parents wanted their children to pursue professional careers, and Zinkoff's parents were no different from their neighbors and friends. It was the classic struggle between immigrant parents and their American children, one that Zinkoff recounted many years later.

> My parents were typical hard-working Jews who came from Russia. Dad had a delicatessen in Philadelphia, the finest in the neighborhood, cooked his own corned beef, pickled his own pickles. Being typical Jewish parents and I being their son, my dad wanted me to be a physician, or a dentist, or a lawyer, or at least a CPA so I could do his tax forms for nothing.
>
> Me, I wanted to be a policeman on a mounted horse, for a while. But as this microphone got a tighter hold on me in college, it became more difficult for me to explain to my parents what I was doing.
>
> Neighbors would come in and say to my father, "Did you see the paper, your boy, look at his picture, his announced this, announced that." My Dad would always answer, "What is a screamer? Who needs a screamer in the family? I want my boy to be a professional man."

Being a faithful son and not wanting to upset his parents, Zinkoff explored a professional career, however brief it was.

> I was unhappy because I did want to please my parents. So for a year I went to law school. I got good grades. But the hold was stronger, and I finally had to admit to them that I had to get out and do what I'm doing.

Still, Zinkoff wanted to please his parents, or at least have them understand his profession and why he loved it so.

> Dad loved music, the opera, and he was a regular patron at the Academy of Music, where he bought the cheapest seats, which in those days were 75 cents. I'll never forget this particular day. He was so downcast and my mother said, "Jake, what is it?" "Rose," he said sadly, "I waited in line for hours to get a ticket for *Aida* and they were sold out. There are none."
>
> So, I put my thinking cap on. I didn't say anything, but the next morning, I ran down to see the ticket man at the Academy. "Zink," he said, "what are you doing here? This is music, there is no basketball here."
>
> I said, "Harry, my dad wanted to see *Aida*." He looks up at the chart and tells me they were sold out, but if however it was my dad, fine. He got out a piece of paper and wrote some hieroglyphic on it and told me to have my dad give the paper to an usher and my dad could hear *Aida*.
>
> I went back home and had dinner and said, "Pop, you are going to see *Aida*." I offered my dad the piece of paper. He cuffed me, one of the few times he ever did that. He said, "You are making a fool of your daddy and I don't like that." It took me and my mother three hours to convince my dad to go. We waited that night for Dad to return. He didn't walk into the room; he floated.
>
> My mother says, "Well, Jake?"
>
> My dad answered, "Rosela, you won't believe what happened."
>
> "What happened?" my mother asked.
>
> "I was afraid," Dad said. "I handed the paper to the usher. 'Come with me,' the usher said, and he led me right down the center aisle. We kept walking and walking and walking, right up to the front, where they have the brass rail. There was a wooden chair, all these people with tuxedos, women in furs, and he seats me in front, violins

were right in my nose. *Aida* was wonderful. I was afraid to get out of my seat at intermission. I was afraid somebody would take my chair. So I stayed there from the first note to the last."

My father had never had a seat on the main floor. What they did, they took a folding chair; we do the same thing at a basketball game. There's always room for another chair. What did my father say to me? "Son, I don't know how you did this, but you did it. Maybe this announcing business you're in is not such a bad thing."[28]

The announcing business was not so bad, and it eventually landed him a job announcing for Eddie Gottlieb's SPHAS, a job that became the springboard for the rest of his career, both professionally and personally. Zinkoff heard that the SPHAS were looking for a public address announcer. Naturally, he was recommended for the job. "I was a student at Temple and was announcing games there. Gotty needed an announcer and someone told him about me. I remember going down to Passon's Sporting Goods Store at Fifth and Market where Eddie had his office."

Zinkoff walked into Gottlieb's office and introduced himself. "So he says, 'Stand over there and say 40 words.' Then he says, 'Face the wall and say 40 words.' By this time, I figure he's meshuga. But I got the job. At first, he wouldn't let me ad lib, but then he got used to my little jobs. Anyways, I used to give out a little program called the *Sphas Sparks*. It had news about the team and who had a baby and who was getting married. And there was always a lucky number in one of the programs, and the winner got a $19.95 suit from Sam Gerson's store at Sixth and Bainbridge."[29]

After a while, Zink, who had been announcing SPHAS games, told Eddie he wanted a raise. Simcha Gersch, a distant cousin of Gottlieb's and former president of the Jewish Basketball League, recounted this story:

> He's making five dollars a week and he wants six. Why? Because he's doing a good job and people are coming to see him. So Eddie says, "Let's see." So he fires Zink, gets a new announcer, and gives Zink a job handing out programs. After two weeks, Zink can't stand it anymore so he asks for his old job back. So Eddie looked around at the full house and says, "It doesn't look like we lost any customers." But Zink gets his job back and a week later six dollars shows up in his pay envelope.[30]

Soon after joining the SPHAS, Zinkoff developed a close relationship with Gottlieb that lasted until Eddie passed away in 1979. For years, Zink was as instrumental to the success and popularity of the SPHAS as Eddie Gottlieb. Together, the Zink and Gotty were inseparable. They knew everyone, worked the crowd, schmoozed with the media, and developed close relationships with all the players.

"Dave Zinkoff was a good friend of Gottlieb. They were nice to Bernie Opper and me," Dutch Garfinkel recalled in a 2007 interview. "They always took us to the Jewish community. They would sit with us at the deli and have franks, corn beef, and knishes. They took care of us and treated us to late dinners. Eddie always wanted to win."[31]

Bernie Fliegel recalled:

> Dave Zinkoff was like a ball boy for the SPHAS. He loved Eddie Gottlieb and always carried his bags. One night we were getting ready to go to Chicago, and Eddie told a few of us to go to Dave Zinkoff's father's deli and grab a bite and have some sandwiches before we travel. So, we get to the deli and go behind the counter and we ate everything. We must have eaten $2,000 worth of food. When Eddie gets there and it's time to leave, he says, "Will $10 cover it?" I know myself that I ate about $50 worth of food that night. But Zink was a good guy, and he always remembered us.[32]

Working with Gottlieb, Zinkoff soon assumed control of the game-day operations, including publishing the *Sphas Sparks*, serving as the public address announcer, and organizing the halftime entertainment. "Besides the dances, we used to give out a program during the game that I was more or less responsible for, that not only gave the fans vital statistics on the players but also included engagement, marriage, and birth announcements of fans who were regularly in attendance. It was our own little social register," Zinkoff said.[33]

The *Sphas Sparks* was only four pages in length, but in those four pages, Zinkoff gave everyone a lifetime of information. It included information about upcoming games; birth, death, and marriage announcements; biographical information on the players; and advertisements for Jewish-owned businesses. Short and informative, it provided the fans with part gossip column and part basketball program. According to Stephen M. Kolman, "The gossip column contributed greatly to the sense of community that existed around the SPHAs and was one of the consistent draws of SPHAs games."[34] As Peter Levine writes, "Above all, [Zinkoff] remembers [SPHAS games] as a rich community experience that bound people together in common

Sphas Sparks

Edited by DAVID ZIN

VOLUME 3 — NUMBER 20 | SATURDAY, MARCH 8, 1941 | Philadelph

SPHAS Resume League Rivalry Against Brookl
Celtics In Crucial Second Half Contest At
Broadwood Hotel Court Next Saturday

SPHAS - WORLD'S CHAMPIONS

VISITORS STARS I
ACTION TONITE

GLOBE TROTTE

SUNNY BOSWELL
LOU PRESSLEY
TED STRONG
BERNIE PRICE

N. Y. JEWELS

WILLIE RUBENSTEI
MAC KINSBRUNNE
HAGEN ANDERSO

CELTICS

CHICK REISER
BERNIE FLIEGEL
MICKEY KUPPERBER

NEXT GAME
SATURDAY, MARCH 15
BROOKLYN CELTICS

TICKETS
509 MARKET STREET

Shown here is the cover of the March 8, 1941, *Sphas Sparks*, the team's program and newsletter. (*From the ABL Collection, courtesy of Naismith Memorial Basketball Hall of Fame.*)

affection for a Jewish basketball team. Even the game program he put out, 'The SPHAs Sparks,' reflected it."[35]

The October 19, 1940, edition of the *Sphas Sparks* is, in many ways, typical of all of the programs published. The headline on the front page announced in big, bold capital letters:

> GREETINGS TO THE NEW SEASON WITH THE N.Y. JEWELS TO-NITE, AND THE SPHAS TOUGHEST OPPONENT, RENAISSANCE, NEXT SATURDAY.

The cover shows a photo of the 1939–1940 ABL championship team in a V-formation. Gottlieb kneels in front, and behind him are the players: Moe Goldman, Cy Boardman, Red Rosan, Leo Gottlieb, Petey Rosenberg, Red Wolfe, Cy Kaselman, Shikey Gotthoffer, and Inky Lautman. To the right of the photo is a brief description of the SPHAS' next two opponents.

> Tonight our opponents are the highly vaunted New York Jewels, who sparkle brightest when pitted against the SPHAS. The rivalry between both clubs is intense, and a thrilling game is always in store when they meet.
>
> Next Saturday night the SPHAS clash with the brilliant Negro stars—RENAISSANCE! Without a doubt, they are the outstanding Colored team in the world and the tussles on the Broadwood Floor have always been fast and furious, leaving nothing to be desired!
>
> Last season's standing between the clubs was SPHAS: 7 victories; Rennies, 6![36]

The bottom of the front page provides information on how to purchase a ticket.

The program's second page contains basketball information and some advertisements. In 1940–1941, the SPHAS welcomed Irv Torgoff to the team. Along with a photograph of him, the program contains a brief write-up about his background, including, "Welcome Irv Torgoff! Newest addition to the local line-up! Irv was the outstanding star of the National Championship Long Island University team and was selected on every All-American five during the season of 1938–1939. Last season he played with the Detroit team of the National League and was the leading scorer in their drive for championship honors. As a matter of record he was selected on the All-Star National League team and will no doubt prove a valuable cog in the SPHAS wheel."[37]

Other newsworthy tidbits include the following:

> The new V formation shot of the SPHAS is the artful brain-child of Marty Harris, who always does a nice piece of picture-snapping.[38]

The advertisements focused on Jewish-related businesses. Jackie Gordon advertised shirts. Former SPHA player David Ingber had an advertisement for his Ingber Bag Company, which stated, "Tonight and every Saturday Night a Lucky Number Holder will receive an Ingber Ladies Bag! Bags for Fastidious Women!" Other announcements stated, "Those interested in advertising in the *SPARKS* should contact Dave Zinkoff." "Pay Your Jewish League Alumni Dues To Dave Dabrow Now!"

Turning to the third page, there is a large advertisement for Sam Gerson, a men's clothier whose store was located at the corner of Sixth and Bainbridge. "If your number corresponds to the one called by the announcer between the first and second periods please make yourself known and obtain your Manchester Suit or Overcoat." The bottom half of the page contains the scorecard for those who want to keep their own score. On the left is the roster for the SPHAS, and on the right is the New York Jewels. The prize drawing number is included as well.[39]

The final page, with the headline "All for Fun and Fun for All!" is the gossip page and the one that many of the spectators looked at first in order to catch up on any community information they might have missed. The column begins "Good Evening Ladies and Gentleman! And all the young ones, too! . . . The Zinky Kid greets you once again and gives you a hasty resume of the summer that has just flown by."

Zinkoff quickly brought everyone up to speed on what had happened since the end of the last season.

> South Mountain Manor was fruitful in increasing the circle of ever-widening acquaintances.
>
> Sol Kodner met Dolly for the first time at the Manor during the season of '39. This summer he brought Dolly up for the Honeymoon to the premises.
>
> A little baby girl is changing the lives of Irv and Jesse Buck.
>
> Make with the unfinished business of the 1939–1940 season and it consists of the following bits: Harry Steinman has a peculiar affinity for One Penny . . . Lanse McCurley eats Charms—cellophane and All! . . . Jane Yeo is to be put into the CUTIEPIE Category! . . . Sara and Bob Goffman became a unit on April 6 (as this column predicted).[40]

Besides the gossip column, one of the more popular features of the program was the lucky number drawn every game. As Zinkoff remembered, "In addition, each program had a lucky number in it. If your number was drawn, you won a suit. The big deal back then was to come to a Sphas game, meet a nice girl at the dance, win the suit and get married."[41]

Picking the lucky number was a rite of passage for Diane Radel Moskowitz, Abe Radel's daughter. In 1938, 6-year-old Diane Radel often accompanied her mother by trolley car to the SPHAS games. "The only thing that I ever saw at the Broadwood Hotel was the ballroom and the pool. My mother would take me swimming before the games," Moskowitz remembered. After swimming, "we would go up in the elevator to the ballroom. Most of the spectators would take the stairs to the ballroom. They would take tickets at the top of the set of stairs. The ballroom was usually full and I guess the seats were bleacher type seats. The floor was very shiny, which was not good for basketball."[42]

As the gun sounded to end play between periods, Diane swung into action. She jumped off the seat next to her mother and ran onto the court to meet her father, the team's business manager. Diane was a regular for the show between periods. Her job, which she guarded with all her might, was to pull the lucky number out of a box:

> Everybody received a program when they entered. There were numbers on each of the ticket stubs. Numbers went into the box and the box was big enough to hold me. I did that once a game at halftime.

> I remember one night I was not the girl in the box. Red Wolfe, one of the players, had a daughter, Nessa, and they let her be the girl who pulled the numbers out. I sure was mad. My feelings were hurt, and my mother calmed me down.
>
> I was born in 1932, and the SPHAS were a part of my life as soon as I was old enough to remember. I was about 4 or 5 years old when I started going to SPHAS games. We lived in West Philadelphia. I remember going to the games on Saturday night and pulling the lucky number out of the big box. I remember watching the games and staying afterwards to watch the dancers.[43]

Staying after the game was also a chance for Diane to see her father, who went directly from work to the Broadwood Hotel to meet Gottlieb and Zinkoff and set up for the games. "My father worked as a bookkeeper for a stockbroker during the day, and he moonlighted in the evenings with the SPHAS. I think it was for the pleasure of being in sports as much as it was to make some extra money. You have to remember that this was during the Depression."[44]

Working hard to earn extra money was a trait Abe learned early as a child. Born in the late 1890s in Ukraine, Radel immigrated with his family as a young child to Philadelphia. The family, which included Abe, his parents, and four siblings, lived on South Mildred Street. When he was young, his mother died, leaving his father with five young children in their new country. "He quit school after the eighth grade to help support the family," Moskowitz recalled years later. "He attended night school and became a bookkeeper."[45] Sports, though, were not far from his mind. With all the baseball fields in the city, Radel was

Abe Radel, who served as the business manager for the SPHAS, was a close friend of Eddie Gottlieb's for many years. In the 1920s, Radel did a write-up about the SPHAS for the *Reach Official Basket Ball Guide*. (*Courtesy of Diane Moskowitz.*)

not at a loss to find a team. He played for an industrial team in 1918. Somehow Radel and Gottlieb connected, and the two were together well into the 1950s, with Radel serving as the business manager for many of Gottlieb's enterprises.

> He was the business manager for the SPHAS. He was in charge of counting up the money and keeping the books. He also fired the starter guns, the blank pistols, before each home game. He was involved with the team for as long as I can remember and probably until they stopped playing.
>
> My father traveled with the team on the weekends. They would pack themselves into a car. He had the responsibility of keeping the driver awake, which was usually Eddie Gottlieb. My father was also involved with Gottlieb and the Negro Leagues. The team was the Philadelphia Stars, and Ed Bolden was in charge of the team. He said that the team would stop to eat and Bolden would ask my father if he could bring him out a sandwich from the restaurant. My mother wondered why and Bolden said, "I am not allowed in there." The black players were not allowed to stay in the hotels. I remember my father talking about that."[46]

Saturday nights at the Broadwood Hotel were a magical time for Philadelphia's Jewish community. The game was often incidental, as the dancing and social aspect allowed young Jewish singles an opportunity to become American. No matter one's reason for attending—dancing, watching the game, serving as an usher, reading the *Sphas Sparks*, or pulling the lucky number—the SPHAS provided entertainment for everyone.

8

THE DARLINGS OF PHILADELPHIA

We were well loved. Even William Penn's statue on the top of City Hall used to bow to us. Every time the SPHAS came by, he'd bow to us.

—Shikey Gotthoffer,
interview by Robert Peterson

On November 28, 1939, with the Thanksgiving holiday past and the 1939–1940 basketball season just underway, newspapers and radios across the country reported that James Naismith, the game's founder, had died of a cerebral hemorrhage. He was 78 years old. The *New York Times*, in its obituary, noted that more than 20 million people were now playing the game worldwide. "The fast, sprightly, colorful basketball of today, enjoyed in many lands by the young of both sexes in college, school, club, association, and society gymnasiums and on professional courts, bears at least the same resemblance to the early game as that of a modern airliner to the Wright brothers' first 'flying machine.' The father of basketball had the distinction of originating the only major sport created in the United States."[1]

As games were played over the next several days, moments of silence were observed. Cities all across the country remembered Naismith. One such city was Troy in upstate New York, which had been one of the early hotbeds of basketball activity and had become a center for great teams and players. From 1905 through the 1915–1916 season, the Troy Trojans annually ranked as one of basketball's top teams. First in the Hudson River League and later in the New York State League, Troy was a dominant team, winning numerous league titles. Ed Watcher, one of the best players during the pioneer years and Troy's leader, was later inducted into the Naismith

Memorial Basketball Hall of Fame. At the time of Naismith's death, Troy fielded a team in the ABL, the Troy Haymakers, coached by one of the early game's best players, Max (Marty) Friedman.

The SPHAS' first league game after Naismith's death was on December 9 at home to the Troy Haymakers. The SPHAS had opened the season strong at 5–3, including wins over Wilkes-Barre, Kingston, Jersey, and Washington. Gottlieb's big acquisition prior to the season's start was Phil Rabin, an outstanding offensive player and one of the league's best young talents.

Born Phil Rabinowitz in 1913 in Paterson, New Jersey, Rabin—short, quick, and tough—was the epitome of a Jewish basketball player during the 1920s and 1930s. From the time he was old enough to run around with his brothers, Rabin could always be found with a basketball nearby.

> Growing up, we were very poor. There was no money in those days. Ninety percent of the people then were poor. We hung a peach basket in the backyard. My brothers and I would get wooden planks and put them on the ground so we could dribble the basketball. When I was 10 or 11, there was a playground nearby, and it had a basket. I went there to play basketball. I was short but very tough.[2]

Whenever time permitted, Rabin could be found playing basketball, perfecting his shooting, and holding his own on the playground. During his high school years, Paterson fielded a team in the first ABL. From 1928–1929 until 1930–1931, when the league folded, the Whirlwinds and later the Crescents played, usually finishing at the bottom of the standings. "There was a professional team called the Paterson Crescents. I would carry the bags for a few of the players. Later in life, I played for them," Rabin recalled decades later.[3]

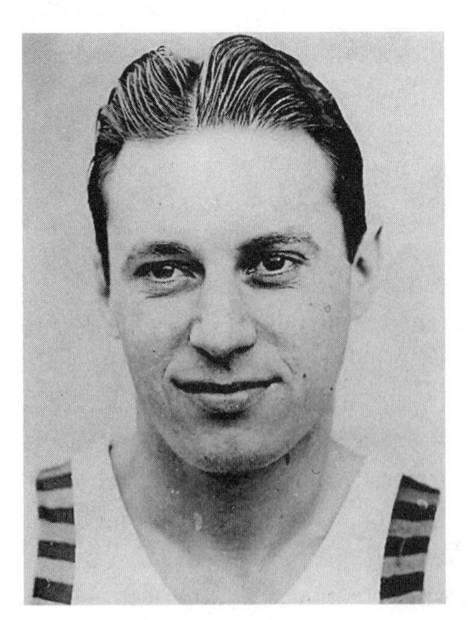

Phil Rabin, who grew up in Paterson, New Jersey, played briefly for the Philadelphia SPHAS. An exceptional scorer, Rabin led the American Basketball League in scoring on multiple occasions. (*Courtesy of Bill Himmelman.*)

After high school, Rabin enrolled at Long Island University (LIU) to play for legendary coach Clair Bee.

> In 1936, I was playing for Long Island University. We were rated in the top three in the country. We played at Madison Square Garden on Saturdays and there would be 20,000 people who would come. Teams such as CCNY, Fordham, NYU, Manhattan, and LIU would play.
>
> At the time, I was playing professional basketball for the team in Atlantic City in the Eastern League. I was way ahead of my time in playing basketball. Someone told Nat Holman, the coach at CCNY, about me. I got a call from Holman.
>
> "You are playing at Long Island University. What are you doing playing pro ball?" Holman demanded.
>
> Shortly thereafter, Coach Bee confronted his star player. "Phil, we are playing Stanford this weekend, but I cannot let you play because you are playing professional basketball."
>
> I told the coach that I needed the money, so I did not play. I did not play and they beat us by 2 points. Stanford had Hank Lusetti.[4]

Rabin's need to play for pay on the side was not unusual for many players of his generation. The only problem was that he was caught.

Having played professionally, Rabin's college career came to an abrupt end. His next logical move was to sign a contract with the ABL. Naturally, he joined his hometown team, Paterson.

After finishing the 1935–1936 season with Paterson, Trenton, and Passaic, Rabin moved to Kingston, New York, for the following year. Playing under future Basketball Hall of Famer Frank Morgenweck, he blossomed into arguably one of the finest players in the league. Over the next three seasons, the first two with Kingston and the last with Jersey, Rabin led the league in scoring each season. Over thirty-seven games in 1936–1937, Rabin averaged 13.2 points per game, although the Colonials finished the second half with a 9–11 record, fifth place in a six-team circuit. The following season, he again averaged 13.2 points, this time over thirty-nine games, but the Colonials did not fare much better. Playing on a Kingston team going nowhere, Rabin yearned for his scoring ability to benefit a playoff-bound club. The next year, he signed with the Jersey Reds, winners of the 1937–1938 championship. His scoring punch aided the Reds considerably, and he again led the league, this time with a 10.3 points per game average, helping the team get back to the championship round only to lose to the New York Jewels.

"When I was playing for the Jersey Reds, we played the SPHAS and beat them for the championship. I wore a jacket with Jersey Reds World Champions on it. Eddie Gottlieb, who was the manager of the SPHAS, saw that I was instrumental in beating the SPHAS, went to the Jersey Reds' owners, and bought me for $100. That is how I went to the SPHAS."[5]

By the time of the Troy game, Rabin had proven to be a good pickup for Gottlieb and was among the team's leading scorers. In the SPHAS' sixth victory of the young season, Rabin tallied 11 points. "Phil Rabin showed improvement in his shooting and landed five long-distance goals," the *Philadelphia Inquirer* noted, as the SPHAS captured a 59–45 victory.[6]

Over the next month, the SPHAS continued to play well and lead the league. The team was playing balanced basketball, as Gotthoffer, Goldman, Rosan, Petey Rosenberg, Rabin, and Lautman all took turns leading the team in scoring. In mid-January, Gottlieb sent Rabin to the Washington Brewers. Despite Rabin's leading the team in scoring in five games, Gottlieb sensed a chemistry problem existing between his new pickup and his core group. No record exists as to why Gottlieb was so quick to jettison one of his better scorers. Seventy years later, Rabin provided his own interpretation, largely based on money, of why his stay in Philadelphia was less than half a season:

> When I was with the SPHAS, we won lots of games. We would be playing and I would be free, and I did not get the ball. So, I asked Shikey Gotthoffer, Red Rosan, Red Wolfe, Inky Lautman, and Cy Kaselman why they would not pass me the ball. They said that I was making $35 a game and they were making only $27.50. Until Gottlieb would pay them an extra $7.50, they were not going to pass me the ball. When I was with the SPHAS, I made $35 a game. I was the highest-paid player in the league. Eddie was tight with money with them. In those days, there was no big money in basketball.[7]

Whatever the reasons might have been, Rabin made an immediate impact with his new teammates. Quickly a two-team race emerged as uncertainty plagued many of the other franchises. The Kingston Colonials and Troy Haymakers merged to form the Troy Celtics, while the Jersey Reds and the New York Jewels combined forces and continued under the New York Jewels name. The Baltimore Clippers, in their first season since transferring as the Brooklyn Visitations, finished 15–16, while the Wilkes-Barre Barons dropped out with a 5–17 mark. Without any serious competition, the SPHAS and Brewers waged a brilliant regular-season battle that came down to the final game.

Four times in the regular season, the SPHAS and Brewers had met, each winning twice. In their first meeting against Washington after trading Rabin, the SPHAS had pulled out a 38–31 win to take a one-game lead over the Brewers. The game had marked the return of Mike Bloom and Phil Rabin, two former SPHAS, to the Broadwood. "Many fans were turned away from the door," the *Philadelphia Inquirer* wrote the following day. "Every available seat was taken and standing room was at a premium. Both players looked good with the visitors, Rabin stunning the crowd in the opening minutes with the first goal of the game."[8] Each scored 9 points to pace the Brewers.

Rabin always had some of his finest games against the SPHAS, both before and after his short stint with the team. In early February in Washington, Rabin tallied five field goals and six foul shots for 16 points to lead the Brewers to a 10-point win over the SPHAS, 43–33. At one point, Washington had led by 24 points. Two weeks later, Washington edged Philadelphia, 31–30, behind Rabin's game-high 12 points. The loss dropped the SPHAS to third place in the standings with a 15–12 record with only five games left in the regular season.

With their season on the line, the SPHAS responded brilliantly, posting a 4–1 record down the stretch. On the last day of the regular season, Philadelphia and Washington stood even with identical 19–13 records. The teams played in a doubleheader at Convention Hall in Philadelphia, where the season's outcome would most likely be settled. In the first game, Washington, behind foul shots by Mike Bloom and Ben Kramer, edged Baltimore, 22–20. Down 16–12 entering the third period, the Brewers outscored the Clippers 10–4 the rest of the way.

Needing a win to force a one-game playoff, the SPHAS came out strong against the New York Jewels, who had since been eliminated from top honors. "Petey Rosenberg was the 'sparkplug' of the SPHAS attack, deflecting passes, cutting with lightning-like speed, and caging four long shots at critical moments early in the battle," wrote the *Philadelphia Inquirer*.[9] The SPHAS won going away, 44–27, to force a one-game playoff with the Brewers the following Saturday.

After a thrilling end to the regular season, few thought that it could be topped. They were mistaken. The one-game playoff was one of the more hard-fought and vicious games played all year. With first place on the line, Washington and Philadelphia fought to the bitter end. As the SPHAS held a 17–13 lead entering the third period, tensions erupted as Mike Bloom and

Moe Goldman "had a regular battle down to the far end of the court. But, quick interference by Referee Max Begovich and other players stopped the encounter before any great amount of damage had been done."[10]

The SPHAS kept their lead as "Moe Goldman, with his side-arm tosses and Red Rosan, on lightning dribbles, each contributed three baskets to further increase the SPHAS' lead." With three minutes remaining, "Shikey Gotthoffer and Ash Resnick, both heavyweights, became involved in a fight and were pummeling each other hard before other players and the referee could interfere. These two combatants were chased from the game."[11] Despite Gotthoffer's ejection, Rosan's 15 points proved enough for the win.

For the first time in league history, a round-robin tournament would decide the championship, and all five teams made the playoffs. Each team had two games against each opponent for a total of eight games.

The rough play from the one-game playoff carried over to the first game versus Troy, where "Cy Boardman was punched so hard by Mickey Kupperberg in the final period that the Sphas' forward staggered and had to cover his face to save himself further punishment. Then he had to retire for repairs, having six stitches put over his eye."[12] The SPHAS edged the Celtics, 32–29. One game was down, and seven more remained. The SPHAS' teamwork and ability to play through various forms of adversity were, in part, a result of the team's having been together for a number of years.

Since 1933–1934, when the ABL resumed after a two-year hiatus, Eddie Gottlieb had carefully assembled a well-balanced team whose core had been together through championships and barnstorming trips. Inky Lautman, Cy Kaselman, Shikey Gotthoffer, Moe Goldman, and Red Wolfe had all played together since that first season. Red Rosan arrived two years later, and Petey Rosenberg was in his second year with the team. The players knew each other, understood their roles, and played exceptionally well together. They played as a unit.

Nobody who saw the SPHAS play would ever forget them. Their style would long be remembered after the games stopped and the fans went home. Through the years, the SPHAS developed a reputation as a team that played as a unit. Basketball in those days was a team concept. Players moved without the ball, worked the ball around until a good shot materialized, and never took a bad shot that would hurt the team.

Nearly fifty years after he stopped playing, Shikey Gotthoffer vividly remembered how he and his teammates played in those days:

> We moved as a team, not as an individual. The man who had the ball would pass it as we moved up the court, not dribble it as they

> do today. Today the man with the ball is in the backcourt and the rest of the ballplayers are down in the area where the basket is. We played on the supposition that if all the men were advancing they had to guard us that way. When we came sweeping down, we came down in full force. They didn't know where the ball was going to go or who was going to handle it. The ball always moved. The ball was off the floor. That was what we advocated. Of course we dribbled, but most of the action the ball was being moved. That brought about opportunities because of the changes that were taking place.[13]

Ed Lerner, a regular at the Broadwood, always sat in the balcony, where he watched the SPHAS unfurl their attack from high above courtside. "When the SPHAS played, it was poetry in motion. The ball never touched the ground. There was the five-man weave, and every player would run around touching the ball. Sometimes they would change direction, and Petey Rosenberg would be under the basket alone. Inky Lautman and Moe Goldman were in the pivot and Cy Kaselman would shoot his set shots."[14]

A key component of their game was passing and the precept that the ball would arrive more quickly to your teammate if you passed it rather than dribbled it. "They played defense and took good shots. If you had to dribble, then you did. If you did not, then you didn't," Dutch Garfinkel recalled. "You looked to pass to the other guy who was in position to shoot. They always wanted to win and had great teamwork."[15]

It would be a stretch to say that a sense of Jewish solidarity was the only explanation for the extraordinary achievements of the SPHAS during 1939–1940. The team did possess the best players and were well-coached. Nonetheless, the events in Europe were clearly on the minds of the Jewish community of Philadelphia, as elsewhere, and indeed helped the sense of brotherhood those men displayed on the basketball court.

Teamwork was what set the SPHAS apart from the other teams in the league. "The style was teamwork, moving, passing, and running, shooting the ball," Ralph Kaplowitz remembered. "It was about making sure you were getting free of your opponents by helping your teammates, by blocking out for them, by blocking out the defense and allowing your teammates to get free as well as yourself to get free of your opponent."[16]

In this bygone era, teams did not feature twelve to fifteen men sitting on the bench. Rather, teams carried between five and seven players, depending on the circumstances. Payrolls were small, and players were paid on a game-by-game basis. Teams did not practice as much as they do today. The players knew their roles and the fundamentals. As Phil Rabin remembered, "It

The 1939–1940 Philadelphia SPHAS captured their fourth American Basketball League championship by winning a round-robin tournament for the title. (*Courtesy of Diane Moskowitz.*)

was too expensive to practice. I played with the Jersey Reds for three years, and we never practiced. But the SPHAS were all from Philly, and Gottlieb got them to practice. In those days, you played on your own merits."[17]

"We had seven ballplayers. It was not like today where they have a bench of 15 or whatever it is," Gotthoffer noted. "You played because you were being paid. When you came out of a game, it was because you weren't conscious of the fact that you were playing in it. It had to be pretty bad."[18]

As Moe Goldman recalled, "We didn't need coaching. We worked together. Everybody knew what to do. We did not need coaches. Very few teams had a coach. [Gottlieb] made the lineups and did the substituting and all the rest of that."[19]

With the championship at stake, the SPHAS responded with a balanced effort that spoke to their experience. In their eight wins, five players—Rosenberg, Gotthoffer, Lautman, Goldman, and Rosan—took turns leading the team in scoring. Red Wolfe came off the bench in the third period of the second game to spark a rally that led to victory. Cy Kaselman proved his usual reliable self with his outside shooting. With their seven-man rotation, the SPHAS dispatched all comers and garnered their first title since their thrilling seven-game win over the Jersey Reds in 1936–1937.

In their final victory, the SPHAS thoroughly dismantled the Washington Brewers, their nemesis for most of the season. Leading 25–20 at the close of the second period, the SPHAS erupted for 23 points while holding Washington to only 10 points in amassing a 48–30 victory. Phil Rabin, who had tormented his former team after being jettisoned to Washington, was held scoreless for the first time all year. Despite his best efforts, Rabin could not overcome a well-balanced SPHAS attack. Rabin would continue playing, but unbeknownst to him, his best days had already passed:

"I played from 1935 to 1940, until I tore my Achilles tendon. I played another four years but I was not as good. My best years were 1936, 1937, and 1938, when I led the ABL in scoring and assists. I had torn cartilage in both knees, and I was the first person in the state of New Jersey to have both knees operated on at the same time. From 1940–1945, I was in Defense. I was 4-F for the Army. I could not jump off a bench. I played until 1945."[20]

9

ROSENBERG TO THE RESCUE

Rosenberg had a great hook shot and was a smart player.

—Louis (Red) Klotz,
interview by the author

On December 29, 1940, just a few days before the New Year, the Philadelphia SPHAS headed out for a brief four-city tour of Ohio. Gottlieb had scheduled games in Cleveland, Cincinnati, Dayton, and Columbus. It was a short visit. Only four games were scheduled, including two on January 1 in Dayton and Columbus. The SPHAS had played in Ohio many times before, and the trip at the end of the year was nothing new for the team. For a number of years, Gottlieb had taken his club out barnstorming the Midwest between Christmas and New Year's. Facing the SPHAS were the New York Renaissance, one of the top teams in all of basketball. The Rens, as they were known, originated in Harlem, New York, and were an all-black team.

By 1940, the Rens had established themselves as one of the top teams in all of basketball. Each season, the Rens and SPHAS played a series with each other and often traveled through the Mid-Atlantic and Midwest regions. Moe Goldman was a regular in this series:

> We'd play the Harlem Renaissance maybe 20 times a year. We'd go up to the Renaissance Casino maybe four or five times. They'd come to our place four or five times, and we'd play in other places four, five times.
>
> At the Renaissance Casino all the people would sit around and they would have big crowds. They wouldn't start the game until

> about 11:00 P.M. They had dancing first. I think we were about the only team that beat them there. At that time, they were the only black team. In the Midwest, the Harlem Globetrotters were just beginning. They took the best of the blacks at that time. I played against Willie Smith and Tarzan Cooper. They were the two center men. They used to drive me crazy.[1]

The Rens were an exceptionally talented team that often put on displays of passing and some showmanship when the game was handily won. Ossie Schectman played for the SPHAS in some of those games:

> We sometimes played exhibition games with the Harlem Renaissance, an all-black team. We would have a game in Troy, New York, then the next night in Albany, New York, and then we would go to Cleveland, Ohio. They were very good. Some of them could have played in the American Basketball League. Eddie was also involved with Negro League Baseball. Eddie and Bob Douglas, owner of the Rens, worked out the exhibitions. When we played in Harlem, we were the only white people in the building.
>
> The Rens loved to make us look bad. They would put on a display of ball movement, and we would be chasing after them. Douglas would call a timeout with a minute left just to prolong the show time.[2]

In their first game on this Ohio swing, the SPHAS and Rens played before 7,000 fans in Cleveland. The games marked the fifth time that season that the teams had faced one another, with each team previously winning twice. In the Cleveland game, the SPHAS held a 1-point lead, 19–18, at the end of the first half. The teams traded baskets in the second half, with the lead seesawing back and forth. The score was tied 32–32 with a minute remaining to play. The Rens worked the ball around to Wilmeth Sidat-Singh, who scored two baskets as the Rens won, 36–32.

The following day the teams traveled to Cincinnati, where they played at the Freeman Avenue Armory. The game mirrored the contest the previous day, except the SPHAS were able to rally and pull out a 36–32 win. The teams were now even on this Ohio trip.

The contests between the teams were often close and came down to the final moments. Because they played together so often, the members developed a close bond on and off the court. Bernie Fliegel was not a regular member of the SPHAS, but was signed by Eddie Gottlieb to travel with the team during their trips to the Midwest. On one of those trips, Fliegel remembered the joking nature of the Rens players:

> One year, we went to Ohio to play the Harlem Renaissance for four games. The first game was in Cincinnati, and before the game started, the referee called a foul on me. I told the referee, "I didn't foul him." He told me to shut up. A few minutes later, I was called for another foul. I said, "I did not do anything." He said, "I heard about you." At halftime, I went up to the referee and I said, "I really am a nice guy. Who told you I wasn't?" He pointed to the Rens team, who were all laughing. I told the referee that they are kidding you.
>
> The Rens had great players. We always played against each other. When they got ahead late in the game, they would get the ball and you would never get it back. They liked to make you look like fools. They were a super team and the first real good black team.[3]

The teams continued to play against one another well into the 1940s, and Ralph Kaplowitz participated in a few of those contests:

> There was one game in Troy, New York, with the SPHAS against the Rens, and it was a feature game. There was twenty seconds to go and we were ahead by 8 points. They scored a basket, and one of the players took the ball out from underneath their basket. As he threw the ball in, the Rens intercepted it, and they scored in two seconds. Now, we only had a 6-point lead. The same player threw the ball in, was intercepted, threw it in again, and the same thing happened. The ball was intercepted, and they scored a basket. Now we only had a 2-point lead. The same player threw the ball in the third time, and they intercepted the ball and scored. Now the score was tied, and with ten seconds left, they scored the winning basket and won the game.
>
> The reason I tell this story is because ultimately the basketball players of New York had a dinner honoring the owner of the Renaissance, Hall of Famer Bob Douglas, and at the end of the dinner, they asked each player to stand up and tell a story that he knows about the Rens. I stood up and told this story, and I did not want to mention whom that player was. Suddenly, Eddie Gottlieb stood up and yelled out, "That player was Irv Davis." I said that I know but I did not want to mention his name. Eddie remembered everything about every game that was played.[4]

After the first two games, both teams took December 31 off and resumed the following day with two games. The doubleheader began in Dayton and finished in Columbus. In the game in Dayton, the SPHAS won a tight 34–33 contest as Irv Torgoff led the way with 9 points. Later that evening in Columbus, the SPHAS capped off the doubleheader with a 40–35 victory to claim three of four in this short series through Ohio.

The games versus the Rens came just past the midway point of the first half of the 1940–1941 season. The SPHAS began the season as the defending ABL champions and looked to become the first team to repeat as champions since they themselves had done it in 1935–1936 and 1936–1937. At the beginning of the season, the ABL had five teams, its smallest roster of franchises to start a season since the league reconstituted in 1933–1934. Along with the SPHAS, the New York Jewels, Washington Brewers, Troy Celtics, and Baltimore Clippers were ready for another season of action. The Troy Celtics, who had played as the Troy Haymakers the previous season, were a team in transit. The Troy Armory, where the Haymakers had played the previous season, was no longer available, so the Troy Celtics were transferred to the New York City area. At the November 8, 1940, ABL Board Meeting, Marty and Ed Connors, who represented the Troy franchise, conveyed to their fellow board members the problems of securing a home venue. It was noted in the Board minutes that, as "it was not possible for them to secure an auditorium in Troy, New York, for the continued operation of the Troy club of the American Basketball League, they had made arrangements to transfer the team known as the Troy Celtics to either Brooklyn or White Plains, New York."[5] By December, the Troy Celtics had found a permanent home in Brooklyn and became known as the Brooklyn Celtics for the remainder of the year. The city of Troy did not have another professional team until the Troy Celtics appeared in 1946–1947 for one year of play in the ABL.

Eddie Gottlieb's roster was nearly identical to that of the previous season, with only one new addition. Irv Torgoff, a star player for Clair Bee at LIU, joined the team. Torgoff led LIU to its second NIT championship during his senior year in 1939. He scored a game-high 12 points as LIU defeated Loyola for the title. His college career over, Torgoff signed to play with the Jersey Reds for the 1938–1939 playoffs. He made little impact as the Reds were swept in three games by the New York Jewels as the Jewels won their only ABL championship. The following season, Torgoff joined the Detroit Eagles of the NBL, where he averaged 6.6 points in twenty-six games. After one season in Detroit, Torgoff returned to the East Coast and was signed by Gottlieb. The 1940–1941 season was the first of his six seasons with the SPHAS; during this time, the SPHAS won three championships and made five trips to the finals. He was a key contributor and became the first of a new wave of New York players who made up Gottlieb's roster through the end of World War II.

With Torgoff on board, the SPHAS started a new campaign on November 16. The season began on a disappointing note, a 38–31 loss at home to the New York Jewels. The Jewels were the only team to defeat the SPHAS during the preseason schedule, and their mastery over Eddie Gottlieb's team continued as the season began. It was one of the few down moments in the first half of the season. The SPHAS then reeled off six straight wins and stayed in the hunt for first-half honors. On December 14, the SPHAS hosted the Jewels in the final game of a tripleheader played at Convention Hall. The Jewels came into the game with a perfect 4–0 record, while the SPHAS were 4–1, their only loss being to the Jewels on opening night. The SPHAS jumped out to a 20–5 lead and held on for a 42–34 win and a half-game lead in the standings. The following night, the SPHAS traveled to New York and trounced the Jewels, 40–20, to open a game-and-a-half lead in the standings.

Their six-game winning streak was snapped by the Brooklyn Celtics on December 21, as the SPHAS lost for the second time at home. Petey Rosenberg twisted his kneecap, and the SPHAS played catch-up all evening. After a win the following week against the Washington Brewers, the SPHAS headed out on the road for their series with the Rens during the Christmas/New Year's break.

When the SPHAS returned home on January 2, six games remained in the first half. The SPHAS compiled a 4–2 mark to finish at 11–4, good for first-half honors over the second-place New York Jewels, who finished at 9–5. The season's second half began late, on January 24, 1941, and the SPHAS met with defeat, losing to the Baltimore Clippers, 38–33.

The league was facing problems with the Brooklyn Celtics franchise. Despite relocating from Troy, the Celtics had difficulty scheduling home games in Brooklyn. The ABL Board agreed that "such members of the American league, as can best afford to do so, will try to schedule several of the Celtics home games on their courts during the second half of the 1940–1941 season."[6] Thus, the game on February 2 between the SPHAS and Celtics was hosted by the New York Jewels. Finally, the league discussed the issue of drafting college players who would graduate by June 1941. It was determined that Sy Lobbelo of LIU would be available for Gottlieb and the SPHAS.

The opening loss to Baltimore did not bode well for the SPHAS. They lost their next three games to drop to 0–4 after a tough 42–41 double-overtime loss to the Brooklyn Celtics on the road. The momentum and good vibes that the team had enjoyed in the first half seemed to vanish overnight. The second half was becoming a struggle, and after a key road win in Washington on February 23, their record stood at 5–5. Three weeks later, on March 15, the Brooklyn Celtics easily defeated the SPHAS, 44–32. The SPHAS' record fell to 6–7. The team needed a break to clear their minds and get back to playing solid basketball. The SPHAS then embarked on their third big road trip of the season. This time, Chicago was the destination, and the games were part of the third annual World Professional Basketball Tournament.

By 1939, the NIT and National Collegiate Athletic Association (NCAA) tournaments were each less than two years old. Crowds loved watching doubleheaders and following teams from around the country. Still in their infancy, both tournaments were successful and eventually reached unimaginable heights in the decades to come. The concept of organizing a single-elimination tournament of the nation's best professional teams appealed to Harry Hannin and Harry Wilson, local Chicago businessmen. Hannin was in the clothing business, while Wilson was a promoter of local sports.

Sponsored by the *Chicago Herald-American* (a merger of the *American* and the *Hearst-Examiner*) and backed by William Randolph Hearst's money, the first tournament in 1939 had been designed as an invitational to be held March 26–28 at the Madison Street Armory. Billing it as the "World Series" of professional basketball, the organizers invited eleven teams to participate in the "greatest array of cage talent ever assembled in one place."[7] Enough funds were raised to award $10,000 in prize money. The players recognized the tournament as the championship of professional basketball.

The *Chicago Herald-American* operated all facets of the tournament. Wilson served as tournament secretary and Hannin was the director of arrangements. They brought in Leo Fischer, a journalist, to serve as publicity chairman. The supervising chairman was Edward W. Cochrane, who was also the sports editor for the newspaper, which gave unlimited coverage to the tournament, with Fischer writing preview articles on each team and continuing to hype the tournament up until the final game.

Although teams were added days before the start, the tournament did assemble a number of the nation's stronger squads. The eleven teams that first year were the New York Renaissance, Harlem Globetrotters, Sheboygan Red Skins, Oshkosh All-Stars, New York Celtics, Chicago Harmons, Illinois Grads, New York Yankees, Fort Wayne Harvesters, Benton Harbor House of David, and Clarksburg Oilers.

During its ten years, the World Professional Basketball Tournament showcased the best professional basketball talent. Sellout crowds of upward of 12,000 annually filled Chicago Stadium, the International Amphitheater, and Madison Street Armory. Great stories and individual performances left lasting impressions while propelling the growth and acceptance of professional basketball by the century's midpoint. The players and teams who built the game during the 1930s were passing the torch to a new generation of players, college trained and better skilled, who would transition the game by the late 1950s to new stars like Bill Russell, Jerry West, and Wilt Chamberlain.

John Schleppi, who wrote *Chicago's Showcase of Basketball: The World Tournament of Professional Basketball and the College All Star Game*, argues that

> professional basketball was in disarray in the late 1930s due to poor financial backing, quixotic leadership, and the effects of the Depression. Against this background entrepreneur Harry Hannin and Leo Fischer of the *Chicago Herald-American* promoted the World Tournament of Professional Basketball, which began in March 1939. Attracting the best available teams, they included the leading black and integrated teams. This was the first time blacks competed with whites on an even footing for a professional team championship. Using major facilities, including the Amphitheatre and the Stadium, attention was drawn to the game during the war years.[8]

The early years of the tournament, though, belonged to those players who, playing in unheated armories and driving seven players to a car, built professional basketball during the 1930s. Players such as LeRoy (Cowboy) Edwards, Harry (Buddy) Jeannette, Bobby McDermott, and George Mikan all played on teams that won the tournament at some point. Jeannette won tournament MVP honors twice (Detroit Eagles 1941 and Fort Wayne Zollner Pistons 1945), as did Mikan (Chicago American Gears 1946 and Minneapolis Lakers 1948). The Oshkosh All-Stars made five trips to the finals, winning once, while the Fort Wayne Zollner Pistons won the tournament three times from 1944 to 1946.

Three teams—the Oshkosh All-Stars (1942), Fort Wayne Zollner Pistons (1944 and 1945), and Minneapolis Lakers (1948)—won the tournament in the same year they captured the NBL title. Seven teams who competed—Fort Wayne Zollner Pistons, Minneapolis Lakers, Sheboygan Red Skins, Anderson Duffey Packers, Tri-Cities Blackhawks, Syracuse Nationals, and Baltimore Bullets—later became NBA franchises. Towns such as Clarksburg, Toledo, and Kenosha also fielded teams at some point during the tournament's ten-year run.

Although teams from the East participated, the tournament definitely possessed a midwestern flavor. Leo Fischer, who covered the tournament for the paper, also served as the commissioner of the NBL for a brief time. As such, the tournament served as a showcase for the NBL and the better independent and barnstorming teams of the Midwest. Seven of the tournament winners were NBL teams. This Midwest focus may have alienated some easterners like Eddie Gottlieb, who felt that the SPHAS, as perennial champions of the ABL, were the nation's best team.

Insight into how John J. O'Brien and the ABL viewed the tournament can be gleaned from a letter O'Brien wrote in 1945, in which he discussed the tournament:

> We have never recognized it as such for the reason that it is of one week's duration and specially recruited clubs have been secured for participation therein, some with established reputations and others drawn together only for this tournament, so that it is nothing more than an outstanding professional competition with the ultimate winner having no particular claim to territorial supremacy than would be true of many other tournaments promoted in other parts of the country; such as Cleveland, Rochester, and Worcester, Mass.[9]

Despite any misgivings that might have existed, the tournament proved wildly popular and successful. Each March, for ten consecutive years, the best teams traveled to Chicago for several days. Huge crowds, upsets, and record-setting performances thrilled players and fans alike. In the decades to come, the NCAA basketball tournament would grow to become a sporting fixture marketed all over the country as March Madness. But, for several days each March in Chicago from 1939 to 1948, the World Professional Basketball Tournament was the original March Madness.

The true legacy of the tournament resided in its desire to be a world series of basketball by inviting the best teams regardless of race. From the beginning, tournament organizers invited the nation's best black teams. The New York Renaissance was the only team to participate in all ten tournaments, winning the inaugural title in 1939. Incidentally, future Basketball

Hall of Fame guard William (Pop) Gates was the only player to have played all ten years. The following year, the Harlem Globetrotters captured the championship. In 1943, the Rens, playing as the Washington (D.C.) Bears due to wartime travel restrictions, won. In the final tournament in 1948, the Rens lost, 75–71, in the championship game to George Mikan and the Minneapolis Lakers.

In addition to all-black teams, two integrated teams played in the tournament. In 1942, the same year the Chicago Studebakers fielded an integrated team in the NBL, the Toledo Jim White Chevrolets and the Long Island Grumman Flyers played with African American players. Bill Jones and Jimmy Johnson played for Toledo, while Dolly King and Pop Gates were star players for Grumman. Toledo lost in the first round to eventual second-place finisher Detroit Eagles. The Grumman Flyers, meanwhile, garnered third place with a 43–41 victory over the Harlem Globetrotters.

With the success of the black teams naturally came great performances from their players. In all but two years (1946 and 1947), there was at least one African American player named to the first and/or second all-tournament teams. Clarence (Puggy) Bell, Zach Clayton, Babe Pressley, Pop Gates, Sonny Boswell, Dolly King, Bernie Price, Johnny Isaacs, Robert (Sonny) Woods, Nat (Sweetwater) Clifton, and George Crowe garnered attention for their all-around performances.

For the decade prior to the 1939 tournament, the New York Rens and Harlem Globetrotters coexisted in separate universes, each laying claim to the moniker as the best black team in the country. The teams had yet to face each other. But they were on a collision course, and the finals of the first tournament saw the Rens edge the Globetrotters, 27–23, to claim the title. The following year, the Globetrotters got their revenge and slipped past the Rens, 37–36, in the semifinals. The next night, they captured the title by defeating the Chicago Bruins, 31–29.

In the first two years, the two best black teams won. Could the best Jewish team win the 1941 tournament?

On February 25, 1941, a headline in the *Chicago Herald-American* declared "Philly Five to Seek Laurels." Announcing the SPHAS' entry into the field, Leo Fischer wrote, "The Philadelphia Hebrews, famous Hebrew Eastern quintet which has dominated the Atlantic seaboard for the past four years, became entry No. 14 in the big basketball show sponsored by the *Herald-American*."[10]

Noting that the World Professional Basketball Tournament often coincided with the ABL playoffs, Fischer went on to explain, "During the previous two tournaments, the Philadelphia team was unable to get here. This year, however, even the title playoff in the American Basketball League has been delayed so that the organization's standard bearer can come here to uphold the honor of Eastern professional basketball."[11] Examining the schedules of the ABL and World Professional Basketball Tournament reveals that this is only somewhat true. In 1939, the organizers had extended an invitation to the SPHAS. On March 22, the SPHAS were listed in the newspaper to play in the tournament. On March 25, a day before the start of the tournament, the final schedule was posted with game times, and the SPHAS had been replaced. During those three days, Eddie Gottlieb more than likely withdrew the team for reasons unknown. John Schleppi surmises that injuries caused Gottlieb to pull his team out.[12] It is possible that Gottlieb did not want to be bothered: the SPHAS' season had ended early that week, and he wanted to focus his attention on promoting baseball. The tournament did not coincide with the ABL playoffs since the SPHAS lost a two-game playoff series to the New York Jewels on March 18 and 19.

In the following year, 1940, the start of the tournament coincided with the ABL round-robin playoffs, and the SPHAS chose to play in their league championship. The SPHAS would go on to capture their fourth ABL title and the first since the 1936–1937 season. By 1941, the schedule was favorable for the SPHAS, who had a week off between league games to travel to Chicago and participate. With no conflict, Gottlieb, along with Red Rosan, Irv Torgoff, Mike Bloom, Inky Lautman, Petey Rosenberg, Shikey Gotthoffer, Red Wolfe, Moe Goldman, and Nat Frankel, made the trip to Chicago to test themselves against the nation's best teams. Now in its third year, the World Professional Basketball Tournament was considered a major sporting event in Chicago.

In the first round, the SPHAS drew the Bismarck Phantoms, "the wonder team of the great Northwest," which had "an imposing record that should spread the fame of Bismarck and give it its rightful place in the basketball sun."[13] The team comprised former college stars at the University of Minnesota, North Dakota State, and the University of North Dakota. One of the team's promising young stars, John Kundla, would later gain fame as a future Basketball Hall of Fame coach for the Minneapolis Lakers, where he would guide George Mikan, Jim Pollard, and Vern Mikkelsen to championships in three separate leagues. Along with Kundla, the Phantoms consisted of Emmet Birk, Bob Finnegan, Russ Anderson, Acey Olson, Paul Maki, Marty Rolek, Pete Burich, and Larry Tanberg. In its review of the Bismarck team, the tournament program noted, "The team is under the capable management of Mayor N. O. Churchill, who finds time, in addition to making Bismarck one of the best governed cities in the United States, to guide the affairs of the town's great basketball club."[14]

Once on the court, the Phantoms did not measure up to the platitudes extolled in the game program or advance press. After a first period that ended with the teams tied at 11, the SPHAS assumed command of the game and cruised to a 48–30 victory. "Mike Bloom and Howard Rosan began hitting from far out, and the Hebrews quickly assumed command of the situation."[15]

Next up for the SPHAS were the Oshkosh All-Stars, champions of the NBL and one of the Midwest's best teams. Since joining the NBL in 1937–1938, Oshkosh had been one of the league's premier squads. After three straight losses in the NBL finals, Oshkosh finally broke through with a championship in 1940–1941. The following year, they won their second consecutive championship. The team had also advanced to the championship game in the inaugural World Professional Basketball Tournament.

Billed as "the 'little world series' between the National and American League champions," the game more than lived up to the advanced billing as the crowd left "marveling at the type of basketball displayed by these pro quintets."[16] With evenly matched teams and a close score throughout, the game was decided by a final spurt at the end.

The game opened with Petey Rosenberg connecting on two long shots to give the SPHAS an early lead. Oshkosh came back to take an 11–10 lead at the end of the first period. The second period seesawed back and forth, with each team looking for an advantage, before a foul shot and "long ringer" by Moe Goldman gave Philadelphia a 1-point halftime lead.[17] As the second half started, Oshkosh exerted itself, and its well-balanced attack ultimately proved too much for the SPHAS. Led by LeRoy (Cowboy) Edwards, who "hit three sensational hook shots," Oshkosh forged ahead in the third period.[18]

With the game on the line, it was automatic for the Oshkosh players to find Edwards and get him the ball. His patented hook shots with either hand often proved too difficult to defend. By the time of this tournament, Edwards had established himself as one of the game's top centers. A tough, physical player who left the University of Kentucky after his sophomore season, Edwards quickly established himself as one of the best young big men the game had seen in years. In 1935–1936, his first season as a professional, he averaged 10.5 points in thirteen games for the Indianapolis U.S. Tires. The following year, he joined Dayton of the Midwest Basketball Conference, a forerunner to the NBL, and played in eleven games, averaging 8.9 points. The following year, he joined the Oshkosh All-Stars, where for the next ten years, he blossomed into a great player, while transitioning the center position from Joe Lapchick of the 1920s and early 1930s to George Mikan of the postwar years. He led the NBL in scoring for three straight years (1937–1940), and his hook shot became one of the game's most potent offensive weapons.

Leading the SPHAS by 4 points to begin the final period, Oshkosh quickly extended its margin to 7 points on a foul shot by Bob Carpenter and a basket by Connie Mack Berry. With one final push left in them, the SPHAS "brought the crowd to its feet with a rally that cut the Oshkosh lead to 33–31."[19] A few baskets by Oshkosh eliminated any chances Philadelphia might harbor for a come-from-behind victory. With their win, Oshkosh advanced to the semifinals while Philadelphia packed their bags for a trip back East.

In their lone appearance in the World Professional Basketball Tournament, the SPHAS acquitted themselves well. They defeated the Bismarck Phantoms, a team they were clearly better than, and played a tough contest against the Oshkosh All-Stars, one of the game's premier teams. In subsequent years, the SPHAS would play Oshkosh in nonleague games and continue their close contests.

Despite their strong showing, the SPHAS never again played in the World Professional Basketball Tournament. Over the next seven years, the war, the formation of the BAA, and the team's relocation to Atlantic City all served to diminish the SPHAS as a top-flight team. Whether this caused the tournament organizers not to extend an invitation or Eddie Gottlieb to pursue other exhibitions is unclear. Although the SPHAS would go on to garner two more ABL titles by the end of World War II, their best days were behind them.

When the SPHAS returned from the World Professional Basketball Tournament, the season was in its home stretch, and the SPHAS were already ensured a place in the championship round versus the second-half winner. The SPHAS dropped two of the remaining three contests to close out a lackluster second-half performance. The one bright spot in the remaining three-game stretch was the play of Alexander (Petey) Rosenberg, in his third season with the SPHAS. Twice during those games, Rosenberg led the team in scoring, and his offense was peaking at the right time.

Little is known about Rosenberg prior to his joining the SPHAS. He grew up in Philadelphia and attended South Philadelphia High School from 1932 to 1936. He enrolled at St. Joseph's College and played varsity basketball for the 1937–1938 season. The team compiled a 13–5 record, which ended with a loss to cross-town rival Temple in the final game of the season. Rosenberg returned for his junior year in September, but a month later in October, he withdrew. Shortly thereafter, he signed to play professionally with the SPHAS.

Sam (Leaden) Bernstein, who grew up watching Rosenberg, remembered him as a player and a person:

> Petey Rosenberg was a heavyset kid, and nobody thought of him as a ballplayer. But he had a lot of ability and nice moves. Everyone liked him. He had gangsters and racketeers around him all the time. He got better and better and then went to high school and became a high school star. He never bragged. Later on, he had a store, and he was in the rackets. He owned a taproom or beat-up restaurant. He used to do business in the restaurant. As a player, he was deceptive. One time, he faked me, and I moved, and my shoes were still there. He had a beautiful fake.[20]

"Petey Rosenberg was my roommate with the Warriors. He broke me in and told me what to do. He was a very friendly guy," Jerry Rullo recalled. "He was also a good baseball player. He played baseball with my brother Joe with the Philadelphia A's. My brother had an appendectomy and Petey came to see him and that is when I first met him. A few years later, I would be his roommate. He was a good all-around player."[21]

"Petey was short and a dribbler. We played together on the Philadelphia Warriors," Ralph Kaplowitz remembered. "He always came into the game to freeze the ball in the last few

After playing one year of college basketball at St. Joseph's College, Alexander (Petey) Rosenberg joined the Philadelphia SPHAS for the 1938–1939 season. He went on to help the team win two championships in three years. (*Courtesy of Bill Himmelman.*)

minutes by dribbling around so nobody could touch him and we kept possession of the ball."[22]

When Rosenberg joined the SPHAS for the 1938–1939 campaign, the team was coming off a season in which they had missed the playoffs. Their archrival Jersey Reds rebounded from a crushing defeat in the finals in 1936–1937 to win the 1937–1938 championship over the New York Jewels. Gil Fitch had finally retired from the game to focus on his music career. In stepped Rosenberg to fill his shoes.

The 1938–1939 season got off to a great start as the SPHAS won their first three games and set a blistering pace. By the New Year, the team's record stood at 11–4. The SPHAS continued their winning ways and finished the regular season with a 24–9 mark, good for second place behind the Kingston Colonials, who stood at 28–7. Rosenberg averaged 7.2 points in thirty-three games and finished in the top ten in the league scoring race. The top four teams made the playoff, and in the first round, the SPHAS faced the fourth-place Jewels while the Kingston Colonials played the third-place Jersey Reds. In two stunning upsets, the Reds defeated the Colonials, and the Jewels swept the SPHAS in two games. The SPHAS had compiled a glittering 16–1 home record but lost the home advantage by dropping the first game at the Broadwood to the Jewels.

A season under his belt, Rosenberg continued to be a key contributor for the SPHAS. The following year, Rosenberg averaged 6.7 points in thirty games, as the SPHAS won the 1939–1940 title in a round-robin format. Rosenberg was now entering his prime, and during the 1940–1941 year, he led the league in scoring with an 8.9 average over thirty-one games. It would be the best year of his career. In twelve games during the regular season, he led the team in scoring, and his offense would be needed as the SPHAS faced the vagabond Brooklyn Celtics in the championship series.

The series opened on April 5 in Philadelphia, and the game was a sloppy affair from the start. Tentative play, poor shooting, and many fouls marred play. The SPHAS committed twenty-one fouls while the Celtics had eighteen of their own. Gotthoffer and Torgoff fouled out for the SPHAS, while Fliegel, Shaback, and Frankel of the Celtics were in foul trouble and on the bench. A strong opening period carried the SPHAS to a 48–38 win in Game 1.

Brooklyn continued to face problems scheduling home games in New York City, so the second game was played in Saratoga Springs, New York. The lack of a home court did not faze the Celtics, who opened a 10–9 advantage after the first period. In the second period, the Celtics increased their margin and thoroughly outplayed the SPHAS in the second and third periods. The Celtics had evened the series as it headed back to Philadelphia.

After a poor showing in the opening game, Petey Rosenberg was starting to make his mark felt in the series. In the first game, he scored 2 points, and in the second game started to find his range, as he tallied 7 points. His offense would be needed as the pivotal third game was set to be played. Game 3 was a wild affair right from the start. In the first period, Red Rosan and Chick Reiser got tangled up under the basket and started throwing punches, "which brought one excited Spha fan rushing on the floor to take sides with Rosan. This started a general rush from many fans and it required several policemen to restore order and let the game proceed."[23] Once play resumed, Rosenberg led the attack and "scored six goals, five of which were made on his famous sidearm shots."[24] His 14 points pushed the SPHAS to a 50–43 win.

In an abbreviated regular season, cut short by World War II, the 1940–1941 Philadelphia SPHAS defeated the Brooklyn Celtics to capture another championship. (*Courtesy of Bill Himmelman.*)

The series shifted to Brooklyn for the fourth game, and with their season on the line, the Celtics came ready to play. The Celtics outscored the SPHAS 15–8 in the first period and 12–8 in the second stanza. They held an 11-point lead entering the last session and looked to force a deciding fifth game in Brooklyn. The SPHAS had other ideas and scored 11 consecutive points to even the score at 27. An Inky Lautman foul shot gave the SPHAS their first lead since the opening period. The Celtics quickly answered and held a 29–28 lead in the waning moments. With possession and a chance to end the series, the SPHAS looked to Rosenberg, who had carried the team for the past two games. The team worked the ball around to Rosenberg who "clinched the game with his one-arm side toss."[25] His shot to win the series harkened back to Red Rosan's heroics in the overtime of the seventh game in 1936–1937 versus Jersey.

In their win, the SPHAS outscored the Celtics 14–2 in the final period. A 30–29 victory gave the SPHAS their second consecutive title and sixth in eight years. In so doing, the SPHAS had become the first team to repeat as champions since they themselves had done it in 1935–1936 and 1936–1937. By now, the SPHAS were regarded not only as the finest team in the ABL but also as one of the best in the country. Their style of play, teamwork, and ability to perform under pressure made them a model for other teams.

10

BASKETBALL AND WAR

> Gottlieb was called the Mogul. During the war years, he wanted the league to continue so he called his players and other players and had them play for other teams. He did that so the league could go on.
>
> —JACK (DUTCH) GARFINKEL,
> INTERVIEW BY THE AUTHOR

In the early morning hours of December 7, 1941, while the country slept, the Japanese attacked Pearl Harbor, jolting America out of its isolationist mentality. The U.S. Navy, unprepared for an attack, suffered tremendous losses, as the Japanese, with an armada of sixty ships, crossed the Pacific Ocean undetected, launching a surprise attack. More than 300 Japanese planes shattered a quiet Sunday morning on Oahu and firebombed the Navy's fleet and military installations with an arsenal of bombers and fighters. In little more than two hours of fighting, the devastation and loss were beyond comprehension. More than 2,400 Americans died that day. Another 1,100 were wounded. The Navy suffered its worst one-day attack in history as 188 planes, 8 battleships, and 3 cruisers and destroyers were all rendered useless. Another 159 planes were significantly damaged. The following day, President Franklin Roosevelt addressed the nation and a joint session of Congress with the famous "day that will live in infamy" speech. Soon thereafter, Congress overwhelmingly voted to authorize war against Japan, and within days, the United States was mobilizing. A country that had been deeply divided through much of the 1930s was now united and intent on winning the war.

America's entry into the war affected all aspects of society over the coming four years. Sports adapted to the demands of war, and basketball was no different from baseball, football, or golf. Players were drafted into military duty, leagues contracted, travel was restricted, and charity games were arranged to support the national effort. Basketball became an important part of the wartime plan to raise morale and generate revenue for the country. Charity basketball matches sponsored by the American Red Cross featured many of the leading stars of the day, including college players and future Hall of Famers George Mikan and Bob Kurland, who played in relief games at Madison Square Garden. Caught up in the fight to make the world safe, young men went to their local draft boards and enlisted. The loss of players greatly impacted the college and professional ranks and had long-lasting effects on the game in the decades to follow.

By 1942–1943, the war had seriously impacted the ABL and its midwestern counterpart, the NBL. Travel restrictions and the military draft made it increasingly difficult for both leagues to operate at full capacity. Some teams folded, while others suspended operations for the duration of the war. Fielding teams on a regular basis became a challenge for owners and coaches, who shuffled players in and out of the lineup almost daily. Continuity was lacking, but the ABL took a proactive approach to sustaining operations despite a number of challenges.

Team withdrawal was a huge concern for league owners. In a board meeting on December 2, 1942, ABL President John J. O'Brien announced the suspension of play for two teams. The Washington Heurich Brewers informed the board that they were unable to obtain an auditorium for the coming season and, thus, would not be able to play. Robert Carpenter, representing the Wilmington Blue Bombers, champions the previous season, made it known that "the Armory in Wilmington had been commandeered by the Army for the housing of approximately 195 soldiers, and that, therefore, this building would not be available for other than military for the duration."[1] Wilmington would stage its return in 1943.

With the Heurich Brewers and Blue Bombers out, five teams started the season, but only four would last. The New York Jewels, who had withdrawn the previous season after a 1–6 first-half record, returned with the hopes of rekindling their franchise. It was not to be. The Jewels finished the 1942–1943 season with an identical 1–6 record and ceased operations. A charter ABL member who had won the 1938–1939 championship, the Jewels ended their affiliation with the ABL and with professional basketball.

Not only did O'Brien and the Board confront the issue of teams withdrawing, but the debate over new franchise applications proved an equally important and complex matter. Representatives from Providence (Rhode Island), Hartford (Connecticut), and Springfield (Massachusetts) all applied for licenses. As the ABL Board minutes noted, due to "the inability of these cities to play other than mid-week games, the applications were dropped for the duration because of traveling restrictions." John (Honey) Russell, seeking to place a team in Paterson, New Jersey, had his application tabled for future discussion because "the high school gymnasium in that city could not be heated after 3:00 P.M. on any weekday because of fuel restrictions."[2] Still, the Philadelphia SPHAS, Trenton Tigers, and New York Jewels welcomed two new members into the league. The Camden Indians of New Jersey jumped to a 2–1 record before transferring to Brooklyn, where they played out the remainder of the 1942–1943 season and the next. The Senators from Harrisburg were granted a franchise and finished with four wins and eight losses. The SPHAS, with the Tigers, Jewels, Indians, and Senators, opened in quiet fashion, just hoping that the league would survive the year.

Aside from fewer teams, other changes signaled that this season would be different from previous ones. First, the schedule was reduced so that each team played fewer games, and the season started a month later, a week before Christmas. Instead of dividing the season into two halves and having the first-half winner play the second-half winner for the championship, this season reverted to one session with the top two teams facing off for the title. Finally, not all of the teams played the same number of games. The SPHAS played fifteen games, while the Tigers (thirteen), Senators (twelve), Jewels (seven), and Indians (eight) all played fewer.

One other accommodation was made. The Trenton, Camden, Harrisburg, and Philadelphia teams all were located within a relatively short drive from one another. The New York Jewels played in Brooklyn, and the expense of traveling a further distance would be greater due to the costs associated with fuel restrictions. In an effort to assist the Jewels, the other franchises agreed "in the financing of the New York Jewels at Brooklyn to the extent of $15 each per home game played by the New York Jewels. If this contribution is not necessary it will not be paid and if any contributions are paid and the New York Jewels enjoy a profitable year it is the understanding that reimbursements are to be made by the Manager of the New York Jewels for such advances previously made to him."[3] The economic hardships facing the league made it imperative that all franchises work together to ensure the league's survival.

With those changes in place and the nation at war, on December 19, 1942, barely a year after Pearl Harbor, the SPHAS opened the season with a 40–36 victory over newcomer Harrisburg before 2,500 fans at the Broadwood Hotel. Lost in the excitement of their season-opening win was the debut of South Philadelphia native Louis (Red) Klotz. In his rookie season, Klotz played twelve games, averaging a modest 3.7 points per game. A fan favorite for his play at South Philadelphia High School, Villanova University, and as a member of the SPHAS Reserves, Klotz electrified the crowd with his speed and passing ability.

In the season's third game, Klotz's all-around play led the SPHAS to a 50–45 victory over the New York Jewels. "Paced by the diminutive star, Herman 'Red' Klotz, the SPHAS had the fans cheering for fully five minutes by the back-hand, over-hand and sidearm passes by Klotz, aided by Schectman, Rosenberg and Irv Davis," William Scheffer wrote the next day in the *Philadelphia Inquirer*.[4] Sixty years later, Klotz still entertained crowds with his pinpoint passing and court vision as he traveled with the Harlem Globetrotters and the Washington Generals promoting basketball to all reaches of the globe.

The rest of the season for the SPHAS proved lackluster, as the team was unable to find its rhythm. Other than a three-game winning streak in January and another to finish the season in February, inconsistency plagued the SPHAS, who followed nearly every win with a loss. During the regular season, only Irv Davis, Inky Lautman, and Red Rosan played in every game. The war affected Gottlieb's ability to count on his regulars; Petey Rosenberg (seven games), Red Wolfe (eight games), Ossie Schectman (three games), and Shikey Gotthoffer (six games) played abbreviated schedules due to their armed service commitments. Gottlieb faced a game-by-game challenge of fielding a five-man lineup.

A loss in late January to Harrisburg dropped the SPHAS out of second place with a 5–4 record with six regular-season games remaining. After a two-game winning streak over Harrisburg and Brooklyn, Philadelphia stood at 7–4. Over the next two games, the SPHAS suffered two of their worst defeats all season. Eddie Gottlieb was vacationing/recuperating in Hot Springs, Georgia, the site where President Franklin Roosevelt would later die in April 1945, and the management of the team was left to the players. On February 13, Shikey Gotthoffer coached the squad as they dropped a 50–34 game to front-runner Trenton. A week later, Red Wolfe assumed the coaching reins, although the team still lost, this time 37–32 to the New York Jewels.

On February 21, the SPHAS traveled across the Delaware River to face their archrivals the Trenton Tigers. The Tigers had already clinched a playoff berth and were waiting to see who their opponent would be in the championship series in early March. Coming off a two-game losing streak, the SPHAS needed a win to earn a trip to the playoffs. The game began with both teams trading baskets, and the first period ended with the SPHAS holding a slim 14–13 lead. The second period seesawed back and forth, and when the dust settled, the teams were tied at 21 entering the final period.

The third period was marred by three fights that threatened to spread into the stands and involve the fans. Early in the third period, Trenton's Mike Bloom squared off against Red Wolfe, but order was quickly restored as referee Chuck Solodare called a double foul. Moments later Irv Davis and Trenton's Dick Fitzgerald started throwing punches and both were ejected from the game. These two incidents were a mere warm-up for the main event, in which Irv Torgoff and Allie Esposito began throwing punches at each other. "This battle threatened to become a real Donnybrook, spreading to the players of both squads and some spectators. But order was restored and the two principals banished."[5] The physical play clearly disrupted the Tigers, who were outscored 15–4 in the third period as the SPHAS cruised to a 36–25 win and clinched a playoff berth.

After completing the season with a 43–34 victory over a lackluster Brooklyn Indians team, the SPHAS returned to the championship round after a one-year hiatus. Facing them were the Trenton Tigers, who finished the shortened season with a league-best 11–2 record and only one loss at home. Ten years had passed since the SPHAS faced a Trenton team for the ABL championship, and the renewed rivalry evoked memories of their hard-fought battles in the Eastern Basketball League in the late 1920s and early 1930s.

Fans and players on both sides of the Delaware River figured the series would be close. The teams had split their four regular season games, each winning once at home and once on the road. Indeed, the trend continued in the opening game as Trenton went into Philadelphia and claimed an impressive 36–27 victory. The SPHAS, as was their playoff tradition, jumped out to an early 15–9 first-period lead, flashing their trademark style and setting the tone.

As the second period began, the game's complexion turned quickly when Matt Goukas came off the bench for Trenton. Running all their plays through Goukas, who scored the first of his three field goals in his first minute on the court, Trenton turned the tables, outscoring the SPHAS 15–8 to claim a 1-point lead entering the final period. The Tigers dominated the third period as Goukas "worked the pivot play to perfection, his handling of the fast whirling sphere was on par of the one-time great Dutch Denhert who was famed for his pivot playing."[6]

The series resumed the next night in Trenton, and the SPHAS looked to regain their first-period form from the previous night. In key situations, the team often looked to Inky Lautman for his steady play. When Louis (Inky) Lautman had first joined the SPHAS in 1933–1934, he was a high school sensation who skipped college to play for Eddie Gottlieb and the SPHAS. He joined a veteran team that had won three titles in four years in the Eastern Basketball League. He was a rookie that season with Moe Goldman and Shikey Gotthoffer, two other key figures who would play large roles for the rest of the decade. Inky played 14 seasons with the SPHAS, second only to Red Wolfe in longevity, and in that time, he missed only nine regular season games. He retired as the team's all-time scoring leader for the regular season and the playoffs. A durable player, Sam (Leaden) Bernstein remembered watching Inky, "He was so good under the boards with either hand. He was very aggressive. He was a scorer. He was always under the basket. He never took outside shots."[7]

Ralph Kaplowitz, a rookie in 1945–1946, played with Inky toward the end of his career:

> [Inky] was a terrific player for the SPHAS. When we played, Eddie Gottlieb used to pick on Inky Lautman a lot. We were playing a game at the Broadwood Hotel, and Eddie says to Inky during a timeout, "Inky, you are playing terribly. You are not getting the ball off the backboard. You are not clearing the ball. You are not passing the ball. You are not doing anything right. What is wrong is with you?"
>
> "Eddie, you insulted me," Lautman said.
>
> "I would never insult you," Gottlieb replied.
>
> "You called me a horse's ass," Lautman responded.
>
> "You are wrong. I never called you a horse's ass. I said you are playing like a horse's ass," Gottlieb remarked.[8]

Despite the tough love from Gottlieb, Inky was an invaluable member of the team, as Bernie Fliegel recalled. "He played the pivot a lot. He was not fast, but was tough. He was an important guy for the SPHAS."[9]

Initially, he came off the bench and as the years passed, he had become a clutch performer to be counted on in key situations. Now, down one game and looking to even the series with a road win, the SPHAS turned to Lautman. He delivered.

Lautman, who had a quiet 6 points in Game 1, set the tone with some early baskets as the SPHAS raced out to a quick lead and were never seriously challenged. The only remaining SPHA from the team's first ABL title against Trenton, Lautman, now in his tenth season, provided the necessary championship experience. Behind his 13 points, the SPHAS evened the series, with the third game set for the following Saturday night in Philadelphia.

Louis (Inky) Lautman went directly from high school to the SPHAS. In fourteen seasons with the team, Lautman missed only nine regular season games and one playoff game. (*Courtesy of Naismith Memorial Basketball Hall of Fame.*)

By now the Tigers and SPHAS had each won one game easily. The series progressed, and both teams prepared for tougher contests. Close throughout, the third game saw the SPHAS take the lead in the third period before a late rally by the Tigers transferred control of the game. Mike Bloom, now the starting center for the Tigers, led the way.

Growing up in New Jersey, Bloom was a tall, scrawny kid who at an early age was on his own. His parents were Russian immigrants who had settled in Trenton after arriving in the United States. His mother died when he was young, and his father, a carpenter, remarried. Basketball became his salvation, and he learned the game at the YMHA on Stockton Street in Trenton. Lacking direction or guidance, Bloom quit high school and moved to New York City, where he laid linoleum floors. His extra salary helped his family during the bleak years of the Depression. On one of his trips home, he ran into one of his childhood friends, and this chance encounter forever changed his life for the better.

"And when I came home a former Trenton High basketball star, and I remember like it was yesterday, we stood on the corner of Lambert and Market. His name is Scotty Moscovitz. And Scotty was the one that kicked me to the right side of the road. And I've been grateful about it ever since," Bloom recalled prior to his induction into Temple University's Hall of Fame in 1986.[10]

With Moscovitz's encouragement, Bloom reentered high school and soon became an important part of Trenton's basketball team. A contributing factor was a growth spurt that put him at 6'5".

> When I went back to high school I was not a basketball player. I was big. He [Coach LeRoy (Red) Smith] worked on me, kicked me

After helping lead Temple University to the first National Invitational Tournament championship, Mike Bloom joined the Philadelphia SPHAS. During his years in the American Basketball League, he was considered one of the league's best centers. (*Courtesy of Bill Himmelman.*)

> around a little bit. And, somehow, I came out all right. I played with a bunch of boys in those days that were just about the best in the world—unselfish, giving to one another. And consequently it paid off. I made all–South Jersey three years in a row, All-State two years in a row. At 6-5, I was big for those days. But I worked very, very hard at it. The one thing that stuck in my mind through all those years is that I was respected. Not only by my teammates, but by most of the people that I played against. And that includes high school, college and the pros.[11]

In high school, he came into his own as a player. During his three years (1932–1934), he led Trenton to a 71–2 record, including forty-one consecutive wins, three South Jersey championships, and three state championships. "I was probably one of the first big men that could shoot two-handed set shots from the outside. That was the big kicker. But, what I took a great deal of pride in was in my opposition not scoring any points. The Big D."[12] His achievements and his defensive ability caught the attention of Temple's basketball program, and he soon enrolled in college.

In his first year, he played on the freshman team for Coach Harry Litwack. With this season coming to a close, Bloom headed home to Trenton for a weekend. A particularly nasty winter made for bad conditions, and Bloom slipped off the icy porch at his parent's home and fractured his skull. It took some time, but Bloom recovered and was able to rejoin the varsity as a sophomore.

The winning tradition that Bloom had enjoyed in high school stayed with him as he made the varsity squad. In his three seasons at Temple, he was twice a Helms Foundation All-American, three times Eastern Intercollegiate Conference team, and three times all-Philadelphia. He twice led Temple in scoring. As a sophomore, he led the Owls to an 18–6 record, and had an immediate impact on his team. In only his third varsity game, Bloom scored a key basket that propelled the Owls to a 44–43 victory over Georgetown. A month later, in a highly anticipated matchup against NYU, Bloom scored 9 points in a 34–31 upset of the defending national champions.

The following year, Bloom's junior season, Temple compiled a 17–6 record and advanced to the Eastern Intercollegiate Conference basketball playoffs. After two impressive seasons, Bloom and the Owls figured to be one of the nation's top teams entering the 1937–1938 season. Two early-season tune-ups, a 54–26 victory over St. John's of Maryland and a 51–38 win versus Illinois, had Temple prepared for one of the most highly anticipated matchups of the season. Stanford University, led by Angelo (Hank) Luisetti, arguably the most exciting basketball player in college, came to Philadelphia as part of their early-season tour of the East Coast.

"Hank Luisetti changed the whole game of basketball with his one-handed shot," Moe Goldman remarked.[13] A native of California, Luisetti gravitated to basketball at an early age, and by the time he entered high school, had developed a reputation as a prolific scorer. A three-year player at Galileo High in San Francisco, Luisetti once scored 71 points in a game against rival Mission High. He enrolled at Stanford University, where he continued his winning ways. Players still shot the ball two-handed in the 1930s, but Luisetti is often credited with introducing and popularizing the one-handed shot. This was unorthodox at the time, although nobody could say it wasn't entertaining. Luisetti took his show on the road, often drawing huge enthusiastic crowds. In 1936, he scored 15 points as Stanford snapped LIU's 43-game winning streak in a game at Madison Square Garden. The New York crowd gave him a standing ovation as he walked off the court.

His college career was stellar, and he was instrumental in revolutionizing basketball. He averaged 14 points as a sophomore, 15 as a junior, and a remarkable 19.4 points in his senior season. He helped lead Stanford to three straight Pacific Coast Conference championships and was named a two-time College Player of the Year and a three-time consensus Helms Foundation All-American.

None of Stanford's trips east garnered more attention than their matchup with Temple University on December 30, 1937. The night before, Stanford had played their annual game at Madison Square Garden against LIU, defeating them handily, 49–35. With LIU in their rearview mirror, Stanford boarded a train for Philadelphia for their matchup with Temple. The game was held at Convention Hall, and the newspapers reported that the crowd of 11,793 was the largest ever to see a basketball game in Philadelphia. Dave Wilson, writing the following day in the *Philadelphia Inquirer*, noted, "The Philadelphia police deserve plenty of credit for the way they handled the enormous outpouring of basketball fans. Only people with tickets were allowed in the building, and as early as five o'clock in the afternoon there was a line a block long outside waiting for the ticket windows to open."[14] It was estimated that 14,000 people were turned away.

The game lived up to the anticipation as Temple won a close contest, 35–31, to snap Stanford's five-game winning streak to open the season. Temple came out of the gates quickly and held a 21–13 halftime lead. Focusing their defensive efforts on Luisetti, Temple held Stanford's top player to no points in the first half. In the second half, Stanford found its rhythm as Luisetti scored 11 points on five field goals and one foul shot. But Temple's first-half lead was too much for Stanford to overcome. Mike Bloom's defensive play, particularly on Art Stoefen, proved instrumental, as Temple won by 4 points in one of college basketball's best early-season games.

With their marquee game behind them, the Owls jumped head-first into their schedule. The team had two slip-ups, one in January on the road against Georgetown and one at home versus city rival Villanova. The Owls then went undefeated in February.

After their season-closing victory over city rival St. Joseph's on March 4, Temple set their sights on the inaugural NIT championship at Madison Square Garden. In the first round, Bradley Tech from Peoria, Illinois, posed little threat, as the Owls "had an amazingly easy time, leading by 20 points in the middle of the second half."[15] Temple coasted to a 53–40 win, as Don Shields paced the Owls with 12 points.

In the semifinals, the Owls faced off against the champions of the Missouri Valley Conference, Oklahoma A&M. With a "brilliant shooting barrage," the Owls netted 25 baskets and put the game out of reach with an early second-half surge.[16] Bloom scored 11 points as Temple won, 56–44.

Standing in the way of Temple's first NIT championship was Colorado, co-champions of the Rocky Mountain Conference. As in their first two games, Temple had little to worry about, embarrassing Colorado, 60–36. Within the first ten minutes, the Owls, with their "fast cuts and magnificent shooting barrage," effectively put the game out of reach.[17] Byron (Whizzer) White, future U.S. Supreme Court Justice, scored 10 points for Colorado. "We kept attacking the ball from one side to another with two men all the time and it worked well for us," Bloom remembered forty-seven years after the game.[18]

Temple finished off an outstanding season that saw them win their fourteenth straight game and twenty-three out of twenty-five games. Playing in his last college game, Bloom scored 6 points and "played a stellar game around the backboards."[19] Bloom had scored in his seventy-second consecutive game. For his efforts, he was an all-NIT selection. He scored 249 points in his senior season and 661 for his college career. He averaged 10 points a game his senior season and was named East Player of the Year.

With five games left in the 1937–1938 ABL schedule, Bloom joined the SPHAS. The season had been a struggle from the beginning. After starting 6–0, the team went 6–10 to close out the first half 12–10. The SPHAS suffered through three 3-game losing streaks, which halted any sense of momentum. The second half was not much different from the first. The team started out 6–2, but again, inconsistency plagued them, as they finished 5–7 down the stretch to complete the second half with an 11–9 record. When Bloom arrived on March 19 for a game against the New York Jewels, the SPHAS sported a 9–6 record and were fighting for second-half honors. Two straight losses effectively eliminated the SPHAS from contention. Bloom played well, scoring a career-high 9 points against the Brooklyn Visitations, showing signs of a promising professional career.

After leaving the SPHAS, Bloom moved around from team to team before returning to his hometown to play for the Trenton Tigers. He had played the entire 1938–1939 season for the SPHAS, who lost a two-game playoff series to eventual champion New York Jewels. Several games into the 1939–1940 season, Bloom moved to the Washington Brewers during that team's second ABL campaign. His scoring average improved from 4.1 points per game to 5.8 points per game as the Brewers finished with a 19–14 record. The SPHAS, his former team, captured its first championship in two years by winning a round-robin playoff series. They defeated the Brewers in consecutive games to win the championship, as Bloom scored 6 points each game in defeat.

Despite his offensive improvement and strong all-around team play, Bloom would find another team to call home for the 1940–1941 season. Less than three weeks into the new season, Bloom "was sold outright to the Baltimore Clippers of the American Basketball League, in an unexpected move."[20] Failing in their attempt to acquire John Pelkington, a 6'7" center for the Akron Goodyears of the NBL, Washington sold Bloom to make room for former George Washington University player and local star Ben Goldfaden.

While the Brewers were looking for a more seasoned big man to keep pace with frontrunners New York and Philadelphia, Baltimore was merely searching for its first win. The *Baltimore Sun* wrote, "As each contest was played the need for a first-rate center became more and more evident, until now it is a question of obtaining a top-flight pivot or giving up any hope of the spurt for a playoff run."[21]

Baltimore tried a center-by-committee approach in the season's first three weeks. Frank Conaty, George Newman, and Allie Schuckman each took their turn in the middle. With the purchase of Bloom, the Clippers played better. In their first game with Bloom anchoring the center position, the Clippers played their best basketball of the season despite dropping their eighth straight game. Bloom "seemed to be the man they needed, and with his aid under the backboard the others appeared to gain in confidence. It was a keen team while it lasted."[22] Bloom scored 9 points to pace his new team.

But the boost was short lived, and despite Bloom's arrival, Baltimore played dismally. Bob McDermott resigned due to a bad knee early in the season. Without McDermott, Baltimore lacked a veteran scoring presence late in games. The Clippers, as a result, lost a number of close contests and finished the first half with a 3–11 record. They fared slightly better in the second half, posting a 6–10 record.

In three full seasons as a pro, Bloom had played for three teams. His play and scoring average increased each year, but the fortunes of his team progressively worsened. The 1941–1942 season was on the horizon, and Bloom found yet another team, this one in his hometown of Trenton, New Jersey. One of professional basketball's founding cities, Trenton had lacked an ABL entry since the Trenton Bengals played five games in 1935–1936 before transferring to Passaic, New Jersey. Not since the early 1930s had Trenton fielded a contending team.

Now Trenton was back in the ABL. Along with Bloom, the Trenton team consisted of Ace Goldstein, Herb Gershon, Allie Esposito, newcomer Jack (Dutch) Garfinkel, Matt Goukas, and Rusty Saunders. Playing a shortened season due to World War II, the Tigers finished with an 11–14 record as the Wilmington Blue Bombers claimed the championship.

After a season adjusting to the league, Trenton became a serious challenger to the SPHAS and one of the league's top teams the following year. The emergence of Bloom, now in his fifth season, propelled the Tigers as a first division team. A great college player, it took Bloom several seasons to adjust to the professional game and find the right team to showcase his skills. Once he realized his potential, Bloom finally became the star that everyone knew he could be. Trenton finished with a league-best 11–2 record as Bloom paced the Tigers with an 8.8 points per game scoring average.

Now stationed at nearby Fort Dix in New Jersey, Bloom played with Trenton on the weekends. His presence and familiarity with the SPHAS had caused problems for his former team in two of their four regular-season matchups.

In the season's second game, played on Christmas night, Bloom nearly outscored the entire SPHAS team in the third period by himself. Scoring 12 of his 13 points in that period to pace Trenton to victory, Bloom and the Tigers asserted themselves as top challengers to the SPHAS. The SPHAS scored only 13 points in that final period as Bloom converted two 3-point plays in the final seven minutes. Two months later, at the end of February, in their last tune-up against the SPHAS before the championship series, Bloom scored 11 points in defeat. Fights, including one between Bloom and former teammate Red Wolfe, marred the game. The loss was Trenton's only home defeat all season.

With the score now tied in the closing minutes of the third game of the 1942–1943 championship series, Bloom dribbled around his former teammate Lautman for a basket to break the tie, giving Trenton a lead they would not relinquish. After a defensive stop, Bloom drove the length of the floor for another score. A late basket from Herb Gershon on a "beautiful pivot play" from Matt Goukas sealed the victory.[23]

A pattern was developing after three games. Trenton won an easy game and then Philadelphia countered with an easy victory of its own. Trenton then won a close game with a late-period flurry. Now, it was Philadelphia's turn to claim a tight victory with clutch play down the stretch. True to form, the fourth game saw the SPHAS stage a late rally. With the score tied at 37, Chink Morganstine overpowered the Trenton defenders and scored his team's final 5 points. The 3-point win, 42–39, evened the series at two games apiece.

The series was deadlocked with the pivotal fifth game the following week. The prevailing wisdom favored the first team to win a home game. Both teams had protected their home court advantage in the regular season. Trenton had lost once at home, while Philadelphia had done so four times. In the championship series, the SPHAS' two victories had come across the river in Trenton, while the Tigers had scored two wins at the Broadwood. Would the SPHAS break the pattern and claim the pivotal fifth game on their home court? Could Trenton continue its stellar play on the road?

The fifth game got off to a quick start as both teams played a brisk period that ended with the SPHAS holding a slight 15–12 lead. Equally strong play throughout the second stanza left the SPHAS with a 2-point lead entering the final period. At critical points throughout the series, the

SPHAS often self-destructed in one crucial period. In the first game, the SPHAS trailed 24–23 before being outscored 12–4 in the final period. In their Game 3 defeat, the SPHAS fell behind 17–8 in the opening period, forcing them to play from behind the rest of the way.

Holding a 2-point margin entering the final period of a series tied at two games apiece, the SPHAS played their worst basketball. Reduced to five players because of the wartime commitments of some teammates, the SPHAS simply collapsed. On offense, the team went cold; defensively, the team lost its focus. The Tigers outscored them 22–10, and cruised to an easy 10-point victory, putting themselves one victory away from claiming their first championship. Mike Bloom, who had hurt the SPHAS all series with key baskets, came through again in the clutch with "two successive long shots that sent Trenton into the lead for good."[24]

Victory was waiting for Trenton. One more win and the city and fans could celebrate their first professional basketball championship since 1932–1933, when the Trenton Moose defeated the SPHAS three games to one in the final season of the Eastern States Basketball League.

From the opening tip-off, Game 6 was a bitterly fought contest. Trenton jumped to an early lead, but the SPHAS soon took control and held off a valiant Tiger squad the rest of the game. With five seconds to play, Dick Fitzgerald hit a foul shot to bring the Tigers within a point, 34–33.

After Fitzgerald's foul shot, the Tigers gained control of the ball on the ensuing center jump. Even though the center jump after each basket had been eliminated in 1937, the ABL had instituted the rule for the last five minutes of games. Trenton tried a few unsuccessful desperation shots. Breathing a sigh of relief, the SPHAS walked off the court with a 1-point victory, knowing they were lucky the series was not over.

The seventh and deciding game was scheduled for April 3 in Philadelphia.

Anticipation filled the air as 3,600 Philadelphians arrived early for the seventh game. For three previous contests, the SPHAS faithful had watched as Trenton outplayed their team on their home court. But the Broadwood crowd knew seventh games. Twice before, Gottlieb's crew had played do-or-die winner-take-all games. Both times, they had won. Each time, the deciding games had been at home. Against the Brooklyn Visitations in 1935–1936, the SPHAS prevailed by a single point. A year later, facing a formidable Jersey Reds squad, the SPHAS fought back from a three games to one deficit to win a thrilling seventh game in overtime by 2 points.

For long stretches in the series, the Tigers outplayed, outexecuted, and outhustled their Philadelphian counterparts. If one of their shots had fallen at the end of Game 6, the series would have been over. The SPHAS knew that. The players also knew their previous success at home in seventh games.

Trenton jumped out to a quick 6–0 lead on two baskets by Ace Goldstein, who was enjoying a fine series, and two foul shots by Dick Fitzgerald. The SPHAS' first points came on a basket by Lautman. For the remainder of the period, the SPHAS outscored the Tigers 12–4 to take a 14–10 lead.

The second period was close throughout with the score tied at 20 and at 21. Mike Bloom paced the Tigers with several tough pivot shots. The Tigers took a 24–23 lead with a second left on the clock. At times during decisive games, key moments hinge on improbable plays or the efforts of unsung players. Irv Torgoff was one of those players. A terrific addition from LIU, he had joined the team in 1940–1941. He had participated in thirty-one games that first season and averaged 6.8 points per game, third on the team. The following season, he had played twenty-two games while averaging 7.6 points per game. Wartime commitments and injuries affected Torgoff for the 1942–1943 season, and he was able to suit up in only nine regular-season games. In the playoff, he found action in four games, and in Game 6, he scored 4 points, his first points of the series. He tallied 8 points for the series.

Torgoff would now have his moment. He gained possession of the ball with the second period winding down. With the timers yelling, "just one second to go," Torgoff turned and with one hand instead of his customary two, shot the ball.[25] Everyone in the arena turned to watch the ball, and his 70-foot shot went straight through the basket as the gun sounded. His teammates mobbed him coming off the floor. Hysteria engulfed the crowd. His improbable shot shifted momentum entering the final period of the deciding game of the championship series.

Midway through the final period, Red Wolfe hit a corner shot to break a 27–27 tie. The SPHAS grabbed a 38–31 lead and, as in the previous game, held off a late Trenton rally. Down 43–42 with seven seconds to play, Trenton called a timeout to set up their final play; however, they were out of timeouts, and the SPHAS were awarded a foul shot. Sol Schwartz calmly stepped to the line and made it. Schwartz, who led all scorers with 14 points, gave his team a 2-point lead and the championship. Several missed foul shots and calling a timeout they did not have cost the Tigers the title. Philadelphia celebrated another championship.

A tough season for professional basketball had come to a close. The ABL and the NBL had managed to survive. Five ABL teams had started the season and with the New York Jewels dropping out, four had made it to the finish line.

For the SPHAS, the season was deemed a success. Gottlieb shifted players in and out of the lineup due to armed or civil service commitments, and by all accounts did an admirable job. The team played fifteen regular season games, but only Inky Lautman, Red Rosan, and Irv Davis played in all fifteen games. Butch Schwartz, Red Klotz, and Chink Morganstine played in twelve contests. Irv Torgoff played in nine, while regulars such as Petey Rosenberg, Red Wolfe, and Shikey Gotthoffer had their seasons significantly curtailed. And the team introduced a new player in Red Klotz. As a rookie trying to provide a spark off the bench, his season had been largely forgettable. Klotz would make his mark in decades to come, playing far longer than all of his teammates.

11

THE INFLUX OF NEW YORK PLAYERS

> Dutch Garfinkel was a terrific passer. He loved to play with me. I would run without the ball, be free and he would get me the ball. He used to call me the Rabbit.
>
> —Jerry Fleishman, interview by the author

World War II fundamentally altered basketball in America. The 1930s witnessed a game that was growing nationally in popularity, where different parts of the country were following the exploits of a team or certain star players thousands of miles away. College doubleheaders at Madison Square Garden and other arenas showcased the talents of rising players from across the nation. The NIT and NCAA tournament proved wildly popular and generated additional national exposure for college basketball. Even the World Professional Basketball Tournament attracted an annual following, as teams descended on Chicago for a month-long basketball extravaganza.

But the war took the game and pushed these developments to new heights. Whereas college doubleheaders and tournaments allowed teams from different parts of the country to play against each other, armed services basketball allowed players from different parts of the country to play with each other. The armed services had leagues and teams stationed throughout the country, and the games became a way to build morale among the troops. As this happened, the game homogenized, which led to a sport that truly became national in the postwar years. Service basketball brought together disparate forms of the game and flattened it out, producing a game that was easily recognizable to anyone.

"Service basketball loosened the game up. In the beginning of WWII to the end of WWII, scoring picked up. The game became more modern,"

Bill Himmelman, a basketball historian, explained. "Service ball promoted the integration of the sport. When they came out of WWII, they did not give as much thought to integration as football and baseball did. Basketball players did not give it a thought. It was considered natural."[1]

Service basketball was a product of Special Services, which was formed by the Joint Army and Navy Committee on Welfare and Recreation in 1942. Its mission was simple, as stated in its publications and promotional literature: "Every red-blooded American youth, in and out of uniform, is a lover of sports. The Army has found it desirable to maintain and foster this competitive ideal. Mass participation in sports and games of every description is the Army goal."[2] With this charge, Special Services had a presence on every base, both stateside and overseas, and created leagues and teams. Sports, particularly basketball, were played everywhere during World War II. Teams were created, leagues were formed, games were set, equipment was available, and players were ready to participate.

Over the next four years, some of the best basketball teams were found on armed forces bases. Professional players, in addition to playing with their pro teams, also competed in the armed services, and those teams regularly competed against and defeated college teams. One of those teams was Great Lakes Naval Training Station.

The Greats Lakes Naval Training Station, located in North Chicago, Illinois, was a powerhouse when it came to fielding basketball teams. The squad of 1941–1942 produced one of the finest seasons of any team during the war—college, professional, or service. In compiling a 31–5 record, they established a level of excellence both on and off the court that was difficult for any team to match throughout the rest of the war. Led by Hall of Famer Tony Hinkle, head coach at Butler University, the team included Bob Calihan, Forrest Anderson, and Frank Baumholtz. They defeated colleges and other service teams, often winning with great ease.

The importance of basketball to the war effort cannot be overstated, as evidenced by a letter that T. DeWitt Carr, Captain, U.S. Navy Executive Officer, wrote to Robert Calihan, EM2c of the U.S. Naval Training Station at Great Lakes, in March 1942:

> Never for one moment have you and the rest of the boys on the team been anything but the finest examples of Navy manhood. On trains, in hotel lobbies, at luncheons and on the basketball court your conduct has been so splendid that the entire Navy recognized you and your team as the best recruiting "poster" in the Ninth Naval District. You carried the Navy story to colleges and towns and you did

> it in the Navy way. You ignored inconveniences, you fought harder when you were tired, and you asked for no special privileges during all the time you were doing a double job for your Navy.
>
> In traveling on the road, your basketball activity was comparable to a fleet arrangement of the United States Navy. Like our own fleet, the further you got from the home base of supplies the more difficult was the attainment of victory. Yet, in foreign "waters" you met the enemy and scored victory. True, five games were lost, but only five out of 36. In Navy terms, losing five while sinking 31 of the enemy ships means complete victory.[3]

Every Saturday morning after inspection, Jack (Dutch) Garfinkel left West Point and drove with a few other enlisted men to New York City, where he picked up the train. From there, he traveled to Philadelphia to play for the SPHAS for the next two seasons and part of a third (1943–1944 to 1945–1946). With player shortages due to the war, Gottlieb looked to stock his roster with players on military bases, and Dutch Garfinkel quickly became one of those men. In his two-plus seasons with the SPHAS, Garfinkel directed the offense for Gottlieb's squad, showing the all-around play and passing ability that had made him a college star at St. John's University.

Growing up in east New York, Garfinkel lived within a large Jewish immigrant community struggling to make a living. His family lived in an apartment with a tenants-share bathroom down the hall. "My mother would take my brother and I to the public baths, which were three blocks away about two to three times a week. During the summer, there was no air conditioner so we slept on the fire escape," Garfinkel remembered. Like other immigrants of the time, his parents always worked to provide for

Jack (Dutch) Garfinkel was a consummate floor general who was a mainstay for the Philadelphia SPHAS during World War II. (*Courtesy of Bill Himmelman.*)

their children. His father was an undertaker and drove the horse and wagon. When an influenza epidemic broke out, his father was especially busy and "would take five or six caskets at a time."[4]

Garfinkel was no different from the other children that he met on the streets or in the playgrounds. Once he found sports, he found his passion, his avocation, and ultimately, his entry into American society. He played at community centers and Public School 82 during the winters. His summers were spent outdoors on the playground playing basketball with the neighborhood kids. "I played ball every chance I had. I loved it, and I made up my mind I wanted to be a basketball player," Garfinkel said. "My parents did not mind me playing basketball as long as I did not get hurt. I just wore out my sneakers once a year. In the summers, they surely did not mind. In those days, my parents were busy. My father worked all the time and women were in the house cleaning and cooking."[5]

Eventually, his family moved and settled in Brighton Beach in Brooklyn. As he matured, he became a better player and set his sights on high school. Abraham Lincoln High School was a short distance from his apartment, about seven or eight blocks, but he wanted to challenge himself and grow as a player. He was looking for the best competition he could find. Thomas Jefferson High School, which had fielded many competitive teams through the years, was a top program, so Garfinkel chose to attend Jefferson, which was quite a distance away. For the next four years, he commuted one hour each way by train from Brighton Beach to East New York.

The commute was worth it. He made the team his final three years:

> In my first year, the team was mediocre. In my second year, we were co-champs of the PSAL with James Monroe of the Bronx. That year was the first time that the PSAL came out with new alignments for its championship. Five teams were competing: James Monroe from the Bronx, Textile from Manhattan, Newtown from Queens, and Samuel Tilden and us from Brooklyn. It was a round-robin tournament. We only lost once and so did Monroe. So, Jefferson and Monroe were in a playoff for the city championships. I cannot remember, but I think a Jewish holiday was coming up so they called it off and made us both co-champs. In my third year in 1936–1937, we were the Brooklyn champions, but lost in the first round to DeWitt Clinton, which was a top team.
>
> After high school, I went to college. A man called with an offer from George Washington University. I made an appointment to meet him in a New York hotel. I got on a train, went to New

> York, and waited. He never showed. Meanwhile, the Athletic Director at St. John's called and asked me if I would like to play for them. This was the second year for Joe Lapchick as coach. I said yes immediately.[6]

Garfinkel enrolled at St. John's and blossomed into one of college basketball's better point guards. He joined the team in 1938–1939 as a sophomore and led the Redmen to an 18–4 record, including key wins over Northwestern and local rivals CCNY and Manhattan. St. John's, which would eventually capture a record six NIT championships, earned its first NIT bid that season as Garfinkel was named first team All-Metropolitan. The Redmen defeated Roanoke College in the first round but eventually finished in fourth place in the tournament.

Fresh off their first postseason appearance, high expectations accompanied the Redmen and Garfinkel into the 1939–1940 campaign. The team finished the regular season 15–4 and received its second straight invitation to the NIT, where they lost in the first round to Duquesne. Garfinkel, who was third in team scoring, was named second team All-Metropolitan. He had distinguished himself as a great point guard, adept at scoring, controlling the tempo, and involving his entire team with his accurate passing. No less an authority on the game than Coach Lapchick believed Garfinkel possessed all the skills to be a great player and ranked him "as second only to Nat Holman as an all-around player."[7]

Playing for Lapchick provided Garfinkel with an opportunity to learn not only from a great coach but also from one of the game's greatest players. Lapchick had starred with the Original Celtics, one of basketball's finest teams, and was a teammate of Nat Holman during the 1920s. For a brief time, he played in the original ABL. Lapchick retired in the early 1930s, and the ABL folded for two years because of the Depression. When it resumed in 1933–1934, the league fielded two teams in Brooklyn. Garfinkel soon made his way to those games:

> There were no big leagues then. There was one league, the American Basketball League. There were teams like the Brooklyn Jewels and the Brooklyn Visitations. When I was at St. John's, I used to see the SPHAS play the Jewels. Eddie Gottlieb was the coach then. I would watch all the teams. They were a great team and won many championships. They had great shooters. Cy Kaselman was a great set shooter. Shikey Gotthoffer was a strong defensive player. They had terrific ball players.

> At Halsey Street, there was a hall called Arcadia Hall, where the Jewels played. Every Saturday night, there were games and if you brought your G.O. [General Organization] cards, you paid twenty-five cents to see the game. I watched the games all the time. I watched attentively. They played three fifteen-minute periods, so they played forty-five-minute games. At the end of each period, the teams would go into the corner and I would get near and listen to what they were saying. This was my learning experience. I learned by watching and picking things up myself.[8]

After seeing the SPHAS play, Garfinkel had made up his mind. "I used to watch the SPHAS as a kid when they would play in Brooklyn. It was always my secret ambition to play with them. They really played good ball."[9]

A quick study, Garfinkel developed into a fundamentally sound player who could do it all. But it was his passing that stood out. From the beginning, he had a knack for finding the open man, and his passing ability could be traced back to show how he received his nickname (Dutch).

> As a kid, I lived for basketball and followed it closely. One of my heroes was a player by the name of Henry (Dutch) Dehnert who, after a good college career, played for the Original Celtics along with Nat Holman, Davey Banks, and the other greats. Now this was the top pro team in the country and it received considerable press. One of their favorite offensive plays was to put Dehnert in the pivot with his back to the basket, and have two men, from either side, cut off him for a pass. This maneuver began to be called "doing the Dutch," and the name was applied to Dehnert, who became well known as Dutch Dehnert. There was no three-second violation back then and Dehnert stayed under the basket for as long as he wished.
>
> When I learned of this maneuver and how successful it was for the Celtics, I began to use it in my own schoolyard play. I played a lot of 3-on-3 in the schoolyard back then, and I always liked the challenge of playing with the two worst players to see if we could win. I began to instruct them on "doing the Dutch" and it usually worked. Of course, I was the one in the pivot feeding off to my cutting teammates, which really helped me to become a very good passer. If I passed to the right cutting man, I could cut left myself, after the pass, and be in perfect position for rebounding a missed shot. Since I was so enthusiastic about this strategy, and I became

> adept at it, my friends, kiddingly at first, began to call me Dutch. The name stuck.[10]

"Doing the Dutch" followed Garfinkel into his senior season with great anticipation. After two trips to the NIT, Lapchick and the Redmen targeted a third straight postseason appearance. It was not to be. Late-season losses to George Washington and St. Francis doomed any chances St. John's had of making the NIT. That did not stop Garfinkel, who was named to the All-Metropolitan team for the third straight year and was the recipient of the Frank Haggerty Award for outstanding college player in New York City. Attending St. John's, as opposed to George Washington, proved to be the right move for Garfinkel. "I played at Madison Square Garden, I got publicity, it made my name, and I played for Lapchick."[11]

His name made, Garfinkel was able to fulfill his childhood dream of becoming a professional basketball player when he joined the Baltimore Clippers of the ABL in 1940–1941. "I was paid $25 a game and I had to pay all my own expenses. I did not care. I was playing ball."[12] The following year, Garfinkel joined the newly formed Trenton Tigers and played well, although the team finished poorly.

After his second season in the ABL, Garfinkel was drafted in the military and served for 2 years as part of the West Point Armored Detachment Team. During this time, Eddie Gottlieb found Garfinkel and signed him up to play. Garfinkel followed a regular routine on weekends during basketball season; as he recalled, after inspection:

> I took the railroad from Long Island to Philadelphia. There was a hotel, the Broadwood Hotel, and they had a ballroom with dances. The guys would meet the girls, and the girls would meet the guys. I would check in, get a few hours sleep, and get up and put my uniform on. I would take the elevator to the ballroom, and there was a court. After the game, I would go back to my room, shower, and go back down to the dance. I would dance with the women. I would pick up a date. That was the life of the hotel.[13]

For two seasons, he followed this same schedule, playing a Saturday night game at the Broadwood, then usually two games on Sunday before heading back to base for check in. "Afterwards, we would drive back to West Point for inspection on Monday morning," Garfinkel noted. "I never slept in those days."[14]

When he arrived at the start of the 1943–1944 season, the SPHAS were defending ABL champions, having outlasted the Trenton Tigers in a thrilling seven-game series the previous April. Shikey Gotthoffer, one of the team's stalwart players, had retired after ten seasons. But things were looking up for the ABL. After curtailing its season dramatically the year before, the league returned to the two-half regular season format and expanded its schedule to twenty-six games, an increase from the previous season. The Brooklyn Indians and Trenton Tigers accompanied the SPHAS; the New York Americans and the Wilmington Blue Bombers, who resumed play after a one-year absence, joined these three, making it a five-team league. Brooklyn subsequently folded during the first half, leaving four teams to complete the season.

It was an odd season for the SPHAS. The team started inauspiciously, as Gottlieb's crew dropped its first two games to the New York Americans and Trenton Tigers. They won their next three contests. Another loss and then a win brought the team to 4–3. Despite the positive record, the team was not playing well. Inconsistency from game to game hurt the team initially. Then, the wheels fell off. Seven consecutive losses left the SPHAS with a 4–10 first-half record and in last place in the standings. The most noticeable characteristic during the losing streak was poor defense. A team that prided itself on defense—something that Gottlieb constantly stressed in the locker room and on the bench—simply ceased to defend. In that seven-game losing streak, the SPHAS allowed 40 or more points six times, including four consecutive times when they allowed 50 or more, during which they dropped games to New York, Trenton, and Wilmington twice. The games were not even close. They lost to New York 57–37, Trenton 50–33, and Wilmington 50–36. With a week before the start of the season's second half, the SPHAS looked to regroup and get back in the hunt for a postseason berth.

The second half began much like the first half, with another loss in which the SPHAS were playing catch-up from the start. Back and forth the SPHAS went, and after seven games, the team had a 4–3 record. In the first half, the team proceeded to lose seven consecutive games after starting the season 4–3. Now, the SPHAS found their offense, which had been missing for much of the season, and posted a 4–1 mark down the stretch for an 8–4 record and second-half honors. The offense was now in sync, and three times, the team tallied 50 or more points. Twice they defeated the Trenton Tigers, their nearest competitors, in hard-fought victories to give them a one-game lead over Trenton. Throughout their surge, the player leading the way was Ossie Schectman.

Ossie Schectman is best remembered for scoring the first basket in the BAA (forerunner to the NBA) on November 1, 1946, when the New York Knicks traveled to Canada to play the Toronto Huskies. Long before Schectman made basketball history in 1946, he was building his reputation on the streets of Brooklyn.

"I started playing basketball in Brooklyn at an early age, and I was involved with settlement house teams. That was my early competition. I had an older brother who was a good athlete," Schectman recalled years later. "I watched various teams in the neighborhood, amateur clubs, teams in Brownsville, and I picked up different moves from the players. I grew into my game. I improved a great deal. I was a dedicated athlete, and I played hard. I was a pretty good point guard who would run the offense and play strong defense."[15]

As a youngster, Schectman was not the biggest guy on the court, but his playing style was shaped by the physical areas where he played. "Playing basketball in those days was confined to smaller areas. The physical setup was not too much. The ceilings were low, and there were ten men on the court. You played in a figure-eight, and there was lots of movement. It was devoid of long set shots."[16]

Schectman and his friends often improvised, using old balls and anything that might resemble a basket. "Sometimes somebody gave us a worn-out ball, all thin-skinned and shiny. We just taped up all the holes and used it as long we could. When we didn't have a ball, we used to tape some rags together in the shape of a ball. The gyms in the settlement houses were the only places that had baskets, and when we wanted to play on our own, we had to improvise."[17]

There were no baskets in the neighborhood, so Schectman and his buddies used their imagination, such as hanging a basket on a street lamppost or using a fire escape. "We didn't mind that this goal was square-shaped, horizontal, and perpendicular to the brick wall that served as a backboard. We were just happy to have someplace to play."[18]

As a teenager, Schectman started attending professional games in Brooklyn to see what he might pick up:

> When I was in junior high and high school, I went to Arcadia Hall in Brooklyn to see the Brooklyn Jewels play in the American Basketball League. The Jewels were represented by the St. John's Wonder Five. I got to see the SPHAS play. With them, it was more of a team concept. I tried to emulate certain players. That was the way I learned to play. A couple of the SPHAS were from Brooklyn, like

> Moe Goldman, who played at CCNY, and Irv Torgoff, who played at Tilden High School. Shikey Gotthoffer was from the Bronx. I used to follow them.[19]

Soon enough, he was ready for high school; he chose to play for a powerhouse:

> In high school, I lived in Flatbush and played for Tilden High School. My senior year in Brooklyn, we won the championship. I was a fairly good student. In 1935, during the Depression Years, Clair Bee, coach at Long Island University, managed a beach club near Brighton Beach. It was a private club and he recruited local players to get them jobs. They earned decent salaries and worked at the private beach and played exhibition games. It was one of the factors why I attended Long Island University and played for Hall of Famer Clair Bee. I could have gone to other schools like St. John's and City College of New York. LIU became a powerhouse. My sophomore year, we played the best teams in the country and went undefeated. The 1938–1939 team was the best group of players that New York saw in those days.[20]

Under head coach Clair Bee, LIU developed into one of the finest college basketball programs of the 1930s and 1940s. At one point in the 1930s, his teams compiled a forty-three-game winning streak, and went undefeated in 1935–1936 and in 1938–1939. His 1939 and 1941 squads won the NIT championship, making Bee the first coach to win it twice. The team's dominance stretched to their home court, where over a thirteen-year span, LIU compiled a 222–3 record.

Bee's 1939 team was led by Irv Torgoff and sophomore sensation Ossie Schectman. Captained by Torgoff, LIU finished the regular season 21–0 and set their sights on the NIT championship. LIU won its first two games against New Mexico State and Bradley, setting up a finals match against Loyola (Illinois), the only other undefeated team in the country. LIU came out strong and swarmed Mike Novak, Loyola's big man, holding him to 1 point. Schectman scored 9 points as LIU captured the championship. The following season, Schectman captained the Blackbirds, who finished 19–4 and lost in the first round of the NIT. He led all scorers in the NIT game with 12 points. In 1941, LIU again won the NIT with a convincing 56–42 victory over Ohio.

> When I got out of college in 1941, there was some type of draft in the American Basketball League. A New York team chose me. I got a call from Eddie Gottlieb, and he wanted to know if I would like to play for the SPHAS. I told him I would if he could work it out. He arranged it, and I went to the SPHAS.
>
> I enjoyed playing with the SPHAS. It was a haphazard league and players were paid on a per-game basis. With the SPHAS, it was a stable situation. If you got hurt, you would get paid. Eddie was very understandable. I played for Grumman Aircraft after graduation from LIU in 1941–1942 and then went into the service in 1943 and came out in 1946 after the war.[21]

Schectman joined the SPHAS for the 1941–1942 season and played in twenty games. Since Wilmington had won both halves, they were declared league champions, and the SPHAS did not make the playoffs. Schectman would have to wait for his playoff debut, but he led the team in scoring in two games that season and became an important contributor to the squad. The following year, Schectman joined the service and was limited to three games all season. He made the most of his playing time, tallying 18 points in the three games. In 1943–1944, Schectman saw more action. Playing in nineteen regular-season games, he led the team in scoring in six of the team's twelve second-half contests. His offense allowed the SPHAS to make a late-season push and face the Wilmington Bombers in the championship series.

Wilmington joined the ABL for the 1941–1942 season and quickly established itself as one the top teams. The Bombers raced out to an early lead that season and cruised to a 10–3 first-half mark. The second half was no different, as they again posted the league's best record. Because they won both halves, they were declared league champions and no playoffs occurred that year for the first and only time in league history. As the Wilmington Blue Bombers official program noted, "Barney [Sedran] guided the Blue Bombers—the name given the Wilmington team—to a clean sweep of both halves of the circuit. This shattered the dynasty of the Philadelphia SPHAS, rulers of the Eastern and American Leagues for so long that the celebrated hirelings of Ed Gottlieb had come to be regarded as the invincible monarchs of all they surveyed in the basketball world."[22]

War-related issues prevented Wilmington from competing in league play in 1942–1943. After a season spent on the sidelines, the Bombers were eager to rejoin the league, and when they did, it hardly seemed as if they had been away. The Bombers jumped out early and coasted to a 12–4 first-half record. Assured of a spot in the championship series, Wilmington eased up in the second half and finished with an average 5–5 record.

Meeting the Bombers in the finals were the rival SPHAS. In the short time Wilmington had been in the league, their battles with the SPHAS were known for their intensity, physical nature, and high quality of play. Even Ossie Schectman got into the act. "One incident I remember as a player occurred in Wilmington, Delaware. It was quite a rivalry between the SPHAS and Wilmington, although I didn't know what created it. It was a Sunday afternoon in the Armory, and there was a skirmish on the court. The closest guys were wrestling with each other, and I stepped in to separate them. Some fan came out of the stands and punched me in the jaw. I had an impacted wisdom tooth and was taken to the hospital."[23]

The Bombers and SPHAS split their eight regular-season games, and the series figured to be a tightly contested affair. Both teams also sought to retain their titles. Wilmington had won the crown in 1941–1942, but sat out a year before rejoining the league. The SPHAS, without Wilmington to challenge them, had defeated Trenton in seven games to win the 1942–1943 title. Prior to the start of the series, Wilmington bolstered its roster by adding Jake Ahearn, Ed Sadowski, and Jerry Bush. Gottlieb, meanwhile, filled his starting lineup with three former New York college stars in Jack Garfinkel, Ossie Schectman, and Irv Torgoff.

Game 1 opened in Philadelphia, and the Bombers outclassed the SPHAS, easily winning, 44–31. The following night, the series shifted to the State Armory in Wilmington, and the SPHAS evened the series with a well-earned 42–35 win. The SPHAS had jumped out to an early lead on a long field goal by Ossie Schectman and led 9–8 at the end of the first period. They held a small lead throughout, and each time the Bombers made a run, the SPHAS had an answer. The SPHAS kept the Bombers at bay, and midway through the third period, Jerry Fleishman "broke loose with three straight field goals to practically end the Bombers' chances for victory."[24]

Over the course of the next two games, the SPHAS found their groove and were on the verge of winning another championship. In the third game, Schectman quickly had the SPHAS off and running. He opened with a layup, then a one-handed shot, and followed that with a set shot from mid-court to give the SPHAS a 6–0 lead. The Bombers battled back, but the SPHAS kept their advantage and pulled out a 50–44 win. The Bombers were playing without two regulars in Angelo Musi and Ben Kramer, while the SPHAS had nine players, and their fresh legs and regular substitutions wore down Wilmington. The winning ways continued for the SPHAS, who triumphed in Game 4, 56–51, in a similar fashion. Schectman led all scorers with 17 points, as the SPHAS pulled ahead in the third period by outscoring the Bombers, 21–15.

As quickly as the SPHAS won two games in a row, the Bombers discovered their rhythm and won two consecutive games to tie the series. Twice facing elimination, the Bombers played with a balanced attack from beginning to end. In the fifth game, the Bombers won, 45–38, and in the sixth game, they absolutely crushed the SPHAS, winning easily, 57–36. The game was no contest and after two wins, momentum had shifted. The SPHAS were reeling.

From the moment that Wilmington joined the league, the Bombers seemed to have the SPHAS' number. Bernie Fliegel periodically played for the SPHAS during the team's annual trip to the Midwest between Christmas and New Year's. Fliegel recalled:

> Eddie liked the way I played. The SPHAS never had good rebounders, not enough strong guys. Between Christmas and New Year's, the SPHAS would travel to the Midwest and play games, and Eddie always needed an extra big man. Moe Goldman was not a good rebounder. He did not have the strength. Gottlieb liked my rebounding and my scoring and team play, and he would always want me to play when available and they were not playing league games. Eddie always wanted me to play, so I did. Eddie was always fair. If you played for Eddie, you knew you would be paid that night.[25]

Hired on occasion to bolster the SPHAS' front line, Fliegel was an original Wilmington Bomber in 1941–1942, but by the championship series in 1943–1944, his service commitment prevented him from participating. His early years with the Bombers provide insight into the strategies used to defeat the SPHAS and into how Wilmington became a power.

Born on May 13, 1918, in New York City at Twentieth Street and First Avenue, Fliegel grew up with his family—his father was Lithuanian, and his mother was from Odessa, Russia—on the East Side of Manhattan. His father was a kosher butcher and had his own shop on 28th Street. Basketball was not an activity to which Fliegel gravitated immediately. Only when his father became ill and retired to the Bronx did Fliegel find basketball in junior high school. "I did not play basketball in Manhattan when I was growing up. My family moved to the Bronx when I was 12 years old. We lived at 208th Street and Bainbridge Avenue. I was first introduced to basketball when I was in Crescent Junior High School and then at Clinton High School. I was taller than most, and it was rare for a Jewish player to be over 6' tall. We had a schoolyard, and I always played against older guys."[26]

As he played, he became better, and the game came more naturally to him. He was seeing improvement regularly. "I learned to play in the schoolyards. I was smart enough to use the feint move. I would practice basketball in the schoolyards. I was like a standing guard. I was a defensive player. I never went past half court. I learned to defend two or three guys."[27]

His defensive ability, one that would later help him as a professional, proved crucial during his high school career. As a sophomore and junior, he played on the junior varsity and was elevated to the varsity level as a senior. "In 1933–1934, we won the city championship by defeating Thomas Jefferson in Brooklyn. I made one foul shot. It was a surprise victory."[28] His defense was pivotal in the win, and he was named to the All-City third team.

> When I was growing up in the Bronx, I did not know about professional basketball. The kids in Brooklyn knew about professional basketball because the American Basketball League had two teams, the Jewels and the Visitations. Moe Goldman, who was from Brooklyn and played at CCNY, later played for the SPHAS. He graduated CCNY in June 1934, and I started in September 1934.[29]

Fliegel joined the varsity as a sophomore in 1935–1936 and led CCNY to a 10–4 record. The following season, he made significant progress as an offensive player, as he scored 119 points, even though the Beavers finished with a disappointing 10–6 record. As a senior, he was regarded by peers and the media as the city's best player. He led the Beavers to a 13–3 record and scored 205 points. For his efforts, he was named first-team All-Metropolitan, was the recipient of the Frank Haggerty Award as the best player in New York, and was voted as the outstanding player in Madison Square Garden.

After his college career ended, Fliegel made the decision to continue playing on the professional level.

> The American Basketball League was the only league around. It was a tough and rough league. The Brooklyn Visitations was a tough bunch. The women would throw beer and trip us with their umbrellas. It was tough. I was the first big guy to play under the basket.
>
> In March 1938, I was 19 years old, and I finished college, and I went to play for the Kate Smith Celtics. She bought the Original

> Celtics, and Ted Collins, the manager and promoter, asked me to come to his office. He wanted me to play.
>
> "We will be the first team to score 100 points," Collins told me.
>
> "Ted, how do you expect us to do that?" I asked.
>
> "You could score 25 points, Jerry Bush could score 25 points, and two other players could score 25 points. Between you and them, we will score 100 points," Collins countered.
>
> "Do you realize that when I played and scored 25 points, I was the only guy in my team shooting? With one ball, we cannot do that," I answered.
>
> I realized that Collins could not be persuaded. But Collins went for shooters, and he was ahead of his time. Eventually, teams scored 100 points in a game.[30]

Fliegel was intrigued by Collins and his vision and soon signed a contract:

> I was with the Kate Smith Celtics, Kingston/Troy Celtics beginning in 1938–1939 and went to Wilmington in 1941–1942. I always played for Barney Sedran. After the service, I was married, a practicing lawyer and had one kid. I coached and played two years with the Jersey City Atoms.
>
> In 1940–1941, we were kicked out of the armories because the U.S. Army needed it for the war effort. We had no place to play. We were playing in the Broadway Arena. Out of the blue, Barney Sedran called and said that the franchise was going to transfer to Wilmington. The team was owned by the DuPont family, and there was no problem in getting us into the armory down there. The governor and the Army had granted permission.
>
> So, we went to Wilmington. Sedran was the coach and owner. I was the captain and Sammy Kaplan came because he always played with Sedran and me. At our first game there, everyone welcomed us. It was a tremendous crowd. This was in 1941–1942.[31]

When the Wilmington franchise began its first season, the SPHAS were the two-time defending champions. They were the class of the league. As Bernie recalled, "The SPHAS were a smart team. They had good shooters who passed the ball well, did give and goes, and were good underneath the boards. Gotthoffer was a bull. They were a great team and one of the best teams in the ABL for many years. After I went to Wilmington, we got

Jerry Bush and Ed Sadowski and beat the SPHAS nine out of ten times one year."[32]

Fliegel's memory of Wilmington's dominance was mostly correct, but in that 1941–1942 campaign, the Bombers defeated the SPHAS seven out of eight times. The SPHAS lost their first seven tries to the Bombers and won the final regular season game only by scoring 25 points in the last period. As a Wilmington Bombers program noted, "In sweeping to the crown in straight heats, Wilmington made the Sphas their chief victims. Seven straight times the Blue Bombers met the Sphas and on as many occasions humbled them in decisive fashion. It was not until the last meeting of the year that the Sphas were finally able to beat their new foes."[33]

The key to beating the SPHAS was having a strong front line that could continually pound the ball inside and wear them down. Fliegel remembers how the Bombers achieved their goal:

> The Detroit team had won the World Professional Basketball Tournament the previous spring, and we were able to sign a few of their players. We signed Jerry Bush, who was 6'3", and Ed Sadowski, who was 6'5" or 6'6". For the first time, I did not have to play center. We had a great team because of our height. The SPHAS at that time always had two or three big guys in Mike Bloom, Irv Torgoff, and Moe Goldman. In our first game against the SPHAS, Bloom outplayed Sadowski. We won, but Sadowski played poorly. Afterward, I said, "Ed, we got you because you are a big, strong guy. You let Bloom push you around." He was steamed. The next time we played the SPHAS, he just killed Bloom. We beat everybody that year. We won both the first and second halves of the regular season, so we won the championship.[34]

The key to the Bombers' success was simple. They had one play and dared the other team to defend against it:

> On our team, we had one standard play. Chick Reiser would block for Charlie Hoefer, who would shoot it. Three of us would get under the boards and bat the ball back and forth. He would shoot, and we had three big guys who would bat the ball around if he missed, and finally one of us would tip it in. That was our sure point play. It was a great year. Years later, the *New York Times* ran an article that said we were the best professional basketball team prior to the Los Angeles Lakers with Wilt Chamberlain and Elgin Baylor.[35]

With the seventh and deciding game for the 1943–1944 championship to be played in Wilmington, the Bombers looked poised to complete a comeback down 1–3. Only once before, when the SPHAS defeated the Jersey Reds in 1936–1937, had a team fought back from a 3–1 deficit. The Bombers made sure this was accomplished a second time. Riding the momentum from the night before, the Bombers picked up where they left off. Wilmington edged out to a 12–8 lead after the first period and then increased their margin to 27–22 entering the final period. From then on, the game was no contest, as the Bombers outscored the SPHAS 30–11. "In the last five minutes the Bombers really 'poured it on' as they passed and shot rings around the defending champions who were clearly outplayed most of the way," the *Wilmington Morning News* wrote the following day.[36] Leading the way for Wilmington was team captain Moe Frankel, who scored 17 points and "sent up shots from far and near, stole a pass and dribbled in for a lay-up, dropped a couple from the side court, and on several occasions sank long open ones from the center of the court."[37] A chance to have won a second title in a row, fourth in five years, and seventh in eleven seasons fell agonizingly short for the SPHAS.

Joining Dutch Garfinkel on the 1943–1944 SPHAS was former NYU star Jerry Fleishman. By 1943, Fleishman was enlisted in the U.S. Army and stationed in Fort Jackson, South Carolina. Gottlieb was always on the lookout for players who could help his team regardless of how many games they could contribute due to their wartime commitments. As Fleishman remembered, "Eddie Gottlieb lured me to the SPHAS after seeing me play against Penn State University. He saw my ability. He would fly me in on the weekends to play ball."[38]

Jerry Fleishman joined the Philadelphia SPHAS during World War II. Later he played for the Philadelphia Warriors when they won the 1946–1947 Basketball Association of America championship. (*Courtesy of Bill Himmelman.*)

With Fleishman on board, Gottlieb now had a roster of individuals to call on for games. All told, nineteen players suited up for Gottlieb that season. Fleishman played in only seven regular-season games for the SPHAS, but was available for four games during the championship series against the Wilmington Bombers. In those four games, he averaged 7 points and proved to be a nice complement off the bench.

Born on February 14, 1922, Jerry Fleishman grew up with his parents and sister in Brooklyn. His family was poor and did not have the money to provide clothes and food for him and his sister, much less for any extra spending. Instead, he learned to improvise. "When we were growing up, we were poor kids. We did not have basketballs. We rolled up newspapers and tied it together with a cord. There were fire escapes on the building, and the lower rung had a hole there, and we threw it through the lower rung. If it went through, it was either a basket or a touchdown. That was our football and basketball."[39]

His parents, immigrants from Europe, worked every day, seven days a week. They struggled to provide for their family. "My parents were from Europe and they did not think basketball was something to look forward to. They said, 'Jerry, don't get hurt.' It was safer than football, though."[40] Despite his parents' objections, Jerry continued playing basketball, and during junior high school, his family moved to a nicer section of Brooklyn. Despite the better circumstances, it was still difficult for his parents. "My folks moved to Florida but I stayed in Brooklyn with my sister."[41]

Fleishman entered Erasmus High School and quickly joined the basketball team.

> I went to Erasmus High School. The coach was Al Badain. One day, I walked into the gym, and there were 20 basketballs, and everybody was shooting. It was free shooting. So, I started to shoot, and the coach says, "Let's start a game." We start the game, and someone passes me the ball, and I run with it like it is a newspaper under my arm. The coach stops and says, "You need to dribble." I said, "What is a dribble?" Coach Badain taught me everything I know about basketball and how to act socially. He was my mentor. He was a wonderful man.[42]

Despite his inauspicious beginnings, Fleishman quickly caught on and soon became adept. He enjoyed a fine high school career and became an integral member of the team:

> At Erasmus, we played against Madison High School in Madison Square Garden. They were coached by Jammy Moskowitz. They had won thirty-six games in a row over two years. There were five high school games on a Saturday afternoon. We were the underdogs. We played well, and towards the end of the game, they put in a basket to win. Afterwards, we came into the locker room, and Coach was laughing and thanked us for playing so hard. He said the next time we play them, we will win. And the next time we played them, we beat them. I had 17 points.[43]

While in high school, Fleishman learned of the SPHAS, a team he was one day destined to join. "It was at Erasmus High School that I first heard of the SPHAS. Irv Torgoff and Dutch Garfinkel would work out against us in the alumni scrimmage. They were our heroes. They were only five years older than we were."[44] Years later, all three would be teammates with the SPHAS.

His exploits soon caught the attention of the local basketball writers, who saw fit to reward his efforts with end-of-the-year accolades. "I was the first ballplayer to make all-city first team in New York City in all the newspapers two times in a row. At the time, the city had eight newspapers."[45]

With the praise and recognition from the local newspapers, Fleishman was bound for college, where he embarked on a great college career. "I went to college at New York University. NYU in those years was like playing for the New York Yankees. I got a full scholarship, which was rare in those days. Usually, you got one year, and if you played well, then you got another. I told them I would not come without a full scholarship. As a freshman, I broke all the records. On the varsity, I broke all the records. In one game at Madison Square Garden, I made ten field goals (nine in a row), which broke the record at Madison Square Garden."[46]

Fleishman joined the SPHAS in 1943–1944 on a limited basis. Due to his service commitment, he played only on weekends and Gottlieb paid for him to travel to play for the SPHAS. "We would play in Philadelphia on a Friday night, and there would be a game and a dance. We would stay over, and on Saturday afternoon, we would play at Wilmington, Delaware, and on Saturday evening, we would play against the Trenton Tigers. I got $100 a game and that would be $300 cash for the weekend. However, if there were not that many spectators, you would have to take a cut or would not be asked back the next time."[47]

When he was not in the service, Fleishman was based in New York and would travel by train to play in Philadelphia. "All the players would meet

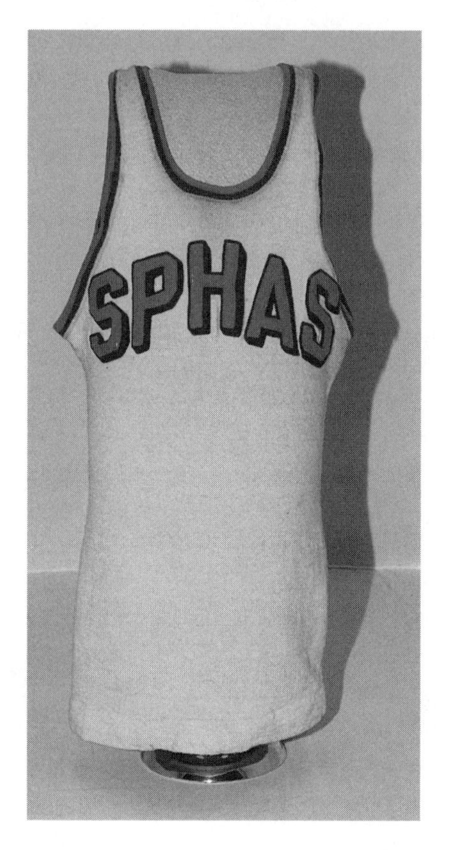

Displayed here is a jersey worn by Jerry Fleishman in the 1940s. (*Courtesy of Naismith Memorial Basketball Hall of Fame.*)

every Saturday night on Track 16 at Pennsylvania Station. You would not need to remind anyone. We would get on the train and play cards until we got to Philadelphia. One time, we are on a train and going to Hartford, Connecticut, and we could not get off. So, finally we get off [in Hartford] and we take a cab from Hartford to Philadelphia. Well, Eddie wasn't too happy but all the people waited around for the dancing at 11:00 P.M."[48]

During the 1944–1945 season, Fleishman would play in even fewer games (two) than he did in the previous season (seven). As Fleishman scanned the box scores each Monday morning, he recognized his fellow New Yorkers. "The SPHAS were the best team in the world. We were better than the Harlem Globetrotters. There was a feeling between each one of us. Lots of the SPHAS players stood together. We played the toughest teams in the towns we went into, and we usually won. We were the same type of fellows, and we played well together. The New York players made the SPHAS the best team in the world."[49]

The 1944–1945 season started with high hopes for the league. Joining the SPHAS were the Wilmington Bombers, Trenton Tigers, New York Westchesters, and two new teams: the Washington Capitols, who became the Paterson Crescents, and the Baltimore Bullets, who would quickly climb to the league's top tier. For the first time since 1942–1943, the ABL decided not to play the season in two halves. Rather, it would be one season, and the top four teams would earn a postseason berth.

The big difference for the SPHAS heading into this season was in the composition of the team. During the 1930s, the SPHAS had Philadelphia and New York players. Gil Fitch, Petey Rosenberg, Red Rosan, Harry Litwack, Inky Lautman, Mike Bloom, and Cy Kaselman were all from Philadelphia or nearby New Jersey. Only Shikey Gotthoffer, Red Wolfe, and Moe Goldman represented the New York contingent that traveled down on Saturdays for the games. The team had a decidedly Philadelphia flavor and was generally regarded as a team representing the city. As the 1940s began, Gottlieb increasingly looked to New York to add players. In 1940–1941, Irv Torgoff joined the team. The following season, 1941–1942, saw the additions of Ossie Schectman, Butch Schwartz, and Irv Davis. Torgoff, Schectman, Schwartz, and Davis were all part of the team for the 1942–1943 campaign. Dutch Garfinkel, Jerry Fleishman, and Art Hillhouse all came aboard in 1943–1944. With the 1944–1945 season set to begin, seven of the top nine players in terms of games played were New Yorkers. Hillhouse, Schectman, Torgoff, Garfinkel, Irv Rothenberg, and Len and Howie Rader all hailed from the New York metropolitan area. Rounding out the top nine were Bernie Opper, a New Yorker who played at the University of Kentucky, and Inky Lautman, who had been with the team since its first season in the league. With many key roster spots now featuring New Yorkers, the SPHAS set their sights on avenging their championship series loss the previous season.

The season opened with a home-and-home rematch of the previous season's championship series against Wilmington. In the first game, played in Philadelphia, the SPHAS got a modicum of revenge by defeating the Bombers, 64–62, in two overtimes. Dutch Garfinkel led the way with 17 points, and solid foul shooting down the stretch helped the SPHAS start the season off with a win, the first time they had done so in two years. The following night in Wilmington, the Bombers jumped in the win column with a 45–35 victory.

The loss did not bother the SPHAS, as they started a three-game winning streak and continued to play well as the new year began. A defeat at Trenton on January 14, 1945, left the SPHAS with an 8–6 mark, enough to keep pace with the rest of the league. From that point forward, the SPHAS gelled as a team, compiling a gaudy 14–2 record to finish the season with a 22–8 mark and a one-game lead over Trenton. An eight-game win streak eventually ended at Trenton with a 51–32 loss, their worst defeat all season. The setback was just a bump in the road, as they quickly jumped back in the win column and closed the season by winning six of seven.

The New York group, particularly Art Hillhouse, Irv Rothenberg, and Irv Torgoff, led the SPHAS all season. During the season, both Hillhouse and Rothenberg played in twenty-nine regular-season games, and Hillhouse averaged more than 7 points per game. Torgoff, meanwhile, saw action in twenty-one games and contributed more than 6 points per game.

Waiting for them in the first round of the playoffs was their nemesis Wilmington. After winning the title the previous season, the Bombers had fallen back to the rest of the pack with a 14–14 record, good for third place. The SPHAS had won the regular season matchup four games to two, including their previous three encounters. Given the short but intense history of this rivalry, the best-of-three series figured to be a tightly contested affair.

The first game was close at the outset, and a pair of baskets by George Glamack and Ben Goldfaden broke a 4–4 tie, giving the Bombers an early 8–4 lead. The SPHAS battled back and claimed a 15–12 lead after the first period. In the second period, the SPHAS increased their advantage and held a 7-point margin heading into the final session. The SPHAS would need that cushion as Wilmington outscored them in the period, making a valiant push at the end. Accurate shooting, especially from the foul line, where the SPHAS held an 11–6 advantage, proved the difference as each club tallied nineteen field goals. Jerry Fleishman and Art Hillhouse combined for 22 points, and their strong second period gave the SPHAS the lead for good.

The second game eerily resembled the previous year's championship series when the SPHAS, one game from closing out the series, ran into a buzzsaw and were easily dispatched. The Bombers came out firing on all cylinders and never looked back. A 13–9 first-period lead swelled in the second period to 18 points, as the SPHAS could score only 4 points. The final period was anticlimactic, as Wilmington won going away, 48–29.

A third and deciding game played in Philadelphia would provide an advantage the SPHAS sorely needed. Balanced scoring, including 11 points from Lautman and 10 each by Hillhouse and Torgoff, proved enough as the SPHAS held off a feisty Bombers squad. The 48–41 victory propelled the SPHAS into the championship round versus the Baltimore Bullets, surprise winners over second-place Trenton in their first-round series.

Newcomers to the league, the Baltimore Bullets had finished in fourth place with a 14–16 record, but surprised Trenton in the first round. The SPHAS held a 5–1 regular-season advantage over the Bullets, and that dominance continued into the first game. The Bullets were overmatched from the opening tipoff as "the Sphas rolled up 15 straight points while holding the locals scoreless in the first eight minutes of play and from there on it was no contest."[50] The Bullets never got closer than 11 points as the SPHAS won handily, 57–32.

As it was already the first week of April by this time, the league decided that the championship round would be reduced from five games to a best-of-three. The final two games were scheduled to be played in Philadelphia, where the SPHAS looked to close out the series. Game 2 started off like the first, as the SPHAS held a 22–9 advantage midway through the second period. Then the Bullets caught fire, and paced by Moe Dubilier, Stan Stutz, and Art Spector, crept back into the game, holding a 2-point margin after two periods. In the final period, the Bullets extended their lead and withheld a late rally to eke out a 47–46 win.

The SPHAS found themselves in a winner-take-all game for the league championship for the second consecutive season. The year before, the SPHAS had been unable to stop the momentum that Wilmington had after tying the series with two decisive wins. Now, another championship was on the line. This time, it was not a veteran opponent, but instead a young, upstart group who planned on being a top team for years to come.

Since the ABL had begun play in 1933–1934, the SPHAS had been the class of the league. Up until this point, they had won six championships. The SPHAS had been the one constant since the league started in 1933–1934 and had defeated all comers along the way. All teams that sought to chip away at the SPHAS' mantle found their efforts thwarted at every turn. The SPHAS had won championship series against the Trenton Moose, Brooklyn Visitations, Jersey Reds, Brooklyn Celtics, and Trenton Tigers, and had bested the entire league in the 1939–1940 round-robin championship tournament. The Baltimore Bullets, in only their first season, had made it to the final game of the championship series. The Bullets wanted to be the next SPHAS. The Bullets would be the next challenge.

The game began, and it appeared that the SPHAS would be in for another hard defeat, as the Bullets staked themselves to an early 10–2 lead. Experience settled in, and the SPHAS slowly clawed their way back into the game. As the first period came to a close, the SPHAS held a 15–11 advantage, one they would not relinquish. Gottlieb played seven players: Lautman, Opper, Garfinkel, Hillhouse, Schectman, Torgoff, and Rothenberg. In the second frame, the SPHAS extended their lead to 33–19, and in the final period withstood a late rally to claim a 46–40 victory. The game was not as close as the score indicated. The SPHAS had captured their seventh championship in twelve years. It would be their last one.

12

LOSING HOME COURT

> At that point, I realized what it was, and I said to myself that the war is over and I am still alive. Thank God.
>
> —Captain Ralph Kaplowitz,
> interview by the author

On August 15, 1945, Philadelphians awoke and grabbed a copy of the *Philadelphia Inquirer*. The banner headline in six-inch capital letters read "PEACE." For the first time since Pearl Harbor, the United States was no longer at war. President Harry Truman, in office less than five months, dropped two atomic bombs on Japan on August 6 and 9, 1945. World War II had finally ended. Philadelphia, like most American cities, went wild with jubilation. City Hall was a mob scene of joy, relief, and utter happiness. Confetti flew, horns were heard everywhere, and people danced in the streets. Rationing was over. Meat, canned goods, and gas soon reappeared. With victory declared, soldiers were eager to return home and resume their careers.

One soldier more than ready to return to the basketball court was Ralph Kaplowitz. Five years of enlistment and conflict in the Pacific theater had left Kaplowitz with a desire to resume his once-promising basketball career, which had been cut short just prior to his senior year of college. Tired of war and with an infant daughter and young wife at home, Kaplowitz longed to get on with his life.

As a child growing up on New York's East Side, Kaplowitz expressed little interest in playing basketball. His older brother, Danny, who later became a star at LIU under head coach Clair Bee, always needed an extra player to even out the teams with the neighborhood kids, so he brought

Ralph Kaplowitz, a standout at New York University, joined the Philadelphia SPHAS for the second half of the 1945–1946 season and helped lead the team to the finals against the Baltimore Bullets. (*From the New York University Archives, Photographic Collection.*)

along his younger brother. "He wanted someone to keep him company. He forced me to go with him to the schoolyard," Kaplowitz remembered decades later. "I did not want to play. I did not want to do anything. He stuck his finger in my ear and dragged me to the schoolyard and forced me to play with him."[1]

Soon enough, though, he found basketball to his liking and no longer needed Danny to encourage him. Kaplowitz played at the Young Men's Hebrew Association (YMHA) on Fordham Road in the Bronx after school and on the weekends. It was three-on-three games mostly, and then five-on-five, and the winning team played until it lost.

Kaplowitz played all day long. "The game of basketball was about friendships in the schoolyards. It was more social than anything," Kaplowitz reminisced decades later. "It was a bunch of kids playing a game." After winning the Public School Athletic League (PSAL) championship with Creston Junior High School, Kaplowitz enrolled at DeWitt Clinton High School and made the team on which his brother starred. "Because of my brother, the coach of the team was willing to look at me. I made the team at DeWitt Clinton, and we had a pretty nice team."[2]

In high school, he "developed his great set-shot, which very seldom missed its target," and grew as a team player.[3] By his senior year, he was an integral member of the team that won the Bronx PSAL championship and advanced to the city championship against Seward Park High School, whose center, Butch Schwartz, was later Kaplowitz's teammate with the SPHAS. In attendance that night was NYU coach Howard Cann, who offered Kaplowitz a scholarship to play for the Violets. Cann viewed Kaplowitz, at 6'2" and 175 pounds, as the next great guard for his squad, one who would eventually replace team captain Bobby Lewis.

As "one of the most promising prospects to enter New York University," Kaplowitz joined the freshman squad in 1938–1939.[4] He quickly became the "sparkplug of his freshman team," scoring 86 points before hurting his knee, as the team finished with an impressive 14–3 record.[5] On the varsity the following year, "the lone sophomore to break into the regular lineup was lanky Ralph Kaplowitz, who promises to be one of the finest basketball players in the Metropolitan area before he graduates."[6] Kaplowitz scored 183 points, second on the team, as the Violets won their first eighteen contests before losing the finale against local rival CCNY. His efforts earned him second-team All-Metropolitan honors alongside future SPHAS teammates Ossie Schectman of LIU and Jack Garfinkel of St. John's. NYU, citing academic reasons, declined an invitation to participate in the third annual NIT championship, depriving Cann's squad of any postseason play.

The next year, his junior season, proved to be his last as a collegian. He made the most of it. "Bobby Lewis, who was an excellent ballplayer the previous season, graduated, and so did some of the other players. So I was left as the fulcrum of the new NYU team,"[7] Kaplowitz remembered. With the offense directed through him, Kaplowitz blossomed, leading the Violets with 193 total points and earning first-team All-Metropolitan honors. The team took a step back, finishing with a 13–6 record. The Violets had opened with eight straight wins, but staggered down the stretch, losing six of their last eleven games. This year a postseason invitation was not forthcoming.

In August 1941, weeks before the start of another academic year and a few months prior to the start of his senior season, Kaplowitz was drafted by the Army Air Corps, a forerunner to the Air Force. Cann knew immediately that his team would struggle without "the services of its best playmaker, highest scorer and most experienced floorman."[8] "We haven't got much. We lost a good man in Ralph Kaplowitz, and we'll be lucky to win half of our major games," Cann noted with a sense of resignation.[9] He exaggerated slightly, however, as the team did post a 12–7 record, only one game worse than the previous year.

Now that his college career was behind him, Kaplowitz embarked on an odyssey that started in the States and eventually led him to the front lines in the battle against Japan. After passing his cadet examination, Kaplowitz enrolled in Air Mechanics School in Illinois. "I was in Chicago on a weekend when the announcement on the radio said that we were attacked at Pearl Harbor. Therefore, all the soldiers—I was a private at the time—had to report back to the barracks. I went back to the barracks, and I found out more about Pearl Harbor. Meanwhile, we went about our normal duties."[10]

At the time, Kaplowitz was stationed at Chanute Field in Illinois. He kept in shape by playing basketball games against other military bases, whose teams were stocked with former college All-Americans. "We had a game with Chanute Field against Scott Field, another team in the Air Corps. The fellows said to me, 'Before you go, we are making you the captain of the team.' I scored 37 points and I did not miss a shot. That was my going-away present. Then, I got on the train and went to Kelly Field, Texas, where I had six weeks of preliminary training."[11]

After those six weeks, Kaplowitz went to Fort Worth for primary flying school.

> This was three months primary, three months basic, and three months advanced. In flying school primary, you had light airplanes where you learned to fly. So we flew in the morning. In the after-

> noon, we went to classes. In the second half, we flew in the afternoon and went to classes in the morning.
>
> I used to get airsick in the airplane, so the instructor would bank the airplane to one side for me to heave. Fortunately, he was in the front and I was in the back, so when I threw up in the back, it went elsewhere and not to him. After we finished, I would be all right for a while. We would do some maneuvers. My instructor realized I was a good learner, and I was a good pilot so he did not report me. He said that if you threw up, they washed you out. But he did not say anything. Ultimately, I got used to it, and I did not throw up anymore.[12]

Kaplowitz was someone who loved to take chances. It was part of his personality. At times, he would fly low to the ground, knowing that if he was caught, the Army Air Corps would throw him out. His luck ran out one day, and he was caught. Kaplowitz landed his plane and was sent back to the barracks and told to pack his bags and catch the first train out of town. While gathering his belongings, Kaplowitz received a call from his instructor. "Kaplowitz, you stupid fool, get your ass down here."[13]

Kaplowitz's meeting with his instructor was tense. The instructor wanted Kaplowitz to provide him with a good enough reason why he should not expel him and send him home. After some discussion and back and forth, it was agreed that he was required to take a flight test with a lieutenant. The goal was simple: if he passed, then he could stay, but if he failed, then his dream of being a pilot would be over.

The following day, Kaplowitz went up with the lieutenant. He performed all the maneuvers and felt he did well:

> When we landed, I went up to the front of the wing, and he was still in the cockpit. I could see that he had a big F on the charts. I had failed.
>
> "Maybe it is not your fault. Maybe your instructor was not so good," the lieutenant declared.
>
> "Lieutenant, I cannot blame my instructor. If I am not good enough, then wash me out, and I will thank you for saving my life, because I think I am pretty good. If you do not think so, then I do not want to be any part of flying."
>
> "We will see what we can do."
>
> The instructor approached later that day and said, "We decided to give you another chance."

"If I am not a good pilot, I do not want to be here."
"We will see. We will manage."[14]

Getting a second chance, Kaplowitz behaved himself for the rest of the term. He was a model soldier, obeying all orders and passing all his flight tests.

He made it to graduation. At the graduation party several months later, the dispatcher approached him and said, "Kaplowitz, you are a good pilot. You could fly anything the Air Corps could give you. We pulled a shitty on you and made you worry. But do not worry anymore. You can fly, and if you pay attention, you will not have any problems."[15]

Kaplowitz was relieved to have graduated, and he went on to the next phase, which was flying BT-13s. "I finished and did well and graduated. Then I went to advanced flying school. At advanced, you had fast airplanes called AT-6s. It was a small fighter plane. So, I did well there, and I graduated and got my wings on August 5, 1942."[16]

Next stop: Savannah, Georgia. Prior to the start of classes on how to fly a British dive-bomber, Ralph had thirty days off, so he proposed to his girlfriend, Norma. A judge married the couple on August 29, 1942.

During his training in Savannah, Kaplowitz became friendly with a Jewish family off base named Rosensweig. They invited Jewish soldiers every Friday night to celebrate the Sabbath. Kaplowitz attended every so often, and in the course of conversation, he mentioned that a judge had recently married him and his wife.

"Ralph, if you have children, they won't be considered Jewish unless you are married by a rabbi," Mrs. Rosensweig declared one night at dinner. "I will take care of it."[17] In October, Ralph and Norma were married a second time, under a chuppah by a Rabbi and with the other Jewish soldiers as witnesses.

Over the next several months, Kaplowitz trained extensively throughout the Southeast. He made stops in Waycross, Georgia, Tampa and Lakeland, Florida, and finally Dalhart, Texas. He gained great experience on a number of planes, including A-36s, B-39s, B-61s, and P-47s. His final stop was Galveston, where he was promoted to captain since he was a flight leader. Kaplowitz's wife, Norma, and young daughter headed home to New York while he prepared to go overseas.

Kaplowitz, now a captain, was finally heading to the Pacific Theater. His first mission, a fighter sweep, was a two-hour flight to Kyushu, the southernmost island of Japan. While flying in formation, somebody radioed "Bogeys," indicating that Japanese fighters were nearby. All the other planes dropped their wing tanks, indicating their intent to fire, except Kaplowitz, who was not quite sure that the planes were Japanese. As the planes came closer, it was learned that they were American. Kaplowitz was the only one who had his wing tanks. The Americans flew for several hours without any incidents, and he dropped the bombs on the island before returning to base. His first mission completed. Kaplowitz would have twelve more missions before the war ended.

Like others who experienced firsthand combat, Kaplowitz had his share of close calls. One day, he was leading a flight of eight planes to Shanghai, when he realized that his guns did not work.

> On the way there, I tested my guns, and they would not fire. They were jammed for some reason. I did not want to report it, because you had to wait several days to go on another flight. After a few hours of flying, I did not want to have to abort and go back. So I stayed without the guns. We got to Shanghai, and I saw three Japanese destroyers tied up at the docks. I called out that I am going after them, so I started dive-bombing. I got to where I felt it was the right moment, and I dropped my two 500-pound bombs. I shot the middle destroyer and it blew up in flames. I got out of there. Nobody fired at me. I reported it. Ultimately, the other flights concurred that a ship was sunk, so I received credit for sinking the Japanese destroyer. They gave me a medal. I already had two air medals. Now, they gave me a third.[18]

The other close call happened when Kaplowitz and his flight were passing by a heavily fortified island, the name of which escapes him more than sixty years after the fact.

> This island was well-fortified with coastal guns, which we did not know about. On the way back from every mission, my commanding officer would come by and strafe the island. I had just come back from a mission to try and locate a missing pilot. I received word to go back and try to dive-bomb the coastal guns on the corner of this island. My commanding officer was shot down between this island and the next island. He was stranded on a buoy that was in the middle of the water.
>
> Meanwhile, those guns were shooting down seventeen American pilots who were trying to rescue this major. Unbeknownst to me, I am now going to the area that I was told from 12,000 feet, to drop

> the bombs at 4,500 feet. I go into my dive at 12,000 feet and my guys are going to follow me. All of a sudden, the bullets are flying by my cockpit. I look up, and I do not see anybody there. I realize that fire is coming from down below. There is a wall of fire, and I cannot get out. I cannot pull out. I am thinking that I will go the other way. By this time, I am now 8,500 feet and I can see my altimeter going round and round. My airspeed is 550 miles an hour. There is nothing I can do. I press the button to drop the bombs, and all of the sudden, the firing stopped. I pull out and got out to sea and watch from there. I do not know where my other planes are. When I returned to the base, I heard that the Japanese picked up the major.[19]

On August 6, 1945, Kaplowitz

> was leading a flight of four, escorting a B-24 over the island Kyushu. I was flying back and forth over the island, taking pictures for the eventual invasion of Japan. Meanwhile, at the briefing that morning, they told us to stay away from the west side. As I was flying, I looked over to the west and saw terrific clouds, which I thought must be thunderstorms in the area. When I got back to the base, they said over the loudspeaker that a bomb was just dropped on a Japanese island that was 20,000 times more powerful than anything we had. At that point, I realized what it was and I said to myself that the war is over and I am still alive. Thank God.[20]

In early November 1945, Kaplowitz finally received orders to return home. He first flew overnight to Guam, and from there to Hawaii, piloting the plane while the lieutenant slept. He spent a day in Hawaii before going on to the States. He arrived on November 27 and was feted with parties and gifts on base. Soon, he boarded a train for Mitchell Field, where he was formally discharged. He bought flowers for his wife and daughter as he walked home for good.

Kaplowitz was home for only a short time before his phone started ringing. Eddie Gottlieb, who had a bead on basketball players on the East Coast and seemed to know when they were coming and going, invited him to a SPHAS game. The SPHAS, sporting an average 6–5 mark to start the 1945–1946 campaign, were playing the New York Gothams at the Saint Nicholas Arena in New York City.

Gottlieb sought to stock his roster with military veterans and college graduates who were returning from service. No shortage existed in the number of players seeking to resume their careers. A player like Kaplowitz made perfect sense and Gottlieb wasted no time trying to recruit him.

> "I am ready to play you tonight," Gottlieb said to Kaplowitz on seeing him before the game.
>
> "No, I want to hear what you have to say," Kaplowitz replied.
>
> "I would like you to play for me," Gottlieb said. "I will pay you $150 a week whether you play two games or three games."[21]

Kaplowitz and Gottlieb shook hands, and Kaplowitz joined the SPHAS.

Growing up in New York during the 1930s, Kaplowitz knew well the reputation of the SPHAS. "I had heard about them before I played with them. They were great players like Shikey Gotthoffer, Moe Goldman, and Red Wolfe, all terrific names. All the old-time basketball players knew about them," Kaplowitz recalled.[22] He would now have a chance to revive his basketball career and play for one of the storied teams from his teenage years.

When Kaplowitz joined the SPHAS, the team held a 7–5 record (they had won the night he saw them against the Gothams) and were searching for a winning streak and an identity. Kaplowitz was the answer. The SPHAS won seven of their next eight contests and reasserted themselves as the team to beat. He scored 15 points in his first game as a professional, as the SPHAS crushed the Trenton Tigers 86–61. "I played a half season with the SPHAS. I joined them in December, 1945, and the season ended in April, 1946. I played half a year and did rather well."[23]

Now a member of the team, Kaplowitz asserted himself quickly and apparently had not lost his shooting touch. The team pushed their record to 15–6. Kaplowitz led the team in scoring in two of his first eight games. After their brief burst of energy with Kaplowitz, the SPHAS quickly lost four straight, as their record fell to 15–10. February was nearing an end, and the season's final run was in front of the team. Down the stretch, the SPHAS posted a 6–3 record, finding themselves in a battle with their newest rivals, the Baltimore Bullets.

Waiting for the SPHAS in the championship series were the Baltimore Bullets and former teammate Mike Bloom.

Since losing a tough seven-game series to the SPHAS in 1942–1943 as a member of the Trenton Tigers, Bloom had developed into one of the league's best big men, claiming consecutive MVP awards. He led the league with 273 points in 1943–1944, good for an average of 10.5 points per game. The following season, he tallied 321 points, raising his average to 10.7 points per game. In the process, he had developed into one of the league's most complete centers and a bona fide all-star, according to his peers and coaches.

The 1945–1946 campaign for the Baltimore Bullets started slowly. On January 10, the Bullets sported a pedestrian 8–8 record, a mere two and a half games behind league-leading Philadelphia, who, in winning four straight games, had begun widening their first-place lead. The Bullets, looking to make a move to jumpstart the team and challenge the SPHAS, traded seldom-used Art Spector and cash to Trenton for Mike Bloom. The Bloom acquisition marked the second time that Baltimore had upgraded its personnel via a trade with Trenton, a team whose season was quickly falling apart. Earlier that season, the Bullets had swapped Ben Goldfaden for Ace Abbott. Six years earlier, the Washington Brewers had traded a young Bloom to make room for local star Goldfaden. Now, Bloom was the most in-demand center and was viewed as the key acquisition to push Baltimore over the top.

In acquiring Bloom, the Bullets now had the one player who had singlehandedly tormented them since they joined the league the previous season. Bloom had scored 84 points for Trenton in six victories over Baltimore; in three wins prior to his trade during the 1945–1946 season, he had tallied 34 points. With "sharpshooter string bean"[24] Bloom on their side, Baltimore looked to make a second-half push at front-runner Philadelphia.

Bloom was immediately put to the test as the Bullets faced a home-and-home weekend series with the SPHAS. In the first game at Baltimore, the Bullets waged a third-period comeback with a 32-point scoring outburst, the highwater mark for the season. Bloom "turned in a finished performance for his new owners and for once Bullet fans were able to cheer each time Big Mike swished the cords or battled for possession of the ball on rebounds off the backboard."[25] Bloom tallied 16 points, while Ace Abbott's 3-point play gave the Bullets a 45–41 lead that they would not relinquish.

The following night at the Broadwood Hotel, the SPHAS exacted their revenge, capturing their first win in four tries against the Bullets. Led by Ossie Schectman, Art Hillhouse, and Inky Lautman, the SPHAS earned a split of the weekend series, while Bloom was held to 9 points in the second game. The acquisition of Bloom had proven pivotal for Baltimore, and the two-team race would not be settled until the last day of the regular season.

The SPHAS and Bullets waged a hard-fought battle for the best record over the season's final twenty games. The two teams clashed four more times in the regular season, each winning twice. In the SPHAS' two losses, the balanced scoring of Ace Abbott, Jake Ahearn, Mike Bloom, Stan Stutz, and Hagan Andersen had proven difficult to contain. On February 2, strong interior defense by the Bullets had forced the SPHAS to score from the outside, which they had trouble doing. The Bullets always had an answer for the SPHAS, and their versatility would ultimately prove too much.

First place came down to the regular-season finale on March 13 in Baltimore, as the Bullets sought to continue their dominance over their foes from the Quaker City. In seven regular-season matchups, the SPHAS had two wins, both times in Philadelphia. Their three losses in Baltimore had been by an average of 8 points. A victory by the 21–12 Bullets would ensure them the regular-season title, while a SPHAS (20–13) win would force a one-game playoff.

Their season on the line, the SPHAS were "loaded and primed for their best performance."[26] Led by Ossie Schectman and Jerry Fleishman, who combined for 39 points, the SPHAS claimed an easy 70–46 win and forced a one-game playoff the following Saturday night in Philadelphia. In the first fifteen minutes of play, the SPHAS built leads of 13–3, 21–5, 27–9, and 29–12, and coasted the rest of the way. Baltimore, meanwhile, had their worst shooting night of the season, making only 12 of 63 shots. Mike Bloom (1-for-10), Jake Ahearn (1-for-11), Ace Abbott (0-for-8), and Moe Dubilier (0-for-6) were the main culprits.

The one-game playoff was set. At stake was the top seed in the playoffs. Eddie Gottlieb was no stranger to winner-take-all games, and had "his Philadelphia squad playing brilliant basketball, and more than primed to successfully defend its title."[27] The Broadwood Hotel crowd was frenzied, and the two teams waged a ferocious third period before Stan Stutz hit a shot from 4 feet beyond midcourt with six seconds to play to give Baltimore a 63–61 victory. "The teams engaged in a crushing point-for-point battle which saw the score change hands nine times in the last period and tied on four different occasions at 49, 54, 55, and 61."[28]

The score was knotted at 55 with four minutes to play before Abbott and Stutz connected on foul shots to push Baltimore ahead, 58–55. Fleishman and Kaplowitz answered with free throws of their own to narrow the gap to one, 58–57. Jackie Peters, replacing Abbott, who had committed his fifth foul, "launched a long set shot for a 60–57 margin." Stutz increased the Bullets' lead to 61–57 on a foul shot, but a basket by Kaplowitz and two foul shots by Hillhouse tied the score at 61 with forty-five seconds remaining. The game came down to the last possession. As detailed in the *Baltimore Sun* the following day, "The Bullets got possession of the ball off the center jump, waiting for an opening, and then Stutz came through with his Frank Merriwell toss from the middle of the floor to give the Bullets the title."[29]

The pressure of the game spilled over into the stands, as several fights broke out among the spectators; twice, officials stopped play to clear the floor. But it was Stutz who rose to the occasion, as his 24 points, including the game winner, offset Jerry Fleishman's 20 points. Victory in hand, the Bullets celebrated top honors as the playoffs started.

The SPHAS quickly dispatched the Wilmington Blue Bombers in two games, while the Bullets did likewise with the New York Jewels. The SPHAS now set their sights on defending their ABL title. The best-of-five championship series began on March 30 in Philadelphia. The SPHAS had reached the finals for the fourth straight year and were seeking their third title in that time. Not since the first four years of the ABL (1933–1937), when Gottlieb's crew won three titles, had the SPHAS dominated league play for such an extended stretch.

In Game 1, the SPHAS picked up where they had left off in their last two regular-season meetings versus the Bullets. A tight first period that ended with the SPHAS leading 15–14 proved as close as the Bullets would get. A 25–12 second period was all the SPHAS needed as they coasted to a 63–48 victory. The Bullets were playing their third game in four nights, following their two victories in the World Professional Basketball Tournament in Chicago, and "failed to give the Sphas much of a contest."[30] Ossie Schectman led the SPHAS with 18 points, including a game-high eight field goals. Ralph Kaplowitz chipped in with 13 and proved instrumental in the win. The first game was in the books, and the SPHAS looked to take control by winning the next game in Baltimore, where they had won the last time they played there.

Their opening-game rout marked the high point of the series for the SPHAS. Over the next three games, the SPHAS lost by an average of 18 points. The Bullets, "clicking from the outside and under the boards with neatly executed cut plays," simply beat the SPHAS.[31] The Bullets held a 27-point lead in Game 2 after humiliating the SPHAS 30–7 in the second period.

In the third game, Philadelphia fell behind, 25–7, in the first period, and Baltimore coasted to their second straight blowout win. The game was never a contest. "The Baltimoreans were hitting the net with amazing consistency, and their man-to-man defense prevented the Sphas from getting set for balanced shots either from the outside or underneath the hoops."[32] Ahearn, Andersen, and Stutz all scored in double figures to pace the Bullets to a 68–45 win. The Bullets now stood one victory from an improbable championship, the "culmination of a season-long uphill fight to the pennant."[33]

The Bullets, in only their second season, had transformed themselves from a .500 club who had lost in the previous year's finals to the SPHAS into the ABL's top team. Winning the league championship seemed unfathomable after starting the season with four straight losses. Instrumental in that turn-around had been Bill Dyer, who became the team's general manager in 1945. Prior to joining the Bullets, Dyer was a native Philadelphian who began his radio career announcing SPHAS games at the Broadwood Hotel.

Sitting courtside, Bill Dyer was the voice of the SPHAS during the 1930s. A native of Ardmore, Dyer graduated from Brown University in Rhode Island before returning to his native state to begin a career as a sports announcer. For five years, Dyer was a fixture on WCAU, where he broadcast both Philadelphia Phillies and A's baseball games. He teamed with Dolly Stark in 1936 and Taylor Grant in 1937 to announce the Phillies. Superstitious, Dyer had a habit of walking around his chair before the start of a game. When asked, he often replied that it was for good luck. He broadcast the World Series in 1936, 1937, and 1938 for CBS as well as baseball's All-Star games. Due to Eddie Gottlieb's strong connection with baseball, particularly as a booking agent, he decided that Dyer would be the perfect person to announce Saturday night SPHAS games at the Broadwood Hotel.

The year 1941 became a turning point for both WCAU and Dyer. The station moved toward broadcasting soap operas in the afternoons and dropped baseball from its programming schedule. At the same time, Dyer renewed his sponsorship contract with Wheaties. Since he was a baseball guy and the station would no longer be broadcasting either the Phillies or A's, Wheaties gave Dyer the option of relocating to Milwaukee, Baltimore, or San Francisco to fulfill his contract. He chose Baltimore, a town expanding its professional sporting landscape and in close proximity to his hometown.

When he arrived in Baltimore, he joined station WITH, and his afternoon variety show included news, sports, and music. Baseball was quickly becoming popular with the Orioles in Triple A, and with his experience with the Phillies and A's, he made the Orioles a popular draw. "Oriole Bill," as he became known, is often credited with assembling a record minor league crowd of more than 50,000 fans for one Junior World Series at Memorial Stadium. The record attendance coincided with the same day that the St. Louis Browns and Cardinals were playing in the World Series. During the war, Paul Himmer's aunt worked for WITH and often wrote her brother (Paul's father) about life in Baltimore. In one of her letters, she wrote, "We sure had an exciting time here last week. They [the Triple AAA Orioles] carried huge crowds and must say a lot of credit is due Bill Dyer, the announcer for he sure built that club up with his enthusiasm."[34]

At roughly the same time, WITH purchased the Baltimore Bullets basketball franchise of the ABL, and Dyer found himself working in basketball again. During the next five seasons (1945–1950), as the Bullets played in the ABL, BAA, and NBA, Dyer served as general manager of the team. Worried about any semblance of a conflict of interest, neither the station nor Dyer made mention of his involvement with the team. Under his leadership, the team signed future star Paul Hoffman from Purdue University. The team captured the 1947–1948 BAA championship over Eddie Gottlieb's Philadelphia Warriors, the reigning BAA champions.

In his prime years, Dyer was the single most important sports voice in the city. Along with the Orioles and Bullets, he could also be found broadcasting the Baltimore Colts, boxing, wrestling, bridge, horse racing, and table tennis tournaments. "WITH Radio owned the team. Bill Dyer did the broadcast, and he was also general manager of the team, but that was kept quiet," Seymour Smith, then a young newspaper reporter in town, recalled. "He had an afternoon show from 4:00 P.M. to 6:00 P.M. that was quite popular. He gave race results, played music, gave national and sports news, and he was also the voice of the International League Orioles. In the evenings, he broadcast the Bullets games. There were enough sponsors to keep it going for awhile. I worked at the newspaper in the evening, so I never listened to the games."[35]

Assisting Bill Dyer with the rebuilding of the 1945–1946 team was club president Jake Embry. Embry shook up the roster with a series of bold trades and player signings and completely remade the team. By season's end, only three players remained from opening night. It was a testament to coach Red Rosan, former SPHAS player, that he was able to integrate all the new players so quickly and to develop the necessary chemistry during a pennant race. Along with acquiring Bloom and Abbott in separate trades with Trenton, Embry signed Jake Ahearn after his discharge from the service and purchased Jack Peters from Wilmington. The team signed former Hamline University star Johnny Norlander in early March. Norlander had starred nearby at the Bainbridge Naval Training Station for the past two seasons. Along with Stan Stutz, Hagan Andersen, and Moe Dubilier, these new players proved too much for the SPHAS to overcome. Writing late in the season, sportswriter Frank Cashen, who would later be the general manager for baseball's Baltimore Orioles and New York Mets, summed up the Bullets well. "The Bombers have a young and ambitious ball club. They are always scrapping and you can never count them out of a game."[36]

Beginning January 1, the Bullets won twenty-five of thirty-three games, including a fifteen-game home winning streak. "The new players gave the

Bullets an inspirational lift, which has been characterized by their frequent whirlwind rallies after appearing headed for defeat." Bloom scored 233 points in his first twenty games with his new team and "is worth that many points and more on the defense."[37] He became the final piece of the puzzle for the surging Bullets.

Although Bloom acted as a key ingredient on the front line, Stan Stutz anchored the team's play. Stutz had been a college star at Rhode Island State and had twice led the Rams to a postseason appearance in the NIT. A prolific scorer due to the team's fast-breaking style, Stutz was named Helms Foundation All-America three times and was regarded as one of the best scorers in New England during the early 1940s. After graduating, Stutz signed with the New York Gothams of the ABL in 1943–1944. He moved to Baltimore the following season, where he helped the Bullets advance to the finals against the SPHAS. In his second full season with Baltimore in 1945–1946, he averaged 12.6 points in thirty-two games. But he saved his best for when he played the SPHAS. In a January 12 loss, he led the team with 18 points; on February 2, he led all scorers with 14 points; in March, he tallied 15 and 17 in separate games; and in the one-game playoff victory marked by his half-court winning shot, he scored 24 points.

Stutz was relatively quiet in the first three championship games, but scored 12 points as the "Bullets laced the Philadelphia Sphas, 54 to 39," to win the championship. "Well versed in each other's style of play, the Bullets performed exceptionally well as a unit, and appropriately their three mainstays, Bloom, Hagan Andersen, and Stutz, shared high-scoring honors at 12 points apiece." Leading 29–25, the Bullets extended it to 40–29. Ahead by 17 points with four minutes to go, "the Bullets put on a polished freeze to win eased up."[38]

The series marked a turning point for both franchises. Thirteen years earlier, the SPHAS were the upstart team defeating an old Trenton club whose style of play was more characteristic of the 1920s. Now, Baltimore featured a young, well-balanced team looking toward the future. The Bullets would play one more season in the ABL and then would become the only ABL team extended an invitation to play in the newly formed BAA. The Bullets captured the 1947–1948 BAA championship over the Philadelphia Warriors, coached by Eddie Gottlieb. A reserve guard on that Baltimore team was Louis (Red) Klotz. The Bullets joined the NBA in 1948–1949 and played five seasons before disbanding after the 1953–1954 campaign. The SPHAS, meanwhile, played three more seasons in the ABL before withdrawing after the 1948–1949 campaign. They missed the playoffs the last two seasons. Their best days ended with the 1945–1946 championship series.

13

THE END OF THE LINE

There was always a big crowd to watch the SPHAS. That changed when the Warriors were formed.

—JERRY RULLO, INTERVIEW BY THE AUTHOR

On June 6, 1946, some two months after the Bullets defeated the SPHAS for the ABL championship, a group of hockey owners gathered at the Hotel Commodore in New York City to discuss the formation of a new professional basketball league.

Hockey, both the National Hockey League and its minor league counterpart, the American Hockey League, enjoyed great success in large eastern cities like Boston, New York, Philadelphia, and Pittsburgh. When the teams were on the road, ice shows and college basketball doubleheaders attracted strong attendance and earned sizable profits. Despite that, the arenas stood empty many nights, and owners of the hockey teams and arenas sought to supplement their income. Professional basketball became an attractive option in the postwar era.

In attendance that day were the following members of the Arena Managers Association of America: Walter Brown, Arthur Morse, Al Sutphin, James Norris, Peter Tyrell, John Harris, Lou Pieri, Emory Jones, and Mike Uline. Franchises were granted to Cleveland, Chicago, Detroit, Boston, New York, Philadelphia, Pittsburgh, Providence, St. Louis, Toronto, and Washington, D.C. Ned Irish was in charge of the New York Knickerbockers, while Eddie Gottlieb oversaw the Philadelphia Warriors. Gottlieb was the only one in attendance that day with professional basketball experience.

With a new team in a new league, Gottlieb had to decide who would make up the Warriors' roster. Would Gottlieb transfer the SPHAS franchise? Would he take some of the SPHAS players? Would he take none of them? Would he try to manage two teams in two leagues? Gottlieb faced many questions, and his answers were not easy.

In the end, while he stayed somewhat involved with the SPHAS, he concentrated his efforts on the Warriors. A businessman at heart who never turned down an opportunity, Gottlieb sensed new promise with the BAA and wanted to field the best possible team he could.

With the formation of the BAA in 1946–1947, the ABL no longer held the status of premier basketball league. Rather than continue to be a major basketball league, the players voted to continue as a weekend league. Most of the players worked during the week and played league games on the weekends. Work during the week provided a steady paycheck, and no guarantees existed that the BAA would allow the players to quit their jobs and become full-time professional basketball players. No guarantees existed that the BAA would survive more than a few years.

Not since the ABL in 1925–1926 had a professional basketball league sought to establish a national circuit. With BAA teams in eleven major cities, John J. O'Brien and the ABL could not recruit elite players to the smaller markets, which made it hard to maintain fan bases and exposure. In the BAA's first year, the ABL fielded franchises in Paterson, Trenton, Newark, Jersey City, Brooklyn, Wilmington, Baltimore, Troy, and Elizabeth. Only Philadelphia had a team in both the BAA and ABL, and that was solely due to Gottlieb.

With the start of the inaugural BAA season a few months away, team owners and coaches needed to stock their rosters with players, and quickly. Along with returning servicemen and college stars, the upstart league lured away the best players from the ABL. Better competition, larger salaries, bigger cities, and a deeper schedule proved difficult for the players to turn down. Over the next few seasons, O'Brien tried to establish working relationships with the BAA and NBL in terms of player movement and a championship series between the ABL and the other two circuits, but those efforts proved futile. The ABL had become reduced to secondary status.

In looking to fill his Warriors roster, Gottlieb held a distinct advantage over his fellow owners. He already owned the SPHAS and knew his roster and the ABL better than anyone. He selected young players he thought could make an immediate impact on his new team. Art Hillhouse, George Senesky, Jerry Fleishman, and Petey Rosenberg joined Gottlieb on the Warriors. In perhaps a nod to the team he fielded in the ABL in 1926–1927 and 1927–1928, Gottlieb named the club the Philadelphia Warriors.

Basketball historian Bill Himmelman, who has studied the early development of professional basketball for decades, says that by the time the BAA came along after World War II, the ABL had lost its importance:

> In 1946–1947, the ABL became a minor league to the BAA in an unofficial way that it could grab players. The BAA was using the ABL and the newly founded Eastern League for players. Basketball never had a farm system like baseball did. Contracts were not long-term, so when players were sent to the EBL [Eastern Basketball League] or ABL, they would find who was in need of a good player and where he was most likely to get playing time. That is where they would send him. The player did not have any long-term contract with the minor league so the player could come back to the BAA any time he was summoned.[1]

While the Philadelphia Warriors began their inaugural BAA season, the SPHAS continued playing in the ABL. At the ABL Board meeting held shortly after the formation of the BAA, it was stated that "Mr. E. Gottlieb of Philadelphia announced that the operation of the Philadelphia Sphas has been placed in the hands of A. Radel, 5833 Pentridge Street, Philadelphia, Pa."[2] Gottlieb stayed involved with the SPHAS, although he turned over the head coaching reins to Harry Litwack, who was also coaching Temple University's basketball team. Abe Radel, his long-time friend and business manager, assumed control of the team and began attending league meetings.

Coinciding with the start of the BAA season was another year of the ABL. The 1946–1947 ABL season saw a few changes in the franchises. Returning were the Philadelphia SPHAS, Baltimore Bullets, Wilmington Bombers, Trenton Tigers, and Paterson Crescents. The New York Gothams became the Brooklyn Gothams. Four new franchises were added: the Troy Celtics, Newark Bobcats, Jersey City Atoms, and Elizabeth Braves. It was the first time since 1933–1934 that Newark had a professional basketball franchise. For Jersey City, it marked the first time since 1932–1933, and for Troy the first since 1940–1941. It was the only year for a team in Elizabeth. The league, probably taking a cue from the BAA's two-division structure, decided to create a Southern Division and a Northern Division. The Northern Division consisted of Brooklyn, Jersey City, Troy, Paterson, and

Newark. The Southern Division comprised Baltimore, Philadelphia, Trenton, Elizabeth, and Wilmington.

For Gottlieb, the SPHAS roster included old stalwarts Inky Lautman, Red Klotz, Irv Davis, and Bernie Opper. Newcomers Len Weiner, Morris (Mendy) Snyder, Mort Freemark, and local sensation Stan Brown joined the squad. "Stan Brown was the premier young guy who played with the SPHAS. He was a great player," Jerry Rullo, a former teammate, remembered.[3]

The season opened on October 26 at home versus the Paterson Crescents, who handily defeated the SPHAS 71–54. The SPHAS then strung together a four-game winning streak and started to build some momentum. The team continued to play well, and by December, sported a respectable 10–7 mark. In the season's second half, the SPHAS had a three-game winning streak in February to propel them to a 19–14 finish, good for second place in the Southern Division behind Baltimore, who had a 31–3 record, easily the best in the league. For the fifth season in a row, the SPHAS made the playoffs, and this time, they looked to avenge their loss to the Baltimore Bullets in the previous year's finals.

The end of World War II brought a fresh start for the country and returning servicemen. Everyone's attention was focused toward the new BAA and professional basketball in large cities. "There was always a big crowd to watch the SPHAS. That changed when the Warriors were formed," Jerry Rullo recalled. "The Warriors played at Convention Hall and Philadelphia Arena. Arenas like those in Detroit and Chicago backed many of the teams in the BAA. Pete Tyrrell ran the Philadelphia Arena. They would put the portable boards over the ice because the next day, they would have a hockey game. On a hot day, the floor became very slippery."[4]

Not coincidentally, the ABL immediately dropped off the front pages of the sports section. This was the case with the SPHAS, whose loyal coverage in Philadelphia newspapers quickly waned. The lack of attention the SPHAS received can be understood by how the team was covered during their playoff run. In order to generate more excitement with the public, the league decided to have more teams participate in the playoffs than in past years. The six teams with the best records were invited to play for the championship. In 1946, at the September 22 ABL Board meeting, the new playoff format was agreed upon: "The first team in each division will play in a series of the best three out of five games; the second place clubs in each division will play in a preliminary playoff series of the best two out of three games; the third and fourth place clubs in the official standing of the league at the termination of the 1946–1947 season, regardless of the division in which they are entered by computed on their percentage rating, will play in a preliminary series of the best two out of three games."[5]

This new playoff format got under way as Baltimore, with the best record (31–3) in the Southern Division, faced the Brooklyn Gothams, who sported the top mark (24–10) in the Northern Division. The SPHAS opened with a three-game series against Jersey City, while Trenton faced Elizabeth. Baltimore, which defeated Brooklyn, earned a bye into the finals while Trenton, who bested Elizabeth, waited for the winner of the Philadelphia and Jersey City series.

The matchup between Philadelphia and Jersey City did not conjure any memories of the epic seven-game series between the SPHAS and Jersey Reds in 1936–1937. Instead, Philadelphia was facing a Jersey team with a 14–22 record. The series opened on March 13, 1947, and the SPHAS were the first game in a doubleheader. In the other game, the Warriors, who were on their way to winning the first-ever BAA championship, routed the Boston Celtics 81–57 behind Joe Fulks's 25 points. The *Philadelphia Inquirer* covered both games together and in a nine-paragraph article devoted only two paragraphs to the SPHAS game. In the third paragraph, Allen Lewis wrote, "In the other game of the doubleheader the Sphas defeated the Jersey City Atoms, 56–47, in their first American League playoff contest. Both teams finished second in their respective divisions."[6] In the last paragraph, it notes that the team was led by Inky Lautman's 16 points. Despite another playoff run by the SPHAS, fans in Philadelphia had lost interest. In the span of only a year, it was a quick reversal of fortune for the SPHAS, who had always been the featured game and who had garnered all the attention.

The second game of the series took place March 16 in Jersey, as the Atoms defeated the SPHAS, 67–60, to even the series at one game apiece. The score of the game was reported in the *Philadelphia Inquirer*, but there was no article. The winner-take-all final game was again played as part of a doubleheader that also featured the Warriors. The game was close throughout, and the Atoms took a 44–43 lead late in the contest. The SPHAS responded behind Sol Schwartz and Mendy Snyder, who each tallied 6 points to push the SPHAS to a 56–50 win and a second-round matchup versus the Trenton Tigers.

The big battles between Trenton and Philadelphia in professional basketball's early years were a distant memory as this series got underway. The contest against Trenton opened across the Delaware River on March 23. The Tigers withstood an early SPHAS lead, 21–12, cruising to an 81–64 victory. The SPHAS were able to even up the series in the second game with a 46–42 win. The game was close throughout, and with a little over a minute left, Inky Lautman scored a layup to give the SPHAS the lead for good. Red Klotz and Bernie Opper converted on their foul shots for the game's final margin. The last game was played as a preliminary match to the Warriors, and in a back-and-forth battle, the SPHAS fell, 48–46. Trenton was to face Baltimore in the finals, but due to scheduling conflicts, Baltimore did not play, and Trenton was declared the winner. The SPHAS had been 3 points away from winning their eighth ABL championship, but it was not to be. Instead, this marked the team's last hurrah; in their remaining two years in the league, they did not make the playoffs again. The game also marked Inky Lautman's last as a member of the original SPHAS. After fourteen seasons, he scored only 6 points in his final appearance.

It was clear by now that the ABL was a minor league, and for the next two seasons, the SPHAS were a nonfactor. Changes were afoot for the 1947–1948 season, as Troy, Elizabeth, Newark, Trenton, and Wilmington withdrew. Baltimore, based on their play over the previous few seasons, was invited to join the BAA. They made the most of it and won the league championship. Their roster included Red Klotz, who came off the bench all season. New ABL teams were added in Lancaster, Scranton, Wilkes-Barre, and Hartford. The SPHAS welcomed a few new players, including Elmore Morgenthaler, a 7'1" center, and local product Jerry Rullo.

Jerry Rullo was another in a long line of Philadelphia players and Temple University stars who played briefly with the SPHAS. According to Rullo, his interest in basketball began at an early age:

> When I was young, I had good influences in basketball, and that is how I developed an interest in the sport. A guy named Howard Cullen got us involved in sports. He was the type of guy that would organize you and get you involved in teams and leagues. He got me connected with a team in the recreational league. They were looking for players, and they called Howard, and I started playing. From there, I became involved in independent ball with Nat Passon, who had a sporting goods store.
>
> When I started playing, the game was individual and very aggressive. You made sure your man did not score on you, and you played hard. You were pretty aggressive. If a guy scored on you, it was a challenge to tighten up a bit. You worked harder and became better. On offense, it was give-and-go; you screened for one another.
>
> In high school, I was involved with a coach named Menchy Goldblatt, who was an All-American at the University of Pennsylvania and was a pretty good basketball coach. He was a great defen-

> sive player. He taught the basics of the game like defense and team ball. From there I was able to get a scholarship to Temple University. I had a great line of coaches who gave me a lot of encouragement and taught me the game and how it should be played.[7]

When Rullo entered Temple, he was assigned to the freshman team, where

> Harry Litwack was my freshman coach. Litwack was a great fundamentalist. When you made a mistake, he would correct you and teach you the proper way. He had a great influence on me, and when he told you something, you paid attention. I knew from hearsay that he played for the SPHAS, but he did not talk about it. I played and made the team. The war broke out, and I had to go in for a while, and after getting out of the service, I went back to Temple and continued to play. I received my degree in teaching.
>
> After college, I was able to try out for the Philadelphia Warriors of the Basketball Association of America. I made the team. I was fortunate at the time, there was a style of play that I was used to playing, and that helped me. The first year in the BAA was a continuation of the college style of play, but on a higher level. The only difference was that you were playing against all the top-notch players. It was about defense and team ball.[8]

When Rullo joined the Warriors, his teammates included some former SPHAS players like Jerry Fleishman, Ralph Kaplowitz, Art Hillhouse, and George Senesky. Coached by Gottlieb, the Warriors finished with a 35–25 mark, good for second place in the Eastern Division behind the Washington Capitols, who were led by

Philadelphia native Jerry Rullo played and later coached the SPHAS in the years after World War II. (*Courtesy of Bill Himmelman.*)

a young Red Auerbach. In the first round of the playoffs, the Warriors defeated the St. Louis Bombers, 2–1, before besting the New York Knicks, 2–0, in the next round. In the championship series, the Warriors easily beat the Chicago Stags in five games to claim the first BAA title. Eddie Gottlieb had won another championship in yet another league.

Rullo was a key contributor off the bench and played in fifty regular-season games and seven playoff contests. According to Rullo:

> We won the BAA championship in 1946–1947. The team gelled. Joe Fulks was great. Everyone got along with one another. I do not think that Fulks got the recognition that he should have. He helped make the league what it is today. He was great the first four years of the league.
>
> In 1947–1948, the Warriors released me, and I went down to play with the Baltimore Bullets. I made the team. In my first year with the Warriors, we flew to all the games. We had a lot of different escapades flying, like being lost in the fog, fire on the plane, and one motor would go out. I went down to Baltimore, and I thought they would not fly. I made the team and played in a few exhibition games. We get set to take our first trip, and it was the same thing with flying, and I could not do it. So, I came back to Philadelphia and played with the SPHAS.
>
> The SPHAS needed players. Gottlieb ran the Warriors and the SPHAS, and he said I could play with the SPHAS in the American Basketball League. They tried to make the American Basketball League a minor league to the Basketball Association of America. I guess it became too much of a problem with all the teams trying to get their franchises together. Some teams did use the ABL as a minor league, like the New York Knicks used Paterson, New Jersey, for extra work or for players to develop more. Some of the players that played with the SPHAS eventually wound up with the Warriors. After that, we had the Eastern League, which was a weekend league.[9]

When Rullo joined the SPHAS, the league was set to begin another campaign. Unfortunately for Rullo, his new team would not be competing for a league title any time soon. The SPHAS opened the 1947–1948 season with a road win against Lancaster, 59–57. After that, the team lost five straight games and played catch-up the rest of the season. The team finished with a 13–19 mark, although the record was deceptive, as ten of their losses came by 4 points or fewer. The team was sixth out of eight in the final standings and was not part of the league race. Rullo played well all year and in thirty games averaged 10 points per contest. Newcomers Elmore Morgenthaler and Aaron Tanitsky finished in the top ten in scoring. They were the lone bright spots for the SPHAS.

The 1948–1949 season would be the last for the SPHAS in the ABL. The SPHAS did not begin the season in Philadelphia that year, but in Atlantic City. Due to Gottlieb's commitment with the Warriors and arrangements with the Arena, it was agreed that the SPHAS would relocate to the Jersey coast. The SPHAS would play their home games either Tuesday or Thursday nights at the Million Dollar Pier in Atlantic City. The team would be known as the Atlantic City Tides.

The Tides, who represented the first professional basketball team in Atlantic City since the Sand Snipers in 1936–1937, initially generated a lot of excitement. Prior to the Tides' league opener, the *Atlantic City Press* excitedly noted, "Coach Harry Litwack, who formerly prepped the Temple freshman and later the Philadelphia SPHAS, has molded together an exceptionally powerful club for the Tides, which consists of several ex-collegiate stars and former members of the SPHAS along with two local players who will endeavor to make the grade in pro ball."[10] The roster consisted of Stan Brown, Elmore Morgenthaler, Ed Lyons, Aaron Tanitsky, Bill McCahan, Frank Stanczak, and Len Weiner. The two local players were Bobby Barnett and George Herlich.

"We had Bill McCahan, who was pitcher for the Philadelphia Athletics who hurled a no-hitter the summer before basketball season," Rullo recalled. "Eddie put him on the team and when he was announced, the crowd got a kick out of that."[11]

The season began on a promising note for the Tides. The team won its first three games. In their season-opening win over the Hartford Hurricanes, the Tides were led by Elmore Morgenthaler, who tallied 33 points. In seventeen games that season, he averaged 21.6 points and was one of the team's better players. Jerry Rullo was a teammate of Morgenthaler for a few seasons and remembers his unique personality. "Elmore Morgenthaler was a real character. The more he played, the better he became. He always had a way to lighting a cigarette, where he would flip it in the air, and the match would strike, and he would light it and put it in his mouth."[12]

Behind Morgenthaler, the team continued to win and posted a 6–1 mark in early December. Then, the wheels fell off. A sixteen-game losing streak over two months effectively squashed any hope that the SPHAS might have one last run. The team found all kinds of ways to lose.

On January 1, the Tides traveled to Hartford for a New Year's Day matchup. The Hurricanes featured Ralph Kaplowitz, who was enjoying a fine season. Kaplowitz remembered, "While I was with the insurance company the first four years, I joined up with the American Basketball League. I played for Paterson Crescents, and Ossie Schectman was on that team. I found out that my contract was sold to Hartford. So I went to Hartford and stayed with them for the next four years. I was a star. Every time I met the coach, Leo Merson of Paterson, he admitted the worst move he ever made as a coach was getting rid of me to Hartford. At Hartford, I averaged 25 points a game."[13] In that New Year's game, Kaplowitz led all scorers with 36 points, which accounted for half of the points the Tides scored in losing, 83–72.

Thirteen games into their losing streak, the SPHAS relocated to Philadelphia, where they would finish up the season. The final game in Atlantic City came on January 11, when the Tides hosted defending league champion Wilkes-Barre. Even the league's top team could not generate much enthusiasm. The poor attendance caused the team to lose $800 on that game. In an article on January 14, 1949, Al Sofer, manager of the Tides, stated, "We endeavored to give Atlantic City the best in the way of professional basketball, but unfortunately it wasn't appreciated by local sports fans who for two years had clamored for a league team. At least that's the way it appears from the poor attendance at all of our home games."[14]

Eddie Gottlieb stepped in, and at an ABL board meeting on January 16—two days after the Tides ceased operation—stated that he "would make an effort to play as many home games in Philadelphia between this date and the close of the 1948–1949 season as was possible."[15] In their final sixteen games after returning to Philadelphia, the SPHAS played five home games. After a win over the Brooklyn Gothams on February 10 to stop the worst losing streak of their franchise history, the SPHAS lost their next five games and nine of ten to finish with an 8–26 mark. Their last home game was March 2, a 104–84 loss to Wilkes-Barre. Their last game was a 118–116 defeat at Trenton on March 25, 1949. The SPHAS finished in last place.

Despite the disappointing season, Gottlieb still wanted to give it one more try. Throughout the summer, he worked diligently to arrange games in Philadelphia and even thirty minutes south in Wilmington. He had no luck. "I ran the SPHAS for about one year for Gottlieb and after me, Harry Litwack came in and ran it for a while," Rullo noted. "Gottlieb still wanted to keep the SPHAS in the American League, hoping that it would catch on as a farm for the team in the NBA. It did not work out because it became too much of an expense."[16]

Gottlieb realized that he would not be able to field a team in the ABL for the 1949–1950 season and asked permission to terminate the franchise for a period of one year, which would give him time to find a suitable home for the SPHAS for the 1950–1951 campaign. The ABL Board, led by O'Brien, agreed "that the franchise of the Philadelphia Sphas be suspended for the season 1949–1950, and in view of the fact the Sphas will continue playing throughout the United States as a traveling team, that Mr. Gottlieb be permitted to continue the use of such players as remained on his roster at the close of the 1948–1949 season, with the understanding that if any present American Basketball League club is interested in acquiring any one or more of these men, he make that fact known to Mr. Gottlieb, and obtain the rights to place players under contract."[17]

The following year, Gottlieb sold the SPHAS franchise to a Utica syndicate led by Leo Ferris of Buffalo, who was a part of the Syracuse team of the NBA. As Gottlieb explained, "We had a nonoperating franchise in the American League. Utica only wanted the franchise and was not interested in the team name. Last year, under the coaching of Mike Bloom, we played 106 games, barnstorming with the Globetrotters. The most we ever played as a league member was 100. We will continue the tie-up with the Globetrotters."[18]

After thirty-two years as a professional basketball team, the SPHAS were no longer affiliated with a league, and with this memories of the golden years for the Philadelphia SPHAS came to an end.

14

PLAYING IT STRAIGHT

> The SPHAS were a good team. They were a good bunch of guys, and some of them could have played in the NBA. However, there weren't nearly as many teams as there are today. But they were playing against a show team and they played along with the routine. The SPHAS did win a few games, but not many.
>
> —Marques Haynes, interview by the author

Eddie Gottlieb and Abe Saperstein became fast friends. Both were short, heavy-set, Jewish men. They were born promoters who loved to make a deal. And they made many deals in their lifetime. In the mid-1920s, each was getting his start in the world of sports. Saperstein assumed control of the Savoy Big Five of Chicago and renamed them the Harlem Globetrotters. Games were scheduled all through the Midwest. Saperstein did the driving, promoting, and coaching. Gottlieb, meanwhile, took over the SPHAS from friends Hughie Black and Chickie Passon. He, too, arranged the games, drove the car, and set the starting lineup. Along with basketball, both soon became involved in Negro League baseball. By the end of World War II, Gottlieb and Saperstein were hugely successful. Gottlieb was an instrumental member of the BAA and later the NBA, and Saperstein was owner of the most popular basketball team in the world. Gottlieb brought Saperstein on as a team stockholder for the Philadelphia Warriors. While the Globetrotters became the toughest ticket in basketball circles, the SPHAS were on their last legs, limping to the finish line. Seeking to keep the SPHAS on the playing circuit, Gottlieb and Saperstein decided to incorporate the SPHAS into the Globetrotters' larger operation.

"Eddie and Abe were very close and they arranged for the SPHAS to travel with the Globetrotters," Jerry Rullo, a former player and coach with the SPHAS, recalled.[1]

By 1949, the Harlem Globetrotters were the most popular and entertaining sports team in the country, and a national phenomenon that knew no bounds. Wherever the team traveled, sellout crowds awaited them. Large arenas or small gyms, big cities or small towns; it did not matter. Everyone wanted to see the Globetrotters. Everyone wanted to see the Globetrotters win. The Globetrotters did not disappoint. They always won. Part of the Globetrotters' traveling routine included putting on doubleheaders in which they always played in the featured game. Traveling with the Globetrotters were the Boston Whirlwinds, Toledo Mercuries, New York Renaissance, and eventually the SPHAS. As Rullo recalls, "There was a Hawaiian and a team from Kansas City that traveled with us. The SPHAS would play the Hawaiian team, and the Globetrotters would play the team from Kansas City."[2]

The 1949 season was the last for the SPHAS in the ABL, despite Gottlieb's great effort. Rather than fold the team, Gottlieb and Saperstein arranged for the SPHAS to be one of the regular traveling teams with the famed Globetrotters, which they were for ten years, until the SPHAS team ceased operation in October 1959.

During this time, the SPHAS' routine was largely the same. They either played the preliminary game against one of the other traveling teams, or they faced the Globetrotters in the marquee matchup. It was a looser operation for the SPHAS. Gottlieb was less hands-on, as he focused mostly on the Warriors and on helping to develop the NBA. At times, he assigned different players to oversee the team, including Mike Bloom, Pete Monska, and Jerry Rullo.

"It would be a two-week tour and play them every night in different towns. All of our games were competitive, and we played hard, but people came to see them because they had what they called Showtime," Rullo recounted.

> When they had the game won, they would put on their antics—put the ball under the shirt and make-believe type of stuff. We played against them so much that we knew their routine. They would beat us and put the Showtime on. Then we would beat them, but they could not put their Showtime on. I ran the team for a while for Gottlieb, and he said, "Run the team. Play the game, and you will get paid after the tour. People come to see them put on Showtime, so go through the routine, and let them win, and you will still get paid." That is what we did.
>
> The relationship between the SPHAS and Globetrotters was great. The Globetrotters had great guys. The personnel were great.

> They had Marques Haynes, Babe Pressley, and Ermer Robinson. We all got along. The only guy who was hard to get along with was Goose Tatum. I do not even think his players got along with him, but he was a big draw. He was a good ballplayer; he put on all the acts, but he was tough to get along with. He was always miserable.[3]

Rullo was not the only player to have a difficult time with Tatum. Bob Lojewski, who played with the SPHAS in the early 1950s, remembers his encounter against the man known as Goose:

> When I joined the SPHAS in '52, there were three exhibition teams that played the Globetrotters. The other two were the Washington Generals and the Toledo Mercuries. We played about eight games a week, and on the weekends we played both afternoon and evening games. I played my first SPHAS game in the Madison Square Garden. I was about 19, could jump over the roof, but knew nothing about the Globetrotters or their style of play. They put me on Goose Tatum, and the first time he tried the patented hook shot, I blocked it. He tried it again and I blocked that, too. So he turned and spit at me. I was shocked. I couldn't believe it. Here was this established star and he couldn't take the heat. At the time-out, Pete [Monska] instructed me to give him more room. But Pete wasn't too upset about it. I think he got pleasure out of watching Goose Tatum get his shot stuffed.[4]

Although the SPHAS generally followed instructions to play along, there were times when they deviated from the script, which usually brought a quick reprimand from Gottlieb or Saperstein. George Dempsey, another SPHAS player from the 1950s, recalled his encounter against Goose. "When I would cover Goose in the pivot, he did this act where he would place the ball on the floor, pretend to look for it, and we were supposed to go along with the act and pretend to look for it, too. But I never pretended. The minute I saw the loose ball, I would pick it up and dribble down the floor with it, and that would ruin their act. After I did it a few times, Abe Saperstein told Pete Monska I had to go along with the act or I was off the tour."[5]

One of the highlights of a Globetrotter game was the halftime show. As Rullo remembers:

> Their halftime shows were great. They would get internationally known ping-pong players and acrobats. The halftime shows ran

thirty to forty-five minutes. They always drew and had these vaudeville shows at halftime.

When we toured with the Globetrotters, [Olympian] Jesse Owens was the announcer. He would introduce the players from both teams. We would travel with him on the bus, and he would sit next to you and talk to you like a regular guy. He was a good man.

During my time, the SPHAS as a team did not travel internationally with the Globetrotters. Individual players and Eddie Gottlieb would travel. The Globetrotters had maybe four teams because there was such demand. The other teams would play in the small towns. The top team would play in the big cities like Pittsburgh, Syracuse, and Virginia. If those guys behaved themselves during the season and no problems, Abe Saperstein would get a team of all those guys and put them together as a unit, and they would travel all through Europe. He did that to reward those guys who played well and behaved well.

I remember the game when we beat the Globetrotters after their big win against Minneapolis after they had won like 105 games in a row. On the bus going to Pittsburgh, their manager Tom was saying, "When the other team plays slow, we play fast, and when we play fast, the other team plays slow." We beat them in Pittsburgh, and we are going to the next town. Elmore Morgenthaler from the SPHAS, he starts mouthing off and says, "When the other team plays slow, we play fast, and when we play fast, the other team plays slow." I told Elmore to take it easy. The next town, we get a message from Eddie, who tells us to go through the motions and let them win.[6]

Winning a game against the Globetrotters, however infrequently, was frowned upon, as fans wanted to see the Globetrotters win and put on Showtime. Along with the different acts, the players put on great performances. Nobody was better than Marques Haynes. "Marques Haynes was a great dribbler. He would dribble, and you would make believe that you could get the ball, and he would pull it back and then make a basket," Rullo recounted years later. "They had another act with a bucket full of confetti and make believe that it was water. The guy would run toward the crowd and throw the bucket and make you think it was water. They had great routines."[7]

The halftime shows proved entertaining, mainly because of Marques Haynes. Considered the world's greatest dribbler, Haynes grew up playing basketball in Oklahoma and soon became one of the feature players for Saperstein's team. Haynes recalled:

I started playing against the SPHAS in 1949 or 1950, when I was with the Harlem Globetrotters. In those years, there were four teams that traveled together—the Harlem Globetrotters, Boston Whirlwinds, New York Renaissance, and the Philadelphia SPHAS. There was a preliminary game and then a feature game, which always starred the Globetrotters. The Globetrotters seldom played the Rens, so we either faced the SPHAS or the Whirlwinds. It was always a good relationship between the SPHAS and the Globetrotters.

In those days, there were four Globetrotter teams that traveled throughout the country. After I left the Globetrotters in 1953, there were two or three teams. When Goose Tatum left in 1955, it was reduced to two teams. But in those years, there was only one SPHAS team. I do not remember the SPHAS ever traveling with us internationally.

All of the games and tours were arranged through the Globetrotters office. The touring season ran from October to April, and if we went overseas, it ran another two or three months. In 1949–1950, Abe Saperstein took over the Rens from Bob Douglas. He ran it for two or three years and then dissolved the team. I believe that Eddie Gottlieb still ran the SPHAS, but had others help him when the team was on the road.

The SPHAS were a good team. Elmore Morgenthaler wasn't a bad player. I remember him being tall, and he also played for the Hartford Hurricanes of the American Basketball League. Stan Brown was a good, solid player. He was one of the SPHAS' outstanding players. Jack Stein was a fine fellow. Dave Zinkoff got involved with the SPHAS through Eddie Gottlieb. He was an announcer for one or two of our trips overseas. He toured the country with us for a few years. Red Klotz was a good, quick player who could shoot the two-handed set shots. There was never an off moment with Red.[8]

Basketball and Red Klotz are synonymous. As a young child growing up, Louis (Red) Klotz quickly discovered basketball, and when he did, he never gave it up.

"I grew up in South Philadelphia, and that neighborhood was all about basketball. I lived in a Jewish area. Basketball was a sport that excited us," Klotz recalled decades later. "We were poor families, and all we needed was a pair of sneakers and ball and pair of shorts. You could play soccer or basketball. I got interested when I was 10 years old, and I never stopped. The game was for poor people. So, we played basketball, from morning to night. We played it right. We played fundamental, smart basketball."[9]

Growing up in South Philadelphia, Klotz had two choices. "Where I was raised, you either earned a scholarship to college or became a gangster."[10] For Klotz, the choice was easy.

"Everything was outdoors then. You did not have indoor courts then. We played outdoors from morning to night, as long as the weather was right. I watched the better players, and you learned from observation. Then you would practice what you saw, and that is how I learned. It paid off."[11]

It most certainly paid off, and despite Klotz's love for the game, his parents, Robert and Lena, believed their son's time could be better spent with other activities. They were concerned for their boy, who stood only 5'7", weighed 140 pounds, and was nearsighted. They felt he would be injured playing basketball. They wanted him to pursue a hobby that was safe, but Klotz knew what he wanted to do and needed to resort to a bit of deception to accomplish his goal.

> My parents did not even know I was playing basketball. I had to sneak out of the house. I would drop my bag out the back window and get on the trolley and go to Fifth and Bainbridge. Fifth and Bainbridge played in a cage, the ceiling was low and you had to shoot the ball right between the ceilings to get it in. While we were playing, if you got pushed into the cage, you bounced off and kept playing. That was the beginning of playing in the cage. We played at Fifth and Bainbridge, and we learned a lot by playing in the cage. I could shoot that ball.[12]

Not surprisingly, Klotz became a very good player and enrolled at South Philadelphia High School. In his junior (1938–1939) and senior (1939–1940) years, he helped lead the team to consecutive city championships. For his efforts, he was named the city's player of the year twice.

> In high school, I was the best player in the city. I was a little Archibald of Philadelphia. I was probably one of the first point guards. They did not have point guards, but if you had put a finger on me and say point guard, I had 15 assists and 15 points. I was happy to set everybody up, and we beat everybody. We won city championship after championship.
>
> I was supposed to go to Temple University for college, but they had a racial quota. I had to wait for Mendy Snyder to graduate. They

Louis (Red) Klotz joined the SPHAS for the 1942–1943 season and in eleven regular-season games averaged 3.8 points. The team went on to win the championship that season. (*Courtesy of Naismith Memorial Basketball Hall of Fame.*)

> wanted me to go to Brown Prep; that was like a pre-college, and in my case, it was a stall. My best friend, Chuck Drizen, who was a great star, went to Villanova. He was a great player for Germantown, and he said, "Come over here; Coach Al Severance would love to have you." So I went over there, and we were heroes at Villanova. We were the only two Jewish players in the whole university, I think.[13]

Klotz spent two years at Villanova. The first season, he played on the undefeated freshman team and then joined the varsity for his sophomore season. In his lone varsity season (1941–1942), Klotz was the second leading scorer with 183 points. During his freshman year, he had eloped and married his girlfriend, Gloria. At the time, schools regarded marriage as an infringement on financial aid, so Klotz lost his scholarship. However, it was time to move on, and beginning in 1942–1943, Klotz became the next in a long line of Philadelphia natives to join the SPHAS.

"I played preliminary games with the SPHAS Reserves before the SPHAS would play. While I was in high school at South Philadelphia High School, I was playing for this team on the side that played preliminary games to the SPHAS. Before that, I played with a midget team called the Outlaws, who played exhibitions in the ballroom where the SPHAS played. We were a smart little team and nobody could beat us for our age and height."[14]

When Klotz joined the SPHAS for the 1942–1943 campaign, they were regarded as the top team in the league:

> The SPHAS were the Lakers of the day in Philadelphia. Philadelphia played in the American Basketball League, which was the equivalent of the NBA today. The SPHAS won championships after championships in the American Basketball League. Cy Kaselman and Petey Rosenberg were great players. I played with them. I was the youngest player on the team. We had a fellow on the team, Red Wolfe from New York, who later coached in a New York college. He was the oldest red-head on the team, and I was the youngest. Eddie kept that group together for years, and to get on that team you had to prove it. I did. I proved I belonged on that team and, gradually, I became part of that team.[15]

Part of that team he was, and during the regular season, Klotz played in eleven games and averaged 3.8 points per game. In the playoff series versus Trenton, he saw action in three games and scored one basket. Prior to his first game that season on December 19 against Harrisburg, the *Sphas Sparks* featured a photo of Klotz on the cover with the caption, "Perpetual motion performer . . . already showing signs of stardom . . . expected to blossom into one of the best local products."[16] He helped the SPHAS win the title, and his brief taste with the big club would be beneficial after the war.

> We won the championship before I went into the military. It was a great team. Scoring in those days was half of what it was today, maybe even less. It was a different game then. We did not have a shot clock. So you can run the clock off and win the game without even shooting if you had the lead. It was a smaller game than played today. It was a team game. We did not stress one star even though we had them.
>
> The team was very popular with the Jewish people, but we also had other people and gradually had non-Jews on the team. For a while they we were all Jewish. It was not that Eddie Gottlieb wanted all Jewish players, but it just so happened that they were the best players of the time.
>
> He was a tough coach. You would not want to be in halftime listening to what he had to say. He was a fundamental smart coach, but he was strict, and if you made a mistake, you were in trouble. In those days, the ball moved around. It would not hit the ground unless you were going to drive. The movements were smart; there were picks and blocks.[17]

Klotz played that one season with the SPHAS and then was drafted into the military, where he spent the next two years.

> I was in the military for a few years, and my Commissioned Officer was Cy Kaselman. He played for the SPHAS and was a great star. We had Petey Rosenberg, who played for the SPHAS and for the BAA champion Philadelphia Warriors. I was stationed in Las Vegas, New Mexico. It was Camp Luna, air transport command. We had a very good team and played all around New Mexico and Arizona and Texas until they shipped us overseas. After the war, I returned to the SPHAS and became player/coach, and I took them everywhere until I formed my own team, the Washington Generals.[18]

When the war was over, Gottlieb brought Klotz back to the team. Klotz returned for the 1945–1946 season, and by then, the makeup of the SPHAS was changing. Gottlieb was tapping into the New York basketball market and had stocked his team with many great New York players.

> Eddie liked New York players. We had Ralph Kaplowitz from New York, Irv Torgoff, and Butch Schwartz. Dutch Garfinkel was a great player. He was good all around—defense, offense, and team player. He is one of the all-time greats to me. Cy Boardman was another great set shooter type player from New York. These two cities, New York and Philadelphia, mixed to form the SPHAS.
>
> The BAA formed in 1946. Eddie had the first franchise in the BAA with Philadelphia. They were the Warriors. I took the SPHAS on exhibitions against the Globetrotters. I first went to try out for the Boston Celtics, and they had a full group. So, I went over to the Baltimore Bullets and we beat the Warriors for the title in 1948.[19]

The 1945–1946 SPHAS team that Klotz joined still had one final push left in them. The team finished with a 21–14 record and won the first round of the playoffs versus Wilmington. Klotz played in thirty-one regular-season games and six playoff contests, where he averaged 5 points per game, but the team lost to Baltimore in the finals. The following year, he again played for the SPHAS, who lost in the playoffs. By now, the BAA dwarfed the ABL, and Klotz signed with the Baltimore Bullets, who moved to the BAA. After winning the title with the Bullets in 1947–1948, Klotz joined the Cumberland (Maryland) Dukes of the All-American Basketball League, where he averaged 11.3 points in thirty games as the team won the league championship.

Despite the success he had for two years in Maryland, the lure of the SPHAS again found Klotz, who returned to Philly in 1949 at Gottlieb's request to coach the team on a two-week exhibition tour with the Harlem Globetrotters. As Klotz explains it, the Globetrotters did not always have the best competition.

> The Globetrotters used to go out and play local teams, but the opposition wasn't consistent. The Trotters played anyone they could sign up back then. That was bad because they'd get good competition in the smaller places. This really angered Abe Saperstein because he didn't want his players going through the motions. He liked good games. The local players had no sense of humor, either; and when they lost to the Globetrotters, they always wanted to fight.[20]

One night, at a game at the Broadwood Hotel, Klotz's SPHAS upset the Globetrotters. As the teams walked off the court, Goose Tatum walked up to Klotz and said, "That'll never happen again."[21] In fact, it did the next night in Syracuse as the SPHAS won by 12 points.

"We played them in a two-week exhibition tour," Klotz remembers. "We played them and beat them in Philadelphia. Abe Saperstein was quite impressed. I chased Marques Haynes, their dribbler, letting him do his thing. We were like Fred Astaire and Ginger Rogers. I was just as fast or maybe faster step for step than Haynes."[22]

After those games, Saperstein approached Klotz about creating his own team to play against the Globetrotters on a regular basis. Klotz jumped at the opportunity and named his team the Washington Generals. As Klotz recalls, "Ike had just thumped Adlai Stevenson, and generals were pretty popular at that time. I thought the name might win us some fans."[23]

> In 1952–1953, I formed the Washington Generals. Abe Saperstein asked me to form a team, because when I took the SPHAS out on exhibition, I was beating the heck out of the Globetrotters. He knew that was the type of opposition he needed to tour all over the world. The teams they were playing were local, and they were not good enough competition. After I formed my own team, I turned the SPHAS over to one of my players, Pete Monska, who continued to coach the team for another year or two until it disbanded. There is no truth to the rumor that Eddie Gottlieb sold me the SPHAS. Whoever had that story and how it got out, I have never known. Eddie Gottlieb took the team with him when he left this earth.
>
> People don't know, but the NBA was a failure for a lot of years. We kept them alive for years as we toured with the Harlem Globetrotters. They were begging us for doubleheaders. We played for Eddie and Philadelphia and then Ben Kerner in St. Louis. They needed that money to stay alive. They lost franchise after franchise after franchise for years before they made it to the age of television.[24]

Minus Klotz, the SPHAS continued to serve as a traveling team to the Globetrotters until they disbanded in October 1959. The Washington Generals, meanwhile, became the touring team with the Globetrotters and traveled the world, spreading the gospel of basketball. In the process, Klotz lost more games in basketball history than anyone else.

As Klotz recalls:

> We played so many years overseas that we introduced basketball to a lot of the world. We carried our own baskets and plywood floors. They did not even have them in those countries. We played in bull-rings and soccer fields, wherever we could put the court down. The people loved it, and gradually, each year, the kids started playing. When we first started, there was nothing but kicking the soccer ball around. They are still kicking it around and soccer is still the top sport in the world. But now, if you go, there are baskets hanging everywhere. They love basketball. They have had American coaches and the right ones. They learned the fundamentals, and we gave clinics for years. We played all around the world, including China right to Japan and Korea. We played everywhere. What you see coming into the NBA today, a hundred players from overseas playing solid fundamental basketball.
>
> It all started with players like the SPHAS. Then it went to the west coast with Hank Luisetti from Stanford, who introduced the new style of basketball, the one-handed shot. He introduced back dribbling. He sensationalized the East, and he came and played against Temple University, who were the national champions that year. Temple had beaten them in Philadelphia in a tight game. He played against Long Island University in Madison Square Garden, and he scored 50 points. He dribbled behind his back and was taking one-handed shots. The whole country from that point came on. Later, you had Jerry West taking jump shots. That was unstoppable. Basketball was born with people like Eddie Gottlieb and Clair Bee. Ned Irish and Walter Brown made it go, but the hard way.[25]

Basketball was born the hard way with teams like the SPHAS who left the game to the next generation of stars. For the SPHAS, it began as World War I was nearing completion as a group of high school friends wanted to continue playing after graduation. They formed their own team and found a sponsor to donate uniforms in exchange for using the association's name. After a few years, the organization ended its affiliation, but the players, now more seasoned and confident, continued playing. They called themselves the SPHAS so everyone would know where they had their start.

The SPHAS soon became a dominant team and until the end of World War II, they established themselves as one of the best professional teams in the country. They won multiple championships, barnstormed around the East and Midwest, and were instrumental in growing the game professionally. Their success was set against the backdrop of the 1930s, the Great Depression and the rise of anti-Semitism. Through it all, the team not only persevered, but succeeded. By the end of the World War II, the game of basketball was changing and the SPHAS no longer were dominant. Their contributions were still evident as they toured throughout the 1950s with the Harlem Globetrotters, who played doubleheaders with the NBA, which helped save the financially strapped league. When the SPHAS bowed out in 1959, the game was changing and the newest sensation was Wilt Chamberlain. Their legacy was still apparent in the popularity of the game, and in the style of play predicated on passing and teamwork. Basketball owes a debt of gratitude to teams like the SPHAS.

EPILOGUE

MEMORIES LIVE ON

> The SPHAS were one of the first great teams. Next to the Original Celtics, they were the best white team. They played great team basketball and were a great bunch of guys.
>
> —Bernie Fliegel, interview by the author

On a warm Saturday in the summer of 2007, I drove to Philadelphia to meet with Harry Boonin, a retired lawyer who devotes much of his spare time to Philadelphia Jewish history. Harry offers walking tours of the Jewish neighborhood, and he had agreed to show me South Philadelphia. Armed with a list of places affiliated with the SPHAS, I hoped that we would be able to find some remaining marks of one of basketball's greatest teams. We drove around with Parry Desmond, himself a researcher, and tried to locate some of the original buildings associated with the SPHAS. In our travels, we found the YMHA at Broad and Pine Streets, the South Philadelphia Hebrew Association at Fourth and Reed, Musical Fund Hall (which is now a condominium) at Eighth and Locust, the original building of Passon's Sporting Goods at Fifth and Market, Southern High School at Broad and Jackson Streets, and the original building for Sam Gerson's store at Sixth and Bainbridge.

Two years later, on another trip—this time by myself—I went to the corner of Broad and Wood Streets, the site of the old Broadwood Hotel. Today, it stands as a parking garage for Hahnemann Hospital. I walked around the garage, up the stairs, and I even drove my car to the top level before descending. At each stop, I looked for any signs of the old Broadwood Hotel. None were found. No marker, no plaque, nothing. I asked the parking attendant if he remembered the Broadwood Hotel. He did not. I suspect he had never heard of the SPHAS, the greatest Jewish basketball team ever assembled.

As I stood there, there were no signs indicating that for more than a decade, the Broadwood Hotel was the site of some of the greatest basketball feats during the 1930s. Cars passed by and people hurried about their business. The garage was busy as cars went in and out.

In the commotion of daily life, I closed my eyes and saw the long lines forming to enter the Broadwood Hotel. The men were wearing top coats and hats, and the women were dressed in their best, high heels and dresses. The excitement and energy in the air was palpable. It was Saturday night, SPHAS night. Everyone entered and walked up the stairs to the third floor, where they paid for their ticket, grabbed a copy of the *Sphas Sparks*, and found their seats. Down on the court, the SPHAS, wearing fancy mackinaws and jackets, were warming up, shooting layups and practicing their foul shots. Tip-off was nearing. Another game was set to begin. Another dance with young Jewish singles would close out the evening.

Long after the SPHAS stopped playing and the Broadwood Hotel closed, the memories of the SPHAS still live on. Their story is our story, the search for the American Dream.

Edwin (Hughie) Black

According to his son Marvin:

> Hughie taught physical education at Tilden Junior High School. He started the camp in 1931, and that kept him very busy. It was a girls' camp in northern Pennsylvania. A co-gym teacher told him a camp was for sale, and they went to look at it and bought it. Eventually, his partner went to another camp, but my father stayed. It was called Rhod Arlene. It was a religious girls' camp from New York named for Rhoda and Arlene. My father changed the name to Pine Forest Camp because of all the pine trees. It has expanded to three camps. My generation started two other camps on my father's land. My father was a very enterprising guy. As a teacher, he would go to the bank and borrow money to buy a hundred acres. It was $50 an acre, and he would do that every year. He accumulated over 700 acres. We added to that, and our camps are now in the third generation. Our son Mickey and his wife, Barbara, run the show now.

> He became very successful in the camp business, but he continued to teach. He taught in an area that was not very good, at Tilden Junior High School. My dad became financially successful with the camp. I remember he started to take vacations in Florida, and that was unheard of for physical education teachers to do that. First, he would go for a few weeks, and then for a month, and they decided it was not a very good thing for him to be doing. So, they had an agreement to discontinue teaching, and he was just as happy because he was getting more and more busy with camp. He would go up every Saturday, and when I got out of college, we would go up every Saturday. Up and back, four hours each way. When he went, there were no heaters in cars. He would go up in the wintertime and wrap a blanket around his legs. He would go up to the mountains and spend an hour there and would come right back. He never stayed overnight. He had a car, a Whippet that had to be parked on the top of a hill. If it didn't, we would have to get out and crank it and get it started. We always looked for a spot on a top of a hill, so we could coast and then start the car.[1]

Black continued working with the camps and in 1986 was honored by the American Camping Association for his work in the field.

He died in 1986 at the age of 92.

Meyer (Mike) Bloom

After helping the Baltimore Bullets defeat the SPHAS for the 1945–1946 ABL title, Bloom was a member of the Bullets when they moved to the BAA in 1947–1948. After thirty-four games, 33-year-old Bloom was traded to the Boston Celtics (coached by John [Honey] Russell) for 22-year-old Connie Simmons. At the time of the trade, Bloom was averaging more than 11 points per game. He joined a Celtics team that eventually lost in the first round of the playoffs to the Chicago Stags. His former team, the Bullets, won the BAA championship. The following year—his last as a professional—he began with the Minneapolis Lakers as a backup to the game's biggest star, George Mikan, and finished the season with the Chicago Stags. In forty-five total games that season, he averaged 2.8 points per game. He missed joining the NBA by one year.

After his playing days ended in 1950, Bloom moved to Baltimore, where his wife, Lillian, had grown up. He was a large-appliance salesman for many years. His wife died two years before he was inducted into the Temple University Hall of Fame in 1986. His two sons died tragically, one in a car accident and the other in a gun accident at home.

Bloom died on June 5, 1993.

Bill Dyer

By the end of the 1940s, Dyer's radio empire had begun to wane and lose its influence. The Bullets were sold, and his afternoon show was the victim of new formats and restructuring. He no longer broadcast the Bullets. In his place were Chuck Thompson, John MacClean, and Joel Chaseman, who covered the team until its demise in 1954. Shortly thereafter, Dyer and his family picked up and moved to California, severing all ties to Baltimore.

Gil Fitch

Fitch played six years with the Philadelphia SPHAS, from 1932–1933 to 1937–1938. His best years were 1934–1935, when he averaged 3.5 points per game in thirty-eight games, and 1935–1936, when he averaged 3.4 points per game in thirty-six games. His interest in music was even stronger than basketball, as he began playing music at an early age. He played both the clarinet and saxophone on the Orpheum Circuit, supporting his mother and two sisters. While playing with the SPHAS, he formed the Gil Fitch Orchestra, which played the dances after the games. He left the SPHAS after the 1937–1938 season to focus on his music career full-time. Fitch moved to Los Angeles after World War II and owned and operated the Robin Hood Day Camp and Camp Roosevelt.

He died in 2005.

Jerry Fleishman

After playing for the SPHAS during the war, Fleishman joined the Philadelphia Warriors of the fledgling BAA. In his first season, he averaged 4.5 points during fifty-nine regular-season games. In the playoffs, he increased his scoring to 6.3 points per game, as the Warriors defeated the Chicago Stags to claim the first BAA championship.

> We won the first BAA championship by defeating the Chicago Stags. I signed for $7,500 and got a $2,100 bonus for winning the

championship. In the off-season, I worked for Cedars Country Club, which was like the Catskills. Every Friday night, we had basketball games, and I would get ten ballplayers to come for the weekend with their wives, and we would play some games.

My contract for the following year was $5,000. I called Eddie and told him that I played my heart out for you, and we won the championship, and I made $7,500. He says, "But now, I own you." See, in those days, there were no representatives or agents like today.

Fleishman played three more years with the Philadelphia Warriors, from 1947–1948 to 1949–1950. In 1950–1951, he returned to play in the ABL with Scranton. In 1951–1952, he began the season in Scranton and finished in Schenectady, New York. The following year, 1952–1953, he began the season with the Philadelphia Warriors and later joined the New York Knicks. In thirty-three games, he averaged 9.0 points and helped lead the Knicks to the top record in the Eastern Division. The Knicks lost to the Minneapolis Lakers in the championship series.

They gave me a contract for 1953–1954, but I went to work with my father-in-law. I had played for 18 years, since I was 14 years old.

After I retired from the NBA, I would play games on the weekend with Scranton of the ABL. It was like a minor league, and if someone in the NBA got hurt, they would pick up a fellow for a few weeks. We had jobs and played on the weekend.

After our playing days were over, we became part of the Retired Players Association, and everyone was like a brother. We would meet once a year, either in the Bahamas or Puerto Rico, and they would have golf and tennis tournaments. I won the tennis tournament two years in a row. One year, it was Dave Bing and I versus Bill Russell and Patrick Ewing. In the second year, it was Jason Collins and I versus Patrick Ewing and Dave Bing. I got two beautiful watches for winning.

Fleishman died in 2007.

Bernie Fliegel

Fliegel was a member of the Wilmington Blue Bombers in 1941–1942 when they won both halves of the season and were declared league champions. Afterward, he entered the service.

I went into the service, but I had an enlarged heart, so I sat out a year. The next year I went in. I played on a basketball team in the service. We beat the Navy [Great Lakes] team that had Bobby Davies from Seton Hall. I played on a team called the Five By Five. We had Bruce Hale, who was a great player for Santa Clara and later coached at University of Miami. He is Rick Barry's former father-in-law. We also had Jake Ahearn and Dwight Eddleman. Our team was located in Miami Beach.

I began my time in the service at Fort Dix in New Jersey. Mike Bloom was there. Nobody wanted to leave because you were not in harm's way of the fighting. They had an extra person and announced that someone would have to go. Since I had twisted my knee and was out, I elected to go only if they would send me to a warm climate. The first stop was Miami Beach, and I stayed there for two years. The Long Island University sent their freshman team down and they needed a team to play against. That is how we started Five By Five. We played games in Tampa and then would come back. It was easy duty, and we played games.

For the first few months, I had a bad knee. I was in the aircraft specialization field. I was in Miami, then I went to Clearwater, and from there, I arrived in North Carolina at Fort McCullough. I was given a broom and put on KP duty. I ran into a friend, Captain Angie Monitto, who said that I should call him. Every day, I asked the sergeant if I could make a call, and he said to go back to work. After a few days, Captain Monitto came to the office and asked why I had not called. I told him to speak to the sergeant. He said, 'The general wants to see you.' This was during the Battle of the Bulge and a lot of the men were having horrible nightmares of what they had witnessed, so the general wanted me to put together a basketball team to help raise the morale of the troops. I said that I would if I could have a five-day furlough to visit my wife in Miami. Once I returned, I looked at a roster and found some players. One of them was Sy Lobello from Long Island University. It turns out that he was shipped out two days before. He died in the first day in battle in Europe.

After that, I had a job in which I would go to the hotel and offer them to buy back their furniture that was stored away when the Army came in and used the hotels during the war. I did this for a year and it was a cushy job.

I traveled with the furniture man in Miami Beach in 1944, before I went to Clearwater and Fort McClellan. I was married in St. Petersburg in November 1944, and played at Largo High School gym the day after I was married.

When I was discharged from the Army, I was already married and had one child. The New York Knicks wanted me to play for them, but I could not afford to play. They offered me $6,000. I had just opened a law office. I thought I could make more money playing in the American Basketball League on the weekends. I was getting $90 a game and playing three games each weekend.

When the war ended, Fliegel rejoined Wilmington for the 1945–1946 season and scored 11 points in two games. The following year, he played with the Jersey City Atoms and averaged 8.7 points in thirty games.

He died in 2009.

Jack (Dutch) Garfinkel

Ten games into the 1945–1946 season, Garfinkel was sent to the Rochester Royals of the NBL. He joined a team that featured future Hall of Fame members Al Cervi, Bob Davies, and Red Holzman. In his first season, the Royals won the NBL championship over the Sheboygan Red Skins. He began the following year with the Royals before being traded to the Boston Celtics of the newly formed BAA. He played there through the 1948–1949 season before being let go. He rejoined his old coach, John (Honey) Russell, and played the 1949–1950 campaign with Schenectady in the New York State League and with Hartford of the ABL.

After I finished with the SPHAS, I joined the Rochester Royals of the National Basketball League. It was one of the greatest teams I played for. They had Red Holzman, Al Cervi, Bob Davies, Fuzzy Levane, John Mahnken, and Bobby Fitzgerald. We won two championships in a row.

After I left the SPHAS, I played for the Royals and then the Boston Celtics of the NBA. Honey Russell was the coach then, and he coached at Seton Hall. He developed great players. Then Doggie Julian from Holy Cross came in. He let me go. Honey called me, and he was in upstate New York near Schenectady, Glens Falls, and Saratoga. I got $50 a game and ended my career there.

I met my wife, Lillian, and I was looking toward the future. I became a physical education teacher for 27 years. I retired and have a pension. I was also a salesman until 2 or 3 years ago. I sold advertising specialty items. Anything with an imprint on it, I sold it. I also get a pension from the NBA, which helps me.

I was also a referee for 27 years. I got $2 or $4 a game. I took the IAABO [International Association of Approved Basketball Officials] test and passed, so I was eligible to referee New York high school games. I also passed the CBOA [Collegiate Basketball Officials Association], so I could referee college ball. One year, Maurice Podoloff, the commissioner of the NBA, calls me and asks if I would like to referee a few professional games. It was a tryout for a weekend in Maine. I just made it back for Monday morning to teach. It would interfere with my teaching job, so I did not do it.

Moe Goldman

Goldman played nine seasons with the SPHAS and retired after the 1941–1942 season. He was a member of five championship teams. An injury in 1940–1941 significantly reduced his playing time that season and the next, and it led to his retirement at the age of 29. He spent the next three years in the service. After being discharged, he tried to resume his basketball career. In 1945–1946, he played nine games with the Baltimore Bullets and old teammate Red Rosan, and he averaged 4.6 points per game. The following year, he split his time with Troy and Newark of the ABL, and in only six games, averaged 7.8 points per game. He played two games with Troy of the New York State League and scored a total of 13 points.

Goldman was also a high school teacher and coach in New York City from 1936 to 1958. Afterward, he served as Chairman of Physical Education at Bushwick High School in Brooklyn. He also was Commissioner of Basketball for the Public School Athletic League of the New York City Board of Education between 1965 and 1975.

He died in 1989 at the age of 76.

Joel (Shikey) Gotthoffer

The 1941–1942 season marked the last full season for Gotthoffer, who was then drafted into military service. He played six games in 1942–1943 before officially retiring. His basketball career effectively over, he played in only six games the following season and none in the championship series loss to Wilmington.

During WWII, I was a supervisor at Wright Aeronautics in New York. I built engines for B-21s. When my local board called me, they told me I was going in as 1A. I made the request to go to officer school in the physical education area. I was sent to New Jersey, and I was questioned as to what I wanted to do. I told them I wanted to go into the health education program in Miami. They told me it was filled in Miami. They told me there was availability in the tanker destroyer unit. I told them I was not interested. I told him I would wait for an opening in Miami. My supervisor said that is not the way we do it.

I went back to work, and I received a 1A from my local board. I took it to the Colonel at Wrights Aeronautics. He tore it up. He told me to go back to my job and forget about it. Two weeks later, I was called down to my local board. This guy had the hots for me. He thought I was avoiding it. He said they would not let me get away with anything. I said, "I wasn't trying to get away with anything. I took it to the Colonel and he tore it up, not I." He said, "You will not get away with it. You'll go in as a private." I was there until the end of the war. I was working double shifts. I didn't play any basketball. I had to sleep sometimes.

After the war, Eddie Gottlieb asked me if I wanted to coach Philadelphia in the BAA. I gave it a lot of thought and came to the conclusion that I didn't want to do it, because I felt that if I didn't make the grade there, I would have to go looking for another coaching job in another city. I had two young kids and my wife, and I didn't want to put them in a position where they would never have any friends in school because their father was moving around, and they'd have to start all over and make other friendships, and my wife would be in the same category. I decided that I didn't want to do that to my family. As a matter of fact, even in business, I chose not to become a salesman with territory, which would have yielded me a tremendous amount of dollars as opposed to being in the metropolitan area. So I stayed, to be in contact with my family and be home every night.

So I told Eddie that I didn't want to do it and gave him my reasons, and he said, "Suppose you make good in Philadelphia and stay forever?" I said, "That's a challenge, and it might, but then again,

> it might not." I said, "I think basketball, right now, at this stage, is fickle because there's no solidity in basketball." I didn't even know if the BAA would succeed. So I never went back into basketball.[2]

During the summers Gotthoffer returned to the Catskills, where he supervised basketball games. At some point, he met a gentleman in the garment industry who gave him a job. Gotthoffer became a salesman for Peter Pan bras and girdles and eventually became a vice president of the company.

He died in 1987 at the age of 76.

Eddie Gottlieb

Gottlieb was a prominent figure in the early development of the BAA and NBA. He coached the Philadelphia Warriors when they won the 1946–1947 BAA championship. The team later won the 1954 NBA title. He bought the Warriors in 1952 for $25,000, and ten years later, when they were the San Francisco Warriors, sold them for $850,000. He served as chairman of the NBA Rules Committee for 25 years and helped oversee the implementation of the 24-second clock, the ban on zone defenses, and the "penalty shot" bonus free throw concept. He was also responsible for organizing the NBA schedule each year. He did so for more than thirty years, without the aid of a computer. Instead, he wrote everything on paper by hand. The Eddie Gottlieb Trophy, named in his honor, is awarded annually to the top rookie in the NBA. He was inducted into the Basketball Hall of Fame in 1972.

He died on December 7, 1979, at the age of 81.

Kitty Kallen

By the late 1930s, Kallen's career began building momentum. In 1938, she worked with Artie Shaw, and two years later, in 1940, she joined Jack Teagarden's band. Soon thereafter, she married Teagarden's clarinetist, Clint Garvin, and the two left the group. The marriage was annulled, and she later married publicist and television producer Bud Granoff. She enjoyed a short stay accompanying Bobby Sherwood, and by 1942 was with Jimmy Dorsey's orchestra. She replaced Helen O'Connell and began singing duets with Bob Eberly. Still a teenager, she was a vocalist on a number of songs, including the hit "They're Either Too Young or Too Old" and the duet

"Besame Mucho" with Eberly. A year later, in 1943, Eberly joined the service, so she left Dorsey and joined forces with Harry James, with whom she sang two popular songs, "I'm Beginning to See the Light" and "It's Been a Long, Long Time."

After the war, Kallen's career kept growing. She became a regular on television shows, including *The Danny Kaye Show, The David Rose Show,* and *Alec Templeton Time.* She recorded under her own name and teamed up with Richard Hayes to sing a song from the 1951 film *Two Weeks with Love* called "The Aba Daba Honeymoon."

At the height of her career, it was reported that she lost her voice and dropped out of sight for two years. By the mid-1950s, Kallen was a regular guest on Fred Allen's television show *Judge for Yourself.* In 1954, she made her comeback with her hit "Little Things Mean a Lot," and *Billboard* and *Variety* voted her most popular female singer. With her success re-established, she continued a long and prosperous singing career.

Ralph Kaplowitz

Winning the 1946–1947 BAA championship with the Philadelphia Warriors marked the high point in Kaplowitz's professional basketball career. After his half season with the SPHAS in 1945–1946, Ralph joined the New York Knickerbockers along with Ossie Schectman, Leo Gottlieb, and Hank Rosenstein. Years later, he remembered how he negotiated his contract with the New York Knicks.

> During the summer of 1946, it was rumored that a big league was being formed. By August, it came true. Ned Irish from Madison Square Garden sent me a telegram stating that a professional league is being started, and he would like me to play for his team. So, I called the number, and I spoke with Fred Podesta. He offered me $4,000 for the season to play. I told him I was not interested. I figured that I could make $4,000 playing for a local team instead of the big leagues. He insisted that I speak with him. I said that "I am not ready to talk for $4,000." He said he would get back to me. The next six weeks, he called me practically twice a week to speak with me. Each time, he raised the amount. Norma was walking up and down the living room saying, "Take it; take it." I kept saying, "Not yet, not until I am satisfied that we settled." I told him I wanted $8,000. Before long, we settled on $6,500, but I insisted on $1,500 up front,

> and they agreed. I got a check for $1,500 and a contract for $5,000. Norma sat down with a sigh of relief.

Kaplowitz joined the Knicks and earned the distinction of playing in the first BAA game. "When I played for the Knicks, I played in the very first game against Toronto. I scored 6 points. We won that game, 68–66. During the first year of the Basketball Association of America, Toronto was not used to basketball, only hockey. They would call the jump ball a face-off like in hockey. They probably never saw a Jew, and the Knicks were mainly a Jewish basketball team. We had Schectman, Gottlieb, Kaplowitz, and Rosenstein. Fans were yelling, not against one ballplayer, but all ballplayers, 'Abe, throw the ball to Abe. Abe, throw the ball to Abe.' This kept going on, which we ignored."

Midway through the season, he received a call from Gottlieb, who said his contract had been sold to the Philadelphia Warriors. Happy to be back in Philadelphia, he quickly joined a very good team featuring Joe Fulks, Howie Dallmar, George Senesky, Angelo Musi, and Art Hillhouse. Along with Jerry Fleishman, he was one of the first off the bench. In the playoffs, Philadelphia defeated his old New York team and then cruised past Chicago to win the championship. "When it came to the playoffs I saw lots of action and I felt that I was really helping the team," he recalled.

"The next season, I got a contract from Eddie for $5,000. I said, 'We won the championship. I should get more. Last year I got $6,500.' He said, 'That is all I can afford to pay.' I did not like it. I felt that $5,000 was not enough. I played that year and my heart was not in it. I did not do too well. It was the worst season for me. As a result, when the season was up, I did not get a contract renewal, and I was out."

In his last season with the Warriors, Kaplowitz started to think about his future, knowing his basketball career would not last forever.

"During our trips to Philadelphia, I would have a chance to talk to other players. Hank Benders was on the team. He said to me, 'Ralph, you would make a good insurance man. Why don't you get in contact with Herbert Angstreich from the Equitable Life Insurance Company? All you have to do is sell one $5,000 policy, and you make enough money for a week; then you can take off and go to the beach.' I said, 'That sounds pretty good to me.' When the season ended, I got in contact with Herbert and he told me about the insurance business. I liked what I heard, and I signed up and that is how I got into the insurance business, which I did for 55 years and did rather well."

Kaplowitz finished out the 1947–1948 season with the Philadelphia Warriors and averaged 3.9 points per game over forty-eight games. The following season, he joined Paterson of the ABL and finished the season with Hartford. He played the following year with Hartford and then finished his career in 1950–1951 with Bridgeport.

"While I was with the insurance company the first four years, I joined up with the American Basketball League. I played for Paterson Crescents, and Ossie Schectman was on that team. I found out that my contract was sold to Hartford. So I went to Hartford and stayed with them for the next four years. I was a star. At Hartford, I averaged 13.9 points a game. I also played with Bridgeport for one year, and I do not remember too much about that."

With his basketball career over, Kaplowitz embarked on a career in the insurance business.

He died in 2009 at the age of 89.

David (Cy) Kaselman

Kaselman played 13 seasons with the SPHAS, from 1929–1930 to 1941–1942, and led the SPHAS to eight championships in the Eastern Basketball League and the ABL. A prolific scorer, he tallied 425 points during the 1931–1932 season, the most ever for a SPHAS player. In World War II, he attained the rank of captain in the Air Force and was stationed at Camp Luna in 1943–1944. When the BAA began, Eddie Gottlieb asked him to be an assistant coach of the Philadelphia Warriors. He served as Gottlieb's assistant for three years until 1948–1949. Kaselman also served as an NBA referee from 1949–1950 to 1952–1953. Kaselman was a great foul shooter and was asked by Gottlieb to help Wilt Chamberlain improve his technique and accuracy. Each year, the Cy Kaselman Trophy is awarded to the most accurate free throw shooter among the Big 5 schools in Philadelphia, which include Temple, Villanova, LaSalle, St. Joseph's, and the University of Pennsylvania.

He died in 1971 at the age of 62.

Louis (Red) Klotz

After Klotz formed the Washington Generals in 1952–1953, his life changed and he soon became a global ambassador for the game of basketball. The touring teams might have changed, but the one constant was Klotz, who continually traveled the world spreading the gospel of basketball.

> We played so many years overseas that we introduced basketball to a lot of the world. We carried our own baskets and plywood floors. They did not even have them in those countries. We played in bull-rings and soccer fields, wherever we could put the court down. The people loved it, and gradually, each year, the kids started playing. When we first started, there was nothing but kicking the soccer ball around. They are still kicking it around and soccer is still the top sport in the world. But now, if you go, there are baskets hanging everywhere. They love basketball. They have had American coaches and the right ones. They learned the fundamentals, and we gave clinics for years. We played all around the world, including China right to Japan and Korea. We played everywhere. What you see coming into the NBA today, a hundred players from overseas playing solid fundamental basketball.

Klotz outlived all his SPHAS teammates. No person since 1950 has traveled more around the world to promote the game of basketball.

Louis (Inky) Lautman

Lautman played his entire 14-year professional basketball career with the SPHAS and was second only to (Red) Wolfe in longevity with the team. He was an iron man who missed only ten games in his fourteen years. His last season was 1946–1947, the first year of the BAA. The following season, he played independent ball, and in 1948–1949 was a member of the SPHAS All-Timer independent team that played around Philadelphia. After his playing career, he owned Point Bar at Twenty-second and Federal Streets.

He died in 1976 at the age of 61.

Harry Litwack

After retiring from the SPHAS as a player, Litwack began focusing on his coaching career at his alma mater, Temple University. He coached the freshman team and later served as an assistant head coach before finally taking over as varsity coach for the 1952–1953 season. Litwack retired after the 1972–1973 season after compiling a 373–193 career record. In 21 seasons, his teams had only one losing season; he led his teams to thirteen postseason tournaments. While serving as the freshman and assistant varsity coach, Litwack developed the box-and-one zone defense that later gained acclaim.

That defense was instrumental in limiting Stanford's Hank Luisetti to 11 points as Temple defeated Stanford 35–31 during the 1937–1938 season. That same Temple team won the first NIT championship that year.

As head coach, Litwack developed many outstanding teams. His 1955–1956 squad featured Guy Rodgers and Hal Lear; they compiled a 23–3 regular-season mark before losing to Iowa in the NCAA semifinals (Final Four). Two years later, in 1957–1958, Litwack was back in the NCAA semifinals as his team had a 24–2 regular-season record. Temple lost to eventual champion Kentucky in the semifinals. But he was finally able to win a postseason tournament when Temple won the 1968–1969 NIT championship over Boston College. The defeat was Bob Cousy's last as a head coach.

Litwack built a solid basketball program at Temple that continues to this day. His approach to recruiting was markedly different from recruiting today. As Bill Kelley, one of his former players, remembered, "The Chief didn't promise his recruits anything—not playing time, playgirls, cars, or money. They were offered only a solid education and a chance, if they worked hard, to play in a nationally respected basketball program."[3] He was inducted into the Naismith Memorial Basketball Hall of Fame in 1976.

He died in August 1999 at the age of 91.

Herman (Chickie) Passon

Passon played basketball from 1917–1918 to 1933–1934, when the SPHAS joined the ABL. He played independent ball with the SPHAS, Paterson, Washington, Trenton, and other assorted teams during a career that typified the 1920s, with players switching teams and leagues regularly. His best year was 1925–1926, when he averaged 17.7 points in eleven games for the SPHAS and 9.5 points in twenty-two games for Paterson of the Metropolitan League.

A co-owner of Passon's Sporting Goods store, Chickie helped operate it from 1927 until 1978. Throughout his life, he was active in promoting and supporting athletics in and around Philadelphia.

He died in 1989 at the age of 89.

Phil Rabin

In 1941, Rabin injured himself and was never the same again. In 1941–1942, he played five games with Saratoga of the New York State League and averaged 2 points. In 1942–1943, he played four games and averaged 7 points with New York of the ABL. The following year, he played with Brooklyn, and in two games, averaged 4.5 points. By 1944–1945, he was splitting time between Baltimore and Trenton and averaged 1.5 points in four games. The following season, his last as a professional with his hometown Paterson team, Rabin averaged 4 points in sixteen games.

"I played from 1935 to 1940, until I tore my Achilles tendon. I played another 4 years, but I was not as good. My best years were 1937, 1938, and 1939, when I led the American Basketball League in scoring and assists. I had torn cartilage in both knees and I was the first person in the state of New Jersey to have both knees operated on at the same time. From 1940 to 1945, I was in Defense. I was 4-F for the Army. I could not jump off a bench. I played until 1945."

Abe Radel

Radel's career and memory is best explained in the words of his daughter, Diane Moscowitz. "My father was a shy person in general, although I think he felt comfortable with the players. He was a family man, real proud of his family. He made the best of his life, given the formal education he received. My father passed away in 1975."

Howard (Red) Rosan

Rosan played with the SPHAS until the 1943–1944 season, enjoying five championships over his ten-year career. In 1944–1945, he joined the Baltimore Bullets as a player/coach and averaged 2.3 points in nineteen games. The following year, he served as the team's coach when they defeated the SPHAS to win the ABL championship.

He died in 1976 at the age of 65.

Alexander (Petey) Rosenberg

Rosenberg played eight seasons with the SPHAS and won four championships. During 1942–1943, he was stationed at Fort Belvoir, and the following year, he was headquartered at San Diego Marine Base. He rejoined the SPHAS in 1944–1945, and the following year, he averaged 5.7 points in twelve games. He played with the Philadelphia Warriors of the BAA in

1946–1947 and was a member of that championship team. While serving in the Marines in World War II, he recommended to Eddie Gottlieb that he sign Joe Fulks to a basketball contract. Fulks became one of the top players in the BAA/NBA during the league's first few years. After his playing career, Rosenberg ran a steak shop and managed a trucking company in South Philadelphia.

He died in 1997 at the age of 78.

Generoso (Jerry) Rullo

After helping the Philadelphia Warriors win the 1946–1947 BAA championship, Rullo began the following season with Baltimore and played in only two games before returning to the SPHAS in the ABL. In thirty games that year, he averaged 10 points per game. In 1948–1949, he began the season with the SPHAS and then returned to the Warriors for forty-nine games, in which he averaged 3.5 points per game. The next year, he started with the SPHAS but then went back to the ABL with Hartford and Trenton. By 1950, he was playing in the Eastern League and averaging double figures in points. He was also playing with the SPHAS as they toured with the Harlem Globetrotters.

"I went to the Eastern League and played there for about eight years. It fit in perfect with my schedule. I played on the weekend. There were a lot of good ballplayers. If Gottlieb needed a ballplayer, he would inquire. We had a great player in Sudbury named Jackie Moore, who became the first black player for the Warriors. I told Eddie, 'He is great. He had a great attitude, no problems, good rebounder.' He played with them and they won the 1955–1956 NBA championship." Rullo became involved in coaching after his playing career.

Ossie Schectman

Schectman played with the SPHAS until 1945–1946. In his last season with the team, he averaged 9.3 points in thirty-five games. The following year, he joined the newly formed BAA.

"The BAA, forerunner to the NBA, was formed for the 1946 season. I was signed by the New York Knicks and captained the team that year. I scored the first 2 points in NBA history. It was November 1, 1946, with the New York Knicks against the Toronto Huskies in Toronto, Canada."

After his one season with the Knicks, Schectman returned to the ABL with Paterson. In 1947–1948, he averaged 4.1 points in thirty-one games. The following year, his last as a professional player, he tallied 6.4 points per game in twenty-one contests.

Louis (Reds) Sherr

Sherr's career can best be summed up by his daughter, Lynn Sherr, a former correspondent for ABC News.

> When he graduated from the University of Pennsylvania Law School in 1929, he had two choices: clerk for a judge or continue to play basketball. The former would have cost him money; the latter paid up to $450 a week. So he rejoined the SPHAs for two more years, winning the celebrated Eastern Basketball League Championship both times.
>
> He left basketball in 1932 and embarked on his law career, running his own firm for 45 years. But his heart was in the two summer camps for children he co-owned in Pennsylvania: Camp Saginaw and Camp Akiba, a logical outgrowth of his own formative experience as a camp counselor for several seasons (while he was at law school). The Philadelphia Playground System, a network of recreational outlets that gave poor kids like him a place to play and a ladder to climb, had been his leg up. He passed it on.
>
> My dad deeply believed that kids—even middle-class Jewish kids living, by then, in nice suburban homes—needed to be away from their parents, close to nature; they needed to have a chance to be something different. He'd say, "For eight weeks, they aren't little princes or princesses." In a magazine article, he pointed out that camp was a place where a child could "develop in ways not always possible in the city," adding an early warning about the technology just starting to invade the world: "And, for those short weeks or months, he is freed from the hypnotic stare of that one-eyed monster, television."
>
> He also wrote about camping: "It is a child's world; the only place where everything is adapted to the child; the food, movies, plays, games, and all other activities are planned and conducted for the child. . . . I have found nothing as wonderful as working with children. There is real joy in having shy and reticent children start camp and see them gradually adjust themselves and, perhaps,

become leaders of their groups. . . . It is an even greater thrill when, at the beginning of a summer, I find among the new group the children of former campers."

Which happened over and over again. He was one of the pioneers in the camping business and often was honored by the American Camping Association and the Association of Private Camps. More importantly to him, he was Uncle Lou (and my mother was Aunt Shirley) to several generations of ever grateful campers.

It was through basketball and the SPHAS that my dad broke the stereotype of the Jewish immigrant. He integrated the lessons of sports into his daily life, and while he left the streets and moved to the suburbs to give his children—my sister and me—the chances he never had, he became an avid booster of whatever we chose. "Dream big; think big," he said, meaning it.

Sherr died in 1977.

Irving Torgoff

Torgoff played with the SPHAS through the 1945–1946 season. In his six years with the team, he was a part of three championship squads. When the BAA was formed in 1946–1947, he left the SPHAS and joined the Washington Capitols. He averaged 8.4 points in fifty-eight games that season, his best as a professional. He played the following year with Washington and averaged 7.2 points in forty-seven games. In 1948–1949, his last in the BAA, he split his time between Baltimore and Philadelphia. The following year, he played in four games with New York of the ABL before retiring.

Torgoff died in 1993 at the age of 76.

George (Red) Wolfe

Wolfe played his entire 15-year career with the SPHAS and retired at the close of the 1943–1944 season at the age of 39. His longevity helped him attain some notable achievements, including ranking first among SPHAS players in years played (15), second in games played (457), and second in playoff games (62). He coached LIU for two seasons, 1943–1944 and 1944–1945, and compiled a 27–8 record.

He died in 1970 at the age of 65.

Dave Zinkoff

Once referred to as "the original Mouth That Roared," the Zink turned announcing into an art form. Working with Zinkoff for more than forty years, Gottlieb had a close, personal seat for hearing Zinkoff perform all those nights. Gottlieb once called Zinkoff "the only PA announcer who could take on a crowd of 18,000 and outshout them."[4]

Quick to respond, Zinkoff said, "It isn't that I outshout them. I work the crowd. From long experience I can sense when the people are about to take a collective breath and—wham!—I move right in."[5]

During World War II, Zinkoff entered the Army as a private and when he left five years later, he had risen to the rank of captain. For several years, he was stationed in Iceland and helped introduce the country to boxing as a sport. After his two years, the Icelandic government presented him with an award for promoting friendship and goodwill between the U.S. and Icelandic militaries. While in the Army, he also served as master of ceremonies for many programs that included movie stars Bob Hope, Frances Langford, Alice Faye, and Jerry Colonna.

It was during his years in the service that Zinkoff developed his lifelong interest in charity work. He spent considerable time entertaining at VA hospitals. Zinkoff often recruited young, beautiful women—he called them "waitresses"—from the Police Athletic League. With them arm in arm, he visited the VA hospitals and entertained the veterans. At times, he was able to find local sponsors to help defray the costs, but he once estimated that he had to lay out between $5,000 and $10,000 of his own money on a yearly basis.

"Glad to do it. Look, I was in the Army for five years and I came out without a scratch. I figure I owe a huge debt to the men in the hospitals. Whatever it cost me to do my thing, it is only a small payment on that debt."[6]

After the war, Gottlieb introduced his good friend Zinkoff to Abe Saperstein, owner of the Harlem Globetrotters. Zinkoff later became the traveling secretary for the Harlem Globetrotters on their European tour and traveled with them during the 1950s and 1960s. In 1953, he published a book, *Around the World with the Harlem Globetrotters*. Zinkoff was the announcer for the Philadelphia Warriors and Philadelphia 76ers and spent more than 50 years announcing the game of basketball. He was involved in many organizations in Philadelphia and was often known to hand out salamis to players who performed well or people who did a good deed.

He died in 1985 at the age of 75.

ACKNOWLEDGMENTS

My interest in the Philadelphia SPHAS began when I worked as the archivist at the Naismith Memorial Basketball Hall of Fame. I spent much of my time researching and organizing the collection, and in the process I became aware of this team and my curiosity was piqued. As someone who is interested in Jews and sports, I found that not much had been written about them. What had been written tended to be the same information handed down through stories and folklore. I believed there was more to this story. Much is known about Hank Greenberg and Barney Ross, two prolific Jewish athletes during the 1930s; sadly, however, little information is available about the SPHAS. What was it like for the SPHAS, a Jewish basketball team, to travel across the East and Midwest and play basketball games in armories, ballrooms, and unheated gymnasiums? Who were these guys and where did they come from? What was the game of basketball like in those days? How did the team play and succeed in an environment that was hostile to Jews? What was it that kept them going? Finding the answers to these questions led me on a wonderful five-year journey that provided me with a greater understanding of the SPHAS and American Jewish history.

Throughout this process, I had the fortune to meet many wonderful people who opened their doors and allowed me to interview them. These included Sam (Leaden) Bernstein, Marvin Black, Irv Davis, Jerry Decker,

Norm Drucker, Jerry Fleishman, Bernie Fliegel, Jack (Dutch) Garfinkel, Sid Gersch, Lance and Muriel Gotthoffer, Marques Haynes, Bill Himmelman, Ralph Kaplowitz, Louis (Red) Klotz, Mitch Labov, Ed Lerner, Robert Luksta, Diane Moskowitz, Dick Nochimson, Joey Passon, Phil Rabin, Franklin Roberts, Jerry Rullo, Ossie Schectman, Helen Shurr, Seymour Smith, Peter Tyrrell Jr., and Venlo Wolfson. All of these individuals shared their time with me, providing insight into their careers and recollections. Their candor was most appreciated, and I thank them for allowing me to tell their story.

One of the challenges in researching this topic was the inability to interview those who played before World War II. This is a book about a team whose heyday was the 1930s and one that was largely forgotten after World War II. All of those players have since passed. However, I am indebted to Robert Peterson, whose book *From Cages to Jumpshots* continues to be the gold standard for the infancy and growth of professional basketball. Robert donated all of his research material for the book to the Naismith Memorial Basketball Hall of Fame. These documents contain firsthand interviews, including those with Moe Goldman and Shikey Gotthoffer.

The Basketball Hall of Fame provided invaluable access to its collections. These collections, overseen by Robin Deutsch and later by Matt Zeysing, contain extensive files on every Hall of Famer, every individual nominated, scrapbooks, *Reach Guides*, photo files, and clipping files of more than 1,000 players. Both the assistance of the Basketball Hall of Fame and the research materials were extremely valuable. A helpful starting point in compiling the appendixes was the work of Roger Meyer, who documented every game the SPHAS played during the 1930s. Additional research was provided by Parry Desmond, Josh Kantor, and Seymour Smith.

I thank Ron Potvin of the John Nicholas Brown Center at Brown University for helping secure a research fellowship that allowed me to finish the microfilm research.

Two individuals deserve special mention. First, Bill Himmelman, an independent basketball historian who is an expert on the game's early history and formative years, was a great resource. Anybody writing a book on professional basketball prior to 1950 should consult him. His associate Karel de Veer also helped with player and league research. Their extensive knowledge and files on every early player and professional league were indispensable. Second, David Smith, formerly of the New York Public Library, was a godsend in navigating the public library system, requesting hundreds of reels of microfilm through interlibrary loan, and introducing me to the who's who of sports writers. Without his help, I would still be walking aimlessly in the stacks of the New York Public Library.

Researching and writing this book was a team effort that required the assistance of many individuals. Without them, this book would not have been possible. During the early drafts, Suanna Selby Crowley (Grammar Girl) was instrumental in helping to structure the book's argument and tone, always pressing me to find my voice. I hope that I have succeeded. As the book took shape, various drafts benefited from the insights of Robin Deutsch, Dave Hecht, Bill Himmelman, Josh Kantor, Joe Nazare, Seymour Smith, and Peter Wosh (New York University Archives Program), all basketball fans, who helped sharpen the book. I thank them for their time, effort, and encouragement.

I also extend my thanks to Micah Kleit, my editor, who believed in this book from day one. To Lynn Sherr, who generously wrote the Foreword and provided copies of her grandfather's scrapbooks about her father, I extend my sincere appreciation. Photos were supplied by Diane Moskowitz, Philadelphia Jewish Archives Center, New York University, Naismith Memorial Basketball Hall of Fame, Bill Himmelman, Mickey and Marvin Black, Lynn Sherr and Lois Sherr Dubin, and the Athenaeum of Philadelphia. I also thank Mike Trostel and Sam Sheehan for their microfilm assistance and Ellie Kaiser for scanning many of the images.

Family always plays an important role in achieving success, and mine was no different. Rachel Dorman assisted in locating Jerry Fleishman, whom I interviewed prior to his passing. Sunday Clark painstakingly double-checked all the appendixes and patiently retyped all the results to make sure they were accurate. My brothers, Jim and Nick Stark, both assisted by doing online research and locating out-of-print books. To all of them, I extend my deepest thanks.

Finally, I thank all of the SPHAS players, whose pioneering spirit, foresight, and drive shaped a generation and laid the foundation for the wonderful game of basketball that is played by millions of people around the world. My only wish is that I could have seen them play, talked to them about their experiences, or spent a Saturday night at the Broadwood Hotel. I hope this book does justice to their basketball careers.

APPENDIX A

GAME-BY-GAME AMERICAN BASKETBALL LEAGUE STANDINGS FOR THE SPHAS

1933–1934

FIRST HALF

DATE	OPPONENT	SCORE	RECORD
November 18	Hoboken Thourots	34–20	1–0
November 25	Union City Reds	38–41	1–1
November 26	at Bronx Americans	34–23	2–1
December 2	Brooklyn Jewels	26–36	2–2
December 3	at Brooklyn Visitations	30–15	3–2
December 9	Trenton Moose	22–28	3–3
December 10	at Union City Reds	36–33	4–3
December 10	at Brooklyn Jewels	25–27	4–4
December 16	Brooklyn Visitations	31–26	5–4
December 19	at Newark Bears	29–34	5–5
December 23	Newark Bears	38–29	6–5
December 25	at Trenton Moose	32–38	6–6
December 30	Bronx Americans	42–21	7–6
December 31	at Camden Brewers	42–32	8–6
January 6	Camden Brewers	26–22	9–6
January 7	at Brooklyn Jewels	34–20	10–6
January 13	Union City Reds	50–43	11–6
January 14	at Brooklyn Visitations	21–26	11–7

(continued on next page)

1933–1934 *(continued)*

FIRST HALF

DATE	OPPONENT	SCORE	RECORD
January 20	Newark Bears	40–28	12–7
January 21	at Union City Reds	30–33	12–8
January 27	Trenton Moose	36–25	13–8
January 28	at Bronx Americans	30–31	13–9
February 3	Brooklyn Visitations	30–28	14–9
February 10	Brooklyn Jewels	23–29	14–10
February 17	Bronx Americans	45–41	15–10
February 18	at Newark Bears	31–49	15–11
February 19	at Trenton Moose	26–36	15–12

SECOND HALF

DATE	OPPONENT	SCORE	RECORD
February 24	Newark Bears	49–42	1–0
March 3	Bronx Americans	69–35	2–0
March 4	at Brooklyn Jewels	30–24	3–0
March 10	Brooklyn Visitations	41–36	4–0
March 11	at Newark Bears	38–26	5–0
March 17	Trenton Moose	39–33	6–0
March 18	at Brooklyn Visitations	21–17	7–0
March 20	New Britain Palaces	39–25	8–0
March 23	at Trenton Moose	38–35	9–0
March 24	Union City Reds	47–38	10–0
March 25	at Bronx Americans	40–24	11–0
March 31	Brooklyn Jewels	42–19	12–0
April 1	at Union City Reds	48–41	13–0
April 4	at New Britain Palaces	27–25	14–0

PLAYOFFS

DATE	OPPONENT	SCORE	RECORD
April 6	at Trenton Moose	28–21	1–0
April 7	Trenton Moose	21–35	1–1
April 13	at Trenton Moose	32–20	2–1
April 14	Trenton Moose	29–32	2–2
April 15	Trenton at Brooklyn	32–22	3–2
April 21	Trenton Moose	40–34	4–2

1934–1935

FIRST HALF

DATE	OPPONENT	SCORE	RECORD
November 3	Newark Mules	25–20	1–0
November 10	Brooklyn Visitations	27–33	1–1
November 11	at New York Jewels	27–31	1–2
November 15	at New Britain Jackaways	32–29	2–2
November 17	New Britain Jackaways	31–27	3–2
November 24	Jersey Reds	32–24	4–2
November 26	at Boston Trojans	33–35	4–3
December 1	Boston Trojans	44–30	5–3
December 7	at Newark Mules	27–22	6–3
December 8	New York Jewels	31–35	6–4
December 9	at Brooklyn Visitations	23–27	6–5
December 15	Newark Mules	31–22	7–5
December 16	at Jersey Reds	33–44	7–6
December 16	at New York Jewels	22–21	8–6
December 22	New Britain Jackaways	26–21	9–6
December 26	at New Britain Jackaways	28–14	10–6
December 27	at Boston Trojans	20–32	10–7
December 29	Brooklyn Visitations	34–30	11–7
January 5	Boston Trojans	20–34	11–8
January 6	at Brooklyn Visitations	37–27	12–8
January 12	New York Jewels	14–25	12–9
January 19	Jersey Reds	43–23	13–9
January 20	at Jersey Reds	28–35	13–10

SECOND HALF

DATE	OPPONENT	SCORE	RECORD
January 26	Brooklyn Visitations	39–25	1–0
January 27	at Brooklyn Visitations	28–31	1–1
February 2	Boston Trojans	44–18	2–1
February 3	at Jersey Reds	27–24	3–1
February 9	New Britain Mules	22–27	3–2
February 10	at New Britain Mules	26–?	3–3
February 16	New York Jewels	40–37	4–3
February 22	New Britain Mules	22–18	5–3
February 23	Jersey Reds	36–21	6–3
March 2	Brooklyn Visitations	21–19	7–3
March 3	at New York Jewels	18–34	7–4

(continued on next page)

1934–1935 *(continued)*

SECOND HALF

DATE	OPPONENT	SCORE	RECORD
March 9	Boston Trojans	34–29	8–4
March 10	at Jersey Reds	37–32	9–4
March 16	New York Jewels	37–33	10–4
March 17	at New York Jewels	24–36	10–5
March 19	New Britain Mules	19–25	10–6
March 20	Boston Trojans	36–31	11–6
March 23	Jersey Reds	44–30	12–6
March 24	at Brooklyn Visitations	31–39	12–7

SECOND-HALF PLAYOFF

DATE	OPPONENT	SCORE	RECORD
April 5	at Brooklyn Visitations	24–15	1–0
April 6	Brooklyn Visitations	30–39	1–1
April 11	Brooklyn Visitations	25–26	1–2

1935–1936

FIRST HALF

DATE	OPPONENT	SCORE	RECORD
November 2	Kingston Colonials	52–36	1–0
November 3	at Brooklyn Visitations	30–25	2–0
November 9	Paterson Panthers	43–26	3–0
November 16	New York Jewels	29–31	3–1
November 17	at New York Jewels	24–16	4–1
November 20	at Kingston Colonials	34–26	5–1
November 23	Brooklyn Visitations	29–25	6–1
November 30	Jersey Reds	41–31	7–1
December 1	at Brooklyn Visitations	21–25	7–2
December 7	Kingston Colonials	47–37	8–2
December 8	at Jersey Reds	23–33	8–3
December 14	New York Jewels	28–40	8–4
December 15	at New York Jewels	29–25	9–4
December 21	Trenton Bengals	41–30	10–4
December 25	at Trenton Bengals	29–25	11–4
December 28	Brooklyn Visitations	35–33	12–4
January 4	Jersey Reds	37–24	13–4
January 5	at Jersey Reds	19–31	13–5
January 8	at Kingston Colonials	37–26	14–5

1935–1936 *(continued)*

SECOND HALF

DATE	OPPONENT	SCORE	RECORD
January 11	Brooklyn Visitations	43–40	1–0
January 12	at Brooklyn Visitations	33–36	1–1
January 18	Passaic Red Devils	30–25	2–1
January 22	at Passaic Red Devils	18–30	2–2
January 26	at Jersey Reds	41–25	3–2
January 26	at New York Jewels	25–28	3–3
January 29	at Kingston Colonials	34–31	4–3
February 1	New York Jewels	27–35	4–4
February 8	Kingston Colonials	32–36	4–5
February 15	Jersey Reds	31–33	4–6
February 16	at Brooklyn Visitations	21–33	4–7
February 22	Brooklyn Visitations	29–44	4–8
February 23	at New York Jewels	27–20	5–8
February 26	at Passaic Red Devils	41–45	5–9
February 29	Passaic Red Devils	42–27	6–9
March 7	Kingston Colonials	40–18	7–9
March 11	at Kingston Colonials	19–25	7–10
March 14	New York Jewels	28–33	7–11
March 15	at Jersey Reds	25–24	8–11
March 21	Jersey Reds	28–21	9–11

PLAYOFFS

DATE	OPPONENT	SCORE	RECORD
March 28	Brooklyn Visitations	30–28	1–0
March 29	at Brooklyn Visitations	24–27	1–1
April 4	Brooklyn Visitations	30–27	2–1
April 5	at Brooklyn Visitations	24–31	2–2
April 11	Brooklyn Visitations	26–23	3–2
April 12	at Brooklyn Visitations	30–31	3–3
April 13	Brooklyn Visitations	47–34	4–3

1936–1937

FIRST HALF

DATE	OPPONENT	SCORE	RECORD
November 4	at Kingston Colonials	30–27	1–0
November 7	Kingston Colonials	40–27	2–0

(continued on next page)

1936–1937 *(continued)*

FIRST HALF

DATE	OPPONENT	SCORE	RECORD
November 8	at New York Jewels	21–30	2–1
November 14	New York Jewels	27–21	3–1
November 20	at Paterson Visitations	39–31	4–1
November 21	Atlantic City Sand Snipers	45–38	5–1
November 28	Brooklyn Visitations	37–27	6–1
November 29	at Jersey Reds	36–38	6–2
December 5	Jersey Reds	42–30	7–2
December 6	at New Jersey Jewels	25–34	7–3
December 8	at Atlantic City Sand Snipers	34–25	8–3
December 12	Kingston Colonials	43–49	8–4
December 19	New York Jewels	52–38	9–4
December 25	at Kingston Colonials	30–47	9–5
December 26	Brooklyn Visitations	40–34	10–5
December 27	at Brooklyn Visitations	37–29	11–5
January 9	Jersey Reds	49–41	12–5
January 10	at Jersey Reds	33–56	12–6

SECOND HALF

DATE	OPPONENT	SCORE	RECORD
January 10	at New York Jewels	37–36	1–0
January 13	at Kingston Colonials	38–46	1–1
January 16	New York Jewels	50–32	2–1
January 17	at New York Original Celtics	28–35	2–2
January 23	Brooklyn Visitations	31–27	3–2
February 6	New York Original Celtics	44–38	4–2
February 7	at Brooklyn Visitations	31–25	5–2
February 13	Kingston Colonials	48–34	6–2
February 14	at Jersey Reds	35–43	6–3
February 17	at Kingston Colonials	35–26	7–3
February 20	New York Jewels	33–23	8–3
February 22	at New York Jewels	30–24	9–3
February 27	Jersey Reds	42–38	10–3
February 28	at Brooklyn Visitations	38–59	10–4
March 6	Brooklyn Visitations	32–40	10–5
March 7	at Jersey Reds	33–38	10–6
March 13	Jersey Reds	51–34	11–6
March 14	at New York Original Celtics	31–22	12–6
March 15	Kingston Colonials	55–29	13–6
March 20	New York Original Celtics	46–33	14–6

1936–1937 *(continued)*

PLAYOFFS

DATE	OPPONENT	SCORE	RECORD
March 27	Jersey Reds	31–36	0–1
March 28	at Jersey Reds	39–36	1–1
April 3	Jersey Reds	28–34	1–2
April 4	at Jersey Reds	30–34	1–3
April 10	Jersey Reds	34–33	2–3
April 14	at Jersey Reds	45–23	3–3
April 17	Jersey Reds	44–43	4–3

1937–1938

FIRST HALF

DATE	OPPONENT	SCORE	RECORD
October 30	New Haven Jewels	51–30	1–0
November 6	New York Yankees	52–36	2–0
November 13	New York Original Celtics	64–46	3–0
November 14	at New York Original Celtics	41–38	4–0
November 20	Kingston Colonials	47–37	5–0
November 27	Jersey Reds	35–31	6–0
November 28	at Brooklyn Visitations	24–39	6–1
December 2	at Jersey Reds	22–34	6–2
December 4	Brooklyn Visitations	33–34	6–3
December 5	at New York Jewels	44–36	7–3
December 8	at Kingston Colonials	31–36	7–4
December 11	New York Jewels	40–44	7–5
December 12	at New York Original Celtics	27–39	7–6
December 22	at New York Yankees	40–28	8–6
December 25	New York Yankees	46–40	9–6
December 26	at Brooklyn Visitations	29–25	10–6
January 1	Jersey Reds	46–55	10–7
January 2	at Jersey Reds	27–36	10–8
January 5	at Kingston Colonials	29–36	10–9
January 8	Kingston Colonials	42–20	11–9
January 9	at New York Jewels	33–47	11–10
January 15	Brooklyn Visitations	46–42	12–10

(continued on next page)

1937–1938 *(continued)*

SECOND HALF

DATE	OPPONENT	SCORE	RECORD
January 22	New York Jewels	33–42	0–1
January 23	at Brooklyn Visitations	49–46	1–1
January 27	Jersey Reds	65–47	2–1
January 30	at New York Jewels	42–34	3–1
February 2	at Kingston Colonials	46–26	4–1
February 5	New York Original Celtics	42–35	5–1
February 6	at Jersey Reds	27–48	5–2
February 12	Kingston Colonials	45–30	6–2
February 17	at New York Jewels	31–33	6–3
February 19	Brooklyn Visitations	48–39	7–3
February 20	at New York Original Celtics	25–34	7–4
March 5	Jersey Reds	33–38	7–5
March 6	at Brooklyn Visitations	48–24	8–5
March 9	at Kingston Colonials	29–41	8–6
March 12	New York Original Celtics	33–26	9–6
March 19	New York Jewels	30–55	9–7
March 20	at New York Original Celtics	34–37	9–8
March 26	Brooklyn Visitations	53–37	10–8
March 27	at Jersey Reds	34–44	10–9
April 2	Kingston Colonials	45–37	11–9

1938–1939

SEASON (NO FIRST OR SECOND HALVES)

DATE	OPPONENT	SCORE	RECORD
November 5	Brooklyn Visitations	53–35	1–0
November 11	at Wilkes-Barre Barons	31–20	2–0
November 12	Kingston Colonials	33–24	3–0
November 13	at New York Jewels	35–36	3–1
November 19	New York Jewels	35–28	4–1
November 26	Washington Brewers	56–41	5–1
November 27	at Jersey Reds	36–39	5–2
December 3	Wilkes-Barre Barons	45–26	6–2
December 4	at Brooklyn Visitations	23–39	6–3
December 9	at Washington Brewers	43–34	7–3
December 10	Jersey Reds	44–34	8–3
December 14	at Troy Haymakers	43–33	9–3

1938–1939 *(continued)*

SEASON

DATE	OPPONENT	SCORE	RECORD
December 15	at Kingston Colonials	20–43	9–4
December 17	Troy Haymakers	44–41	10–4
December 24	Brooklyn Visitations	50–38	11–4
January 7	Kingston Colonials	34–32	12–4
January 8	at Washington Brewers	48–36	13–4
January 14	New York Jewels	40–37	14–4
January 15	at New York Jewels	40–39	15–4
January 21	Wilkes-Barre Barons	43–39	16–4
January 22	at Jersey Reds	43–36	17–4
January 28	Washington Brewers	62–42	18–4
January 31	at Kingston Colonials	25–40	18–5
February 2	at Troy Haymakers	32–43	18–6
February 4	Jersey Reds	40–36	19–6
February 11	Troy Haymakers	67–41	20–6
February 17	at Wilkes-Barre Barons	49–41	21–6
February 18	New York Jewels	38–40	21–7
February 25	Brooklyn Visitations	61–43	22–7
February 26	at Jersey Reds	33–42	22–8
March 2	at Brooklyn Visitations	49–30	23–8
March 4	Jersey Reds	41–35	24–8
March 5	at New York Jewels	32–33	24–9

PLAYOFFS

DATE	OPPONENT	SCORE	RECORD
March 18	New York Jewels	44–46	0–1
March 19	at New York Jewels	24–31	0–2

1939–1940

SEASON (NO FIRST OR SECOND HALVES)

DATE	OPPONENT	SCORE	RECORD
November 4	Wilkes-Barre Barons	50–34	1–0
November 8	at Kingston Colonials	44–29	2–0
November 11	Kingston Colonials	39–41	2–1
November 16	at Wilkes-Barre Barons	59–42	3–1
November 18	Jersey Reds	47–37	4–1

(continued on next page)

1939–1940 *(continued)*

SEASON

DATE	OPPONENT	SCORE	RECORD
November 19	at Jersey Reds	44–46	4–2
November 24	at Baltimore Clippers	32–38	4–3
November 25	Washington Brewers	51–37	5–3
December 9	Troy Haymakers	59–45	6–3
December 10	at New York Jewels	32–24	7–3
December 14	at Washington Brewers	35–26	8–3
December 16	Baltimore Clippers	35–36	8–4
December 20	at Troy Celtics	38–40 OT	8–5
December 23	Jersey Reds	40–31	9–5
January 6	New York Jewels	39–41	9–6
January 13	Baltimore Clippers	46–44	10–6
January 14	at New York Jewels	44–21	11–6
January 17	at Troy Celtics	36–19	12–6
January 20	Troy Celtics	36–38	12–7
January 27	Washington Brewers	38–31	13–7
January 29	Wilkes-Barre Barons	44–32	14–7
February 3	New York Jewels	39–51	14–8
February 4	at Washington Brewers	33–43	14–9
February 4	at Baltimore Clippers	40–34	15–9
February 10	Troy Celtics	32–38	15–10
February 14	at Troy Celtics	30–43	15–11
February 17	Washington Brewers	30–31	15–12
February 18	at New York Jewels	34–25	16–12
February 22	at Washington Brewers	29–21	17–12
February 24	Baltimore Clippers	51–36	18–12
February 25	at Baltimore Clippers	35–37	18–13
March 2	New York Jewels	44–27	19–13
March 9	Washington Brewers	34–27	20–13

PLAYOFFS

DATE	OPPONENT	SCORE	RECORD
March 16	Troy Celtics	32–29	1–0
March 17	at New York Jewels	33–27	2–0
March 23	Baltimore Clippers	43–36	3–0
March 24	Baltimore Clippers	51–32	4–0
March 30	New York Jewels	37–35	5–0
April 3	at Troy Celtics	32–28	6–0
April 6	Washington Brewers	51–44	7–0
April 8	at Washington Brewers	48–30	8–0

1940–1941

FIRST HALF

DATE	OPPONENT	SCORE	RECORD
November 16	New York Jewels	31–38	0–1
November 23	Troy Celtics	44–30	1–1
December 6	at Baltimore Clippers	44–39	2–1
December 7	Baltimore Clippers	37–35	3–1
December 8	at Washington Brewers	27–20	4–1
December 14	New York Jewels	42–34	5–1
December 15	at New York Jewels	40–20	6–1
December 21	Brooklyn Celtics	31–38	6–2
December 28	Washington Brewers	50–34	7–2
January 3	at Baltimore Clippers	36–34	8–2
January 4	Baltimore Clippers	51–46 OT	9–2
January 5	at New York Jewels	37–38	9–3
January 11	Washington Brewers	43–33	10–3
January 18	Brooklyn Celtics	44–42	11–3
January 19	at Washington Brewers	28–37	11–4

SECOND HALF

DATE	OPPONENT	SCORE	RECORD
January 24	at Baltimore Clippers	33–38	0–1
January 25	New York Jewels	32–45	0–2
February 1	Baltimore Clippers	30–43	0–3
February 2	at Brooklyn Celtics	41–42 OT	0–4
February 8	Brooklyn Celtics	49–44	1–4
February 9	at New York Jewels	40–32	2–4
February 15	New York Jewels	47–54	2–5
February 21	at Baltimore Clippers	48–46	3–5
February 22	Washington Brewers	48–45 OT	4–5
February 23	at Washington Brewers	39–35	5–5
March 9	at Washington Brewers	34–51	5–6
March 12	Brooklyn Celtics at Washington	45–41 OT	6–6
March 15	Brooklyn Celtics	32–44	6–7
March 22	Baltimore Clippers	36–42	6–8
March 23	at New York Jewels	45–43	7–8
March 29	Washington Brewers	38–50	7–9

(continued on next page)

1940–1941 *(continued)*

PLAYOFFS

DATE	OPPONENT	SCORE	RECORD
April 5	Brooklyn Celtics	48–38	1–0
April 6	at Brooklyn Celtics	26–40	1–1
April 12	Brooklyn Celtics	50–43	2–1
April 13	at Brooklyn Celtics	30–29	3–1

1941–1942

FIRST HALF

DATE	OPPONENT	SCORE	RECORD
November 2	New York Jewels	34–31	1–0
December 3	at Wilmington Bombers	24–40	1–1
December 6	Washington Brewers	39–46 2OT	1–2
December 7	at New York Jewels	38–37	2–2
December 13	Wilmington Bombers	36–48	2–3
December 19	at Washington Brewers	27–37	2–4
December 26	at Trenton Tigers	38–35	3–4
December 27	Trenton Tigers	49–42	4–4
January 1	at Wilmington Bombers	36–55	4–5
January 3	Washington Brewers	46–41 OT	5–5
January 10	Wilmington Bombers	27–31	5–6
January 16	at Trenton Tigers	35–33	6–6
January 17	Trenton Tigers	44–31	7–6
January 18	at Washington Brewers	40–32	8–6

SECOND HALF

DATE	OPPONENT	SCORE	RECORD
January 30	at Trenton Tigers	29–26	1–0
January 31	Wilmington Bombers	33–43	1–1
February 5	at Wilmington Bombers	33–50	1–2
February 7	Trenton Tigers	31–34	1–3
February 14	Washington Brewers	46–35	2–3
February 15	at Washington Brewers	27–38	2–4
February 21	Wilmington Bombers	26–42	2–5
February 28	Washington Brewers	40–35	3–5
March 1	at Wilmington Bombers	45–43	4–5
March 2	at Trenton Tigers	30–44	4–6
March 7	Trenton Tigers	40–43	4–7
March 14	Washington Brewers	52–42	5–7

1942–1943

SEASON (NO FIRST OR SECOND HALVES)

DATE	OPPONENT	SCORE	RECORD
December 19	Harrisburg Senators	40–36	1–0
December 25	at Trenton Tigers	34–40	1–1
December 26	New York Jewels	50–45	2–1
January 1	at Harrisburg Senators	36–44	2–2
January 2	Camden Indians	35–48	2–3
January 9	Trenton Tigers	40–37	3–3
January 22	at New York Jewels	38–37	4–3
January 23	New York Jewels	42–29	5–3
January 30	Harrisburg Senators	32–33	5–4
February 4	at Harrisburg Senators	45–38	6–4
February 6	Brooklyn Indians	43–39	7–4
February 13	Trenton Tigers	34–50	7–5
February 20	New York Jewels	32–37	7–6
February 21	at Trenton Tigers	36–25	8–6
February 27	Brooklyn Indians	43–34	9–6

PLAYOFFS

DATE	OPPONENT	SCORE	RECORD
March 6	Trenton Tigers	27–36	0–1
March 7	at Trenton Tigers	42–35	1–1
March 13	Trenton Tigers	30–37	1–2
March 14	at Trenton Tigers	42–39	2–2
March 27	Trenton Tigers	38–48	2–3
March 28	at Trenton Tigers	34–33	3–3
April 3	Trenton Tigers	44–42	4–3

1943–1944

FIRST HALF

DATE	OPPONENT	SCORE	RECORD
November 12	at New York Americans	43–44	0–1
November 13	Trenton Tigers	35–40	0–2
November 20	New York Americans	44–42	1–2
November 21	at Brooklyn Indians	46–35	2–2
November 28	at Wilmington Bombers	39–37	3–2
December 4	Wilmington Bombers	43–48	3–3

(continued on next page)

1943–1944 *(continued)*

FIRST HALF

DATE	OPPONENT	SCORE	RECORD
December 11	Brooklyn Indians	46–43	4–3
December 12	at Trenton Tigers	42–47	4–4
December ?	at New York Americans	37–57	4–5
December 18	Trenton Tigers	33–50	4–6
December 19	at Wilmington Bombers	44–50	4–7
December 25	Wilmington Bombers	36–50	4–8
January 2	at Trenton Tigers	32–38 OT	4–9
January 8	New York Americans	40–48	4–10

The SPHAS played a league game versus the New York Americans sometime between December 12 and 18, 1943; however, a date for this game cannot be found.

SECOND HALF

DATE	OPPONENT	SCORE	RECORD
January 15	Trenton Tigers	42–46	0–1
January 16	at Wilmington Bombers	52–36	1–1
January 21	at New York Americans	37–38	1–2
January 22	New York Americans	52–44	2–2
January 29	Wilmington Bombers	63–42	3–2
January 30	at Trenton Tigers	33–44	3–3
February 5	Trenton Tigers	54–46	4–3
February 12	New York Americans	49–47	5–3
February 19	Wilmington Bombers	39–36	6–3
February 20	at Trenton Tigers	52–51	7–3
February 26	New York Americans	62–49	8–3
February 27	at Wilmington Bombers	30–38	8–4

PLAYOFFS

DATE	OPPONENT	SCORE	RECORD
March 4	Wilmington Bombers	31–44	0–1
March 5	at Wilmington Bombers	42–35	1–1
March 12	at Wilmington Bombers	50–44	2–1
March 18	Wilmington Bombers	56–51	3–1
March 19	at Wilmington Bombers	38–45	3–2
March 25	Wilmington Bombers	36–57	3–3
March 26	at Wilmington Bombers	33–57	3–4

1944–1945

SEASON (NO FIRST OR SECOND HALVES)

DATE	OPPONENT	SCORE	RECORD
November 11	Wilmington Bombers	64–62 2 OT	1–0
November 12	at Wilmington Bombers	35–45	1–1
November 19	at Trenton Tigers	42–31	2–1
November 30	at Baltimore Bullets	39–34	3–1
December 2	New York Westchesters	43–30	4–1
December 9	Trenton Tigers	39–41	4–2
December 16	Baltimore Bullets	44–49	4–3
December 23	Washington Capitol's	60–46	5–3
December 29	at New York Westchesters	39–41	5–4
January 4	at Baltimore Bullets	39–34	6–4
January 6	Trenton Tigers	44–42	7–4
January 7	at Wilmington Bombers	38–41	7–5
January 13	Paterson Crescents	48–36	8–5
January 14	at Trenton Tigers	52–56	8–6
January 20	Wilmington Bombers	32–19	9–6
January 25	at Baltimore Bullets	43–36	10–6
January 27	New York Gothams	47–42	11–6
February 3	Baltimore Bullets	38–37	12–6
February 10	Trenton Tigers	46–37	13–6
February 11	at Wilmington Bombers	42–38	14–6
February 14	at Paterson Crescents	54–46	15–6
February 17	New York Gothams	45–40	16–6
February 23	at Trenton Tigers	32–51	16–7
February 24	Baltimore Bullets	41–36	17–7
February 25	at New York Gothams	37–31	18–7
March 3	Wilmington Bombers	47–39	19–7
March 10	Paterson Crescents	58–52	20–7
March 11	at Paterson Crescents	41–40 OT	21–7
March ?	at New York Gothams	28–45	21–8
March 18	Paterson Crescents	43–20	22–8

The SPHAS played a league game versus the New York Gothams sometime between March 11 and 18, 1945; however, a date for this game cannot be found.

PLAYOFFS

DATE	OPPONENT	SCORE	RECORD
March 17	Wilmington Bombers	49–44	1–0
March 21	at Wilmington Bombers	29–48	1–1

(continued on next page)

1944–1945 *(continued)*

PLAYOFFS

DATE	OPPONENT	SCORE	RECORD
March 31	Wilmington Bombers	48–41	2–1
April 5	at Baltimore Bullets	57–32	1–0
April 7	Baltimore Bullets	46–47	1–1
April 14	Baltimore Bullets	46–40	2–1

1945–1946

SEASON (NO FIRST OR SECOND HALVES)

DATE	OPPONENT	SCORE	RECORD
November 3	Paterson Crescents	63–55	1–0
November 17	Trenton Tigers	60–56	2–0
November 18	at New York Gothams	68–65	3–0
November 25	at Trenton Tigers	47–53	3–1
December 1	New York Gothams	50–48	4–1
December 7	at Baltimore Bullets	62–72	4–2
December 8	Baltimore Bullets	62–66	4–3
December 9	at Wilmington Bombers	49–55	4–4
December 15	Paterson Crescents	76–66	5–4
December 16	at Paterson Crescents	53–40	6–4
December 22	Wilmington Bombers	48–57	6–5
December 23	at New York Gothams	59–54	7–5
December 29	Trenton Tigers	86–61	8–5
December 30	at Trenton Tigers	62–58	9–5
January 5	New York Gothams	60–59	10–5
January 11	at Baltimore Bullets	61–67	10–6
January 12	Baltimore Bullets	61–56	11–6
January 13	at Wilmington Bombers	47–40	12–6
January 19	Paterson Crescents	59–52	13–6
January 20	at Paterson Crescents	57–53	14–6
January 26	Wilmington Bombers	72–60	15–6
January 27	at New York Gothams	61–75	15–7
February 1	at Baltimore Bullets	56–65	15–8
February 2	Baltimore Bullets	55–57	15–9
February 9	New York Gothams	53–60	15–10
February 16	Wilmington Bombers	70–58	16–10
February 17	at Wilmington Bombers	43–58	16–11
February 23	Baltimore Bullets	68–47	17–11

1945–1946 *(continued)*

SEASON

DATE	OPPONENT	SCORE	RECORD
February 24	at Trenton Tigers	48–63	17–12
March 2	Wilmington Bombers	70–61	18–12
March 3	at Paterson Crescents	74–73 OT	19–12
March 9	Trenton Tigers	72–69	20–12
March 10	at Wilmington Bombers	58–62	20–13
March 13	at Baltimore Bullets	70–46	21–13
March 16	Baltimore Bullets	61–63	21–14

PLAYOFFS

DATE	OPPONENT	SCORE	RECORD
March 17	at Wilmington Bombers	69–65	1–0
March 23	Wilmington Bombers	75–72	2–0
March 30	Baltimore Bullets	63–48	1–0
March 31	at Baltimore Bullets	48–65	1–1
April 13	Baltimore Bullets	45–68	1–2
April 14	at Baltimore Bullets	39–54	1–3

1946–1947

SEASON (NO FIRST OR SECOND HALVES)

DATE	OPPONENT	SCORE	RECORD
October 26	Paterson Crescents	54–71	0–1
November 2	Trenton Tigers	68–62	1–1
November 3	at Newark Bobcats	55–54	2–1
November 6	at Jersey City Atoms	51–44	3–1
November 9	Jersey City Atoms	64–57	4–1
November 24	at Brooklyn Gothams	47–68	4–2
November 29	at Wilmington Bombers	77–83	4–3
November 30	Baltimore Bullets	68–63	5–3
December 5	at Baltimore Bullets	46–59	5–4
December 7	Wilmington Bombers	83–77	6–4
December 8	at Trenton Tigers	40–52	6–5
December 14	Troy Celtics	69–59	7–5
December 19	at Troy Celtics	52–49	8–5
December 21	Elizabeth Braves	81–51	9–5
December 25	at Elizabeth Braves	58–67	9–6

(continued on next page)

1946–1947 *(continued)*

SEASON

DATE	OPPONENT	SCORE	RECORD
December 28	Brooklyn Gothams	49–59	9–7
December 29	at Paterson Crescents	58–53	10–7
January 4	Kingston Chiefs	73–55	11–7
January 5	at Brooklyn Gothams	53–70	11–8
January 8	at Jersey City Atoms	51–58	11–9
January 11	Jersey City Atoms	85–66	12–9
January 18	Trenton Tigers	67–57	13–9
January 19	at Wilmington Bombers	71–72	13–10
January 25	Paterson Crescents	89–63	14–10
January 26	at Paterson Crescents	65–67	14–11
February 1	Baltimore Bullets	77–59	15–11
February 2	at Trenton Tigers	86–96	15–12
February 4	Troy Celtics	58–44	16–12
February 8	Wilmington Bombers	88–71	17–12
February 20	at Elizabeth Braves	60–44	18–12
February 27	at Baltimore Bullets	61–86	18–13
March 5	at Troy Celtics	51–57	18–14
March 6	Brooklyn Gothams	60–53	19–14

PLAYOFFS

DATE	OPPONENT	SCORE	RECORD
March 13	Jersey City Atoms	56–47	1–0
March 16	at Jersey City Atoms	60–67	1–1
March 20	Jersey City Atoms	56–50	2–1
March 23	at Trenton Tigers	64–81	0–1
April 2	Trenton Tigers	46–42	1–1
April 12	Trenton Tigers	46–48	1–2

1947–1948

SEASON (NO FIRST OR SECOND HALVES)

DATE	OPPONENT	SCORE	RECORD
November 9	at Lancaster Red Roses	59–57	1–0
November 13	Trenton Tigers	60–71	1–1
November 16	at Brooklyn Gothams	73–74	1–2
November 20	Wilkes-Barre Barons	59–61	1–3

1947–1948 *(continued)*

SEASON

DATE	OPPONENT	SCORE	RECORD
November 23	at Trenton Tigers	74–77	1–4
November 26	at Jersey City Atoms	67–71	1–5
December 2	Jersey City Atoms	88–77	2–5
December 3	Lancaster Roses	56–50	3–5
December 6	at Paterson Crescents	73–75	3–6
December 7	at Trenton Tigers	71–69	4–6
December 16	Brooklyn Gothams	81–71	5–6
December 17	at Wilkes-Barre Barons	57–65	5–7
December 26	Paterson Crescents	43–47	5–8
January 3	at Paterson Crescents	65–76	5–9
January 9	at Hartford Hurricanes	87–85	6–9
January 11	at Brooklyn Gothams	68–61	7–9
January 16	Wilkes-Barre Barons	74–70	8–9
January 18	at Trenton Tigers	76–80	8–10
January 20	Trenton Tigers	75–61	9–10
January 21	at Wilkes-Barre Barons	53–73	9–11
January 31	at Paterson Crescents	65–72	9–12
February 11	at Wilkes-Barre Barons	47–64	9–13
February 12	Hartford Hurricanes	74–64	10–13
February 15	at Brooklyn Gothams	71–73	10–14
March 5	at Hartford Hurricanes	80–73	11–14
March 10	at Scranton Miners	76–83	11–15
March 11	Paterson Crescents	65–59	12–15
March 13	at Paterson Crescents	80–86	12–16
March 14	at Trenton Tigers	84–87	12–17
March 17	at Wilkes-Barre Barons	58–62	12–18
March 18	Brooklyn Gothams	61–52	13–18
March 21	at Scranton Miners	69–74	13–19

1948–1949

SEASON (NO FIRST OR SECOND HALVES)

DATE	OPPONENT	SCORE	RECORD
November 9	Hartford Caps	96–65	1–0
November 12	at Hartford Caps	94–87	2–0
November 16	Paterson Crescents	79–67	3–0

(continued on next page)

1948–1949 *(continued)*

SEASON

DATE	OPPONENT	SCORE	RECORD
November 17	at Wilkes-Barre Barons	58–71	3–1
November 18	Scranton Miners	91–76	4–1
December 1	Brooklyn Gothams	79–69	5–1
December 7	Bridgeport Newfield Steelers	86–71	6–1
December 11	at Brooklyn Gothams	78–91	6–2
December 12	at Bridgeport Newfield Steelers	67–78	6–3
December 17	at Scranton Miners	85–87	6–4
December 18	at Paterson Crescents	75–92	6–5
December 19	at Trenton Tigers	79–86	6–6
December 29	at Scranton Miners	71–85	6–7
January 1	at Hartford Caps	72–83	6–8
January 2	at Bridgeport Newfield Steelers	67–85	6–9
January 11	Wilkes-Barre Barons	95–107	6–10
January 12	at Wilkes-Barre Barons	85–104	6–11
January 15	at Brooklyn Gothams	79–85	6–12
January 16	at Hartford Caps	69–103	6–13
January 30	at Trenton Tigers	82–86	6–14
February 3	Trenton Tigers	78–90	6–15
February 5	at Paterson Crescents	73–88	6–16
February 6	at Scranton Miners	77–82	6–17
February 10	Brooklyn Gothams	58–54	7–17
February 17	Wilkes-Barre Barons	57–87	7–18
February 20	at Paterson Crescents	85–90	7–19
February 26	at Brooklyn Gothams	77–93	7–20
March 1	Paterson Crescents	87–97	7–21
March 2	Wilkes-Barre Barons	84–104	7–22
March 6	at Bridgeport Newfield Steelers	90–83	8–22
March 11	at Trenton Tigers	96–105	8–23
March 13	at Scranton Miners	65–82	8–24
March 23	at Bridgeport Newfield Steelers	85–95	8–25
March 25	at Trenton Tigers	116–118	8–26

Played in Atlantic City as the Tides through January 16 before moving back to Philadelphia.

APPENDIX B

YEAR-BY-YEAR STANDINGS FOR THE SPHAS

1917–1918

AMERICAN LEAGUE (OF PHILADELPHIA)

TEAM	WON	LOST	PCT
Philadelphia St. Columba	14	1	.933
Philadelphia Hancock	9	6	.600
Brotherhood Beth Israel	8	7	.533
Girard Alumni	6	9	.400
Philadelphia YMHA	**4**	**11**	**.267**
Philadelphia Port Richmond YMCA	4	11	.267

1918–1919

AMERICAN LEAGUE (OF PHILADELPHIA)

FIRST HALF

TEAM	WON	LOST	PCT
Philadelphia Yours Truly	7	1	.875
Philadelphia Hancock	6	2	.750
Philadelphia St. Columba	5	2	.714

(continued on next page)

1918–1919 *(continued)*

AMERICAN LEAGUE (OF PHILADELPHIA)

FIRST HALF

TEAM	WON	LOST	PCT
Philadelphia Dobson	5	2	.714
Philadelphia SPHAS	**3**	**4**	**.429**
Philadelphia Victrix C.C.	2	5	.286
Philadelphia Midvale	1	6	.143
Philadelphia Naval Aircraft Wilbar	0	7	.000

SECOND HALF

TEAM	WON	LOST	PCT
Philadelphia St. Columba	7	0	1.000
Philadelphia Hancock	5	2	.714
Philadelphia Midvale	4	3	.571
Philadelphia Dobson	3	4	.429
Philadelphia SPHAS	**3**	**4**	**.429**
Philadelphia Yours Truly	3	4	.429
Philadelphia Victrix C.C.	3	4	.429
Philadelphia Naval Aircraft Wilbar	0	7	.000

SEASON'S RECORD

TEAM	WON	LOST	PCT
Philadelphia St. Columba	12	2	.857
Philadelphia Hancock	11	4	.733
Philadelphia Yours Truly	10	5	.667
Philadelphia Dobson	8	6	.571
Philadelphia SPHAS	**6**	**8**	**.429**
Philadelphia Midvale	5	9	.357
Philadelphia Victrix C.C.	5	9	.357
Philadelphia Naval Aircraft Wilbar	0	14	.000

Yours Truly and Hancock played one game to decide tie for first half.
Yours Truly and Hancock played one extra game.

1919–1920

AMERICAN LEAGUE (OF PHILADELPHIA)

FIRST HALF

TEAM	WON	LOST	PCT
Philadelphia Dobson	6	1	.857
Philadelphia Xavier	6	1	.857
Philadelphia SPHAS	**5**	**2**	**.714**
Philadelphia Hancock	5	2	.714
Philadelphia St. Columba	2	5	.286
Philadelphia Mt. Carmel	2	5	.286
Philadelphia Girard	2	5	.286
Philadelphia Criterion	0	7	.000

SECOND HALF

TEAM	WON	LOST	PCT
Philadelphia Hancock	7	0	1.000
Philadelphia Xavier	6	1	.857
Philadelphia Dobson	3	3	.500
Philadelphia SPHAS	**3**	**4**	**.429**
Philadelphia Criterion	3	4	.429
Philadelphia Mt. Carmel	2	5	.286
Philadelphia Girard	1	5	.167
Philadelphia St. Columba	0	4	.000

1920–1921

AMERICAN LEAGUE (OF PHILADELPHIA)

FIRST HALF

TEAM	WON	LOST	PCT
Philadelphia Post 26	7	0	1.000
Philadelphia Nativity	5	2	.714
Philadelphia Hancock	4	3	.571
Philadelphia SPHAS	**4**	**3**	**.571**
Philadelphia 50 Club	3	4	.429
Philadelphia Logan	2	5	.286
Philadelphia Kaywood	2	5	.286
Philadelphia Girard	1	6	.143

(continued on next page)

1920–1921 *(continued)*

AMERICAN LEAGUE (OF PHILADELPHIA)

SECOND HALF

TEAM	WON	LOST	PCT
Philadelphia Hancock	6	1	.857
Philadelphia 50 Club	5	2	.714
Philadelphia Logan	4	3	.571
Philadelphia Post 26	4	3	.571
Philadelphia Nativity	4	3	.571
Philadelphia Kaywood	3	4	.429
Philadelphia SPHAS	**2**	**5**	**.286**
Philadelphia Girard	0	7	.000

FINAL STANDINGS

TEAM	WON	LOST	PCT
Philadelphia Post 26	11	3	.786
Philadelphia Hancock	10	4	.714
Philadelphia Nativity	9	5	.643
Philadelphia 50 Club	8	6	.571
Philadelphia Logan	6	8	.429
Philadelphia SPHAS	**6**	**8**	**.429**
Philadelphia Kaywood	5	9	.417
Philadelphia Girard	1	13	.071

1921–1922

AMERICAN LEAGUE (OF PHILADELPHIA)

FIRST HALF

TEAM	WON	LOST	PCT
Philadelphia Passon, Gottlieb, Black	**6**	**1**	**.857**
Philadelphia 20th Century	5	2	.714
Philadelphia Holy Name	4	2	.667
Philadelphia American Independence	4	2	.667
Philadelphia Alpha	2	4	.333
Philadelphia Broadway	2	4	.333
Philadelphia Merrill	1	5	.167
Philadelphia East Gnt.	1	5	.167

1921–1922 *(continued)*

AMERICAN LEAGUE (OF PHILADELPHIA)

SECOND HALF

TEAM	WON	LOST	PCT
Philadelphia Broadway	4	0	1.000
Philadelphia Alpha	3	1	.750
Philadelphia Passon, Gottlieb, Black	**2**	**1**	**.667**
Philadelphia 20th Century	2	1	.667
Philadelphia American Independence	1	2	.333
Philadelphia Holy Name	1	3	.250
Philadelphia Corley C. C.	1	3	.250
Philadelphia East Gnt.	0	3	.000

League disbanded before schedule was completed.

1922–1923

MANUFACTURERS' LEAGUE

FIRST HALF

TEAM	WON	LOST	PCT
Philadelphia Keystone Telephone	6	1	.857
Philadelphia M & H Sporting Goods	5	2	.714
Philadelphia Passon, Gottlieb, Black	**5**	**2**	**.714**
Philadelphia H. O. Wilbur	4	3	.571
Philadelphia Colonial Ice Cream	3	4	.429
Philadelphia Overbrook Carpet	2	5	.286
Philadelphia National Metal Edge	2	6	.250
Philadelphia Steel Heddle	1	6	.143

SECOND HALF

TEAM	WON	LOST	PCT
Philadelphia Colonial Ice Cream	7	0	1.000
Philadelphia H. O. Wilbur	5	2	.714
Philadelphia M & H Sporting Goods	5	2	.714
Philadelphia Keystone Telephone	3	4	.429
Philadelphia National Metal Edge	3	4	.429
Philadelphia Passon, Gottlieb, Black	**3**	**4**	**.429**
Philadelphia Steel Heddle	1	6	.143
Philadelphia Overbrook Carpet	1	6	.143

(continued on next page)

1922–1923 *(continued)*

PHILADELPHIA LEAGUE

FIRST HALF

TEAM	WON	LOST	PCT
Philadelphia Cathedral	8	2	.800
Philadelphia SPHAS	**7**	**3**	**.700**
Philadelphia St. Henry	6	4	.600
Philadelphia St. Peter's	3	6	.333
Philadelphia Tri-Council Caseys	3	7	.300
Philadelphia Holy Name	2	7	.222

SECOND HALF

TEAM	WON	LOST	PCT
Philadelphia St. Henry	9	2	.818
Philadelphia Tri-Council Caseys	8	3	.727
Philadelphia Cathedral	5	5	.500
Philadelphia St. Peter's	4	6	.400
Philadelphia Holy Name	3	6	.333
Philadelphia SPHAS	**1**	**8**	**.111**

1923–1924

PHILADELPHIA LEAGUE

FIRST HALF

TEAM	WON	LOST	PCT
Philadelphia Tri-Council Caseys	20	8	.714
Philadelphia Cathedral	17	10	.630
Philadelphia St. Peter's	17	11	.607
Philadelphia Shanahan	15	13	.536
Philadelphia SPHAS	**14**	**13**	**.519**
Philadelphia St. Henry	10	18	.357
Camden Railroaders	10	18	.357
Philadelphia Holy Name	8	20	.286

1923–1924 *(continued)*

PHILADELPHIA LEAGUE

SECOND HALF

TEAM	WON	LOST	PCT
Philadelphia SPHAS	**11**	**3**	**.786**
Philadelphia Cathedral	10	4	.714
Philadelphia St. Henry	8	5	.615
Philadelphia Tri-Council Caseys	6	7	.462
Philadelphia St. Peter's	6	8	.429
Philadelphia Shanahan	5	8	.385
Philadelphia Holy Name	3	7	.300
Camden Railroaders	3	10	.231

The SPHAS won the championship 2–0 over Tri-Council Caseys.

1924–1925

PHILADELPHIA BASKET BALL LEAGUE

FIRST HALF

TEAM	WON	LOST	PCT
Philadelphia SPHAS	**15**	**4**	**.789**
Philadelphia St. Henry	11	9	.550
Philadelphia Cathedral	9	9	.500
Philadelphia Tri-Council Caseys	8	10	.444
Philadelphia Kayoula	7	9	.438
Philadelphia Shanahan	5	14	.263

SECOND HALF

TEAM	WON	LOST	PCT
Philadelphia Tri-Council Caseys	11	7	.611
Philadelphia Shanahan	10	8	.556
Philadelphia SPHAS	**8**	**10**	**.444**
Philadelphia Cathedral	7	11	.389

The SPHAS won the championship 2–1 over Tri-Council Caseys.

1925–1926

EASTERN LEAGUE

FIRST HALF

TEAM	WON	LOST	PCT
Trenton Bengals	12	4	.750
Reading Bears	12	5	.706
Philadelphia SPHAS	**8**	**6**	**.571**
Philadelphia Cranes	5	6	.455
Pottsville Miners	3	9	.250
Camden Skeeters	1	11	.083

SECOND HALF

TEAM	WON	LOST	PCT
Philadelphia SPHAS	**6**	**0**	**1.000**
Philadelphia Quartermaster	4	2	.667
Pottsville Miners	1	5	.167
Exide A.C.	1	5	.167

1926–1927

AMERICAN BASKETBALL LEAGUE

FIRST HALF

TEAM	WON	LOST	PCT
Cleveland Rosenblums	17	4	.810
Washington Palace Five	16	5	.762
Philadelphia Quakers	14	7	.667
Brooklyn Celtics	13	8	.619
Fort Wayne Hoosiers	8	13	.381
Rochester Centrals	8	13	.381
Chicago Bruins	7	14	.333
Baltimore Orioles	1	20	.048
Detroit Pulaski Post	0	6	.000

SECOND HALF

TEAM	WON	LOST	PCT
Brooklyn Celtics	19	2	.905
Fort Wayne Hoosiers	15	6	.714

1926–1927 *(continued)*

AMERICAN BASKETBALL LEAGUE

SECOND HALF

TEAM	WON	LOST	PCT
Washington Palace Five	14	7	.667
Philadelphia Warriors	**10**	**11**	**.476**
Cleveland Rosenblums	9	12	.429
Chicago Bruins	6	15	.286
Rochester Centrals	6	15	.286
Baltimore Orioles	5	16	.238

Brooklyn Celtics defeated Cleveland 3–0 to win title.
Detroit dropped out after first half.
Brooklyn Arcadians transferred to Brooklyn Celtics.

1927–1928

AMERICAN BASKETBALL LEAGUE

EASTERN DIVISION

TEAM	WON	LOST	PCT
New York Celtics	40	9	.816
Philadelphia Warriors	**30**	**21**	**.588**
Washington Palace Five	7	15	.318
Brooklyn Visitations	18	11	.621
Rochester Centrals	24	28	.462

WESTERN DIVISION

TEAM	WON	LOST	PCT
Fort Wayne Hoosiers	27	24	.529
Cleveland Rosenblums	22	29	.431
Detroit Cardinals	5	13	.278
Chicago Bruins	13	36	.265

New York Celtics defeated Fort Wayne 3–1 to win title.
Detroit dropped out January 3, 1928.
Washington Palace Five transferred to Brooklyn January 3, 1928.
New York beat Philadelphia 2–0 in the Eastern Division playoff.

(continued on next page)

1927–1928 *(continued)*

PHILADELPHIA BASKETBALL LEAGUE

FIRST HALF

TEAM	WON	LOST	PCT
Philadelphia Elks	7	1	.875
Pattison	4	3	.571
Philadelphia Quartermaster	4	4	.500
Manayunk	2	4	.333
Philadelphia SPHAS	**0**	**5**	**.000**

SECOND HALF

TEAM	WON	LOST	PCT
Pattison	10	4	.714
Philadelphia Elks	10	8	.556
Philadelphia Quartermaster	10	9	.526
Germantown	9	10	.474
Downington Moose	9	11	.450
Manayunk	8	13	.381

Philadelphia SPHAS dropped out December 15, 1927.
Pattison was expelled from the league on February 19, 1928 for using ineligible players.

1928–1929

The team played independently and was not associated with a league.

1929–1930

EASTERN BASKETBALL LEAGUE

FIRST HALF

TEAM	WON	LOST	PCT
Philadelphia Elks	17	3	.850
Philadelphia SPHAS	**16**	**4**	**.800**
Pattison Coffey-Grinders	10	10	.500
Wilmington Cardinals	7	13	.350
Camden Skeeters	6	14	.300
Kennett Square Farmers	4	16	.200

1929–1930 *(continued)*

EASTERN BASKETBALL LEAGUE

SECOND HALF

TEAM	WON	LOST	PCT
Philadelphia SPHAS	**14**	**3**	**.824**
Wilmington Cardinals	10	8	.556
Philadelphia Elks	8	8	.500
Camden Skeeters	8	9	.471
Kennett Square Farmers	5	11	.313
Pattison Coffey-Grinders	5	11	.313

Philadelphia SPHAS defeated Philadelphia Elks 3–2 for title.

1930–1931

EASTERN BASKETBALL LEAGUE

FIRST HALF

TEAM	WON	LOST	PCT
Philadelphia SPHAS	**17**	**3**	**.850**
Philadelphia Elks	16	4	.800
Camden Skeeters	9	7	.563
Kennett Square	7	12	.368
Philadelphia Turners	3	14	.176
Wilmington Cardinals	3	15	.167

SECOND HALF

TEAM	WON	LOST	PCT
Camden Skeeters	15	5	.750
Philadelphia SPHAS	**14**	**6**	**.700**
Philadelphia Elks	13	7	.650
Reading Bears	7	13	.350
Wilmington Cardinals	6	14	.300
Kennett Square	5	15	.250

Philadelphia SPHAS defeated Camden Skeeters 3–1 for title.
Philadelphia Turners replaced by Reading Bears for second half of season.

1931–1932

EASTERN STATES BASKETBALL LEAGUE

FIRST HALF

TEAM	WON	LOST	PCT
Philadelphia Moose	15	5	.750
Philadelphia SPHAS	**15**	**5**	**.750**
Wilmington Cardinals	8	8	.500
Bridgeton Moose	8	10	.444
Camden Skeeters	4	12	.250
Philadelphia Jasper Jewels	4	14	.222

SECOND HALF

TEAM	WON	LOST	PCT
Philadelphia SPHAS	**14**	**4**	**.778**
Bridgeton Moose	10	5	.667
Philadelphia Moose	10	9	.526
Philadelphia Jasper Jewels	7	10	.412
Wilmington Cardinals	7	10	.412
Camden Skeeters	0	10	.000

Philadelphia Moose defeated Philadelphia SPHAS for first-half title.
Philadelphia SPHAS defeated Philadelphia Moose 3–1 for title.
Camden franchise forfeited on February 15, 1932.

1932–1933

EASTERN STATES BASKETBALL LEAGUE

FIRST HALF

TEAM	WON	LOST	PCT
Philadelphia SPHAS	**12**	**6**	**.667**
Trenton Moose	10	7	.588
Philadelphia Moose	9	7	.563
Bridgeton Gems	10	8	.556
Philadelphia Jasper Jewels	7	10	.412
Wilmington Cats	2	4	.333
Philadelphia WPEN A.C. Broadcasters	1	9	.100

1932–1933 *(continued)*

EASTERN STATES BASKETBALL LEAGUE

SECOND HALF

TEAM	WON	LOST	PCT
Trenton Moose	14	1	.933
Philadelphia Moose	10	4	.714
Philadelphia SPHAS	**8**	**7**	**.533**
Bridgeton Gems	5	5	.500
Philadelphia Jasper Jewels	3	10	.231
Philadelphia WPEN A.C. Broadcasters	1	14	.067

Trenton Moose defeated Philadelphia SPHAS 3–1 to win title.
Wilmington Cats dropped out during first half.

1933–1934

AMERICAN BASKETBALL LEAGUE

FIRST HALF

TEAM	WON	LOST	PCT
Trenton Moose	22	6	.786
Brooklyn Jewels	22	6	.786
Philadelphia Hebrews	**15**	**12**	**.556**
Brooklyn Visitations	12	12	.500
Bronx Americans	10	15	.400
Union City Reds	10	18	.357
Newark Bears	9	17	.346
New Britain Palaces	5	19	.208

SECOND HALF

TEAM	WON	LOST	PCT
Philadelphia Hebrews	**14**	**0**	**1.000**
New Britain Palaces	7	5	.583
Brooklyn Jewels	4	4	.500
Trenton Moose	6	7	.462
Newark Bears	4	5	.444
Union City Reds	4	7	.364
Bronx Americans	2	6	.250
Brooklyn Visitations	1	8	.111

Philadelphia Hebrews defeated Trenton Moose 4–2 to win title.
Hoboken moved to Camden, then to New Britain during first half.

1934–1935

AMERICAN BASKETBALL LEAGUE

FIRST HALF

TEAM	WON	LOST	PCT
New York Jewels	16	6	.727
Philadelphia Hebrews	**13**	**10**	**.565**
Brooklyn Visitations	13	11	.542
Newark Mules	12	11	.522
Boston Trojans	10	11	.476
Jersey Reds	7	14	.333
New Britain Jackaways	6	14	.300

SECOND HALF

TEAM	WON	LOST	PCT
Brooklyn Visitations	12	7	.632
Philadelphia Hebrews	**12**	**7**	**.632**
New Britain Mules	9	9	.500
Jersey Reds	9	9	.500
New York Jewels	8	10	.444
Boston Trojans	4	12	.250

Brooklyn Visitations defeated Philadelphia Hebrews 2–1 for the second-half title.
Brooklyn Visitations defeated New York Jewels 3–2 to win title.
Newark transferred to New Britain Mules.
New Britain Jackaways dropped out.

1935–1936

AMERICAN BASKETBALL LEAGUE

FIRST HALF

TEAM	WON	LOST	PCT
Philadelphia Hebrews	**14**	**5**	**.737**
New York Jewels	11	8	.579
Brooklyn Visitations	10	10	.500
Jersey Reds	9	9	.500
Kingston Colonials	7	12	.368
Trenton Bengals	4	11	.267

1935–1936 *(continued)*

AMERICAN BASKETBALL LEAGUE

SECOND HALF

TEAM	WON	LOST	PCT
Brooklyn Visitations	12	8	.600
Jersey Reds	11	9	.550
New York Jewels	10	10	.500
Kingston Colonials	9	10	.474
Philadelphia Hebrews	**9**	**11**	**.450**
Passaic Red Devils	8	11	.421

Philadelphia Hebrews defeated Brooklyn Visitations 4–3 to win title.
Paterson transferred to Trenton during first half.
Trenton transferred to Passaic during first half.

1936–1937

AMERICAN BASKETBALL LEAGUE

FIRST HALF

TEAM	WON	LOST	PCT
Jersey Reds	14	4	.778
Philadelphia Hebrews	**12**	**6**	**.667**
Kingston Colonials	11	6	.647
New York Jewels	7	10	.412
Brooklyn Visitations	4	12	.250
Atlantic City Sand Snipers	0	10	.000

SECOND HALF

TEAM	WON	LOST	PCT
Philadelphia Hebrews	**14**	**6**	**.700**
Jersey Reds	12	8	.600
Brooklyn Visitations	10	9	.526
New York Original Celtics	10	10	.500
Kingston Colonials	9	11	.450
Brooklyn Jewels	4	15	.211

Philadelphia Hebrews defeated Jersey Reds 4–3 to win title.
Atlantic City dropped out.
New York transferred to Brooklyn during second half.
Paterson transferred to Brooklyn during first half.

1937–1938

AMERICAN BASKETBALL LEAGUE

FIRST HALF

TEAM	WON	LOST	PCT
Jersey Reds	16	6	.727
New York Jewels	12	8	.600
Brooklyn Visitations	13	10	.565
Philadelphia SPHAS	**12**	**10**	**.545**
New York Original Celtics	11	10	.524
Kingston Colonials	5	15	.250
New York Yankees	1	11	.083

SECOND HALF

TEAM	WON	LOST	PCT
New York Jewels	14	5	.737
Jersey Reds	13	7	.650
Philadelphia SPHAS	**11**	**9**	**.550**
Kingston Colonials	9	9	.500
New York Original Celtics	7	11	.389
Brooklyn Visitations	2	15	.118

Jersey Reds defeated New York Jewels 4–2 to win title.
New York Yankees dropped out during first half.
New Haven transferred to New York during first half.

1938–1939

AMERICAN BASKETBALL LEAGUE

TEAM	WON	LOST	PCT
Kingston Colonials	28	7	.800
Philadelphia SPHAS	**24**	**9**	**.727**
Jersey Reds	19	14	.576
New York Jewels	19	15	.559
Wilkes-Barre Barons	14	22	.389
Troy Haymakers	12	21	.364
Brooklyn Visitations	7	20	.259
Washington Brewers	7	22	.241

Jersey Reds defeated Kingston Colonials 2–1. **New York Jewels defeated Philadelphia SPHAS 2–0.**
New York Jewels defeated Jersey Reds 2–1 to win title.

1939–1940

AMERICAN BASKETBALL LEAGUE

TEAM	WON	LOST	PCT
Kingston Colonials	8	4	.667
Philadelphia SPHAS	**20**	**13**	**.606**
Washington Brewers	19	14	.576
Troy Haymakers	3	9	.250
Troy Celtics	19	15	.559
New York Jewels #2	15	15	.500
Baltimore Clippers	15	16	.484
Jersey Reds	7	14	.333
Wilkes-Barre Barons	5	17	.227

Philadelphia SPHAS defeated Washington Brewers 1–0 for first place.
Philadelphia SPHAS defeated Washington Brewers, Troy Celtics, New York Jewels, and Baltimore Clippers in round-robin series to claim the title.
Kingston and Troy Haymakers merged to form Troy Celtics while continuing with the Troy Haymakers' won/loss record.
New York Jewels #1 and Jersey Reds merged to form a new New York Jewels #2 while continuing with the first New York Jewels' won/loss record.
Wilkes-Barre dropped out.

1940–1941

AMERICAN BASKETBALL LEAGUE

FIRST HALF

TEAM	WON	LOST	PCT
Philadelphia SPHAS	**11**	**4**	**.733**
New York Jewels	9	5	.643
Washington Brewers	7	7	.500
Troy Celtics/Brooklyn Celtics	4	7	.364
Baltimore Clippers	3	11	.214

SECOND HALF

TEAM	WON	LOST	PCT
Brooklyn Celtics	11	4	.733
New York Jewels	8	8	.500
Washington Brewers	7	8	.467
Philadelphia SPHAS	**7**	**9**	**.438**
Baltimore Clippers	6	10	.375

Philadelphia SPHAS defeated Brooklyn Celtics 3–1 to win title.
Troy Celtics transferred to Brooklyn Celtics.

1941–1942

AMERICAN BASKETBALL LEAGUE

FIRST HALF

TEAM	WON	LOST	PCT
Wilmington Blue Bombers	10	3	.769
Philadelphia SPHAS	**8**	**6**	**.571**
Washington Brewers	5	6	.455
Trenton Tigers	5	8	.385
New York Jewels	1	6	.143

SECOND HALF

TEAM	WON	LOST	PCT
Wilmington Blue Bombers	8	4	.667
Trenton Tigers	6	6	.500
Philadelphia SPHAS	**5**	**7**	**.417**
Washington Brewers	5	7	.417

New York Jewels dropped out.

Wilmington won regular season to claim championship.

1942–1943

AMERICAN BASKETBALL LEAGUE

TEAM	WON	LOST	PCT
Trenton Tigers	11	2	.846
Philadelphia SPHAS	**9**	**6**	**.600**
Brooklyn Indians	3	5	.375
Harrisburg Senators	4	8	.333
New York Jewels	1	6	.143

Philadelphia SPHAS defeated Trenton Tigers 4–3 to win title.
Camden Indians transferred to Brooklyn Indians.

1943–1944

AMERICAN BASKETBALL LEAGUE

FIRST HALF

TEAM	WON	LOST	PCT
Wilmington Blue Bombers	12	4	.750
New York Americans	9	6	.600
Trenton Tigers	8	6	.571
Philadelphia SPHAS	**4**	**9**	**.308**
Brooklyn Indians	2	9	.182

SECOND HALF

TEAM	WON	LOST	PCT
Philadelphia SPHAS	**8**	**4**	**.667**
Trenton Tigers	7	5	.583
Wilmington Blue Bombers	5	5	.500
New York Americans	2	8	.200

Wilmington Blue Bombers defeated Philadelphia SPHAS 4–3 to win title.
Brooklyn dropped out.

1944–1945

AMERICAN BASKETBALL LEAGUE

TEAM	WON	LOST	PCT
Philadelphia SPHAS	**22**	**8**	**.733**
Trenton Tigers	21	9	.700
Wilmington Bombers	14	14	.500
Baltimore Bullets	14	16	.467
New York Westchesters/New York Gothams	11	15	.423
Washington Capitols	2	8	.200
Paterson Crescents	1	15	.063

Baltimore Bullets defeated Trenton Tigers 2–1. **Philadelphia SPHAS defeated Wilmington 2–1.**
Philadelphia SPHAS defeated Baltimore Bullets 2–1 to win title.
New York Westchesters transferred to New York Gothams.
Washington Capitols transferred to Paterson Crescents.

1945–1946

AMERICAN BASKETBALL LEAGUE

TEAM	WON	LOST	PCT
Baltimore Bullets	22	13	.629
Philadelphia SPHAS	**21**	**14**	**.600**
New York Gothams	18	16	.529
Wilmington Bombers	15	19	.441
Trenton Tigers	14	20	.412
Paterson Crescents	13	21	.382

Baltimore Bullets defeated New York Gothams 2–1. **Philadelphia SPHAS defeated Wilmington Bombers 2–0.**

Baltimore Bullets defeated Philadelphia SPHAS 3–1 to win title.

1946–1947

AMERICAN BASKETBALL LEAGUE

SOUTHERN DIVISION

TEAM	WON	LOST	PCT
Baltimore Bullets	31	3	.912
Philadelphia SPHAS	**19**	**14**	**.576**
Trenton Tigers	17	17	.500
Elizabeth Braves	15	18	.455
Wilmington Blue Bombers	15	20	.429

NORTHERN DIVISION

TEAM	WON	LOST	PCT
Brooklyn Gothams	24	10	.706
Jersey City Atoms	14	22	.389
Troy Celtics	13	22	.371
Paterson Crescents	11	23	.324
Newark Bobcats/Kingston Chiefs/Yonkers Chiefs	7	17	.292

Baltimore Bullets defeated Brooklyn Gothams 2–1. **Philadelphia SPHAS defeated Jersey City 2–1.** Trenton Tigers defeated Elizabeth Braves 2–1. **Trenton Tigers defeated Philadelphia SPHAS 2–1.**

Baltimore Bullets quit playoffs to participate in World Professional Basketball Tournament, and Trenton Tigers were declared league champions.

1947–1948

AMERICAN BASKETBALL LEAGUE

TEAM	WON	LOST	PCT
Wilkes-Barre Barons	26	8	.765
Paterson Crescents	19	16	.543
Trenton Tigers	17	15	.531
Scranton Miners	16	16	.500
Elizabeth Braves/Hartford Hurricanes	11	12	.478
Philadelphia SPHAS	**13**	**19**	**.406**
Brooklyn Gothams	8	20	.286
Jersey City Atoms/Lancaster Red Roses	1	5	.167

Wilkes-Barre Barons defeated Trenton Tigers 2–0. Paterson Crescents defeated Scranton Miners 2–0.

Wilkes-Barre Barons beat Paterson Crescents 2–1 to win title.

Elizabeth moved to Hartford.

Jersey City moved to Union City on January 16, 1948 and Union City moved to Scranton on January 28, 1948.

1948–1949

AMERICAN BASKETBALL LEAGUE

TEAM	WON	LOST	PCT
Wilkes-Barre Barons	29	12	.707
Scranton Miners	26	15	.634
Trenton Tigers	25	16	.610
Paterson Crescents	24	17	.585
Bridgeport Newfield Steelers	24	17	.585
Hartford Caps	13	26	.333
Brooklyn Gothams	10	30	.250
Atlantic City Tides/Philadelphia SPHAS	**8**	**26**	**.235**

Paterson Crescents defeated Bridgeport Newfield Steelers for fourth place.

Wilkes-Barre Barons beat Trenton Tigers 2–0. Scranton Miners beat Paterson Crescents 2–0.

Wilkes-Barre Barons beat Scranton Miners 3–2.

Atlantic City moved to Philadelphia on January 16, 1949.

APPENDIX C

SPHAS VERSUS OTHER PHILADELPHIA PROFESSIONAL TEAMS

	SPHAS	EAGLES	PHILLIES	A'S	STARS
1933–34	Champions	Fourth	Seventh	Fifth	Champions
1934–35	No playoffs	Last	Seventh	Last	Fifth
1935–36	Champions	Last	Last	Last	Second
1936–37	Champions	Last	Seventh	Seventh	Fourth
1937–38	No playoffs	Fourth	Last	Last	Fifth
1938–39	Lost in first round	Fourth	Last	Seventh	Fourth
1939–40	Champions	Last	Last	Last	Fifth
1940–41	Champions	Fourth	Last	Last	Sixth
1941–42	No playoffs	Last	Last	Last	Fourth
1942–43	Champions	Third	Seventh	Last	Fourth
1943–44	Lost in finals	Second	Last	Sixth	Fourth
1944–45	Champions	Second	Last	Last	Fourth
1945–46	Lost in finals	Second	Fifth	Last	Fourth
1946–47	Lost in finals	Lost in finals	Seventh	Fifth	Fifth
1947–48	No playoffs	Champions	Sixth	Fourth	N/A
1948–49	No playoffs	Champions	Third	Fifth	N/A

APPENDIX D

BOX SCORES

BOX SCORE FOR LAST GAME

OCTOBER 17, 1959 VERSUS HARLEM GLOBETROTTERS

HARLEM GLOBETROTTERS (68)	G	F	PF	P
Lemon, lf	10	1	0	21
Hall	0	0	1	0
Harrison, rf	5	2	2	12
Summons	6	0	0	12
Buckhalter, c	2	1	0	5
Burton	0	0	1	0
Milton, lg	2	0	1	4
Wilson, rg	7	0	1	14
Totals	**32**	**4**	**6**	**68**

PHILADELPHIA SPHAS (42)	G	F	PF	P
Brennan, lf	3	0	0	6
Mitari, rf	9	0	1	18
Griboski, c	0	0	3	0
Josephs	0	0	0	0
Schreiber, lg	3	1	0	7

(continued on next page)

BOX SCORE FOR LAST GAME *(continued)*

PHILADELPHIA SPHAS	G	F	PF	P
Schayes	1	0	0	2
Lennox, rg	4	1	0	9
Corey	0	0	0	0
Totals	**20**	**2**	**4**	**42**

Key: **G** = goals; **F** = free throws; **PF** = personal fouls; **P** = points.

BOX SCORE FOR FIRST CHAMPIONSHIP SERIES

1922–1923 IN PHILADELPHIA LEAGUE, WON 2–0 OVER TRI-COUNCIL CASEYS

APRIL 3, 1924, GAME 2

PHILADELPHIA SPHAS (32)	G	F	P
Banks, lf	0	5	5
Passon, rf	1	6	8
Klotz, c	0	3	3
Tettemer, lf	1	1	3
Newman, rg	2	9	13
Totals	**4**	**24**	**32**

TRI-COUNCIL CASEYS (27)	G	F	P
Christian, lf	2	4	8
Gailey, rf	1	1	3
Leler, c	1	1	3
Campbell, lg	1	4	6
Sturgis, rg	0	7	7
Totals	**5**	**17**	**27**

Key: **G** = goals; **F** = free throws; **P** = points.

BOX SCORE FOR LAST CHAMPIONSHIP SERIES

LAST WON IN 1944–1945, DEFEATED BALTIMORE 2–1

APRIL 14, 1945, GAME 3

PHILADELPHIA SPHAS (46)	G	F	P
Schectman, f	4	3–4	11
Opper, f	1	0–0	2
Hillhouse, c	6	3–3	15
Lautman, g	2	4–7	8
Garfinkel, g	4	2–2	10
Totals	**17**	**12–16**	**46**

BALTIMORE BULLETS (40)	G	F	P
Boyle, f	2	2–2	6
Spector, f	2	2–4	6
Stutz, f	3	1–1	7
Nimz, c	0	1–2	1
Knuppel, c	1	0–1	2
Paris, g	1	2–2	4
Dubilier, g	2	5–5	9
Rosan, g	2	1–1	5
Totals	**13**	**14–18**	**40**

Key: **G** = goals; **F**= free throws; **P** = points.

APPENDIX E

ALL-TIME SPHAS ROSTER

This is an alphabetical listing of individuals who played with the Philadelphia SPHAS. The list is by no means all-inclusive, and some of the names are incomplete. I thank Bill Himmelman for his invaluable help in compiling this list.

Anderson, [ ]
Artus, George
Atherholt, [ ]
Baldwin, Oscar
Banks, David "Davey"
Baraz, [ ]
Barlow, Thomas "Tom"
Barnett, Bob
Becker, Morris "Moe"
Beckett, William "Billy"
Beron, Edward "Ed"
Bertman, Solomon "Solly"
Black, Edwin "Hughie"
Bloom, Meyer "Mike"
Boardman, Simon "Cy"
Brophy, [ ]
Brown, Andy
Brown, Stanley "Stan"
Bunin, Mark "Mockie"
Calhoun, Min
Campbell, James "Soup"
Chizmadia, Gaza
Clift, George
Cohen, Saul
Cooney, Roger "Rody"
Davis, [ ]
Davis, Irving "Irv"
Deighan, Cornelius "Neil"
Deighan, Richard "Rich"
Della Monica, Joe
Dessen, James "Jimmy"
Disney, [ ]
Dolin, Edwin "Eddie"
Downey, "Jiggs"
Dubin, Louis "Lou"
Emslie, [ ]
Feigenbaum, George
Fitch, Gilbert "Gil"
Fleishman, Jerome "Jerry"
Flemming, "Buck"
Fliegel, Bernie
Forman, Harry
Forman, Louis "Lou"
Fossett, Russell "Russ"
Fox, Dave
Fox, L. James "Jim"
Freeman, "Bunny"
Freemark, Mooney "Mort"

Gailey, Walter "Walt"
Gaines, Daniel "Bud"
Garber, George
Garfinkel, Jack "Dutch"
Getchell, C. Gorham
Geventer, Schireli
Glasco, George
Gluck, Edward "Sonny"
Goldblatt, Emanuel "Menchy"
Goldfaden, Benjamin "Ben"
Goldman, Morris "Moe"
Gordon, Dave
Gorman, [ ]
Gotthoffer, Joel "Shikey"
Gottlieb, Edward "Eddie"
Gottlieb, Leo
Goukas, Matthew "Matt"
Greenspan, [ ]
Griebe, Robert "Bob"
Gurfein, Arthur "Art"
Hall, Ed
Harris, [ ]
Herlich, George
Hewson, John "Jack"
Hillhouse, Arthur "Art"
Hyde, Joseph "Joe"
Kaplowitz, Ralph
Kaselman, David "Cy"
Kasner, Julius "Jules"
Kearns, Edward "Ted"
Kellett, Alfred "Al"
Kempner, Ed
Kirshner, Harry
Klotz, Louis "Red"
Klotz, Ralph "Babe"
Knorr, Harry
Knuppel, Herman
Kobler, William "Bill"
Krabovitch, Meyer "Moyer"
Kravitz, Ray
Lautman, Louis "Inky"
Leff, Isadore "Izzy"
Lehr, Allen "Al"
Lester, Charles
Levine, William "Bill"
Lewbart, [ ]
Litwack, Harry
Lojewski, Bob
Lyman, Milton "Babe"
Lyons, Eddie
Maister, Michael "Mickey"
Makransky, Eddie
Markoff, Phil
Marshall, [ ]
McCahan, William "Bill"
McGaffney, John "Red"
McNichol, Daniel "Dan"
Meehan, Frank "Stretch"
Miehoff, Solomon "Sol"
Miller, Edward "Ed"
Mondross, [ ]
Monska, Pete
Moorehead, Samuel "Sam"
Morganstine, William "Chink"
Morgenthaler, Elmore
Mosicant, Charles "Charlie"
Murphy, John "Johnny"
Neuman, Charles "Charlie"
Newman, George "Dutch"
Nowak, Paul
O'Connell, Tom
Opper, Bernard "Bernie"
Passon, Harry
Passon, Herman "Chickie"
Patkin, Max
Pierson, [ ]
Platt, Harry
Posnak, Max "Mac"
Possner, Louis "Lou"
Povernick, Joseph "Joe"
Prescott, [ ]
Rabin, Phil
Rader, Howard "Howie"
Rader, Leonard "Len"
Rappaport, Moe
Reagan, John "Inky"
Reichman, Irvin "Irv"
Resnick, Joseph "Beno"
Riconda, Henry "Harry"
Rocker, Jack
Rosan, Howard "Red"
Rosenberg, Alexander "Petey"
Rothenberg, Irwin "Irv"
Rullo, Generoso "Jerry"
Rutt, [ ]
Schectman, Oscar "Ossie"
Schneider, Alfred "Al"
Schneiderman, Louis "Lou"

Schrey, John
Schwartz, Solomon "Butch"
Senesky, George
Sherr, Louis "Reds"
Shires, C. Arthur "Art"
Snyder, Morris "Mendy"
Soltaire, [ ]
Staberg, [ ]
Stanczak, Frank
Swartz, Charles "Charlie"
Tanitsky, Aaron
Tettemer, Charles
Thomas, David "Hank"
Tobey, David "Dave"
Torgoff, Irving "Irv"
Trubin, Edward "Ed"
Van Osten, Wyleys "Bill"
Wallace, Paul
Watman, [ ]
Weiner, Leonard "Len"
Weintraub, Abraham "Butch"
Weller, Frederick "Fritz"
Welsh, Brookman "Yock"
Wesslock, Fred "Fritz"
White, "Doc"
Wiener, Robert "Albie"
Williams, [ ]
Wilson, [ ]
Wisner, Lou
Wolfe, George "Red"
Young, D.
Zeiss, Bill
Zubic, William "Bill"

NOTES

PREFACE

1. "Wilt Scores 29, but Stars Lose," *Philadelphia Inquirer*, October 18, 1959, Sports 13.

2. Deane McGowen, "Knicks Defeat All-Star Five before 17,932 at Garden," *New York Times*, October 18, 1959, Sports 17.

CHAPTER 1

1. Moe Goldman, interview by Robert Peterson, May 3, 1987, Robert Peterson Collection, Naismith Memorial Basketball Hall of Fame.

2. Jerry Fleishman, telephone interview by the author, September 2006.

3. Venlo Wolfson, telephone interview by the author [late 2006/early 2007].

4. Over the years, there were several National Basketball Leagues; none were related. "NBL" is used throughout the text to denote the midwestern league that existed from 1937 to 1949. It should not be confused with the East Coast league that existed from 1898 to 1904, mentioned in Chapter 2.

5. "Revenge Is Wing Hope," *Akron Beacon Journal*, December 28, 1938, 16.

6. "Fisher Plays Hebrew Five," *Flint Journal*, December 30, 1938, 16.

CHAPTER 2

1. "Y.M.C.A. Athletes," *Philadelphia Inquirer*, January 15, 1893, 3.

2. Jon Entine, *Taboo: Why Black Athletes Dominate Sports and Why We're Afraid to Talk about It* (Westport, Conn.: Greenwood Press, 1994), 199.

3. Ossie Schectman, telephone interview by the author, January 2007.
4. Sam (Leaden) Bernstein, interview by the author, Philadelphia [summer 2006].
5. Marvin Black, interview by the author, Philadelphia, October 2006.
6. Ibid.
7. Gloria Hayes Kremer, "The Last of the Legendary Sphas Celebrates His 90th Birthday," *Philadelphia Inquirer*, August 18, 1985, 3N.
8. Marvin Black, interview.
9. Ibid.
10. Ibid.
11. Ralph Kaplowitz, interview by the author, Queens, N.Y., December 2007.
12. "Eddie Gottlieb, 81, Dies: N.B.A. Pioneer," *New York Times*, December 8, 1979, 46.
13. Frank Deford, "Eddie Is the Mogul," *Sports Illustrated*, January 28, 1968, 43–45.
14. Sam (Leaden) Bernstein, interview by the author, Philadelphia [summer 2006].
15. Jerry Fleishman, telephone interview by the author, September 2006.
16. Shikey Gotthoffer, interview by Robert Peterson, May 1987, Robert Peterson Collection, Naismith Memorial Basketball Hall of Fame.
17. Louis (Red) Klotz, interview by the author, Margate City, N.J., August 2006.
18. Jerry Rullo, interview by the author, Philadelphia, July 2007.
19. Deford, "Eddie Is the Mogul," 45.
20. Jack (Dutch) Garfinkel, telephone interview by the author, October 2006.
21. Moe Goldman, interview by Robert Peterson, May 3, 1987, Robert Peterson Collection, Naismith Memorial Basketball Hall of Fame.
22. Abe Radel, "South Philadelphia Hebrew Association," in *The Reach Official Basket Ball Guide, 1926–27*, ed. William Phillips (Philadelphia: A. J. Reach, 1926), 222.
23. Entine, *Taboo*, 200.
24. Louis (Red) Klotz, interview.
25. Sam (Leaden) Bernstein, interview.
26. Ron Avery, "The SPHAs: Basketball Champions Shined When the Stars Were Jewish," *Jewish Exponent*, June 25, 1982, 48–49.
27. Steve Cohen, "They Took Their Shots: Gil Fitch, a Member of Philadelphia's All-Jewish Basketball Team in the 1930s, Reflects on Violence in Sports." *Naked City*, Philadelphia Citypaper, December 30, 2004–January 5, 2005. Available at www.citypaper.net/articles/2004-12-30/naked.shtml.
28. Ibid.
29. Sam (Leaden) Bernstein, interview.

CHAPTER 3

1. Moe Goldman, interview by Robert Peterson, May 3, 1987, Robert Peterson Collection, Naismith Memorial Basketball Hall of Fame.
2. Charles Salzberg, *From Set Shot to Slam Dunk: The Glory Days of Basketball in the Words of Those Who Played It* (Lincoln: University of Nebraska Press, 1987), 3.
3. "Final Contest," n.d., Moe Goldman Nomination File, Naismith Memorial Basketball Hall of Fame.
4. Bernard J. Kremenko, "Times' All-P.S.A.L. Quint Headed by Aaron Liebowitz," Moe Goldman Nomination File, Naismith Memorial Basketball Hall of Fame.

5. Moe Goldman, interview.

6. "Holman: The Early Years," CCNY Library exhibition. Available at www.ccny.edu/library/exhibitions/holman/holman_early_years.html.

7. Moe Goldman, interview.

8. Salzberg, *From Set Shot to Slam Dunk*, 7.

9. Moe Goldman, interview.

10. Ibid.

11. Salzberg, *From Set Shot to Slam Dunk*, 3.

12. "C.C.N.Y Five Tops Temple Quint for 10th Straight Win," *Philadelphia Inquirer*, February 4, 1934, Sports 1.

13. Ibid., Sports 2.

14. Salzberg, *From Set Shot to Slam Dunk*, 3.

15. Ibid., 4.

16. Ibid.

17. Moe Goldman, interview.

18. Salzberg, *From Set Shot to Slam Dunk*, 4.

19. Ibid.

20. Ibid.

21. "Moe Goldman Helps Sphas Defeat Jewels," *Philadelphia Inquirer*, March 5, 1934, 11.

22. "Goldman Gleams as Sphas Defeat Visitation Foes," *Philadelphia Inquirer*, March 11, 1934, Sports 1.

23. Salzberg, *From Set Shot to Slam Dunk*, 7–8.

24. Ed Delaney, "Hebrew Title Cause Tested In Local Game," *Philadelphia Record*, n.d., Moe Goldman Nomination File, Naismith Memorial Basketball Hall of Fame.

25. "Sphas Take Game From Trenton Foe," *Philadelphia Inquirer*, April 7, 1934, 15.

26. Ibid.

27. "Trenton Runs Away from Sphas in Third Period Even Playoffs," *Philadelphia Inquirer*, April 4, 1934, Sports 3.

28. Ibid.

29. Moe Goldman, interview.

30. Letter from Bernie Fliegel to Joe O'Brien, August 15, 1988, in Moe Goldman Nomination File, Naismith Memorial Basketball Hall of Fame.

31. Letter from Jack (Dutch) Garfinkel to Joe O'Brien, March 22, 1988, in Moe Goldman Nomination File, Naismith Memorial Basketball Hall of Fame.

32. Salzberg, *From Set Shot to Slam Dunk*, 9.

33. "Sphas Romp to 32–20 Triumph over Trenton and Take Lead in Series," *Philadelphia Inquirer*, April 14, 1934, 18.

34. Ibid.

35. "Saunders, Spindell Lead Bengal Attack That Tops Hebrews," *Philadelphia Inquirer*, April 15, 1934, Sports 1.

36. Phil Rabin, telephone interview by the author, September 2006.

37. Louis (Red) Klotz, interview by the author, Margate City, N.J., August 2006.

38. "Sphas Trounce Trenton Five, 33–22," *Philadelphia Inquirer*, April 16, 1934, 19.

39. Ibid.

40. "Sphas Down Trenton to Take American Court Crown," *Philadelphia Inquirer*, April 22, 1934, Sports 8.

41. Ibid.

CHAPTER 4

1. Steve Cohen, "They Took Their Shots: Gil Fitch, a Member of Philadelphia's All-Jewish Basketball Team in the 1930s, Reflects on Violence in Sports." *Naked City*, Philadelphia Citypaper, December 30, 2004–January 5, 2005. Available at www.citypaper.net/articles/2004-12-30/naked.shtml.
2. Sam (Leaden) Bernstein, interview by the author, Philadelphia, [summer 2006].
3. Cohen, "They Took Their Shots."
4. Lance and Muriel Gotthoffer, telephone interview by the author, [summer] 2007.
5. Peter Levine, *Ellis Island to Ebbets Field: Sport and the American Jewish Experience* (New York: Oxford University Press, 1992), 272.
6. Cohen, "They Took Their Shots."
7. Ibid.
8. Ibid.
9. Ibid.
10. Bill Ordine, "A Better Team Than Money Could Buy . . . ," *Today* (*Philadelphia Inquirer*), April 17, 1977, 38.
11. Moe Goldman, interview by Robert Peterson, May 3, 1987, Robert Peterson Collection, Naismith Memorial Basketball Hall of Fame.
12. Charles Salzberg, *From Set Shot to Slam Dunk: The Glory Days of Basketball in the Words of Those That Played It* (Lincoln: University of Nebraska Press, 1987), 9.
13. Ibid., 12.
14. Ron Avery, "The SPHAs: Basketball Champions Shined When the Stars Were Jewish," *Jewish Exponent*, June 25, 1982, 48–49.
15. "Hebrew Passers Lose Chance to Clinch A.L. Half Honors When Brooklyn Five Scores," *Philadelphia Inquirer*, March 25, 1935, 13.
16. Minutes of Meetings 1934, American Basketball League Collection, Naismith Memorial Basketball Hall of Fame.
17. Ronald Friedenberg, "Last-Period Rally Wins for Hebrews," *Philadelphia Inquirer*, November 4, 1934, Sports 1.
18. Ibid., Sports 6.
19. Ibid.
20. "Kaselman Dies at 62," *Philadelphia Inquirer*, July 4, 1971, 5.
21. Ronald Friedenberg, "Kaselman's Goals at Psychological Stage of Tilt Assure Sphas First Half Tie," *Philadelphia Inquirer*, March 24, 1935, Sports 3.
22. Marvin Black, interview by the author, Philadelphia, October 2006.
23. Ibid.
24. Louis (Red) Klotz, interview by the author, Margate City, N.J., August 2006.
25. Sam (Leaden) Bernstein, interview.
26. Friedenberg, "Kaselman's Goals," Sports 3.
27. Ronald Friedenberg, "Visitation Takes Second of Series to Even Up Count," *Philadelphia Inquirer*, April 7, 1935, Sports 1.
28. Ronald Friedenberg, "Brooklyn Five Wins Crown in Final Minutes," *Philadelphia Inquirer*, April 12, 1935, 19.
29. Ibid., 21.
30. Ibid.
31. Ibid.
32. Ibid., 19.
33. Ibid.
34. "Sphas Dethroned as King of Courts," *Brooklyn Daily Eagle*, April 12, 1934, 26.

CHAPTER 5

1. Ronald Friedenberg, "Sphas Reverse Jersey Foeman to Snare Title," *Philadelphia Inquirer*, January 5, 1936, Sports 1.
2. Sam (Leaden) Bernstein, interview by the author, Philadelphia [summer 2006].
3. Ralph Kaplowitz, interview by the author, Queens, N.Y., December 2007.
4. Bernie Fliegel, telephone interview by the author, May 2007.
5. Shikey Gotthoffer, interview by Robert Peterson, May 1987, Robert Peterson Collection, Naismith Memorial Basketball Hall of Fame.
6. Ibid.
7. Ibid.
8. Ibid.
9. Ibid.
10. Ibid.
11. Ibid.
12. Lance and Muriel Gotthoffer, telephone interview by the author, [summer] 2007.
13. Shikey Gotthoffer, interview.
14. Ibid.
15. Lance and Muriel Gotthoffer, interview.
16. Ronald Friedenberg, "Sphas Defeat Visitation 30–28 in First of American League Playoff Tilt," *Philadelphia Inquirer*, March 29, 1936, Sports 5.
17. Ibid.
18. Arthur Daley, "Final Olympic Basketball Tryouts Get Under Way at the Garden Tonight," *New York Times*, April 3, 1936, 32.
19. Arthur Daley, "Washington, Wilmerding, Y.M.C.A., Universal and Oilers Basketball Victors," *New York Times*, April 4, 1936, 20.
20. Carrie Kahn, "My Jewish Grandpa's Triumph at Hitler's Olympics," Morning Edition, Aug. 8, 2008, *National Public Radio*. Available at www.npr.org/templates/story/story.php?storyId=93400660.
21. Ibid.
22. Ibid.
23. "U.S. Five Annexes Final Battle, 19–8," *New York Times*, August 15, 1936, 7.
24. Peter Levine, *Ellis Island to Ebbets Field: Sport and the American Jewish Experience* (New York: Oxford University Press, 1992), 9.
25. Ibid.

CHAPTER 6

1. Ronald Friedenberg, "Sphas Classy, Win Loop Starter Here," *Philadelphia Inquirer*, November 8, 1936, 8.
2. Ibid.
3. Ronald Friedenberg, "Players, Fans Mix as Sphas Prevail," *Philadelphia Inquirer*, November 15, 1936, 6.
4. Sam (Leaden) Bernstein, interview by the author, Philadelphia [summer 2006].
5. Ronald Friedenberg, "Jewels' Spurt Tops Trojans in First Tilt," *Philadelphia Inquirer*, March 20, 1935, 17.
6. Ronald Friedenberg, "Sphas in High Gear Top Atlantic City," *Philadelphia Inquirer*, November 22, 1936, 5.
7. "SPHAS Triumph, Take 2nd Place," *Philadelphia Inquirer*, December 28, 1936, 19.

8. Bill Dallas, "Sphas Battle Jersey Reds Tonight for First-Half American Basketball League Honors," *Philadelphia Evening Ledger*, January 9, 1937, 16.

9. Ronald Friedenberg, "Sphas Win to Stay in Hunt for Title," *Philadelphia Inquirer*, January 10, 1937, Sports 1.

10. "Blistering First Period Finally Clinches First Half Title for Reds," from an unknown New Jersey newspaper, collected in a scrapbook donated by Robert Gallo, Naismith Memorial Basketball Hall of Fame.

11. "Reds Score 16th Consecutive Home Victory, Beating Hebrews 43–35," *Hudson Dispatch*, February 15, 1937, 1

12. Ibid., 2.

13. Ibid.

14. Ronald Friedenberg, "SPHAS Stage Rally to Win from Reds and Extend Lead," *Philadelphia Inquirer*, February 28, 1937, Sports 5.

15. Ibid., Sports 1.

16. Ronald Friedenberg, "SPHAS Brilliant, Beat Union City and Tie for Lead," *Philadelphia Inquirer*, March 14, 1937, Sports 1.

17. Ronald Friedenberg, "Hebrews Fail to Reach Top Form and Bow," *Philadelphia Inquirer*, March 28, 1937, Sports 1.

18. Ibid.

19. Ibid., Sports 6.

20. "Reds Gain Even Break with Hebrews in Playoffs over Weekend," *Hudson Dispatch*, March 29, 1937, 9.

21. Ibid.

22. "Reds Will Shift Spahn to Guard Post for Third Game of Title Series," *Hudson Dispatch*, April 3, 1937, 11.

23. Ronald Friedenberg, "SPHAS Collapse after Fast Start, Trail in Playoffs," *Philadelphia Inquirer*, April 4, 1937, Sports 1.

24. "Reds Crush Hebrews Twice and Move within One Game of Championship," *Hudson Dispatch*, April 5, 1937, 11.

25. "Reds Are Beaten, 34–33, in Fifth Game before Delirious Philly Mob," *Hudson Dispatch*, April 12, 1937, 9.

26. Ibid.

27. Ibid.

28. Ibid.

29. Ibid.

30. Ibid.

31. Ibid.

32. "Red Hopes Resting on Al Benson as Teams Wait Whistle," *Hudson Dispatch*, April 17, 1937, 13.

33. Ronald Friedenberg, "Sphas Top Reds for Title: Rosan's Points Give Hebrews League Crown," April 18, 1937, Sports 1.

CHAPTER 7

1. Ed Lerner, telephone interview by the author, June 2007.

2. Helen Schurr, telephone interview by the author, March 2007.

3. Sam (Leaden) Bernstein, interview by the author, Philadelphia [summer 2006].

4. James Rosin, *Philly Hoops: The SPHAS and WARRIORS* (Philadelphia: Autumn Road Publishers, 2003), 15.

5. Venlo Wolfson, telephone interview by the author [late 2006/early 2007].

6. Jerry Fleishman, telephone interview by the author, September 2006.

7. Ron Avery, "The SPHAs: Basketball Champions Shined When the Stars Were Jewish," *Jewish Exponent*, June 25, 1982, 48–49.

8. Ossie Schectman, telephone interview by the author, January 2007.

9. Bernie Fliegel, telephone interview by the author, May 2007.

10. Marvin Black, interview by the author, Philadelphia, October 2006.

11. Stephen M. Kolman, "Courting the American Dream: The Social and Cultural Community of Jewish Basketball in Philadelphia, 1920–1945." master's thesis, University of Wisconsin, Madison, 1991, 70.

12. Sam (Leaden) Bernstein, interview.

13. Ed Lerner, interview.

14. Jerry Rullo, interview by the author, Philadelphia, July 2007.

15. Sam (Leaden) Bernstein, interview.

16. Laurie Hollman, "Thanks to Memories, Athletic Club Demolition Is No Sweat," *Philadelphia Inquirer*, December 10, 1991, B1.

17. Louis (Red) Klotz, interview by the author, Margate City, N.J., August 2006.

18. Ed Lerner, interview.

19. Bill Ordine, "A Better Team Than Money Could Buy . . . ," *Today* (*Philadelphia Inquirer*), April 17, 1977, 40.

20. Rosin, *Philly Hoops*, 15.

21. Avery, "The SPHAs: Basketball Champions Shined, *Jewish Exponent*, 48–49.

22. Bill Lyon, "Always Imitated, Dave Zinkoff Was Truly an Original," *Philadelphia Inquirer*, December 26, 1985, 1D.

23. Sam (Leaden) Bernstein, interview.

24. Quoted in Marilyn Lois Polak, "Dave Zinkoff: Voluble Voice of the Sixers," *Philadelphia Inquirer*, March 18, 1979, Dave Zinkoff Clipping File, Naismith Memorial Basketball Hall of Fame.

25. Larry Merchant, "Zink Prepares Liberty Speech," December 17, 1959, Dave Zinkoff Clipping File, Basketball Hall of Fame.

26. "Introducing . . . the Zink! Look for a Mike, a Blonde or a Redhead, and There You'll Find the Arena's 'Voice,'" February 24, 1948, Dave Zinkoff Clipping File, Basketball Hall of Fame.

27. Polak, "Dave Zinkoff: Voluble Voice."

28. Ibid.

29. Avery, "The SPHAs: Basketball Champions Shined," 48–49.

30. Rosin, *Philly Hoops*, 9–10.

31. Jack (Dutch) Garfinkel, telephone interview by the author, October 2006.

32. Bernie Fliegel, interview.

33. Ordine, "A Better Team," 40–41.

34. Kolman, "Courting the American Dream," 70.

35. Peter Levine, *Ellis Island to Ebbets Field: Sport and the American Jewish Experience* (New York: Oxford University Press, 1992), 65.

36. *Sphas Sparks*, ed. Dave Zinkoff, October 19, 1940, 1. In the possession of the author.

37. Ibid., 2.

38. Ibid.

39. Ibid., 3.

40. Ibid., 4.

41. Ordine, "A Better Team," 41.
42. Diane Moskowitz, interview by the author, Timonium, Md., March 2007.
43. Ibid.
44. Ibid.
45. Ibid.
46. Ibid.

CHAPTER 8

1. "Dr. J.A. Naismith Is Dead in Kansas," *New York Times*, November 28, 1939, 25.
2. Phil Rabin, telephone interview by the author, September 2006.
3. Ibid.
4. Ibid.
5. Ibid.
6. "Sphas Spurt Late to Trip Troy Haymakers, 59 to 45," *Philadelphia Inquirer*, December 10, 1939, Sports 4.
7. Phil Rabin, interview.
8. "Hebrew Five Take First in Circuit," *Philadelphia Inquirer*, January 28, 1940, Sports 3.
9. "Washington, Sphas Triumph," *Philadelphia Inquirer*, March 3, 1940, Sports 2.
10. "2 Fist Fights Mark Sphas Victory," *Philadelphia Inquirer*, March 10, 1940, Sports 3.
11. Ibid.
12. "Fist-Fights, Rough-Housing Mark Sphas' 32–29 Victory over Troy in Series Opener," *Philadelphia Inquirer*, March 17, 1940, Sports 1.
13. Shikey Gotthoffer, interview by Robert Peterson, May 1987, Robert Peterson Collection, Naismith Memorial Basketball Hall of Fame.
14. Ed Lerner, telephone interview by the author, June 2007.
15. Jack (Dutch) Garfinkel, telephone interview by the author, October 2006.
16. Ralph Kaplowitz, interview by the author, Queens, N.Y., December 2007.
17. Phil Rabin, interview.
18. Shikey Gotthoffer, interview.
19. Moe Goldman, interview by Robert Peterson, May 3, 1987, Robert Peterson Collection, Naismith Memorial Basketball Hall of Fame.
20. Phil Rabin, interview.

CHAPTER 9

1. Moe Goldman, interview by Robert Peterson, May 3, 1987, Robert Peterson Collection, Naismith Memorial Basketball Hall of Fame.
2. Ossie Schectman, telephone interview by the author, January 2007.
3. Bernie Fliegel, telephone interview by the author, May 2007.
4. Ralph Kaplowitz, interview by the author, Queens, N.Y., December 2007.
5. Minutes of Board Meeting, November 8, 1940, ABL Collection, Naismith Memorial Basketball Hall of Fame.
6. Minutes of Board Meeting, January 20, 1941, ABL Collection, Naismith Memorial Basketball Hall of Fame.
7. Ben Green, *Spinning the Globe: The Rise, Fall, and Return to Greatness of the Harlem Globetrotters* (New York: HarperCollins Publishers, 2005), 107.

8. Available at www.aafla.org/SportsLibrary/NASSH_Proceedings/NP1989/NP1989Zd.pdf.

9. Letter from John J. O'Brien, dated February 27, 1945. ABL collection, Naismith Memorial Basketball Hall of Fame.

10. Leo Fischer, "Philly Five to Seek Laurels: Famous Hebrew Team to Meet in Amphitheater," *Chicago Herald-American*, February 25, 1941, 19.

11. Ibid.

12. John Schleppi, *Chicago's Showcase of Basketball: The World Tournament of Professional Basketball and the College All Star Game* (Haworth, N.J.: St. Johann Press, 2008), 6.

13. World Professional Basketball Tournament program, March 15–19, 1941, 4, Naismith Memorial Basketball Hall of Fame.

14. Ibid.

15. Leo Fischer, "Trotters Lose; 7 Left in Tourney," *Chicago Herald-American*, March 17, 1941, 20.

16. Leo Fischer, "Toledo Five Eliminates Bruins," *Chicago Herald-American*, March 18, 1941, 20.

17. Ibid.

18. Ibid.

19. Ibid.

20. Sam (Leaden) Bernstein, interview by the author, Philadelphia [summer 2006].

21. Jerry Rullo, interview by the author, Philadelphia, July 2007.

22. Ralph Kaplowitz, interview.

23. "Sphas Win, Fans in Riot," *Philadelphia Inquirer*, April 13, 1941, Sports 1.

24. Ibid.

25. "Sphas Take League Title," *Philadelphia Inquirer*, April 14, 1941, 22.

CHAPTER 10

1. Minutes of Meeting, December 4, 1942, ABL Collection, Naismith Memorial Basketball Hall of Fame.

2. Ibid.

3. Ibid.

4. William J. Scheffer, "Sphas Halt Jewels' Rally to Win, 50–45," *Philadelphia Inquirer*, December 27, 1942, Sports 1.

5. "3 Player-Fights as Sphas Win," *Philadelphia Inquirer*, February 22, 1943, 22.

6. William J. Scheffer, "Trenton Beats Sphas, 36 to 27," *Philadelphia Inquirer*, March 7, 1943, 3.

7. Sam (Leaden) Bernstein, interview by the author, Philadelphia [summer 2006].

8. Ralph Kaplowitz, interview by the author, Queens, N.Y., December 2007.

9. Bernie Fliegel, telephone interview by the author, May 2007.

10. Quoted in Rosemarie Ross, "'The Right Side of the Road' Leads Meyer Bloom into Temple's Hall," n.d., Mike Bloom Nomination File, Naismith Memorial Basketball Hall of Fame.

11. Quoted in ibid.

12. Quoted in ibid.

13. Moe Goldman, interview with Robert Peterson, May 3, 1987, Robert Peterson Collection, Naismith Memorial Basketball Hall of Fame.

14. Dave Wilson, "Temple Beats Stanford Five before 11,793," *Philadelphia Inquirer*, December 31, 1937, 15.

15. "Bradley Quint Easy for Owls in N.Y. Contest," *Philadelphia Inquirer*, March 10, 1938, 19.

16. Dave Wilson, "Temple Upsets Oklahoma, 56–44," *Philadelphia Inquirer*, March 15, 1938, 17.

17. Dave Wilson, "Temple Swamps Colorado, 60–36," *Philadelphia Inquirer*, March 17, 1938, 21.

18. Leonard Lewin, "A Night to Remember," *New York Post*, November 25, 1985, 65.

19. Wilson, "Temple Swamps Colorado," 21.

20. "Brewers Sell Bloom, Center, to Baltimore," *Washington Post*, December 28, 1940, 15.

21. "Clippers, Still Seeking First Victory, Meet Jewels Tonight," *Baltimore Sun*, December 27, 1940, 12.

22. Craig E. Taylor, "Clippers Blow Early Advantage over Jewels to Drop Eighth Straight," *Baltimore Sun*, December 28, 1940, 11.

23. William J. Scheffer, "Trenton Beats Sphas, 37–30; Takes Lead in Title Series," *Philadelphia Inquirer*, March 14, 1943, 3.

24. William J. Scheffer, "Trenton Victor over Sphas, 48–38," *Philadelphia Inquirer*, March 28, 1943, 3.

25. William J. Scheffer, "Sphas Triumph to Take Crown," *Philadelphia Inquirer*, April 4, 1943, 1.

CHAPTER 11

1. Bill Himmelman, interview by the author, Norwood, N.J., August 2007.

2. "Special Services Division" handbook, February 15, 1944, RG 160, Records of Headquarters Special Services Division General Records, 1941–45; RG 353.8, Research File—Sports (Box number not recorded), National Archives and Records Administration II, College Park, Md.

3. Seymour Smith, Jack Rimer, and Dick Triptow. *A Tribute to Armed Forces Basketball 1941–1969* (Lake Bluff, Ill.: Self-published, 2003), 126.

4. Jack (Dutch) Garfinkel, telephone interview by the author, October 2006.

5. Ibid.

6. Ibid.

7. Alex Zirin, "Chuckovitz Lines Up Strong Quintet," *Cleveland Plain Dealer*, March 8, 1942, C-2.

8. Jack (Dutch) Garfinkel, interview.

9. Ron Avery, "The SPHAs: Basketball Champions Shined When the Stars Were Jewish," *Jewish Exponent*, June 25, 1982, 48–49.

10. Stan Friedland, *Play It Again Sam: The Sam Schoenfeld Story* (Self-published, 2004), 154.

11. Jack (Dutch) Garfinkel, interview.

12. Ibid.

13. Ibid.

14. Ibid.

15. Ossie Schectman, telephone interview by the author, January 2007.

16. Ibid.

17. Charley Rosen, "NBA Pioneer Is No Old Fogey," *Page 2, ESPN.com*, 2004. Available at www.espn.go.com/page2/s/rosen/030408.html.
18. Ibid.
19. Ossie Schectman, interview.
20. Ibid.
21. Ibid.
22. Official Program, Wilmington Blue Bombers, 1942–1943, in the possession of the author.
23. Ossie Schectman, interview.
24. John J. Brady, "SPHAS Beat Bombers, 42–35, Keglers Tie for Top Prize," *Wilmington Morning News*, March 6, 1944,12.
25. Bernie Fliegel, telephone interview by the author, May 2007.
26. Ibid.
27. Ibid.
28. Ibid.
29. Ibid.
30. Ibid.
31. Ibid.
32. Ibid.
33. Official Program, Wilmington Blue Bombers, 1942–1943.
34. Bernie Fliegel, interview.
35. Ibid.
36. John J. Brady, "Bombers Win 1943–44 American Basketball League Title," *Wilmington Morning News*, March 27, 1944, 12.
37. Ibid.
38. Jerry Fleishman, telephone interview by the author, September 2006.
39. Ibid.
40. Ibid.
41. Ibid.
42. Ibid.
43. Ibid.
44. Ibid.
45. Ibid.
46. Ibid.
47. Ibid.
48. Ibid.
49. Ibid.
50. Robert Elmer, "SPHAS Thump Bullet Five," *Baltimore Sun*, April 16, 1945, 17.

CHAPTER 12

1. Ralph Kaplowitz, interview by the author, Queens, N.Y., December 2007.
2. Ibid.
3. "Kaplowitz, a Musician, Makes Baskets Hum," n.d., Records of the Athletic Department, New York University Archives.
4. Ibid.
5. 1940 NYU Album, New York University Archives.
6. 1940 NYU Violet, New York University Archives.

7. Ralph Kaplowitz, interview.
8. 1942 NYU Violet, New York University Archives.
9. 1942 NYU Album, New York University Archives.
10. Ralph Kaplowitz, interview.
11. Ibid.
12. Ibid.
13. Ibid.
14. Ibid.
15. Ibid.
16. Ibid.
17. Ibid.
18. Ibid.
19. Ibid.
20. Ibid.
21. Ibid.
22. Ibid.
23. Ibid.
24. Robert Elmer, "Bullets Buy Mike Bloom," *Baltimore Sun*, January 11, 1946, 18.
25. Robert Elmer, "Bullets Come from Behind to Whip SPHAs in 67–61 Pro Basket Battle," *Baltimore Sun*, January 12, 1946, 11.
26. Robert Elmer, "SPHAS Whip Bullets, 70–46 to Force Playoff for Pro Cage Loop Title," *Baltimore Sun*, March 14, 1946, 15.
27. Robert Elmer, "Bullets Seek Title Tonight," *Baltimore Sun*, March 13, 1946, 14.
28. "Bullets Top Sphas, 63–61, to Win Pro Cage Title," *Baltimore Sun*, March 17, 1946, Sports 1.
29. Ibid.
30. "Bullets Lose Playoff Game," *Baltimore Sun*, March 31, 1946, Sports 1.
31. Robert Elmer, "Bullets Subdue SPHAS to Even Professional Basketball Playoff Series," *Baltimore Sun*, April 1, 1946, 14.
32. "Bullets Drub SPHAS, 68–45," *Baltimore Sun*, April 14, 1946, Sports 1.
33. Robert Elmer, "Bullets Seek Title Tonight," *Baltimore Sun*, March 13, 1946, 15.
34. "Bill Dyer," *Broadcast Pioneers of Philadelphia*. Available at www.broadcastpioneers.com/billdyer.html.
35. Seymour Smith, telephone interview by the author, June 2007.
36. Frank Cashen, "Under the Basket," *News Post*, March 7, 1946, 22.
37. Elmer, "Bullets Seek Title," 15.
38. Robert Elmer, "Bullets Beat Sphas, 54–39, for Pro Cage League Playoff Championship," *Baltimore Sun*, April 15, 1946, 16.

CHAPTER 13

1. Bill Himmelman, interview by the author, Norwood, N.J., August 2007.
2. Minutes of Meetings, June 9, July 14, August 16, 1946, ABL Collection, Naismith Memorial Basketball Hall of Fame.
3. Jerry Rullo, interview by the author, Philadelphia, July 2007.
4. Ibid.
5. Minutes of Board Meeting, September 22, 1946, ABL Collection, Naismith Memorial Basketball Hall of Fame.

6. Allen Lewis, "Warriors Rout Celtics, 81–57," *Philadelphia Inquirer*, March 14, 1947, 34.
7. Jerry Rullo, interview.
8. Ibid.
9. Ibid.
10. "Tides Take On Hurricanes in League Opener Tonight," *Atlantic City Press*, November 9, 1948, 15.
11. Jerry Rullo, interview.
12. Ibid.
13. Ralph Kaplowitz, interview by the author, Queens, N.Y., December 2007.
14. "The Atlantic City Tides Quintet Abolished," *Atlantic City Press*, January 14, 1949, 20.
15. Minutes of Board Meeting, January 16, 1949, ABL Collection, Naismith Memorial Basketball Hall of Fame.
16. Jerry Rullo, interview.
17. Minutes of Board Meeting, September 19, 1949, ABL Collection, Naismith Memorial Basketball Hall of Fame.
18. "Sphas Remain Intact But Sever Franchise," n.d., Eddie Gottlieb Clipping File, Naismith Memorial Basketball Hall of Fame.

CHAPTER 14

1. Jerry Rullo, interview by the author, Philadelphia, July 2007.
2. Ibid.
3. Ibid.
4. James Rosin, *Philly Hoops: The SPHAS and WARRIORS* (Philadelphia: Autumn Road Publishers, 2003), 20.
5. Ibid., 21.
6. Jerry Rullo, interview.
7. Ibid.
8. Marques Haynes, telephone interview by the author, May 2007.
9. Louis (Red) Klotz, interview by the author, Margate City, N.J., August 2006.
10. Tim Crothers, "The General Whose Army Never Wins," *Sports Illustrated*, February 20, 1995, 180.
11. Louis (Red) Klotz, interview.
12. Ibid.
13. Ibid.
14. Ibid.
15. Ibid.
16. *Sphas Sparks* 5, no. 2, December 19, 1942, Louis (Red) Klotz Nomination File, Naismith Memorial Basketball Hall of Fame.
17. Louis (Red) Klotz, interview.
18. Ibid.
19. Ibid.
20. Ken Rappoport, "Basketball's Lovable Loser," *Sports Today*, March 1981, 44.
21. Crothers, "The General," 180.
22. Mike O'Hara, "Fall Guys Know Court Roles," n.d., Louis (Red) Klotz Nomination File, Basketball Hall of Fame.
23. Crothers, "The General," 180.

24. Louis (Red) Klotz, interview.
25. Ibid.

EPILOGUE

1. Unless noted otherwise, the quotations in the epilogue are taken from direct correspondence and interviews conducted by the author.
2. Shikey Gotthoffer, interview by Robert Peterson, May 1987, Robert Peterson Collection, Naismith Memorial Basketball Hall of Fame.
3. Richard Goldstein, "Harry Litwack, 91, Dies: Basketball Coach," *New York Times*, August 9, 1991.
4. Edgar Williams, "Sixers Announcer Dave Zinkoff Dies," *Philadelphia Inquirer*, December 26, 1985, 10A.
5. Ibid.
6. Ibid.

BIBLIOGRAPHY

This bibliography includes sources not mentioned in the notes.

BOOKS

Aamidor, Abraham. *Chuck Taylor, All Star: The True Story of the Man behind the Most Famous Athletic Shoe in History*. Bloomington: Indiana University Press, 2006.

Alfieri, Gus. *Lapchick*. Guilford, Conn.: Lyons Press, 2006.

Binzen, Peter, ed. *Nearly Everybody Read It: Snapshots of the Philadelphia Bulletin*. Philadelphia: Camino Books, 1988.

Bjarkman, Peter C. *The History of the NBA*. New York: Crescent Books, 2002.

———. *Hoopla: A Century of College Basketball*. Indianapolis: Masters Press, 1986.

Bloomfield, Gary. *Duty, Honor, Victory: America's Athletes in World War II*. Guilford, Conn.: Lyons Press, 2003.

Bodner, Allen. *When Boxing Was a Jewish Sport*. Westport, Conn.: Praeger, 1997.

Bole, Robert D., and Alfred C. Lawrence. *From Peachbaskets to Slamdunks: A Story of Professional Basketball*. Lebanon, N.H.: Whitman Press, 1987.

Boonin, Harry D. *The Jewish Quarter of Philadelphia: A History and Guide 1881–1930*. Philadelphia: Jewish Walking Tours of Philadelphia, 1999.

Brinkley, Alan. *Voices of Protest: Huey Long, Father Coughlin and The Great Depression*. New York: Vintage Books, 1982.

Bullock, Steven R. *Playing for Their Nation: Baseball and the American Military during World War II*. Lincoln: University of Nebraska Press, 2004.

Century, Douglas. *Barney Ross*. New York: Schocken Books, 2006.

Cohen, Roger. *Tough Jews: Fathers, Sons, and Gangster Dreams*. New York: Simon and Schuster, 1998.

Cohen, Stanley. *The Game They Played*. New York: Carroll and Graf, 1977.

Devaney, John. *The Story of Basketball.* New York: Random House, 1976.
Dickey, Glenn. *The History of Professional Basketball since 1896.* New York: Stein and Day, 1982.
Dubin, Murray. *South Philadelphia: Mummers, Memories, and the Melrose Diner.* Philadelphia: Temple University Press, 1996.
Entine, Jon. *Taboo: Why Black Athletes Dominate Sports and Why We're Afraid to Talk about It.* Westport, Conn.: Greenwood Press, 1994.
Fox, Stephen. *Big Leagues: Professional Baseball, Football, and Basketball in National Memory.* New York: William Morrow, 1994.
Frank, Stanley B. *The Jew in Sports.* New York: Miles Publishing, 1936.
Fried, Albert. *FDR and His Enemies.* New York: Palgrave, 1999.
Friedland, Stan. *Play It Again Sam: The Sam Schoenfeld Story.* Self-published, 2004.
Friedman, Murray, ed. *Jewish Life in Philadelphia 1830–1940.* Philadelphia: Ishi Publications, 1983.
———. *Philadelphia Jewish Life 1940–2000.* Philadelphia: Temple University Press, 2003.
Gilbert, Bill. *They Also Served: Baseball and the Home Front, 1941–1945.* New York: Crown Publishers, 1992.
Gorn, Elliott J., and Warren Goldstein. *A Brief History of American Sports.* New York: Hill and Wang, 1993.
Gould, Todd. *Pioneers of the Hardwood: Indiana and the Birth of Professional Basketball.* Bloomington: Indiana University Press, 1998.
Graham, Tom, and Rachel Graham Cody. *Getting Open: The Unknown Story of Bill Garrett and the Integration of College Basketball.* New York: Atria Books, 2006.
Green, Ben. *Spinning the Globe: The Rise, Fall, and Return to Greatness of the Harlem Globetrotters.* New York: HarperCollins Publishers, 2005.
Gurlock, Jeffrey S. *Judaism's Encounter with American Sports.* Bloomington: Indiana University Press, 2005.
Hammig, Jack G. *A Historical Sketch of Doctor James Naismith.* Lawrence: University of Kansas, 1962.
Hopkins, C. Howard. *History of the YMCA in North America.* New York: Association Press, 1951.
Hubbard, Jan, ed. *The Official NBA Encyclopedia.* New York: Doubleday, 2000.
Isaacs, Neil D. *All The Moves: A History of College Basketball.* New York: Harper and Row, 1984.
———. *Vintage NBA: The Pioneer Era (1946–1956).* Indianapolis: Masters Press, 1996.
Jares, Joe. *Basketball: The American Game.* Chicago: Follett, 1971.
Jay, Kathryn. *More Than Just a Game: Sports in American Life Since 1945.* New York: Columbia University Press, 2004.
Jenkins, Philip. *Hoods and Shirts: The Extreme Right in Pennsylvania, 1925–1950.* Chapel Hill: University of North Carolina Press, 1997.
Ketchum, Richard M. *The Borrowed Years 1938–1941: America on the Way to War.* New York: Doubleday, 1989.
Kirsch, George B., Othello Harris, and Claire E. Nolte, eds. *Encyclopedia of Ethnicity and Sports.* Westport, Conn.: Greenwood Press, 2000.
———. *Sports in North America: A Documentary History.* Volume 4, *Sports in War, Revival, and Expansion.* Gulf Breeze, Fla.: Academic International Press, 1995.
Koppett, Leonard. *24 Seconds to Shoot: An Informal History of the National Basketball Association.* New York: Macmillan, 1968; rev. and exp. ed., 1970.

Kugelmass, Jack, ed. *Jews, Sports, and the Rites of Citizenship*. Urbana: University of Illinois Press, 2007.

Kuska, Bob. *Hot Potato: How Washington and New York Gave Birth to Basketball and Changed America's Game Forever.* Charlottesville: University of Virginia Press, 2004.

Lanctot, Neil. *Fair Dealing and Clean Living: The Hilldale Club and the Development of Black Professional Baseball, 1910–1932*. Syracuse, N.Y.: Syracuse University Press, 1994.

———. *Negro League Baseball: The Rise and Ruin of a Black Institution*. Philadelphia: University of Pennsylvania Press, 2004.

Langfeld, William R. *The Young Men's Hebrew Association of Philadelphia: A Fifty-Year Chronicle*. Philadelphia: Young Men's and Young Women's Hebrew Association, 1928.

Levine, Peter. *Ellis Island to Ebbets Field: Sport and the American Jewish Experience*. New York: Oxford University Press, 1992.

Mayer, Paul Yogi. *Jews and the Olympic Games: Sport—A Springboard for Minorities*. London: Vallentine Mitchell, 2004.

Meyers, Allen. *Images of America: The Jewish Community of South Philadelphia*. Portsmouth, N.H.: Arcadia Publishing, 1998.

Miller, Fredric M., Morris J. Vogel, and Allen F. Davis. *Philadelphia Stories: A Photographic History, 1920–1960*. Philadelphia: Temple University Press, 1988.

———. *Still Philadelphia: A Photographic History, 1890–1940*. Philadelphia: Temple University Press, 1983.

Mokray, William G. *Ronald Encyclopedia of Basketball*. New York: Ronald Press, 1963.

Naismith, James. *Basketball: Its Origin and Development*. New York: Association Press, 1941.

Neft, David S., Roland T. Johnson, Richard M. Cohen, and Jordan A. Deutsch, eds. *The Sports Encyclopedia: Pro Basketball*. New York: Grossett and Dunlop, 1975.

Nelson, Murry. *The National Basketball League: A History, 1935–1949*. Jefferson, N.C.: McFarland, 2009.

———. *The Originals: The New York Celtics Invent Modern Basketball*. Bowling Green, Ohio: Bowling Green State University Popular Press, 1999.

Peters, Charles. *Five Days in Philadelphia: The Amazing "We Want Wilkie!" Convention of 1940 and How It Freed FDR to Save the Western World*. New York: PublicAffairs, 2005.

Peterson, Robert W. *Cages to Jump Shots: Pro Basketball's Early Years*. New York: Oxford University Press, 1990.

Pfleger, Birte. *Ethnicity Matters: A History of the German Society of Pennsylvania*. Washington, D.C.: German Historical Institute, 2006.

Pomerantz, Gary M. *Wilt, 1962: The Night of 100 Points and the Dawn of a New Era*. New York: Three Rivers Press, 2005.

Porter, David. *Biographical Dictionary of American Sports*. Westport, Conn.: Greenwood Publishing Group, 2000.

Postal, Bernard, Jesse Silver, and Roy Silver. *Encyclopedia of Jews in Sports*. New York: Bloch Publishing, 1965.

Putney, Clifford. *Muscular Christianity: Manhood and Sports in Protestant America, 1880–1920*. Cambridge, Mass.: Harvard University Press, 2001.

Rabinowitz, Benjamin. *The Young Men's Hebrew Associations 1854–1913*. New York: National Jewish Welfare Board, 1948.

Rader, Benjamin G. *American Sports: From the Ages of Folk Games to the Age of Televised Sports*, 5th ed. Upper Saddle River, N.J.: Prentice Hall, 2005.

Rains, Rob, with Helen Carpenter. *James Naismith: The Man Who Invented Basketball.* Philadelphia: Temple University Press, 2009.

Reiss, Steven A. *City Games: The Evolution of American Urban Society and the Rise of Sports.* Urbana: University of Illinois Press, 1989.

———, ed. *Sports and the American Jew.* Syracuse, N.Y.: Syracuse University Press, 1997.

Ribalow, Harold U. *The Jews in American Sports.* New York: Bloch Publishing, 1948.

Rosen, Charley. *The First Tip Off: The Incredible Story of the Birth of the NBA.* New York: McGraw Hill, 2009.

———. *The House of Moses All-Stars.* San Diego: Harcourt Brace, 1996.

———. *Scandals of '51.* New York: Seven Stories Press, 2001.

Rosin, James. *Philly Hoops: The SPHAS and WARRIORS.* Philadelphia: Autumn Road Publishers, 2003.

Salzberg, Charles. *From Set Shot to Slam Dunk: The Glory Days of Basketball in the Words of Those Who Played It.* Lincoln: University of Nebraska Press, 1987.

Schaap, Jeremy. *Triumph: The Untold Story of Jesse Owens and Hitler's Olympics.* Boston: Houghton Mifflin, 2007.

Scheffer, William J., ed. *The Reach Official Basket Ball Guide.* Philadelphia: A. J. Reach, 1901–1926.

Schleppi, John. *Chicago's Showcase of Basketball: The World Tournament of Professional Basketball and the College All Star Game.* Haworth, N.J.: St. Johann Press, 2008.

Schumacher, Michael. *Mr. Basketball: George Mikan, The Minneapolis Lakers, and the Birth of the NBA.* New York: Bloomsbury, 2007.

Sherr, Lynn. *Outside the Box: A Memoir.* New York: Rodale, 2006.

Shouler, Ken, Bob Ryan, Sam Smith, Leonard Koppett, and Bob Bellotti. *Total Basketball: The Ultimate Basketball Encyclopedia.* Wilmington, Del.: Sport Classic Press, 2003.

Slater, Robert. *Great Jews in Sports.* Middle Village, N.Y.: Jonathan David Publishers, 1983.

Smith, Seymour, Jack Rimer, and Dick Triptow. *A Tribute to Armed Forces Basketball 1941–1969.* Lake Bluff, Ill.: Self-published, 2003.

Sorin, Gerald. *The Nurturing Neighborhood: The Brownsville Boys Club and Jewish Community in Urban America, 1940–1990.* New York: New York University Press, 1990.

Sting Like a Maccabee: The Golden Age of the American Jewish Boxer. Philadelphia: National Museum of American Jewish History, n.d.

Taylor, John. *The Rivalry.* New York: Random House, 2005.

Taylor, Paul. *Jews and the Olympic Games: The Clash between Sport and Politics.* Brighton, England: Sussex Academic Press, 2004.

Thomas, Ron. *They Cleared the Lane: The NBA's Black Pioneers.* Lincoln: University of Nebraska Press, 2002.

Triptow, Richard F. *The Dynasty That Never Was.* Lake Bluff, Ill.: Self-published, 1996.

Vecsey, George. *Harlem Globetrotters.* New York: Scholastic Book Services, 1970.

Webb, Bernice Larson. *The Basketball Man: James Naismith.* Lawrence, Kans.: Kappelman's Historic Collections, 1994.

Weigley, Russell F., ed. *Philadelphia: A 300-Year History.* New York: W. W. Norton, 1982.

Westcott, Rich. *A Century of Philadelphia Sports*. Philadelphia: Temple University Press, 2001.

———. *The Mogul: Eddie Gottlieb, Philadelphia Sports Legend and Pro Basketball Pioneer*. Philadelphia: Temple University Press, 2008.

———. *Philadelphia's Old Ballparks*. Philadelphia: Temple University Press, 1996.

Wizov, Sandy. *A Corner Affair: 500 Guys from the "Corners" of South Philly*. Self-published, 1999.

Zinkoff, Dave, with Edgar Williams. *Around the World with the Harlem Globetrotters*. Philadelphia: Macrae Smith, 1953.

ARTICLES

Avery, Ron. "The SPHAs: Basketball Champions Shined When the Stars Were Jewish." *Jewish Exponent*, June 25, 1982, 48–49.

Borish, Linda J. "'An Interest in Physical Well-Being among the Feminine Membership': Sporting Activities for Women at Young Men's and Young Women's Hebrew Associations." *American Jewish History* 87, no. 1 (March 1999): 61–93.

Cohen, Steve. "They Took Their Shots: Gil Fitch, a Member of Philadelphia's All-Jewish Basketball Team in the 1930s, Reflects on Violence in Sports." *Naked City*, December 30, 2004–January 5, 2005. Available at www.citypaper.net/articles/2004-12-30/naked.shtml.

Feldman, Steve. "When Jewish Players Ruled the Courts." *Jewish Exponent*, December 9, 1988, 36–37.

Ordine, Bill. "A Better Team Than Money Could Buy . . ." *Today* (*Philadelphia Inquirer*), April 17, 1977, 33–41.

Wittner, Fred. "Basketball Blossoms Out." *Sports Illustrated and the American Golfer* (March 1936): 28–29.

UNPUBLISHED MATERIAL

Kolman, Stephen M. "Courting the American Dream: The Social and Cultural Community of Jewish Basketball in Philadelphia, 1920–1945." Master's thesis, University of Wisconsin, Madison, 1991.

Rayl, Susan. "The New York Renaissance Professional Black Basketball Team, 1923–1950." Doctoral dissertation, Pennsylvania State University, 1996.

Sclar, Ari. "'A Sport at Which Jews Excel': Jewish Basketball in American Society, 1900–1951." Doctoral dissertation, Stony Brook University, 2008.

NEWSPAPERS

Connecticut
Bridgeport Post
Bridgeport Telegram
Hartford Courant
New Britain Herald

Delaware
Wilmington Morning News

District of Columbia
Washington Post

Maryland
Baltimore Sun
Evening Sun
News Post

Massachusetts
Boston Herald
Boston Post

Michigan
Detroit Free Press
Flint Journal

New Jersey
Atlantic City Press
Elizabeth Daily Journal
Hudson Dispatch
Passaic Herald News
Paterson Morning Call

New York
Brooklyn Daily Eagle
Daily Worker
New York Daily News
New York Herald Tribune
New York Journal American
New York Post
New York Times
Rochester Democrat and Chronicle

Ohio
Akron Beacon Journal
Cleveland Plain Dealer

Pennsylvania
Evening News
Intelligencer Journal
Jewish Exponent
Lancaster New Era
The Patriot
Philadelphia Inquirer
Philadelphia Public Ledger
Scranton Times
Times Leader, the Evening News

Wisconsin
Oshkosh Northwestern
Sheboygan Press

ARCHIVES

Free Library of Philadelphia
Historical Society of Pennsylvania
Jewish Exponent Library
New York Public Library
New York Public Library for the Performing Arts
New York University
Philadelphia Inquirer and *Daily News* Library
Philadelphia Jewish Archives Center
Springfield College Archives
Temple University Urban Archives

NAISMITH MEMORIAL BASKETBALL HALL OF FAME

Note: The Naismith Memorial Basketball Hall of Fame in Springfield, Massachusetts, is the premier Hall of Fame for the game of basketball. It covers the game on all levels, including high school, college, professional, and international, for both men and women. The library contains a wealth of information, including a Hall of Famer file, clipping file, and photo file for every member of the Hall of Fame. There are also files on everyone who has ever been nominated to the Hall of Fame, along with scrapbooks, magazines, the Reach and Spalding Guides, archival collections, and personal papers. The library contains the Robert Peterson Collection, which is all the research conducted for his book *Cages to Jump Shots*. The highlight of the collection is all of the interviews—both cassettes and transcripts—he conducted for the book. There are also files on early professional leagues, including the American Basketball League during the 1930s and 1940s. Finally, the Hall of Fame embarked on an oral history program in the late 1980s, and cassettes and transcripts from this program are available.

Clipping Files
Davey Banks
Moe Becker
Mike Bloom
Eddie Gottlieb
Louis "Red" Klotz
Harry Litwack
Ossie Schectman
George Senesky
The SPHAS

Hall of Famer Files
Eddie Gottlieb
Harry Litwack

Nomination Files
Mike Bloom
Moe Goldman
Louis "Red" Klotz
Francis P. "Stretch" Meehan
Moe Spahn

Scrapbooks
American Basketball League 1936–1937
Nat Holman

Archive and Manuscript Collections
American Basketball League

INDEX

Douglas Stark is the Museum Director of the International Tennis Hall of Fame & Museum.